FINDING

ZSA ZSA

FINDING
ZSA ZSA

The Gabors
Behind the Legend

SAM STAGGS

KENSINGTON BOOKS
www.kensingtonbooks.com

Permission to quote the passage from the Yad Vashem website on pages 128-129 is courtesy of Yad Vashem.

Permission to quote the passage on page 134 is courtesy of The New York Post, NYP Holdings, Inc.

Kensington Books are published by:

Kensington Publishing Corp.
119 West 40th Street
New York, NY 10018

All Kensington titles, imprints, and distributed lines are available at special quantity discounts for bulk purchases for sales promotion, premiums, fund-raising, educational, or institutional use.

Special book excerpts or customized printings can also be created to fit specific needs. For details, write or phone the office of the Kensington Special Sales Manager: Attn. Special Sales Department. Kensington Publishing Corp., 119 West 40th Street, New York, NY 10018. Phone: 1-800-221-2647.

Kensington and the K logo Reg. U.S. Pat. & TM Off.

Library of Congress Card Catalogue Number: 2019932235

ISBN-13: 978-1-4967-1959-1
ISBN-10: 1-4967-1959-X
First Kensington Hardcover Edition: August 2019

ISBN-13: 978-1-4967-1961-4 (ebook)
ISBN-10: 1-4967-1961-1 (ebook)

10 9 8 7 6 5 4 3 2 1

Printed in the United States of America

For Tony Turtu

and

in memory of

Constance Francesca Gabor Hilton

Contents

Imagine a horoscope cast for us in our youth that failed to account for the shocking changes awaiting us in the future.
Marcel Proust,
Remembrance of Things Past

She generally gave herself very good advice, though she very seldom followed it.
Lewis Carroll,
Alice's Adventures in Wonderland

Preface

As pop culture icons, the Gabors—Zsa Zsa, Eva, Magda, Jolie—were enormous fun. Watching them was like eating peanuts—you couldn't stop. Even now, though departed, they remain household names. The Gabors are also taken seriously: in recent years, several female academics have written about them as proto-feminists. Indeed, under the frills they were strong, courageous women ahead of their time.

I set out to write a book that embraces this captivating aspect of these women even as it contradicts their frivolous, candy-floss reputation. In doing so, I wrote the book I wanted to read; surely every writer does the same. I hope that in these pages readers finally meet the Gabors nobody knew. Here, for the first time ever, they appear minus the artifice.

Clichés about this legendary family seem indestructible. I hope, however, to have punctured two of the silliest. The first is that they were famous for being famous. On the contrary, the Gabors were famous because they worked at it, and because they worked at their careers, every hour and every day for close to a century.

The other outlandish notion is that they somehow foreshadowed the Kardashians and others of that ilk. This one is nourished by those who know nothing of the Gabors and too much about the Ks, not one of whom has the sophistication, the poise, or the savoir faire of an Eva or a Zsa Zsa. The cosmopolitan Gabors, icons of elegance with color, style, flair, and wit, spoke multiple languages fluently, and their driving ambition landed them in hundreds of movies, TV shows, and stage productions. They ran businesses, raised money for charity, traveled the world, attracted countless friends in society high and low, and their bon mots became as famous as the wisecracks of Dorothy Parker and Mae West. Perhaps the Kardashians, along with Paris Hilton and other vapid celebrities, aspire to Gabor caliber and finesse. All of these no doubt enrolled in Gaborology 101. But they flunked the course.

Introduction: Five Nights in the Fifties

Why, one may ask, only five? After all, the blonde-hungry 1950s belonged to the Gabors as surely as to Marilyn Monroe, Jayne Mansfield, and to all those bottle-blonde starlets, models, and TV personalities. And also, of course, to countless imitators striving to live blonde lives in the postwar, conformist Eisenhower era, all of whom answered "Yes!" to Clairol's advertisement: "Is it true blondes have more fun?"

Every night from 1950 to 1960 belonged to one Gabor or another. Zsa Zsa and Eva laid claim to most, but Magda—the redhead, the older sister—and Jolie, the irrepressible mother, grabbed the leftovers. Since these opening pages must limit the Gabor exploits of that teeming decade, I begin with an hors d'oeuvre: five pungent nights that helped entrench the Gabors in the spotlight. (Once on that magic media carpet, they scrambled and clawed to remain irresistible public *dahlings*.) After this appetizer, like Scheherazade I will unscroll the prodigious, hallucinatory, rollicking, and sometimes bitter lives of these four women, as well as the very different trajectories of Vilmos, father of the Gabor sisters, and Francesca Hilton, Zsa Zsa's troubled daughter.

January 24, 1950

Opening night of *The Happy Time* at the Plymouth The-atre on Forty-fifth Street in New York. Written by Samuel Taylor, produced by Rodgers and Hammerstein, and set in Ottawa in the 1920s, it's the story of Bibi, a French-Canadian schoolboy on the verge of puberty who learns something—but not much—about love. For 1950, however, in Cold War America, the play was looked on as a sex comedy, for Bibi stands accused by his schoolmaster of drawing dirty pictures, and much talk ensues among the grown-ups about nudity and the like. It turns out the boy didn't do it—those doodles were the work of a guttersnipe classmate.

At home, the boy's mother is a straitlaced Presbyterian while his more lenient father is a vaudeville musician and there's an uncle who is—wink, wink—a traveling salesman. Then there's Mignonette, the French maid, who gives Bibi his first kiss and, as *Life* magazine demurely put it, "Bibi feels the first stirrings of manhood." (This plot, of course, is *Gigi* transgendered.)

The French maid, however, speaks with a Hungarian ac-cent, for she is played by Eva Gabor. Making her Broadway debut, Eva the minx outshone other cast members with her sparkle. *Life* again: "The play's most decorative performer is Eva Gabor." Others in the journeyman cast included charac-ter actors Kurt Kasznar, Leora Dana, Claude Dauphin, and Johnny Stewart as Bibi. Eva, too, felt the boy's "stirrings," for Stewart was sixteen years old and when he and Eva em-braced, his manhood saluted.

Eva, who arrived in the United States in 1939 with the first of her five husbands, had appeared in half a dozen forget-table movies from 1941 to the end of the decade. Then, on October 3, 1949, she costarred with Burgess Meredith on CBS in the first episode of the network's new series, *The Sil-ver Theater*. This episode, broadcast live, was titled *L'Amour the Merrier*, and Eva played a French maid with a Hungarian accent. Richard Rodgers, sans Hammerstein, happened to watch television that night, and even in black and white Eva struck him as just the right article for *The Happy Time*. Had he guessed that she was thirty-one years old, he might have switched channels in search of a fresher soubrette.

The play ran for 614 performances, but Eva left the cast after a year and a half, in May 1951. Two weeks after the opening, Eva's flawless face appeared on the cover of *Life*. That stunning portrait was the work of Philippe Halsman, one of the twentieth century's best-known photographers. A few years later, a different photograph from the session, although equally strong, appeared on the cover of Eva's autobiography, *Orchids and Salami*.

Eva's *Life* cover flung open doors for her in New York that had remained shut in Hollywood. For a time, Eva's face, her fashions, and most of all her accent popped up everywhere at once. A feeding frenzy swirled around this new exotic beauty whose past lay locked behind the Iron Curtain. But acting, more than allure, was her great passion. This she cultivated with love and labor, although glamour, and her accent, blocked the route. Like Marilyn Monroe, Eva studied with expert teachers and attended classes at the Actors Studio. Like Marilyn also, no one believed she wished to perfect the craft of acting.

July 23, 1951

Enter Zsa Zsa. With all eyes on Eva, Zsa Zsa was a distant dream that had not yet come true. Her resumé, had she produced one, would have shown that she possessed the requisites for a sort of louche fame, for in 1933, at age fifteen, she had been a contender in the Miss Hungary contest. Two years after that, she married an official in the Turkish government who often visited Budapest on political missions.

With him, she lived in Ankara until 1941, when she embarked for the United States and arrived in New York on June 3rd of that year, along with twenty-one suitcases. In 1942 she married Conrad Hilton, the wealthy but tightfisted American hotelier whose anticipated generosity proved a sore disappointment to his spendthrift young wife.

Having deleted Conrad Hilton, in 1949 she married the actor George Sanders, who taunted and belittled her when she begged him to help her get a toehold in movies. Between Hilton and Sanders, Zsa Zsa cracked up and became the involuntary inmate of a psychiatric institution.

When Eva opened on Broadway in *The Happy Time*, Zsa Zsa had been Mrs. George Sanders for less than a year. Living in Hollywood yet segregated from the studios, Zsa Zsa felt betrayed by her nearest and dearest: George, the man she loved, and also the younger sister who made movies and who now posed for magazine covers and had New York at her feet, as the columnists liked to say. Zsa Zsa secretly accused Eva of a stroke of low cunning, for the *Life* cover bore the date February 6, 1950—Zsa Zsa's thirty-third birthday!

While Zsa Zsa seethed with envy, news came one day of an offer to make a film—an offer for George, of course. They had now been married just over two years, and in the summer of 1951 George left for England to make *Ivanhoe*, in which he costarred with Robert Taylor, Joan Fontaine, and Elizabeth Taylor. Zsa Zsa begged and pleaded to go along. Her supplications echoed like forlorn yodels across the hills of Bel Air, where she lived with George and loved him with a full heart, though he was never under her spell and found her usually quite exasperating. In spite of his ill treatment, or as she later implied, because of it, she loved him until death.

"You stay home," he told her. "You would just be bored and would make it impossible for me to work."

In the empty house, she wept and phoned her mother in New York. But not until long-distance rates went down after five o'clock; the Gabors, even when prosperous, counted their spare change. "Oh, *Nyuszi*," Zsa Zsa wailed, "I cannot live without him. I will kill myself." (The girls sometimes called her "Mama," though more often "*Nyuszi*," or "*Nyuszika*," pet names in Hungarian meaning "bunny rabbit.")

Jolie had heard it all before. "Buy a new frock and charge it to George," she counseled. "And throw in diamond earrings to match."

When George learned of his mother-in-law's advice, he called her "you fucking Hungarian!" But Jolie, having seen husbands enter and exit, knew that greatness lay in store for her Zsa Zsa, along with marital treasures far brighter than this disdainful man who spoke Russian to his brother when he wished to keep secrets from Zsa Zsa.

That brother, the actor Tom Conway, had grown up in St. Petersburg, along with George and their sister. Although Russian citizens, they were said to be descended from English stock and the Sanders family emigrated to England at the time of the Russian Revolution in 1917. (The family's English heritage has subsequently been disputed. Late in her life, George's sister came to believe the family to be pure Russian.)

Tom Conway worked steadily in pictures, although in character roles and smaller parts, unlike George, who had become a real movie star. Between films, Tom was a regular panelist on a new West Coast television show called *Bachelor's Haven*. The show's gimmick was advice to the lovelorn, always lighthearted and the sillier the better. (The heavy breathing of ABC's *The Bachelor* and its spinoffs was unthinkable on fifties TV.)

On July 23, 1951, two days after George's departure for England, Tom Conway phoned Zsa Zsa with an offer that she almost refused. "We've a vacancy on tonight's panel," he said. "Do be a love and help me out of a jam." She balked. True, she was not easily intimidated, for she had traveled alone, during wartime, from Turkey across such risky terrain as Iran, Iraq, and Afganistan, finally boarding a ship in India for passage to the U.S. She had married three times and had woken up in a straitjacket in a mental ward. All that, yet she quailed at the thought of live TV. "No, dahling," she said. "Your dear brother has told me a thousand times I have no talent." Pause. "What would George say?" Two beats. "I'll show that son of a bitch. What time are you picking me up?"

If the camera in that TV studio had been of the male gender, Zsa Zsa would surely have seen its manhood stirring, for it did everything but fondle her. And no wonder. Perfect skin, pure as vanilla ice cream, against her black Balenciaga gown. Diamond earrings and more diamonds around her neck and on her fingers. When she opened her red Cupid's bow mouth, a feral accent spilled out that sounded like a snow leopard learning English.

During the show's opening moments, the host commented on her jewelry. She shrugged. "Dahling, zese are just my vorking diamonds." The audience roared; Zsa Zsa's wisecracks kept them in stitches right up to the closing credits and calls inundated the switchboard. Soon fan letters flooded the station. A week later *Daily Variety* reported that Zsa Zsa was an "instant star" and had been invited as a regular on the show.

Bundy Solt, a childhood friend of the Gabor sisters, had come to Hollywood at the outbreak of World War II. Two days after Zsa Zsa's dazzling debut, he phoned her and said, "Have you read the trade papers?"

She replied, "I do not know what means 'trade papers.'"

"You dope," he replied. "Hold the line." And he read her the raves, which perplexed the brand-new celebrity. As far as she knew, she had done nothing other than being Zsa Zsa Gabor.

When George Sanders returned from his long location shoot in England, he first thought it was Eva once more on the cover of *Life*. But no, it was Zsa Zsa, who adorned the issue of October 15, 1951. She had been too busy to inform him that she now had an agent, a manager, a dramatic coach, a PR team promoting her, and offers to appear in movies.

Back in New York, good-natured Eva felt kicked in the belly. She, who had toiled for years in drama classes, rehearsed scenes and monologues, showed up for cold readings, done screen tests and auditions—all that, and now her bossy, overbearing sister had become one of the greatest overnight successes in show-biz history. And all because of a raucous, unscripted appearance on TV.

January 9, 1953

In the press, Magda was often described as "the quiet Gabor." And so she was, at least in public. In the family, she could raise her voice, flounce out of a room, spew invective, and slam doors as theatrically as the others. She had no theatrical ambitions, however, until one day a producer of plays for a regional theatre phoned to offer her a part in *The Women*, the acerbic comedy of manners written by Clare Boothe Luce. The play's gimmick is that the female characters, in bitchy repartee, dissect husbands and boyfriends—and one another—yet no men appear on the scene. The 1939 film version, directed by George Cukor, starred Norma Shearer, Joan Crawford, Rosalind Russell, and Joan Fontaine.

When the producer told Magda why he was calling, she berated him. "You are an opportunist!" she hissed. "You want only a Gabor for publicity. I have never been in my life on a stage."

He managed to say that he wanted her for the role of Crystal. "She's the girl in the bathtub," he added.

"I can see it now," Magda railed. "Your publicity—'See a Gabor in a Bathtub.'"

The producer didn't flinch. "So you can't take a challenge," he chortled. "You lack the courage of Zsa Zsa and Eva!"

That did it. "I was so mad I signed for the play. But not for

Crystal in the bathtub. I played Peggy, the role of Joan Fontaine in the film." (In this production, the character was described as a "war bride" to account for her accent.)

Magda's stage debut took place January 9, 1953, at the Hilltop Theater in the Round in Lutherville, Maryland, a suburb of Baltimore. The run of the play was thirteen performances, with Magda the only neophyte in a seasoned cast. During one performance, with Magda and four other cast members onstage, an actress forgot her line. It was hardly her fault, however, for in this arena production, the front row of the audience sat only a few feet from the actors. When the script called for this actress to light a cigarette, a man in the front row did it for her. His unwelcome courtesy threw her off. She went blank. At that point, Magda ad-libbed a line that quickly steered her floundering colleague back on script. Backstage after the performance, the entire cast praised her quick thinking. "Magda," they said, "you're a real trouper. Welcome to the theatre!"

Magda said later, after appearing in other plays, that instead of theatre in the round she preferred a traditional proscenium—or, as she called it, "theatre in the square."

February 10, 1953

Unstoppable Zsa Zsa. In spite of her late start in show business, she had almost fifty years ahead during which she would perform in virtually every branch of entertainment, and in many countries, until her final appearance before a camera in 1998.

Among the reverberations from her slam-bang debut on *Bachelor's Haven* were three films made in rapid succession: *Lovely to Look At*, for MGM, filmed in fall 1951; *We're Not Married*, at 20th Century Fox, shot in December 1951 and into 1952; and *Moulin Rouge*, for which Zsa Zsa traveled to Paris and then to London in the summer and fall of 1952.

When *Moulin Rouge* opened in New York on February 10, 1953, Zsa Zsa had star billing second only to José Ferrer. That night, the same New York that had lain stretched out at Eva's feet three years earlier now clamored for Zsa Zsa. If that fickle city spoke with a single voice, it might well have rasped, "Eva who? We want Zsa Zsa, send her out that we may know her!"

She arrived at Idlewild Airport to an aurora borealis of flashbulbs and newsreel cameras. The stampede followed her to the Plaza, where the film's producers had booked a larger suite, and a more lavish one, than anything ex-husband Conrad Hilton had ever shown her—and he owned the Plaza.

Zsa Zsa recalled every instant of her apotheosis: "The morning of the *Moulin Rouge* premiere I climbed a white ladder at Fiftieth Street and Broadway and while the cameras turned, I replaced the street sign with one reading *Rue de Montmartre* in honor of our opening at the nearby Capitol Theatre."

Outside the Capitol, Walter Winchell acted as emcee for the premiere, proceeds of which would go to charity. In later years Winchell would discover that Zsa Zsa could talk faster and say less than he, but on that cold February night in 1953 even he was agog. As crowds of fans pushed against police barricades, and klieg lights outshone the bright lights of Times Square, celebrities arrived in droves, but no one got louder cheers than Zsa Zsa, who loved the adulation so much that she might have forgotten to go inside and watch herself onscreen had not Harold Mirisch, one of the producers, signaled that the show was about to begin and escorted her to what she perhaps mistook for a throne. That night, she was monarch of all she surveyed.

"*Moulin Rouge* began, and I watched myself. How bitterly I had fought with John Huston, how I had struggled with my part, how terrified I had been through all the shooting—now I was repaid. The evening was a triumph. At my staircase scene the audience broke into applause, and when the lights went on, I heard voices: 'Zsa Zsa! We want Zsa Zsa!' "

When she returned at last to the Plaza, she found a telegram: YOU AND TECHNICOLOR SAVED OUR PICTURE. CONTRATULATIONS. JOHN HUSTON.

The audience loved her, and so did New York, and most reviewers singled her out as—well, not knowing exactly what she was, they decided that readers should keep their eyes on this thrilling newcomer.

A short time before the premiere, Zsa Zsa had encountered Porfirio Rubirosa, a roving diplomat for the Dominican Republic and the ex-husband of French film star Danielle Darrieux and also of Doris Duke, said to be the richest woman in the world. But on the night of February 10, 1953, he was there at the Plaza, and when Zsa Zsa returned from her evening of glory, he telephoned to invite her downstairs to the Persian Room. There he and several friends, including Prince Carl Bernadotte of Sweden, were waiting to toast her victory.

This, the fourth one of those five Gabor nights in the fifties, might reasonably count as a double entry, for not only did Zsa Zsa reach the pinnacle of her professional life, but before the night was over, she had captivated the man reputed to be the Greatest Lover of the Century. That night she spent in the notorious, intoxicating arms of Rubirosa.

Too much happiness, however, proved dangerous, for that very night began Zsa Zsa's long, slow decline from her brief pinnacle. If her famous stairway scene in *Moulin Rouge* had flashed a mirror image behind the screen of the Capitol Theatre, the audience might have watched in disbelief as Zsa Zsa shed the adulation of that evening, along with the admiration of the crowd and the promise suggested by reviewers. In time her lovely screen persona would reverse and turn into a caricature and a parody—a hollow husk and a spectre that haunted even Zsa Zsa herself.

October 29, 1958

On a cold autumn Sunday, Eva and Magda arrive at Flughafen Wien, Vienna International Airport, on a flight from New York, and two days later Jolie blows into town. Then, on Wednesday evening, October 29, 1958, Zsa Zsa draws the biggest crowds when she and her eleven-year-old daughter, Francesca Hilton, land in Vienna on a flight from Rome. She has taken a few days off from filming *For the First Time* with Mario Lanza. Zsa Zsa leaves the plane ahead of other passengers, and behind her comes Francesca, clutching a Hula-Hoop. ("The first one in Italy!" she exclaimed more than fifty years later. "The Italians had never seen anything like it.")

They have all come to Vienna for a reunion with Vilmos, Jolie's ex-husband, the father of Magda, Zsa Zsa, and Eva, and Francesca's grandfather. It's the first time the entire family has been together since 1948, when Vilmos, who had spent three years in the United States, decided that Hungary was where he wanted to live out his remaining years. Francesca was an infant then, so that tonight it's as if she has not met him before. Never again will the entire family be together, for Vilmos will die four years later.

Hungary's communist authorities have, at last, issued a visa to the elderly man. His ex-wife and his daughters used every influence available in Washington and elsewhere to obtain his eight-day release from behind the Iron Curtain.

There at the airport to meet Zsa Zsa and Francesca are Vilmos and Jolie. Great throngs of reporters, photographers, police, autograph seekers, and the merely curious make it difficult for Zsa Zsa to embrace her father and cover him with kisses. Not once, but repeatedly. Everyone kisses everyone else—Zsa Zsa kisses Vilmos, then Jolie, Vilmos kisses Zsa Zsa, Jolie kisses Vilmos, Francesca kisses Vilmos and then her grandmother. The crowds, even in orderly Vienna, verge on hysteria like those at the riotous Hollywood premiere in *The Day of the Locust*.

A curious omission: no one sheds tears at this highly emotional meeting. That's because tough-minded Gabors always kept their deepest emotions out of sight. "This is my only real husband," Jolie chimes out, whether to Vilmos or the press is unclear. She kisses him once more—for the cameras, forgetting that thirty years earlier she had called him a savage reprobate. We can't make out what Vilmos thinks of his daughters' candy-floss fame and their display of capitalistic luxury. The choice of fur coats is wide, the jewelry slightly subdued for this dignified occasion in a conservative European city.

For years, his daughters, and Jolie as well, have sent Vilmos as much money as allowed by a rigid communist state, reportedly one hundred dollars a month. They are allowed to ship parcels not to exceed the value of forty dollars, and Zsa Zsa sends a monthly supply of insulin, for Vilmos is diabetic. Until recently, he and his second wife, formerly his secretary, lived in a one-room flat in Budakeszi, a bleak suburb of Budapest. Indeed, all is bleak since the uprising in 1956. Exactly two years ago, in late October, Hungarians revolted against Russian tyranny only to be murdered by the thousands as Russian tanks invaded the country and gunfire ripped Budapest apart. Those men and women not killed in the streets, or lined up before firing squads, were herded into sealed boxcars and sent to the Soviet Union, never to be seen again, or else imprisoned in Hungary under vile conditions.

Tonight the Gabors move toward their limousine but it's like walking through water. The police can barely control the frenzied crowd. Newsmen shout questions through the air in German, English, Hungarian, and Zsa Zsa flings back press-release tidbits in all three languages. *"Ja, natürlich freue ich mich sehr, meinen lieben Vater wiederzusehen!"* and "Yes, we are all happy. Please let us pass." The throng swirls around these famous Gabors like extras in a Fellini movie.

Eventually, airport police push the crowds aside and clear a path into the terminal, to baggage retrieval, and at last to the waiting limousine. Francesca climbs in first, then Jolie and Vilmos, and Zsa Zsa. On to the august Sacher Hotel, where the Gabors occupy four suites.

"No, no, I cannot give any more autographs," Zsa Zsa says, slightly irritated, as she glides through the imperial doors. "I haven't seen my father in years!" Accosted once more, Zsa Zsa snaps, "I am not answering this interview!" Nevertheless, she permits one newsreel photographer into her boudoir for a moment. The next day on Austrian television Zsa Zsa preens and primps before a large mirror, even though hair and makeup have retained their movie star perfection. As always, she is the fairest in the land.

After everyone has freshened up, they gather in Magda and Eva's suite. The press is invited in, flashbulbs go off like popcorn and newsreel cameras whirr and buzz. Three generations! Mink coats out of sight, pearl necklaces on Jolie and her girls, Eva and Magda showing décolletage and bare shoulders in contrast to Zsa Zsa's tailored suit, everyone kissing everyone once more, it's like a champage high on New Year's Eve at midnight. Then Francesca takes out her own camera and photographs the family while press photographers take pictures of her doing so.

She is the only one who will soon go to sleep. Her mother, her aunts, and her grandparents will talk most of the night. On Sunday night, after their arrival, Eva, Magda, and their father stayed up talking until five in the morning. "And we cried and cried," said Magda. They also laughed at his old-country notions. When Magda took out a cigarette, Vilmos jumped. "Oh Magduska, you smoke. How terrible!"

Tonight Magda, with a firm smile, ushers to the door all those who have no Gabor blood. Only then do she, her mother and father, and her sisters, say all the things that Gabors, and others, say when overcome by happiness. During these fleeting hours, the night is perfect. Here in the warmth and comfort and safety of this venerable hotel, it is as if there were no war, no separation, no tears, and no death.

Chapter 1

Gábor úr és Gáborné
(Mr. and Mrs. Gabor)

To locate the beginning of the Gabor saga, we must go to Central Europe at the time of the complicated dual monarchy of Austria-Hungary, which was created in 1867 and ruled by the Hapsburgs. On the other hand, if we accept fanciful family lore, our trajectory jumps to earlier centuries farther east. Zsa Zsa and Eva spoke so often of their high Mongolian cheekbones that this fiction became real to them as they pictured ancestors on horseback who swept across the Eurasian steppe with Attila the Hun and Genghis Khan. From time to time in Zsa Zsa's yarns, a soupçon of Gypsy blood spiced their veins, and she sometimes alluded to an obscure Russian granny perched on a far branch of the family tree. Her kinsmen seemed unaware of this babushka.

In reality, they were Jewish. Francesca maintained, vaguely, that Vilmos, her grandfather, was not, yet he was born Farkas Miklós Grün and, like many Hungarian Jews in the late nineteenth century, changed his name to advance financially and socially at a time of raging anti-Semitism. Unlike some of their relatives, however, who adhered to the Jewish faith, the Gabors were secular and nonobservant. One might say that instead of the God of Israel, they worshiped the King of Diamonds.

Zsa Zsa once said that her father had her baptized a Catholic at birth. If her report was accurate, no doubt her sisters were also baptized in infancy. If not, then at some point Zsa Zsa and Eva converted to Catholicism, and Francesca was raised in the Church. Another possibility is this: the Gabors converted to Catholicism in 1928 for the purpose of upward mobility. I base the speculation on a baptismal certificate that Zsa Zsa produced in 1983 to "prove" her age as fifty-four when, in reality, she was sixty-six. It will surprise many readers that Eva and Francesca were regular churchgoers and that Zsa Zsa sometimes dropped in at Christmas and Easter. Zsa Zsa once explained her many marriages like this: "I can't live in sin. I never stopped being a Catholic in my heart."

Although Budapest had a huge Jewish population before World War II, the prestige religion was Roman Catholicism. Social climbers scouted for members of the clergy, whose presence at dinner or a celebration might well gain a mention in the newspaper. Jolie claimed that Cardinal József Mindszenty, head of the Catholic Church in Hungary, attended her mother's soirées. If true, his attendance would have been prior to World War II and before his elevation to cardinal, which was soon followed by imprisonment under the communist regime.

If Vilmos approved his family's conversion, he later reverted to Judaism. He is buried beside his second wife in the Kozma Street Jewish Cemetery in Budapest. On his gravestone is a Hebrew inscription translated as "Mourned by his wife and family with never-ending love."

It is important to note that assimilation—a new, frightening, but also a tempting phenomenon for many Jews, and often accompanied by conversion to Christianity—was widespread in Hungary in the late nineteenth and early twentieth centuries. Of interest, also, in placing the Gabors in context is this statistic from *The Invisible Jewish Budapest* by Mary Gluck: "In 1900, Budapest had a Jewish population of roughly twenty-three percent, making it the second largest Jewish city in Europe." Only Warsaw surpassed it. A reviewer summarized Gluck's history as an examination of "the vibrant modernist culture created largely by secular Jews in Budapest, in counterpoint to a backward-looking, nationalistic Hungarian establishment and a conservative Jewish religious elite."

In changing his name from Grün to Gabor, Vilmos perhaps intended a coded message to the community he had left. Since "Gabor" in Hungarian means "Gabriel," the name of the archangel who appears in both Jewish and Christian scriptures, Vilmos's subtext might have been, You see, we're still one of you as well as one of *them*.

Motherhood, in the Gabor family, has a curious history. One can observe its transmigration through three generations, beginning with Franceska Reinherz Tillemann, the first matriarch whose likeness comes into focus. In a formally posed photograph from around 1900, she stands like a tall Biedermeier chest of drawers, carved from oak or mahogany and capable of filling up a high-ceilinged room. (The photograph belies reality; Zsa Zsa recalled her as quite short.) Her bell-shaped face, bedecked with a voluminous hat, suggests great intelligence, limited patience, and high spirits. Her keen interest in current Viennese and Budapest fashion is obvious, for she is swathed in a lacy black gown with a triangular sprig of white lace that seems to peer into a daring décolletage. That peek is a tease, however, for beneath the lace is a silk bodice.

Despite her large bosom, she refused to nurse her children: Janette, Dora, Jancsi, Rosalie, and finally Sebestyn, the only boy. Many years later Jancsi (pronounced YAWN-chee) became known to the world as Jolie Gabor. "She had some Jewish blood," Jolie said of her mother, and left it at that. She had much more to say about her mother's parenting skills, many of which she herself practiced with Magda, Zsa Zsa, and Eva, and which Zsa Zsa, in the case of her own Francesca, carried to regrettable extremes. We will come to these presently. Before Franceska Reinherz Tillemann became a parent, however, she worked as a cook, waitress, and then purveyor of jewels.

Franceska Reinherz was born in Vienna, although her birth year is open to debate. Jolie provided no date, and so we must grope in nineteenth-century darkness to locate her probable d.o.b. as 1865. Or 1870. Even on this sliding probability scale, the date would not have been more than a year or two later, for Jolie—the third of five children—was almost certainly born in 1893, the same year as Mae West and Mao Zedong, with both of whom she shared certain traits. Jolie's niece, Annette Tillemann-Dick, recalls her great-aunt saying on a visit in 1988, "Dahling, I'm ninety-five years old." And Jolie would have had no reason to lie to a family member.

The Reinherz family owned a chain of jewelry shops in Vienna and a bit of real estate. "They weren't a rich family," Jolie stated in her autobiography, "just a good family." With typical bourgeois yearnings, they wished their daughter to marry a professional man with shining prospects. Franceska, however, believed in love, which came to her in the form of József Tillemann, a poor university student. After a ruction at home, Franceska and József packed up and eloped to Budapest. In those days, everyone above the peasant class spoke German as well as Hungarian, so the young couple avoided linguistic if not financial tribulation. József became a tutor to the scions of wealthy families, and in less than a year he had saved enough to open a small luncheonette in an obscure quarter of Budapest. With no money for hired help, he and his wife labored without rest. "My mother," recalled Jolie, "who was raised like a queen, worked eighteen hours a day,

cooking, washing dishes, and personally serving the customers." (This backstairs revelation, along with many other
glimpses of kitchen-sink realism, explains why Zsa Zsa and
Eva were incensed with Mama Gabor when her book came
out in 1975.)

Eventually Franceska Tillemann's financial acumen, boosted
by a loan, enabled her to found the Diamond House where, according to Jolie, her parents "made a fortune on a clever new
idea. In those days there were no cultured pearls, only expensive natural ones. Mama didn't see why they couldn't make
good imitations to look genuine, so they created strands of
fake pearls but with real diamond and gem clips." In other
words, dipped pearls. This intertwining of true and false,
with pearls as with facts, could have served as the Gabor coat
of arms.

Franceska and József, growing prosperous, ascended to
the Budapest bourgeoisie. They continued to speak German
at home, and that became the first language of Jolie and her
siblings. Hungarian they picked up from playmates and at
school. Recently I asked Jolie's niece whether, in the Tillemann and Gabor households, German might actually have
been Yiddish. "Oh no," she said. "It was Hochdeutsch [high
German]. Hungarian Jews looked down on Polish Jews and
others who spoke Yiddish."

That niece is Mrs. Annette Lantos, born in Budapest in
1931 and not to be confused with her daughter, Annette
Tillemann-Dick, quoted above. Mrs. Lantos is the daughter
of Jolie's brother, Sebestyn, and the widow of Congressman
Tom Lantos, Democrat of California, who served in the
House of Representatives from 1981 until his death in 2008.
I will call upon Mrs. Lantos in future chapters to help advance the narrative and to clarify certain dissimulations formulated by the press and by the Gabors themselves.

Mrs. Lantos explained that Franceska Tillemann—her
grandmother and Jolie's mother—owned several jewelry stores

in Budapest. This came about because she opened a new store when each one of her children was born, intending every new establishment as the eventual dowry for that particular child. Jolie claimed in her book that by the time she and her siblings were in their teens, their parents owned a chain of thirty-six jewelry shops spread across Europe. Mrs. Lantos, well acquainted with her aunt's exaggerations, adjusted that number downward to half a dozen or so.

One might expect a hard-driving businesswoman like Franceska Tillemann, a female pioneer in a man's world and an innovator in her field of enterprise, to bring home some of her no-nonsense efficiency and high standards of behavior. And so she did. In private, as in the workaday world, she was formidable. Even in adulthood, her daughters and her son, along with her grandchildren, stood when she entered the room. According to Zsa Zsa, no one dared use the familiar form of address to this grandmother, a statement that requires explanation to speakers of English. We have only one word for "you," but in Hungarian and in most other European languages, two forms are used. The familiar form is for children, family members, close friends, and animals. One uses the so-called polite, or formal, "you" when speaking to colleagues, clergy, teachers, acquaintances, and so on. In Hungarian the forms are "te," familiar, "ön" and "maga," formal. Zsa Zsa perhaps meant that no one outside the family dared address Franceska Tillemann as "te." It would be unusual for family members to use formal address with one another unless, for instance, their kindred occupied a high social station.

She seems to have found children distasteful, though she produced five of them and demanded full devotion in exchange for aloof maternity. Scarcely were these infants delivered than Franceska Tillemann turned them over to wet nurses and nannies. Jolie again: "Mama never spent time with her children the way other mothers did. She didn't play with us or take us to school or sit and listen to our problems. She remained always a big distance from us. If any of us called to her when she came home from work, she handled it by replying, 'Keep still. Don't shout. God should only help me that you will someday be out from here.' I don't remember her as ever being involved with us."

Nevertheless, "Mama was our everything. Simple love wasn't enough for how we felt about her. We adored her. We worshiped her." With her own daughters, Jolie replicated this unorthodox parenting. "When they were little girls I would charge them two cents to touch my beautiful complexion. This taught the value of money *and* the value of beautiful skin." Alongside this incipient charm school/credit union, Jolie would sometimes teach the girls pugilism. On a particular rainy afternoon, when Magda was six, Zsa Zsa four, and Eva two, they asked their mother how they might spend the afternoon.

"Why not have a fight?" she suggested.

"With pillows?" Magda chirped.

"No, a fistfight. A fight with hitting one another."

And so they began. Eva ended with a bloody nose, Zsa Zsa with scratches, Magda with pulled hair, and all with weeping and wailing.

Just then Vilmos came home. "What is going on here?" he demanded above Eva's screams. "Are you mad?"

"No," said Jolie. "For me it was very interesting. I like when they fight. I like when they do *everything*."

Jolie's School Without Pity continued in summer when they vacationed a hundred miles from Budapest at Lake Balaton, Hungary's largest body of water. "The lake was calm, I wanted them to know how to swim and so I threw them into the water. They simply had to swim and so they swam. My friend gasped, 'How can you throw them in?'"

" 'They will paddle like dogs,' I said calmly—and they did."

One further example of Jolie's pathological mother love

will convince the most skeptical that Vilmos had a point. She *was* mad. "At the circus," she recalled, "we sat spellbound as an Indian fakir swallowed fire while flames spurted from his mouth and he climbed a ladder of razor-sharp swords on naked feet. I punched my Zsa Zsa in her ribs. 'Now,' I hissed in the darkness, 'when will you be able to do that?'"

Jolie's goal, it seems, was to assure that her daughters turned out extraordinary, and, in their uniqueness, entirely dependent on her. Many children would resent this parental abuse to the point of loathing; the parent would risk estrangment. The Gabor sisters, on the other hand, professed undying devotion to Jolie, and throughout their lives they telephoned her once a day from whatever corner of the world they were in. No marriage took place until Jolie, like a dowager empress, nodded consent.

The obvious explanation for their slavish filial piety is insecurity, which Jolie instilled with mother's milk. Terrified of losing her love, the girls panted for any drop that Jolie squeezed from her leathery heart. Since she also encouraged them early on to compete with one another for their small ration, and to do so forever, the Gabors were never weaned. Into their own senior years—their seventies and eighties—they groped and elbowed one another like a litter of hungry kittens at the bosom of centenarian Jolie, who lived, well past one hundred, until 1997.

With every Gabor, facts are elusive and often reformatted to suit the occasion. In the matter of Vilmos, few exist. According to Zsa Zsa, he was eighteen years older than Jolie. Jolie upped the figure to twenty. If his actual age in 1958, at the time of that final Gabor family reunion, was eighty-four, as reported in the press, then he would have been born in 1874. That makes him a contemporary of Jolie's parents, and a couple of decades her senior.

In a photograph taken when Vilmos was about thirty-five years old, he resembles Harvey Keitel when Keitel was that age: a slightly crooked smile that suggests a lurking sense of sexy mischief; narrow eyes that seem to evaluate—or undress—those who catch his interest; and yes, those high cheekbones that his daughters so valued as their genetic inheritance. In another photograph, taken a few years later and after he had endured Jolie and the added stresses of fatherhood, Vilmos looks older than his fifty years.

As he aged, Vilmos came to look a lot like Conrad Hilton, Zsa Zsa's second husband. Had the Gabors crossed paths with Dr. Freud, whose Viennese couch stood a hundred miles west of Budapest, the diagnosis might have been, for all three sisters: Electra complex. The majority of their husbands were considerably older than they, and a number of them bore similar paternal lineaments. With a few notable exceptions, Zsa Zsa, Eva, and Magda married hard-driving capitalists, like their father. Nor did matrimony provide much fun. Everything wacky and witty that issued from a Gabor mouth was said on television or in interviews. Husbands were there as escorts, financial advisors, bearers of gifts, and scapegoats when plans went awry.

Lacking any chronicle by Vilmos, we must scrutinize every biographical scrap. As if intentionally to complicate the process, during his three years in the United States, 1945 to 1948, his daughters placed him under a virtual gag order: Do not speak to reporters! Later Iron Curtain censorship perhaps seemed benign by comparison. The girls also discouraged his learning English. What if, they whispered among themselves, he spilled the beans in contradiction of the growing Gabor myth invented by press agents and fattened by three hyperactive imaginations, with added calories from Mama? (One example: In the early 1940s, Paramount decided that Eva the starlet had been a champion ice skater and café singer in her native Hungary. In reality, she was minimally athletic and seldom landed on pitch. That imaginary café would have attracted only the deaf.)

According to Jolie, Vilmos was a poor boy who, by his thirties, had made a lot of money. He told his eager fiancée that his growing fortune came from the import-export business. "I own fruit trees," he said, "real estate, and businesses in Sardinia and Portugal." Translation: He had begun as a fruit peddler who operated a stall at the Central Market Hall, the largest and oldest indoor market in Budapest. In later years he prospered as a speculator, optioning entire crops of fruit in Italy and elsewhere when the young trees were planted. In so doing, he acquired rights to future yields at bargain rates. The risk, of course, was that bad weather could devastate the crop. This explains why the Gabor fortunes rose and fell. Eva, however, is the only one who ever alluded to lean times. In her sketchy autobiography, *Orchids and Salami*, she mentions that unlike her sisters, she did not go to finishing school in Switzerland. She hints, also, that 'round about this time the Gabor family gave up their comfortable apartment and moved in with Jolie's parents.

Vilmos, courting Jolie, brought flowers, baskets of fruit, and on one memorable visit "a black velvet jewel box. Inside, on the plush purple velvet, was a diamond choker studded with deep blue sapphires plus a bow of diamonds on the choker. Also, resting on their own carved-out beds were a pair of diamond earrings." This was almost certainly costume jewelry purchased at rhinestone rates, with perhaps a minuscule real diamond winking timidly in the mix.

His gifts impressed her, but not his manners. She considered Vilmos a parvenu, a nouveau riche. Whatever his deficiencies, however, Jolie matched and even surpassed them. "I thought, Wouldn't it be wonderful to have all this jewelry without the man."

Their marriage, in 1914, had nothing to do with love. Jolie, since childhood, had ambitions of becoming an actress, although her only qualification seems to have been the ability to swoon convincingly and collapse on the floor as limp as a feather boa. This talent she had acquired from watching silent-screen heroines such as Blanche Sweet, Lillian Gish, and the Hungarian actress Sári Fedák. Discussing the future with Vilmos, she confessed that she liked him but had no interest in marrying for love, not with him or anyone. She imagined herself in a few years as the First Lady of the Budapest Stage.

Vilmos, owing to his eye for sugar content—and invasive pests—in a given orchard, struck a deal with this silly young sprout of a girl. "Be my wife," he said, "and I promise that at the end of six months if you still want to be an actress I will give you your freedom. If you are not hilariously happy I'll give you a divorce. And you can keep the diamonds." Here we see the start of a family tradition, for Jolie's second marriage, many years later, and more than a few of her daughters', involved a similar quid pro quo. Love, when it happened, was a fringe benefit.

Anticipating her night of ecstasy, lusty Jolie, though still a virgin, sought out a leg waxer. This she kept a secret, for in Budapest in those years the only women with depilated legs were said to be prostitutes. And so she and Vilmos were united as husband and wife, in a marriage from Armageddon. Troths were plighted in the Tillemann family apartment at Rákóczi út 54, a building still standing in Budapest. On the ground floor of this building was Franceska R. Tillemann's emporium, the Diamond House.

From 1914, when they married, until 1918, and the Armistice, World War I engulfed most of Europe. Jolie seems hardly to have noticed, despite the turmoil and suffering. She makes only a passing reference to it in her autobiography:

"The Budapest of those days was a center of enormous zest for living. Even after the First World War, which was so disastrous for Hungary, Hungarians still lived their lives in huge flourishes." This omission seems even more singular in light of the Gabor family's claim that Vilmos had served in the Austro-Hungarian Army. The exact dates of his service cannot be determined. Indeed, his actual service remains in question. Here's why.

In the 1950s, when Gabor publicity resembled twenty-four-hour news, several reporters attempted to dig up the "truth" behind the headlines. At that time, a scattering of Hungarians living in the United States had known the Gabors back in Budapest, and reporters in search of an exclusive story spoke to various ones of them. Their versions often differed dramatically from the Gabors' own.

The consensus of these Hungarian émigrés was that the Gabors lived above their means and were considered on the odd side by neighbors and by the girls' classmates. Several made the unchivalrous claim that, far from the rank of major—or colonel, to which the family often promoted him—Vilmos had been a cook. Not so, ran a counterclaim. He sold fruit to Austro-Hungarian supply wagons and made a fortune with his overpriced produce. How then, these informants were asked, to account for the handsome photograph of Vilmos, in his forties one would guess, resplendent in hussar's uniform, and a chest bedecked with two rows of medals, more even than you'd see on His Majesty the Emperor Franz Joseph? Oh that, they replied. That's a cavalry costume from the operetta *Tatárjárás*, composed by Imre Kálmán in 1908. It was a huge hit all over Hungary, they added, and one of the hussar's costumes found its way to certain photographers' studios whose clients would pose in it for a portrait sitting. (*Tatárjárás* means "invasion of the Mongol Tatars," and the operetta dealt, unrealistically of course, with an important event in Hungarian history. The notion of those

Gabor cheekbones may have originated at a performance of the work.)

Conrad Hilton, Zsa Zsa's husband for a time, met Vilmos shortly after his arrival in the United States in 1945. "I asked him about those medals," said Hilton. "I said to him that he must have been in many battles." Zsa Zsa translated her husband's question, and her father's witty answer. Vilmos laughed and said, "The greatest battle I ever had was getting my wife from twenty-nine to thirty!" This suggests that the family had not yet briefed Vilmos on the newly minted family history, and that his candor might prove problematic to their agenda. No English lessons for Papuska, they decided. From that day forward, as the girls themselves turned his Hungarian into English, much was surely lost in translation.

When not fighting with Vilmos, Jolie was giving birth: Magda in 1915 (some accounts list her arrival as 1914), Zsa Zsa in 1917, and Eva in 1919. One month after Eva's birth, on February 11, revolution swept Hungary, with Budapest as storm center. With the country in postwar chaos, a small but powerful group of Hungarian communists, led by Béla Kun, proclaimed the Hungarian Soviet Republic. This communist regime lasted a mere 132 days.

Before that, however, the official start of the First World War occurred on June 28, 1914, when an ethnic Bosnian, Gavrilo Princip, assassinated Archduke Franz Ferdinand, heir presumptive to the Austro-Hungarian throne, and his wife, Sophie, Duchess of Hohenberg. The assassination took place in Sarajevo, later a part of Yugoslavia and today, since the dissolution of that country in the 1990s, the capital of Bosnia and Herzegovina.

Hungary in 1914 might be compared to present-day Scotland, which has its own prime minister, its own parliament, and yet in the eyes of many citizens, languishes under the heavy yoke of Great Britain. As in present-day Scotland, so in Hungary in the second decade of the twentieth century: agitation for independence, in the latter case from the Dual Monarchy of Austria-Hungary. As an independent nation, Hungary dates only from 1918.

Although outside the epicenter of war, Hungary nevertheless suffered widespread food shortages, high inflation, and other miseries. From *Budapest 1900*, by the eminent historian John Lukacs: "Sometime during the first winter of the war something unexpected began to appear in the streets of Budapest, something that clutched at the hearts of people, no matter how quickly they would turn their heads away from the sight of maimed or blind soldiers back from the front. Less visible at first but more and more evident was the destitution of tens of thousands of the wives and children of the working classes, whose husbands and fathers were at the front. The government support of their welfare was insufficient."

One reason that Jolie remained oblivious to such misery was her feverish fantasy life. She seems to have lived in it much more than in real time. In this regard, she was like Emma Bovary: besotted by romantic dreams, and unable to separate the plots of trashy novels from the less colorful events of daily life. "After four years of marriage," Jolie panted, "I read Elinor Glyn's book *The Three Weeks*, which is about a princess and a commoner and how they make love all day long. I thought, I will die if I don't have three such weeks." (*New Yorker* writer S.J. Perelman called the novel "servant-girl literature" written in Glyn's "marshmallow" style.)

Jolie's endless fights with Vilmos, though vicious, served as aphrodisiac: "He and I were always arguing. For no reason we would have a fight. For instance: 'If I gave you heaven you would not be happy!' Vilmos shouted at me.

" 'That is true,' I shouted back. 'I will be happy only when I find another man.' "

Jolie admits, however, that while life with Vilmos lacked storybook romance, perfumed rooms dimmed by deliquescent candles, and the throb of Gypsy violins, sex was raw and frequent. "He would have sex with me in the morning, in the evening, in the afternoon. We would make love before dinner. Even when we were longtime married he was very passionate and it was good. Even when I didn't like him in the daytime, I always loved him in the night." She loved him especially on the night when he took her in the hallway of their apartment, in front of a large beveled mirror.

They were far happier after their divorce in 1940, for then Jolie could flirt with him as though she were indeed that princess in the marshmallow pages of Elinor Glyn. "After the divorce we not only had lunch together but Vilmos would take me to the theatre and he would take me to dinner and then he would escort me home and sometimes we would sleep together, and then finally I was happy with him for the first time."

Chapter 2

The Mother of Them All

In her autobiography, published in 1975, Jolie narrates a relentless chronicle of faults, primarily those of Vilmos but also the miserable failings of her sisters, her in-laws, neighbors, friends far and near, and her daughters. She alone bears no stain, and from the very first paragraph her boasting soars like a beanstalk that can't be chopped down: "For my age I am a miracle. I am attractive. I am talented. I play the piano. I am the life of a party. I have always friends. I have a younger husband who adores me."

Typical of those who find truth unattractive, Jolie often gives herself away. One example is her repeated assertion that, after an ugly-duckling childhood, she blossomed into a great beauty—a claim belied by photographs in the press and in family albums. In reality, her features resembled an unfortunate blend of Marjorie Main and Caitlyn Jenner. Eventually, after myriad surgeries, her face morphed into the pastel abstraction of a Sherwin-Williams wall.

Jolie's daughters, on the other hand, showed early signs of allure, especially little Zsa Zsa. In a group photograph from around 1922, she has the Cupid's bow mouth that would always be hers, a smoldering look in her knowing eyes that's unsettling on a five-year-old, and a full head of auburn hair. Blonde Eva, still babyish at three, has huge dark eyes and a perfect oval face. Magda, then and later, bore the least resemblance to her parents or to her sisters. Her face was round and chubby. (Magda's childhood nicknames lingered in the family: "*Vörös*," redhead, and "*Duci*," big-boned.) As an adult, however, Magda was the sister who might most convincingly have claimed Mongolian ancestry, for her eyes were smaller and more tapered, her cheekbones higher than Zsa Zsa's or Eva's. Even as children, they showed the feline promise, and threat, of tiger kittens poised to pounce.

All three girls inherited the best features of Jolie and Vilmos, and few of the flaws, though Zsa Zsa always felt self-conscious about her large, pearly ears, and tried to keep them covered with hair, wigs, or hats. Even without the cosmetic enhancements that began in the 1940s and continued for the next fifty years, the Gabor sisters might have stood out as very attractive women.

Had Jolie been a present-day soccer mom, she could not have hovered closer to her girls nor signed them up for more instruction. "I gave them ballet lessons, tennis lessons, riding lessons," she recalled. Then, one glacial day in the Budapest winter, she decided they needed to learn ice skating, so off they went to Városliget, the largest city park in Budapest and as fashionable as the Bois de Boulogne. To these accomplishments were added fencing lessons and tutors in all subjects, for the Gabor girls took but a distant interest in book learning. This relegation of academics they surely absorbed by osmosis from Jolie, who valued the female mission of man trapping above all else. Poise, makeup, hair, jewelry, clothes, furs—Jolie preached the skilled and profitable exploitation of these. She believed, like Joan Rivers, that "no man is ever going to put his hand up your dress looking for a library card."

Some of these childhood lessons paid off. Zsa Zsa became an accomplished horsewoman, and so did Eva to a lesser extent. Both played tennis, and ballet knowledge transferred to the ballroom. Then and later, at parties, in nightclubs, and eventually onscreen, they commanded the dance floor with grace and aplomb, whether in a gliding waltz or an energetic caper—watch Eva, for instance, along with Maurice Chevalier, Joanne Woodward, Thelma Ritter, and several dozen extras in a slightly arthritic cancan in *A New Kind of Love* (1963). In the same picture, she does the twist with George Tobias.

The Gabor fingers, however, proved less agile than their legs, for ten years of piano lessons left the sisters unable to play anything more demanding than "Chopsticks." Jolie recalled fighting off sleep as she sat listening to "my musically untalented daughters as they practiced their terrible piano." Zsa Zsa inadvertently proved her right when, in 1964, on *The Jack Paar Show*, she sat at the piano with Liberace. For their duet, he assigned her a three-note cadenza to play when he gave the signal. "Black keys don't match my dress," she giggled. He launched his florid arrangement of "Night and Day," but Zsa Zsa's three notes soon proved beyond her meager abilities.

"That's the first time I ever saw Zsa Zsa flat," Paar bantered. To Zsa Zsa he said, "Liberace was practicing piano when you were practicing marriage."

Throughout their childhoods, Magda, Zsa Zsa, and Eva contended with their parents' endless fighting, the daily threats of divorce, the maledictions flung by Jolie at her husband's family and by Vilmos at Jolie's. "I will kill your Jewish mother," he stormed during one of their knock-down dragouts, referring to Franceska Tillemann. And he often damned Madame Tillemann as "that *kurva*," the Hungarian (and Yiddish) word for "whore" or "bitch."

"My mother-in-law was an awful woman," countered Jolie. "She was dreadful and common."

If Jolie so much as glanced at another man in the street, Vilmos exploded in a jealous rage. Again his threats, and again her vow to divorce him. The girls, at least, had one another, and being made of tough fiber they became inured to domestic strife. Early on, they joked about the divorce that never happened, at first among themselves and then openly to Jolie and Vilmos. "Divorce today?" caroled Magda, returning from school.

"Why don't you get a divorce so that I can stop piano lessons?" taunted Zsa Zsa.

Vilmos, with conventional ideas about the proper behavior of young ladies, blamed Jolie for their daughters' cheekiness. He surely had a point, for Jolie lived out her actressy fantasies through her girls. "I wanted for them the glamorous life I had so desperately wanted for myself," she said years later. "Your mother is crazy," he said to the girls, in Jolie's presence as in her absence. "She has everything and she still wants more."

Jolie's niece, Mrs. Lantos, who witnessed these goings-on as a young person, had this to say: "Very few men could have dealt with Jolie. She provoked Vilmos, but he was not a likeable man."

Jolie stirred the pot and kept life constantly off-balance for the family. "I always lied to Vilmos. Even when I had not things to lie to him about I would lie." Vilmos, when not goaded to fury by his wife, sometimes displayed a courtly side. He would greet ladies at a party with *"Kezét csókolom,"* meaning literally "I kiss your hand," which in old Budapest was considered gracious and a sign of good breeding. He and Jolie had nothing in common but sex, plus love for their daughters, however screwy that love may have appeared from a distance.

Jolie, then and later, couldn't resist a sharing violation. She incurred Zsa Zsa's wrath with an anecdote in her autobiography about their adventures on the skating rink at Városliget. Flirting with a handsome, uniformed young skater, Jolie became so enchanted with his finesse that she neglected her three small girls, who "screamed as around I went with my captain." Eventually, upon looking more closely, she discovered that her captain wore the uniform of a letter carrier. Deflated in her status search, she suddenly remembered her daughters and slid over to them, where tears were freezing on their puckered faces.

Arriving back home, Jolie said, "I herded my children into their big bathroom. My three treasures were blue with frost. Cuki [their governess] filled the bathroom with steam from the shower and showed me that Zsa Zsa had icicles hanging off her little *pinuska*. She had made pipi in her panties and it was so cold that ice formed." Always one to provide too much information, Jolie failed, in this anecdote and others, to realize that the childhood potty habits of glamour queens can only be read as macabre.

Under duress, however, her Belle Watling bawdiness yielded to the straightlaced notions of her husband. "We never discussed sex with the children," she said. "With prudish Vilmos I was afraid even to mention the word in the house. He had them so frightened that they believed they could get pregnant from a kiss." When pubescent Zsa Zsa plucked her eyebrows and appeared at dinner with her nails painted a garish heart-disease purple, her father shouted, "I won't have my daughters growing up to be bad women!" He accused Jolie of not raising them as normal human beings, a point not easily contradicted.

Along with abundant vulgarity, Jolie also had a charming side. In small doses, she was as amusing as a page from Dan Greenburg's *How to Be a Jewish Mother*. Virginia Graham said of her, "She is the original; her girls were made in Japan." Jolie never ran short of slightly ribald remarks, and she would sometimes lament, "Oh, I'm an old hag"—which everyone, of course, was expected to contradict. Once at a Chinese-themed costume party in Hollywood, she came as Confucius and passed out fortune cookies that advised, among other wise sayings, "Never mistake asthma for passion." On a more personal note, when I was eight years old I wrote her a letter, to which she responded with a glossy color photo of herself and her daughters, with a handwritten reply that read, "Thank you for your nice letter. Sincerely, Jolie Gabor."

And despite her pushiness and rampant egotism, she possessed a sometimes benevolent nature. During the Spanish flu pandemic beginning in 1918, Jolie took in the orphaned daughter of a couple who both had died within days of each other. Unfortunately, Jolie caught flu from the child and spent several weeks in the hospital. In later years, she attracted many friends with her earthy humor, her refusal to be depressed, and her talent for turning ordinary moments into amusing theatrical tableaux.

Some of Jolie's most serious moments came about in 1956, at the time of the Hungarian Revolution. On *The Tonight Show Starring Steve Allen*, November 22, 1956, she spoke in grave tones in her plea for funds to aid refugees who had fled Hungary during the recent uprising against Russian occupation. Then, in December, Jolie recorded another appeal for refugee aid. This one, a seventy-eight-second recording, was played on radio stations around the United States.

Long before the term "dysfunctional family" gained currency, the Gabors lived the prototype. Or did they? One might well ask how different they were from all others of their social class, if other families' secret chambers had been exposed to media scrutiny. No Gabor was beaten or abandoned, none shot, and despite their many stresses everyone spent money, laughed, ate their fill, and kicked up their heels.

During the Gabor sisters' childhood and coming-of-age years, the family lived in a number of locations, all on the Pest side of the Danube and most in neighborhoods identified as traditionally Jewish. Tracing their movements, however, would baffle the most Holmesian biographer. That's because every Gabor, even when giving a specific address, managed to obscure when, why, and how long they lived there. Then, too, much of Budapest was destroyed in World War II, with even more of the city reduced to rubble in the 1956 revolution. Add to that almost fifty years of communist rule, with gimcrack apartment blocks thrown up without thought to aesthetics, followed by Hungary's eventual membership in the European Union and greatly improved architecture replacing many buildings where the Gabors had lived, and the problem of determining their probable economic and social status in the 1920s and '30s is almost insoluble.

As mentioned earlier, Jolie and Vilmos were married at Rákóczi út 54, a building still in place on one of Budapest's principal streets. (Rákóczi has been called the Forty-second Street of Budapest.) Number 54 is a typical Belle Epoque building with a decorative façade, though the street, and the building, now look a bit seedy. Many parts of the city gleam, but that glow has not yet reached number 54.

Everyone in the family agreed that Zsa Zsa was born at Múzeum körút 31, a handsome building destroyed by Allied bombing in 1944 and later replaced by a drab postwar structure. At the time of Zsa Zsa's birth, this neighborhood matched parts of upper Fifth Avenue. The address is directly across the street from the Magyar Nemzeti Múzeum (Hungarian National Museum), a vast neoclassical building completed in 1846.

Jolie portrayed that dwelling in terms that might seduce a

high-end buyer. "The apartment was in one line. It was ten rooms but we had a mirror at the end of the hall and it looked like twenty rooms. It was enormous, with pillars and high ceilings, gigantic burgundy silk brocade upholstered chairs, heavy rosewood furniture, two immense salons, and two pianos."

When I read this description to Jolie's niece, Mrs. Lantos, she laughed and called it inflated. "Jolie counted the closets, bathrooms, and hallways," she said. "It was probably closer to four or five actual rooms." Jolie herself inadvertently revealed that the girls shared a single room. Surely that spacious flat of her imagination would have allowed separate bedrooms for her disputatious daughters.

No matter the location of their home, or the floor plan, one thing is certain. Mama planned her daughters' future. "I was determined not to send my children to college." This statement, chilling today, sounds less cruel when we recall that in many parts of the world, in the 1930s and later, college-educated women—and men—were the exception. Nevertheless, it seems that Magda, Zsa Zsa, and Eva were not consulted in the matter. "To use a checkbook they did not need geometry or algebra," reasoned Jolie. "It was my plan to send them to finishing school to learn to play music and be elegant, accomplished ladies with good manners and obviously good upbringing. I wanted them to be actresses and they are. They're not so talented like me but they are actresses."

She sounds like Mama Rose. If Jule Styne and Stephen Sondheim had had her book in hand as they wrote *Gypsy*, the show might have morphed to *Jolie*: for she, too, had a dream. A dream about Zsa Zsa, Eva, and Magda, who were gonna be stars, though never as good as Mama. For them, everything was coming up diamonds. Then at last, telling her story in 1975, there she was at last, world, and it was Jolie's Turn!

Chapter 3

The Best Little Finishing School in Switzerland

In later years, when asked about her school days, Zsa Zsa's refrain was, "I was raised in a convent." As in so many instances, her childhood memories allowed for sweeping poetic license. In reality, she attended Notre Dame de Sion, a day school in Budapest operated under the auspices of nuns. Classes were taught in French, and there Zsa Zsa, along with her sisters, studied not only French language and French literature (of the morally uplifting sort), but also English, history, and mathematics. The school was located on Mária útca, a short distance from the Gabor apartment. It is interesting to note, in the case of the Gabors, that the Congregation of Our Lady of Sion ("Sion" being French for "Zion") was founded in Paris in the mid-nineteenth century by two priests, the Ratisbonne brothers, who were Jewish converts to Roman Catholicism. The various schools run by Notre Dame de Sion served as outreach to Jewish children, those whose families had converted as well as those who were culturally assimilated but still technically of the Jewish religion. Until recent times, conversion was at least one aim, however submerged, of the schools.

Here we find ourselves again on Gabor quicksand, for one of their contemporaries, a New York woman who knew them in Budapest, had this to say: "They were Jewish. I was in Hebrew school with them." Her statement does not necessarily negate Zsa Zsa's claim to a Catholic education, for the term "Hebrew school" can mean both a full-time curriculum and also the equivalent of a Sunday school that meets for an hour or so each week to teach children Jewish history and the rudiments of biblical Hebrew.

Jolie and her daughters filled their sequined autobiographies with governesses enough to rival P.L. Travers. Their own Mary Poppins, however, was Cuki, whom they sometimes called their nanny; we met her a few pages back as she attended to little Zsa Zsa's ice emergency after Jolie's negligence at the skating rink. Eva described Cuki as "our German governess" who was "warmhearted, lovable, and fat." Since the Gabor fortunes rose and fell during the 'teens, twenties, and thirties, in actuality those governesses were most likely short-term help. According to family legend, they remained but briefly in the household owing to the decibel level of parental quarrels and the ungovernability of the girls. While lack of job satisfaction no doubt played a role in the governess merry-go-round, Hungary's economic crises, and the Gabors' own, contributed to the volatility. But Cuki endured.

When each Gabor daughter reached the age of thirteen or fourteen, it was time to look beyond home instruction, tutors, and Notre Dame de Sion. Jolie, as usual, had a grandiose plan for the advancement of her "treasures," for they were truly valuable investments.

Some girls are thrilled by the prospect of finishing school in Switzerland, but not Magda Gabor, and certainly not Zsa Zsa. Although forced to live Jolie's dream, to learn languages, to acquire social graces, and most of all, as Jolie drummed into the heads of her young show ponies, *to be agreeable to a man,* her daughters disliked Madame Subilia's School for Young Ladies, near Lausanne, from the start. Hoping to win over Vilmos, Jolie veiled from him what she told unhappy Magda and Zsa Zsa: "In Switzerland, you will learn how to make glamorous, rich marriages." Rather, she emphasized to her skeptical husband the high morality of Madame Subilia, for this lady was around fifty years of age, well seasoned in the transformation of tomboys (which Zsa Zsa was) and burnishing the rough edges even of a studious, reticent girl like Magda. "Vilmos," stated Jolie in unusually pious tones, "Madame is very strict. Her girls wear uniforms, proper hats, and black stockings. They pray before lunch and they sing religious songs before dinner. Best of all for our Gabor night owls, they are in bed with lights out by ten o'clock. Why, the discipline is almost like the military. When they come home, they will know how to pour tea and hold a teacup just like Sybil Thorndike!"

A classmate of Zsa Zsa's, who will soon have more to say about their schooldays, realized, many years after leaving Madame Subilia's, that the headmistress was probably a lesbian. She shared an upstairs apartment with another woman, who was either a teacher in the school or otherwise employed there. Those two ladies formed a couple. Each one of the girls had an assigned week of duty during which she brought their dinner up from the refectory. These girls were under strict orders to set down the food tray outside the door, knock, and depart. No pupil ever saw the inside of the apartment, though speculation was rife.

In English, the term "finishing school" carries echoes of Jacqueline Kennedy, Mrs. Astor, and other high-toned ladies. Eva, who did not attend Madame Subilia's, called it a "pension," in Europe an ambiguous term that means anything from a B and B to the down-at-the-heels rooming house in Balzac's *Père Goriot*. She surely meant "pensionnat," a boarding school that does not necessarily imply the snob appeal of a Miss Porter's School in Connecticut. To Jolie's febrile mind, however, it could have been a flophouse so long as the address was francophone Switzerland.

It happened that Jolie's sister Janette had a daughter, Ila, near Magda's age, so the four of them boarded a train for Lausanne. Having deposited the girls, Jolie and Janette charged into town for a day of shopping. When the shops closed, Jolie, prepped for an evening of flirtation *à la suisse*, decked herself out in finery, sprayed perfume on her bosom, admired herself in the mirror, and—the phone rang. It was Madame Subilia.

Young Magda, finding herself in a drafty bedroom on a hallway with a gaggle of girls of international provenance—a sort of adolescent *Magic Mountain* minus the respiratory afflictions and ponderous philosophy—felt herself abandoned in an alien land.

"What am I to do with this girl?" Madame Subilia demanded. "She hasn't stopped weeping since you left. Homesick, desperately homesick and it's only the first day."

"I was delighted," recalled Jolie. "This meant I stayed on in Switzerland without Vilmos." She wired him a dark version of Magda's plight. Among Magda's nicknames in the family were "the Duchess," for her high-minded standards, and "the General," for her stoicism and iron will. And so, after a few days at school, she began to relax into the Swiss orderliness and sanity that struck her as so different from home.

Great ambiguity exists as to the number of prayers offered and the number of hymns sung in chapel at Madame Subilia's. The school seems to have been nondenominational, although for form's sake the girls learned the basics of high-church behavior. More important than theology was the ladylike protocol of covering one's head in a house of worship with a stylish hat and bedecking one's person in Sunday best.

The following year, Zsa Zsa arrived at Madame Subilia's

and shed not a single homesick tear. Her two years there, as recounted by Zsa Zsa and by her roommate, conjure a mix of *Mädchen in Uniform*, the 1932 German film about schoolgirls and their Teutonic teachers, and *The Prime of Miss Jean Brodie*. Despite the restrictions of "long black stockings, penances, and psalms before dinner," as Zsa Zsa recalled, the staff lamented that she still was not quite house trained. In her first letter back to Budapest, she begged Mamuska for two favors: please send me a garter belt, and burn this letter before Papuska can read my request. "I am the only Hungarian girl here, and the others think all Hungarians are Gypsies and are amazed that I know how to use a knife and fork."

Looking back on her teenage self from her early forties, Zsa Zsa admitted that "I was not a good student but I was a quick one. My mind was amazingly fast; I always seemed to know more than I really knew because of a word here, a phrase there, and I was able to catch meanings instantly." When her answers in class fell wide of the mark, the other girls tittered. They also laughed, though not maliciously, at her French, which she spoke with a Hungarian accent, and at her Hungarianized English.

Then and always, Zsa Zsa was an Anglophile. Her closest friend was a British girl named Phyllis who decided one day to tame this feral specimen. "She put her arm around me and announced, 'I'm taking this little barbarian under my wing.'" Zsa Zsa loved it. "I became her slave," she said. Already Zsa Zsa manifested what her third husband, George Sanders, called her "colonial complex," i.e., blind admiration for everything British: men, women, clothes, customs.

Neither at Madame Subilia's nor elsewhere did anyone mistake Zsa Zsa for a polymath. She was, however, always street smart and fearless, a daredevil and an egoist. Despite her unstudious nature, however, in Switzerland she perfected her command of foreign languages. French and German she soon spoke with near-native fluency and minimal accent. In

English, the accent became a trademark, although when she braked the logorrhea she could lose half of it.

A rare example of this: In 1971 she narrated the shaggy-dog saga *Mooch Goes to Hollywood*. Unseen on camera, she sounds like a calmer, less exotic Zsa Zsa Gabor. Eva, the year before, as the voice-over of Duchess in *The Aristocats*, also sounded unlike her ususal self. In that animated film, Eva the cat purred her English with only a fraction of the Gabor accent. One might theorize, therefore, that both sisters were so concerned with how they looked on TV or in movies that they neglected enunciation. Or perhaps they increased the accent for effect, playing it as an instrument. Like Garbo, they were instantly recognizable by the gold in their throat.

Eva, who spoke French, German, and English in addition to Hungarian, said, "I can talk about nothing in four languages." Nor could she spell. On one of her many *Match Game* appearances, the word to match was "burp." Eva knew the synonym "belch" but wrote on her card "belczze." The audience roared and copanelist Richard Dawson leaned over and said, "Eva, 'belch' has only one Z!"

Zsa Zsa once told an interviewer that she spoke Hungarian no better than English and that she couldn't spell in any language. Nevertheless, she learned enough Turkish to get by while married to her first husband and living in Ankara, and later on she could hold her own in Italian and Spanish. At Madame Subilia's, her favorite subject was art, and throughout her life she remained a talented Sunday painter. (As did Eva, several of whose well-executed landscapes fetched enviable prices on eBay a few years ago.)

Report cards did not concern Jolie. When Zsa Zsa returned to Budapest at holidays, her mother inspected her for auguries of a femme fatale in the making. If Madame Subilia, or other teachers, attached a note that Zsa Zsa's deportment fell below expected standards, Jolie shrugged it off, for Zsa Zsa, like her mother before her, read slapdash romance novels under the bedcovers after lights out. Caught up in these bodice rippers, she fancied herself swept off to remote castles by dashing young counts and aging barons. And who cares, sighed Jolie, if young girls climb out of windows at midnight to meet boys. To improve Zsa Zsa's taste, Phyllis lent her a clandestine copy of *Nana*, Zola's novel about a streetwalker who rises to Parisian fame and fortune thanks to the powerful men she seduces. Zsa Zsa, in later life, seems to have updated some of Nana's enticements.

Zsa Zsa's roommate during much of her sojourn at Madame Subilia's was Elisabeth Rucklander, a Swiss girl from Zürich whose native language was German and whose parents sent her to Lausanne to perfect her French. A few years later, Fräulein Rucklander married a Mr. Nussbaum, who had escaped to Zürich from Nazi Germany, and after the war the couple settled in Seattle. Although Mr. and Mrs. Nussbaum are now deceased, I recently spoke with their son, Tom, and their daughter, Dorie.

Asked about his mother during her time at Madame Subilia's, Tom Nussbaum had this to say: "I believe my mom had certain personality disorders. Today she might be placed in a high-functioning level of special education. For example, she just didn't know when to shut up, or when to filter her thoughts."

"Exactly like Zsa Zsa," I said.

"Mom always called Zsa Zsa 'that beast.' Which was her word for 'bitch.' In hindsight, I realize it was because the two of them were so much alike. Mom couldn't stand her, and she probably couldn't stand my mother because they both babbled a mile a minute, giving out every thought and opinion that nobody asked for." In Zsa Zsa's case, this unfiltered flood of talk was an early manifestation of the bipolar disorder that would become more pronounced with passing years, often with scandalous or outré consequences.

It was Elisabeth Rucklander Nussbaum who realized, late in life, that Madame Subilia and her female companion were probably lesbians. Whatever her later feelings about Zsa Zsa, however, as girls they must have shared some good times, for Tom and Dorie Nussbaum showed me a letter that Zsa Zsa wrote to their mother around 1930. My translation from Zsa Zsa's imperfect French and her unwieldy handwriting:

> *My dear Lizon* [i.e., Lizzie]
> *I must write to tell you that I'm happy to be going home even though it's sad to leave behind those I've known for almost a year and a half, and every day, almost every minute. Remember when we shared a room how we laughed and carried on. And on our excursions, what funny things you said. My dear, I will never forget my little chum from Munich* [Zsa Zsa's mistake; her friend had no connection to Munich] *who was so lively and so "obedient." I hope that if one day you come to Budapest you will pay me a visit.*
> *Be happy!*
> *A thousand kisses,*
> *Zsa Zsa*

Eva seemed grateful to have dodged Madame Subilia's. In her tell-very-little autobiography, *Orchids and Salami*, published in 1954, she had this to say: "When my turn came, the money market shuddered. Hungarian pengős went down and Swiss francs went in another direction. The cataclysm in the money market spared me instruction in such matters as cooking, needlepoint, deep-frozen etiquette, and other idiocies whereby a young girl was made totally incompetent." She attended instead the Forstner Girls Institute in Budapest, an establishment later obliterated either by war or urban renewal. Despite many inquiries in Hungary and myriad searches online, I have found not a trace.

No Gabor ever admitted to hard times, though Eva inadvertently revealed an acquaintance with household drudgery that she perhaps acquired with the fall of the pengö. "Life for me has not always been a never-never land. Blonde as I am, I do know the shape of a broom and the function of the wet end of a mop. I have used them both, spiritlessly to be sure, but competently enough."

No precise documentation exists that maps the activities of Zsa Zsa, Eva, and Magda from the early 1930s, when they completed their schooling, to the later thirties, when all three began their adventures in matrimony. Several reports by Hungarian émigrés in the 1950s that were printed in newspaper and magazine articles about the Gabors placed them behind the counter of one family shop or another.

At some point, the Gabors claimed, Vilmos joined his wife's family in the jewelry business, although he loathed his in-laws. Some of those same Hungarian émigrés, however, remembered him as a watchmaker who worked in a cubbyhole of a shop cluttered with watches, clocks, and spare parts for timepieces. Bundy Solt, the childhood friend of the Gabor sisters, modified these claims as well as the more grandiose ones of his friends. "Papa Gabor's main business," he said, "was catering to a middle-class clientele. Young men would come to the shop to buy their engagement and wedding rings. Fathers would come to buy the first gold wristwatch for their sons. It was not the chichi type of Cartier or Van Cleef and Arpels, but rather a jewelry store catering to the masses."

Contradicting what he considered the false witness of anti-Gabor Hungarians in the United States, Solt said, "No group hates the Gabors more than the refugee Hungarians. They cannot forget that the descendants of a bourgeois merchant could become so famous, whereas most of the so-called elegant aristocratic Hungarian refugees in New York and California didn't get anywhere."

According to Zsa Zsa, her father's store, at number 6 Rákóczi út, was down the street from Franceska Tillemann's own Diamond House. Perhaps Vilmos's hatred of his mother-in-law grew out of envy. Hungary, of course, was not spared the hardships of the worldwide Depression in the 1930s, so that it is reasonable to assume that Vilmos tried to keep up his other enterprises. People might pawn their clocks and watches and never replace them, but their hunger for fresh produce would go on.

By the time the Gabor sisters reached their mid- to late teens, Jolie had acquired two stores. Bundy Solt again: "Mama Gabor's shop was called 'Jolie.' She became so successful selling the same type of jewelry that she sells today [he was speaking in 1958]—costume jewelry which incorporated the fine workmanship of genuine jewelry—that she opened a second store around the corner from her little boutique. This was called 'Crystallo.' Here she specialized in selling crystal glass and porcelain." Mrs. Lantos recalls another one of her aunt's shops called "Bijou."

With both parents running busy establishments, it is more likely than not that Zsa Zsa, Eva, and Magda helped behind the counters. Whatever their teenage reluctance, they would have required lower wages than hired shopgirls, or perhaps no cash stipend at all, meaning that money stayed in the family. And under Mamuska's tutelage, they learned that everything comes with a price tag.

Chapter 4

Tempest on the Danube

Zsa Zsa, age fifteen, having learned all she could be taught at Madame Subilia's, returned to Budapest. Scarcely was she off the train than Jolie decided that her middle daughter should become Miss Hungary. And so she did—*but only in the imagination of two Gabors: Jolie, and Zsa Zsa herself.* For the next sixty years, they repeated that fiction so often that to them it became an article of faith. Neither Eva nor Magda, however, fostered the fabrication.

The truth about Jolie's shady machinations to insert Zsa Zsa into the Miss Magyarország contest, as it was officially known, would require an investigation as vast as that of the Watergate scandal. ("Magyarország" is the Hungarian name for Hungary.) Although in later years Zsa Zsa would vow in interviews that she had been chosen Miss Hungary, she didn't specify the year. As she moved up her date of birth—eventually to 1928—journalists began to mock her by pointing out that she would thus have been Miss Hungary at age five. Squeezed by chronology, she pushed forward the phantom event to 1936 . . . 1938 . . . 1939. After so many prevarications, however, savvy writers in the press knew that during those years she was married and living in Turkey. In her first autobiography, published in 1960, Zsa Zsa gave a more accurate account. At the Grand Hotel Royale, the contest venue, "Mother was hugging me ecstatically. 'You've won—you're Miss Hungary!' But I was not Miss Hungary. I was not sixteen and I had to be sixteen. The judges met in emergency session; there was nothing to do but name the runner-up as Miss Hungary, and name me also a runner-up, or first Maid of Honor."

Based on my research in Budapest, and on archival film footage of the event, I submit this report. The year was 1933, in the month of January. Zsa Zsa had recently come home from Switzerland, either having graduated at midterm or, owing to some misdemeanor, been expelled. In that winter month, Zsa Zsa was fifteen years old; she would not turn sixteen until February 6, and sixteen was the minimum age for contestants.

Both she and Jolie later claimed that several of the contest judges had recently attended a party at the home of Franceska Tillemann, Jolie's mother, and that Jolie had engaged in the kind of electioneering that might sway a venal judge or repel the more scrupulous. Vilmos, meanwhile, opposed what he labeled his wife's attempt to sell Zsa Zsa into white slavery. "I won't have my daughter put on display!" he railed.

Archival footage from January 1933 contradicts the Gabor version of Zsa Zsa stripped of her title upon discovery of her true age. In it, the three finalists march onstage, Júlia Gál is crowned as winner, and Zsa Zsa and the other runner-up exit. In the press, she was called "*udvarhölgy*," or "lady in waiting." No doubt this designation rankled. It recalled those trays of hot food left outside the closed door of Madame Subilia and companion, as well as afternoons spent waiting on customers in parental emporia.

A different version of Zsa Zsa's loss appeared in the *New York Post* in 1958, in a series of eleven articles on the House of Gabor. At that time, Sándor Incze, a Hungarian refugee, was living in Manhattan, and available for an interview. Years earlier, in 1933, he had been publisher of *Szinházi Élet* (*Theatrical Life*), whose cover issue for January 29–February 4 that year bore a photograph of the contest winner, Júlia Gál, flanked by the two runners-up. *Szinházi Élet* was sponsor of the beauty contest.

"I came home to Budapest from a trip to London on the morning of the contest," Incze recalled, "and my secretary told me, 'Oh, we have a wonderful girl.' The girl was Zsa Zsa, and the whole staff thought she should be Miss Hungary. But the whole staff also had been over to dinner at Zsa Zsa's house the night before. Her mother, Jolie, had invited them. Well, I was annoyed because it looked like a fix. Zsa Zsa was the most beautiful girl in the contest, but I put on a real fight against her. If people found out about that dinner, they would say it was rigged." According to his account, age had nothing to do with it.

Nevertheless, if tribute had been paid to nubile feminine poise on that January day in the ballroom of the Grand Hotel Royale in Budapest, young Zsa Zsa would have won. The actual winner, Júlia Gál, and the other lady in waiting, Lilly Radó, both seventeen, could pass for middle-aged matrons. Both look rather used-up, with mousy hair, undistinguished facial features, and slightly stooped posture. Sandor Incze again: "When we elected Júlia Gál, she didn't even smile. In fact, all through the contest she kept a serious expression on her face. We started to take pictures, and I told her to smile. 'I can't,' she said, 'because my teeth are bad.'" Incze rushed her to the dentist, then to a later photo shoot.

Zsa Zsa, by contrast, is sweet-faced. If her expression is not exactly innocent, she has nonetheless the patina of virtue. Even then, at fifteen, she possessed the extraordinary Zsa Zsa face in embryo, although her eyebrows, plucked thin, suggested an unfortunate resemblance to Eva Braun, and so did her limp, sallow hair. But those high cheekbones were in place. In Budapest, viewing footage of the event, I wondered who taught Zsa Zsa to walk like that, for even then her gait was the chest-out, movie star stride that continued throughout her life, whether sweeping onstage at the Pantages Theatre to present an Oscar to Edith Head in 1952, making her entrance on Broadway in 1970 in *Forty Carats*, or, at age seventy, greeting Dame Edna Everage on TV in London in 1987 with that same alluring, though slightly macho, prance.

As Jolie told it, Vilmos sent her and Zsa Zsa to Vienna for a week to console their loss. The loss was indeed a joint one, for Jolie suffered more than her child. Zsa Zsa, after all, had a future, whereas her mother bewailed the prospect of bleak years in an empty nest with an even bleaker husband.

That Viennese journey, however, did not take place for over a year. Zsa Zsa's beauty-pageant defeat occurred in January 1933, and not until summer of the next year did she and Jolie end up in Vienna. It is likely that Zsa Zsa spent that gap year once more behind the counter, for Hungary, like the rest of the world, had plunged into the Great Depression. It was just then that Eva, had money been plentiful, would have gone off to finishing school in Switzerland. But instead she stayed in Budapest and perhaps wielded her first broom and mop.

Zsa Zsa and Jolie arrived in Vienna one warm August day in 1934. A few days later they traveled with friends to Grinzing, a suburb near the Vienna Woods. There they attended an outdoor concert, where, Zsa Zsa recalled, "We had all been given tall, thin tumblers of heady wine." Into this romantic setting there suddenly came a handwritten note which, in keeping with romantic stories, proved fateful for the young heroine. It was, of course, from a man, and though Zsa Zsa's narrative of the follow-up to that afternoon seems unlikely, the facts stand up to scrutiny. We've caught Zsa Zsa in the truth.

A waiter brought the folded note to Jolie, telling her that a gentleman at a distant table wished her to have it. That gentleman was none other than Richard Tauber, the world-famous Austrian tenor whose name, and voice, were as familiar in the music world of the day as Plácido Domingo's today. Tauber was forty-four years old, heavy-set, and he bore a resemblance to both Vilmos Gabor and to Josip Broz Tito, the ruler of postwar Yugoslavia. For added distinction, he wore a monocle perched over his right eye. Tauber's vast repertoire included roles in operas and operettas, and his countless worldwide appearances in both, along with recordings, had made him a matinee idol to match any in Hollywood. Adulation by his fans turned him into the rock star of his day. (Tauber's voice can still be heard on CD compilations and on youtube.com.)

The legend of Lana Turner discovered sipping a Coke at Schwab's Pharmacy had not yet been invented. Zsa Zsa's own discovery by Tauber predated that fanciful press agentry by three years. The note to Jolie was written in German. Zsa Zsa's translation ran like this: "Forgive me, Madame, but I am seeking a girl to play an American debutante in my new operetta. If it is your daughter with you, may I have a word?"

Zsa Zsa's animation, fueled by nerves and nerve, had caught his eye, and no wonder. The flightness and the unfiltered chatter that so annoyed her roommate, Elisabeth Rucklander, at Madame Subilia's, gave Tauber the idea of auditioning her for *Der Singende Traum* (*The Singing Dream*), the operetta he had recently composed. The premiere was set for August 31 at the Theater an der Wien, a prestigious historic venue.

Tauber's widow, the British actress Diana Napier, recounted the plot: "The story was not new: it was about a man, terribly in love, who hypnotized an actress. Only under his spell does she sing successfully but he cannot hypnotize her into falling in love with him." Typical of Viennese operettas, Tauber's floated on clouds of honeyed melody with faint suggestions of naughtiness and a plot guaranteed free of realism. The role of the actress was sung by Mary Losseff, Tauber's lover before his marriage to Napier. He wrote *Der Singende Traum* for Losseff, his stated purpose being "to make her the biggest singing star in the world."

Tauber cast Zsa Zsa as Violetta, a teenage soubrette. A problem loomed, however, one that seemed insurmountable: the part required singing and dancing. We have seen Zsa Zsa as a passable dancer but a lamentable chanteuse. An unfortunate singing voice, however, seldom stops the casting of a performer in a musical role, whether on Broadway or in Vienna, especially if the producers find the performer endowed with other qualities, such as stage presence or a star name. In Zsa Zsa's case, not only was the voice unlovely; she was also tone deaf, with a tin ear and vocal cords to match. But Tauber found something he liked. Perhaps her walk, so noticeable a year earlier in the Miss Magyarország competition, won him over. Or was there a quid pro quo?

Jolie knew how things got done, in the theatre and elsewhere. What her zealous imagination didn't supply, she learned from acquaintances among the demimondaines of Budapest who visited her shop. She realized that girls must sometimes make sacrifices, and so must older ladies.

Tauber's love for Mary Losseff did not obviate his attraction to other pleasing females who came into view. He pounced like a bobcat on Diana Napier, whom he married in 1936. They enjoyed an open relationship until his death in 1948. And groupies flocked to his dressing room, to the stage door, to his hotel suite. As for Zsa Zsa, apparently no intimacy took place beyond what she reported: "Now and then as I passed him backstage, he would pat me approvingly on the rear. 'Solid, solid,' he would say teasingly, and burst into laughter." Otherwise, Tauber was involved with Mary Losseff around the clock, onstage and off. And Zsa Zsa had a different admirer, whom we will soon meet.

Had Tauber known the Gabor backstory, he might well have composed an *opéra comique* filled with their antics. What a team he and Jolie would have made, a pair of Falstaffs. Tauber, with schmaltz and schlag aplenty in his music, kept it up offstage, as well. He could have qualified as an honorary Gabor.

The morning after the presentation to Jolie of Tauber's folded note, she and Zsa Zsa kept their appointment at the Theater an der Wien. Seated in the darkened auditorium, Jolie clenched her moist fists in anxiety as insouciant Zsa Zsa began her number, first singing in German, then trying out the dance steps. "I got through it," she recalled. "A dance instructor had coached me for ten minutes; in his arms I stumbled and giggled and somehow managed one of the routines. Perhaps I should have been more awe-struck by it all, but I took it almost as a lark."

Here we see the first indication of Zsa Zsa's refusal to accept the discipline and the drudgery required for an enduring show business career. In 1950s Hollywood, except for *Moulin Rouge* and a couple of other films, she put forth minimum effort for each performance, seldom more. Soon she acquired the reputation of only playing herself.

Onstage in Vienna, also, there appears evidence of how Zsa Zsa's flippant approach differed from Eva's, for Eva toiled to improve her abilities. She sought to burnish her talent so that every performance lifted her above all previous ones. When, in later years, a script called for her to dance on-screen, she rehearsed until her short legs throbbed. For Eva, work was never a lark, though sometimes—as in *Green Acres*—she made it seem so.

Unready for a debut on any stage, let alone in sophisticated Vienna, Zsa Zsa found herself in theatrical boot camp. For three intensive weeks, voice coaches, along with acting teachers and dance instructors, worked to transform this Hungarian sow's ear into lovely Viennese silk. Everyone chorused, "You can't sing, you can't dance, you can't act!" (Eighteen years later, John Huston yelled the same at her on the set of *Moulin Rouge*.) Her vocal coach, who carried a violin bow in his hand to beat out rhythm, rapped poor Zsa Zsa over the head with it while telling her how awful she sounded. Finally he told her to lie supine, and he put three heavy books on her stomach. "Now sing from down there," he ordered. The result did not please him. At length the producer lost his patience. "Since you can't do anything else," he thundered, "at least keep that pretty face of yours to the audience!" This suggests that Zsa Zsa had been demoted to stage decoration while others did the musical heavy lifting.

In view of such staggering lack of talent, I recently asked an experienced vocal teacher whether she could take a student with zero ability and in three weeks squeeze out an acceptable sound. "No," she answered. "I did that with a boy of seven, but it took two years." She also remembered an unlikely man of seventy-five who made somewhat faster progress, but not in three weeks. Finally I said, "Suppose you absolutely had to teach someone to sing in that amount of time. Opening night is up to you. What can you do?"

She said, "If the music was of a very limited range, a few notes around middle C, then it might work. I'm not sure. That student could perhaps sing 'Hot Cross Buns,' or something like it, especially if the orchestra covered her worst blunders."

On August 29, two days before the premiere, Zsa Zsa was fired. Once more Jolie the Tiger, burning bright, leapt onto the producer. No doubt sore from Gabor teeth marks, he relented. On August 31, 1934, *Der Singende Traum* opened, with Richard Tauber and Mary Losseff in the leads, and Sári Gábor billed fifth.

But which Gabor was that? It was, of course, our Zsa Zsa, whose birth name was Sári, a form of the Hungarian Sára. She was named for one of Jolie's maternal aunts, and also for Sári Fedák (1879–1955), Hungary's most famous actress in the early years of the twentieth century. Fedák's nickname, in her family and among fans, was Zsa Zsa, and so little girls with the same name also became Zsa Zsa. Fedák, however, eventually proved an unfortunate namesake. The second wife (1922–1925) of playwright Ferenc Molnár, she became famous in Hungary and elsewhere in Central Europe as a splendid actress and singer. Her politics shifted from left to right until at last she became a Nazi sympathizer. In the 1940s, Fedák made propaganda broadcasts from Vienna in which she urged Hungary to continue as an ally of Hitler's Germany. After the war, she was sentenced in Budapest to an eight-month prison term.

Zsa Zsa offered several coy versions of how she lost her virginity, none involving Tauber. Perhaps the loss was serial, for she once implied that a warm bath restored a woman to her original state.

Zsa Zsa was kept on for the three-month run of *Der Singende Traum* in Vienna. To everyone's surprise, she received positive reviews. "Extremely amusing was the charming Sári Gábor," wrote one critic. "Miss Sári Gábor, who plays Violetta, bears great promise for the future," echoed another. During the run, Zsa Zsa spotted a man in the first row of the orchestra whose eyes seemed to follow her like a key light. "He was a wild, passionate-looking man in his late forties, with a square, Mongolian face and a great mane of iron-gray hair." In other words, just her type. And since Herr Tauber's flirtation stopped at butt-slapping, she returned the gaze of the man in front row center. (Then and later, she didn't hesitate to break character.)

The man was Willy Schmidt-Gentner, a well-known composer of film music. Born in Germany in 1894, he had just turned forty when he and Zsa Zsa met; perhaps to her teenage eyes he looked much older. (Years subtracted from her own age she often added onto others, usually women.) Soon they were seen around town. He plied her with vodka and compliments, eventually revealing that he had a wife in Switzerland. Some girls, learning such news, would have suffered. Not Zsa Zsa, because, as she said later, "In the world in which I grew up, one did not marry for love: a man took as his wife a suitable young woman of good family who became the mother of his children, who was skilled in running his home and entertaining his friends. For love he turned to someone else. Love in marriage was a luxury which only the very poor could afford."

Her recollections, years later, gave this May–December romance the lineaments of—well, a Viennese operetta. Willy didn't hypnotize her, or not literally, but he did use every line in the book except the one about his etchings. "With proper guidance and hard work," he said, gazing into her avid eyes, "you can make a real career." Although he probably didn't believe a word of it at the time, by the end of his life, in 1964, his prophecy had come true beyond his imagination, or hers.

In the final weeks of 1934, Willy was called away from Vienna to compose the score for a new film. He begged Zsa Zsa to come along, and she actually accompanied him as far as Klagenfurt, the last Austrian city before the international border. Frightened at the gravity of eloping to a foreign country with a married man, she left the train at midnight. The next train in the opposite direction, back to Vienna and from there to Budapest, was not due until 5:00 a.m. Sitting in the drafty waiting room on a hard, wooden bench, she pondered her situation: "What was I doing here, away from my home, my parents, my family?" In those snowy predawn hours, the sophisticated young woman deliquesced. Tears rolled down her cheeks and into her cup of black coffee. Like a heavy bell, the question tolled, What now? What now?

Chapter 5

Starter Marriages

Whether by design or coincidence, the Gabor girls almost married in order of age, eldest first, as in a Jane Austen novel. Zsa Zsa, however, like Lydia Bennet in *Pride and Prejudice*, jumped the gun at eighteen and married Burhan Belge, a minor official in the Turkish embassy at Budapest. He was thirty-six at the time of the marriage, which took place on May 17, 1935.

Two years later Magda married, and Eva in 1939. Jolie, like Austen's fluttery Mrs. Bennet, reacted with fulsome pleasure as each daughter made what she, in her rhapsodic mind, fashioned into an exalted match. Each daughter's subsequent departure for a foreign land served to further engorge Jolie's sumptuous fantasies: Zsa Zsa in Turkey and supposedly addressed as "Your Excellency" owing to her husband's diplomatic status; Magda a countess in Poland; and Eva in Hollywood, married to a doctor—what could be more enchanting for Jolie's demented propriety? The only shadow over this Hungarian version of correct Janeite lives is the mouse-like rumor that darted here and there in the fifties, viz., that Zsa Zsa eloped at fourteen with a Gypsy boy. Perhaps the rumor arose when someone spied her innocently climbing out a Swiss window at midnight.

A more potent rumor, this one equally fanciful and unverifiable, is the one that bestows on Magda the title Countess of Warsaw. Her first husband, Jan Bychowski (also given as de Bichovsky, Bychowsky, et al.), was reputed to be a count. But reputed only by the Gabors. He is nowhere in the *Almanach de Gotha*. The closest you'll come to a title for him is a coat of arms for the Bychowsky family, which means only that someone paid to have one designed. (You'll find a plethora of coats of arms for the families Smith, Jones, and any other with money to buy one.)

It is true that Magda married Jan Bychowski in 1937. Before the marriage took place, however, she appeared that year in two films. *Tokaji Rapszódia* (*Tokay Rhapsody*), with a fleeting appearance by Magda, involves a romance in the vineyards. Its title suggests an advertorial for Hungary's most famous wine. Magda's second film that year, *Mai Lányok* (*Today's Girls*) derives from the fluffy musical comedies of Hollywood and those of Germany. By the time of her films' limited release, Magda had left Budapest for Poland, where she lived for a time with her husband in Warsaw.

An enduring Gabor mystery is why no one in the family ever mentioned in interviews, nor in their ghostwritten memoirs, Magda's brief film career. I can only speculate that her later distaste for show business, along with the realization that two insignificant films might detract from her American persona, caused Magda to issue a ukase at a closed session of the Gabor politburo: "*Kuss!*" And when Magda said, "Keep it quiet," even Jolie complied.

Just before the Nazis invaded Poland in 1939, Magda returned to Hungary. Bychowski escaped to England. It seems that their marriage had been troubled for some time. After the fall of France in 1940, Polish units were formed as a part of the Royal Air Force in Britain; these were blended into the

RAF and known as the Polish Air Force. Jan Bychowski was killed in action during a bombing raid on May 22, 1944. He was forty-two years old. Beyond these stark facts, nothing more is known.

Zsa Zsa's versions of her first marriage, how she engineered it, along with the fantastic adventures and disgruntlements that ensued, might be compared to a cluster of tales in the *Arabian Nights*. Whatever her enhancements, however, many events happened more or less as reported. The titles she bestowed in later years on Burhan Belge summon up a one-man governmental bureau: "Press Director in the Foreign Ministry of the Government of Turkey," "former Turkish ambassador to Hungary," "Senator," "Minister of Propaganda," and so on. Here, however, I quote from an email from his son, Murat Belge, a professor of comparative literature at Bilgi University in Istanbul: "He was in Hungary as a minor official in the Embassy. Maybe something like 'political officer.'"

Burhan Belge was later elected to Parliament in 1957, though this took place long after his divorce from Zsa Zsa in 1941. Belge himself told a reporter for the *New York Post* in 1958, "I am a serious man. I do not care to discuss such a frivolus topic [as Zsa Zsa's fantasies]. But I will say this. I have never been a senator. I have never been an ambassador. And I have never been a minister of press and propaganda." And then, added the reporter, "He laughs again."

Murat Belge is more blunt than his late father, who died in 1967: "Zsa Zsa was a great and unscrupulous liar."

At the end of the previous chapter, Zsa Zsa, age seventeen and out of work after *Der Singende Traum*, was en route back to Budapest in December 1934. After the holiday festivities, she boarded another train, this one again headed to Vienna, where she landed a job as a nightclub hostess or, in some accounts, a singer or chorus girl. Zsa Zsa herself omits this career move from her memoirs. Her mother wrote that "she went to work as Mistress of Ceremonies" whose job was to "come out in beautiful dresses and announce the next act. She didn't sing; the truth is she *couldn't* sing."

Let us recall that the profession of nightclub performer has a vivid history as a popular euphemism in Hollywood movies of the 1940s and '50s for a profession that predated all others. Two glaring examples: Rita Hayworth in *Miss Sadie Thompson* (1953) and Jane Russell in *The Revolt of Mamie Stover* (1956). Closer to Zsa Zsa's Vienna in time and space, there's Marlene Dietrich in *A Foreign Affair* (1948) singing her come-hither song, "Black Market" in the shambles of postwar Berlin. Since Zsa Zsa didn't—couldn't—sing a note, the question remains unanswered as to how she delighted patrons of that Viennese night spot, the Club Femina, which was reputed to be a showplace for the display of female flesh. Zsa Zsa appeared there under the name of Georgia Gabor. (Orson Welles, casting her in 1958 as manageress of that sleazy honky-tonk in *Touch of Evil*, was perhaps winking at her résumé.)

Vilmos Gyimes, owner of the tiny club, was living in New York in 1958 when the *Post* ran its eleven-part series on the Gabors. Like Burhan Belge, he spoke to a reporter from the paper, recalling that he hired Zsa Zsa for the chorus but that she was not the star of any revue. Perhaps he shared her delusions, for he said, "Femina was like the Latin Quarter in New York." In fact, it was a pint-size cabaret that employed half-a-dozen young women in the chorus. The Latin Quarter, on the other hand, sprawled like the set of an MGM musical.

Gyimes took credit for introducing "Georgia," as Zsa Zsa then was, to Burhan Belge, who was passing through Vienna en route to Istanbul after a government assignment in Germany. This, surely, makes for a more credible scenario than the one Zsa Zsa later created, viz., that she had met Burhan on many occasions at her grandmother's dinner parties and glittering soirées.

Nor could she leave it there. In her handcrafted tableau vivant, Zsa Zsa proposes to him in the bar of the Hotel Ritz: "Excellency, will you marry me?" He almost chokes on his Scotch, but a short time later they are honeymooners on the *Orient Express*, a fitting first step in the orientalization of Zsa Zsa. As the night deepens, and preparations are made for bed, Zsa Zsa trembles in suspense. Clutching her little dog, Mishka, a Scotty, she awaits the approach of this older man, a virtual stranger to her. But then—he kisses her on the forehead and retires to his own berth. "How could I know," she later said, "that to a Muslim dogs are unclean, that Burhan would never sleep where a dog had lain?"

Such calculated naiveté on Zsa Zsa's part, easily mistaken for wide-eyed daffiness, is one of her fascinations. It's also part of her brilliance as a comedienne. She parlayed this goofy side of herself into decades of froufrou fame.

Dogs, it seems, interfered forever in Zsa Zsa's love life. In 1987, on Dr. Ruth's talk show, she had the audience in stitches with this tale from a couple of years earlier, just before her marriage to the soi-disant prince, Frederic von Anhalt, husband number nine. "One morning I had to ride my horse in the Rose Bowl parade. I said to Frederic, 'Please be on time.' He was staying in my house but he didn't come up from the kitchen until too late. I was furious! I said, 'Go back to Germany!' So he went back, and a couple of weeks later I found out that he tried to eat a piece of salami at breakfast, the salami fell on the floor, and when he tried to pick it up one of my dogs bit him. He was bleeding! He was afraid to tell me he was bleeding because who wants a bleeding prince?"

Readers of Patrick Dennis, and especially of his 1961 parody novel *Little Me: The Intimate Memoirs of That Great Star of Stage, Screen, and Television,* could surely make the case that it's a roman à clef with a certain Gabor as the *clef*. (Dennis's biographer, Eric Myers, wrote that the author had in mind such "pompous Great Female Star autobiographies" of the time as those of Pola Negri, Mae Murray, and Zsa Zsa.) *Little Me*, and of course *Auntie Mame*, are both camp classics, intentionally so. Like those Dennis novels, Zsa Zsa's two autobiographies, *My Story* in 1960 and *One Lifetime Is Not Enough*, 1991, make for delicious camp reading. They are all the more amusing because she expected them to be read as factual accounts.

In spite of such jiggery-pokery in Zsa Zsa's memoirs, it's true that she did live in Turkey as the wife of Burhan Belge for almost six years, and so I will extract the more likely parts of her narrative like a specialist chef serving up edible parts of the puffer fish while shunning its toxic bulk.

In the midst of much vanity and frivolity in *My Story*, she inserted a serious note, and a telling one. Referring to the time of her marriage, she wrote, "These were critical days. The future of Europe, of Hungary, was uncertain. Budapest was gay, because Hungarians hate to face reality. But it was impossible, with Hitler on the march, not to know that anything might happen. For me to be the wife of a high-ranking Turkish government official, protected by a diplomatic passport, was no small thing."

Even though this passage has the advantage of hindsight, it suggests that Zsa Zsa herself, or certainly her parents, considered her removal from Hungary a safety measure quite apart from any prestige the marriage might confer. The same with Eva, whose first marriage, in 1939, took her to California. The Gabors, whatever their level of denial, were known to be Jews, or at least former Jews. From Budapest to Munich, a Nazi hotbed, was some 350 air miles, with no buffer between except German-speaking Austria, Hitler's homeland. Then, too, in 1935 Hungarian fascists founded the Arrow Cross Party, which remained in lockstep with other European fascists, especially those of Germany and Austria. That same year, anti-Semitic agitation increased sharply.

As Hitler gained power in the mid-1930s, Admiral Miklós Horthy, regent of Hungary from 1920 to 1944, maintained an uneasy alliance with Germany. Rabidly anti-communist, yet lacking the fascist fervor of Hitler or Mussolini, Horthy assessed Hungary's untenable position: a small country trapped and helpless between the Soviet Union and the Third Reich. For a host of complex reasons, Horthy, as head of state, leaned toward Germany, so that during World War II, Hungary was an Axis ally. Owing to that official stance, many Hungarians, whether Jewish or not, and among them Jolie and Vilmos Gabor, felt relatively safe. According to this faulty syllogism, Hungary was Hitler's friend; he needed all the friends he could find; therefore, why would he attack? For those who might have left, but didn't, such reasoning proved fatal. When Hitler finally invaded Hungary in March 1944, Jolie, Vilmos, and Magda were arrested. Their hours on the razor's edge, their release from custody, and their spine-chilling escape read like the climax of a Hitchcock thriller, as we will see.

Turkey, far from Germany and considered a fierce opponent in battle, had few immediate worries. Officially neutral, the country maintained correct, though ambiguous, relations with Germany as well as with many countries in Hitler's crosshairs. With Zsa Zsa ensconced in Ankara, the capital, and Eva breaking into movies in Hollywood, those Gabors left in Budapest carried on as before. Almost from the day of his marriage to Zsa Zsa, however, Burhan Belge urged his in-laws to leave Hungary. Keenly aware of developments throughout Europe, he had no illusions about Hitler's neighborliness. Years later, Jolie recalled her son-in-law's dramatic warnings.

"Jolie," he said, "go out from this country. Go to America. Go to Mexico. It is only beginning. All of Europe will burn.

Everyone will be killed. The Jewish intellectuals will be massacred by the Nazis. The Christian aristocrats will be massacred by the Reds. I tell you, Jolie, leave Hungary. Immediately! Today."

If Zsa Zsa heard these conversations, she seems to have brushed aside dire warnings that might interfere with her Turkish romp. From the moment she stepped proudly off the train, she played the role of Madame Belge as grandly as Tallulah Bankhead barging down the Nile as Cleopatra—although without La Bankhead's flamboyance, which Zsa Zsa would perfect only later. In her early days in Turkey Zsa Zsa was held in check by her husband and by her own youthful uncertainty. His restraint accounts for her subsequent description of him as dour and humorless. Burhan no doubt realized early on what he had on his hands. He determined to capitalize on his young wife's assets, for she was pretty, fashionable, vivacious, and easily assimilated into the sophisticated yet provincial society of the Turkish capital. Owing to her youth and the unfamiliarity of her new situation, she seldom rebelled. Soon after their arrival, he hired a tutor to coach Zsa Zsa in Turkish, which she learned readily enough. These assets Burhan valued, though he pondered how to prevent her running loose. Clever, wily, and practiced in matrimony—there were several Madame Belges before this one—he well knew how easily his new wife could create mayhem and make him a laughingstock. He did not covet the title of "husband to that screwy Hungarian."

How could someone like Zsa Zsa *not* stand out in a place like Ankara? Although the city's population in 1935 was 123,000, it retained the rustic character of the outpost it had been since ancient times. In photographs taken that year, Ankara resembles drowsy, remote towns in nearby countries, such as Tirana, Albania, or Plovdiv, Bulgaria. When Mustafa Kemal Atatürk became president of Turkey after the collapse of the Ottoman Empire in World War I, he transformed the country from an essentially medieval to a modern nation in just a few years. His aim, largely accomplished before his death in 1938 at age fifty-seven, was to remake the country as a European entity, a secular state rather than a theocracy mired in the backward, self-defeating politics of the Middle East. In 1923 he moved the Turkish capital from Istanbul to Ankara.

Other photographs of Ankara in the 1930s show Atatürk Boulevard, the so-called Embassy Row where the Belges lived, as the elegant part of town. Wide and spacious, punctuated with young trees and shrubs planted in formal rows as in French cities, this part of Ankara turned its face toward Europe. As a reminder of the town's rural setting, however, diplomats recounted sightings of the occasional wolf when returning at night from government receptions, especially in winter when snow covered the ground several feet deep.

Eva, in tears when Zsa Zsa left Budapest, gave her a code word to use if ever she desperately needed help. "Just send me a wire," Eva sniffed, hugging her sister close. "Use the word *cigány* [Gypsy] and I'll be there as fast as I can." Such reassurance made Zsa Zsa, at age eighteen, feel better about the wild adventure she was about to embark upon. After the honeymoon spent with Burhan's family in Istanbul, however, in their fine old house overlooking the Bosphorus, intuition told her she had triumphed again, although she must wait to see exactly how.

Burhan's father welcomed Zsa Zsa in French. Burhan's dignified and very proper sister, Leman, and her worldly husband, Yakup Kadri, occupied the social position that the Gabors in Budapest so yearned for. Kadri was Turkey's ambassador to Albania when Zsa Zsa first knew him; later he was posted to Czechoslovakia, Switzerland, the Netherlands, and Iran. He and his wife traveled from their home in Ankara to welcome Burhan and his bride to Istanbul.

Since Zsa Zsa, on arrival, understood not a word of Turkish beyond *merhaba*, meaning "hello," we can imagine the buzz of conversation between Burhan and Leman as they stepped aside from Belge *père* with his florid compliments, and his wife, whom Zsa Zsa described as "a tiny woman with a fiery red Mohammadan *säl* [i.e., a square piece of cloth worn as a covering for the head, neck, and shoulders] sitting with her legs crossed under her like an Oriental queen."

"That damn dog," says Burhan to his sister, and explains what happened—or didn't happen—a few nights earlier on the train. "Tonight will be different," his sister certifies. After this tête-à-tête, Leman leads the couple upstairs to their bedroom in the center of which is an enormous double bed. Lush wall hangings, plush bed clothes with tiny blue pearls embroidered on each pillow to ward off the evil eye, draperies as thick as the curtain at the Budapest Opera—this bedchamber could double as a set for *The Abduction from the Seraglio.*

Leman gestures to Burhan to make himself scarce. A servant glides in, and she and Leman help Zsa Zsa dress for dinner in the tailored white satin gown that Jolie packed in the trousseau of her first daughter to require one. After dinner, the ladies retire from the dining room where the men smoke, drink brandy, and perhaps make jokes about the traveling salesman who went to Budapest and. . . .

Leman to Zsa Zsa, when the others had discreetly vanished: "My brother seems to be very fond of you. I think I should tell you that he has been spoiled by many women. You must submit to him and be good to him." A pause. "You must learn to please him. Do you not wish to retire? Now I think you should go upstairs. I will send him to you presently."

Imagine the jokes Joan Rivers or Johnny Carson might have cracked had Zsa Zsa recounted this story on TV, because once again there was that damn dog! "I turned to call

Mishka," said Zsa Zsa, "who was worrying a bone under the table, but my sister-in-law, taking me by the arm, said firmly, 'We will make a place for him in the kitchen tonight.' "

For once, Zsa Zsa had no comeback. Like it or not, she recalled years later, "the honeymoon had begun."

Chapter 6

Turkish Rondo

Burhan Belge's disavowals notwithstanding, he seems to have claimed a more crucial portfolio than "minor official." He surely had duties in the government, along with foreign affiliations, that Zsa Zsa was not privy to. Moreover, his frequent prewar travels to Germany, France, and England suggest missions of a sensitive nature. Fluent in German and several other languages, he shuttled between Ankara and Berlin in the years just prior to World War II. As an expert in foreign relations, Belge made a Saturday radio broadcast from Ankara in which he gave his analysis of world affairs and how various international shifts and upheavals might affect Turkey.

At home, he warned Zsa Zsa not to exaggerate his importance, for he had overheard her boasting, "My husband is Minister of Press and Propaganda." Again and again he told her, "I am only a newspaperman." But even a child bride wasn't so easily fooled. A mere journalist, after all, would not travel on a diplomatic passport, nor would his wife, and yet Madame Belge's Hungarian passport had been replaced with a more commanding one. Looking back on the dangerous intrigues of those years, Zsa Zsa eventually realized that she had landed in a "bewildering world of political intrigue." But she couldn't decipher the arcane static that buzzed about her, whether at gatherings in their home or embedded within the round of embassy parties, dinners for visiting dignitaries, and national celebrations. Her husband warned her to be careful what she said on the telephone. He cautioned never to repeat what she heard in their house, whether half-understood in Turkish or completely clear when overheard in German, French, or English. Ankara, and all of Turkey, resembled *Casablanca*: crackling with secrets, gossip, rumors, and filled with refugees and foreign agents. The ears of Turkey gathered secrets from all corners of the world. Owing to Turkey's quasi-European location and its semi-Asiatic identity, Axis powers and Allied nations viewed it as a strategic bridge between East and West.

"And Burhan played a more important role than he cared for me to know," Zsa Zsa said long after she had left Turkey and when the terrors of war were a fading memory. At the time, however, Burhan's attempts to brief her on the Nazi engulfment of Europe and Hitler's plan for world domination, or the distant but equal threat from Japan, provoked yawns. When not bored, she found his lectures irritating, for they made her feel "like a silly girl called before a schoolmaster."

His own irritation sometimes exceeded hers. At times, perhaps, he wished that he could ship her back to Hungary. One day, after riding Fatushka, the white Arabian mare that Burhan had bought for her, Zsa Zsa strolled into town with Ali, her fifteen-year-old houseboy from Turkestan who, according to Zsa Zsa, had never worn shoes until hired by the Belge household. They passed a gnarled farmer who had something live in the battered old hat he held out to them. "Buy! Buy!" he cajoled. Thinking it a puppy or a kitten, and always eager to increase her menagerie, Zsa Zsa picked up— a tiny bear cub!

"Wait here," she told Ali and the farmer. Cuddling the baby bear, she ran to Burhan's office not far away, pounded on the door, and burst in. "Burhan, darling, may I have this little bear?" she said, mixing Turkish and German. Then she noticed: the room was full of important members of the government, and she had interrupted a conference. Some smiled, others looked stern, and Burhan glared at her. "Let us, please, talk about this later." After the icy discussion at home, and Zsa Zsa's tears, it was decided that before very long a bear might pose a threat to Mishka, and so the cub was donated to the zoo. Not long after that, Eva paid a visit to Ankara and, once back in Budapest, held Jolie and Vilmos spellbound with a thousand details of her sister's life among the diplomats.

According to Zsa Zsa's anecdotes—all of which must be microscoped—at a dinner party she made a catty remark about the Nazis to Franz von Papen, German ambassador to Turkey. Other evenings she played bridge with Lev Mikhailovich Karakhan, ambassador from the Soviet Union. Another remark, this one unfavorable both to his country and to Germany, elicited a veiled warning beneath his handsome diplomatic smile. The warning boomeranged, however, for in 1937, during the Stalinist terror, Karakhan was arrested and shot.

More than three decades after her departure from Turkey in 1941, Zsa Zsa received an invitation to the White House as a guest of President and Mrs. Nixon. The event was a dinner for Haile Selassie, emperor of Ethiopia. Zsa Zsa made the guest list for two reasons: She was a Nixon Republican who added glitter to the evening, and she had first met the emperor in Ankara at a state function around 1938. No one asked Selassie, eighty-one years old, whether he remembered the former Madame Belge. Nor did reporters ask Zsa Zsa what she recalled of her long-ago meeting with the Lion of Judah, one of the emperor's many titles. By this time she had come to rely on talk-show shtick, and so she babbled to the press about being "a bride of fifteen who was hostest-with-the-mostest in Turkey." Flinging back her head with a laugh and caressing her blonde hair—or perhaps it was an Eva Gabor wig that she caressed—she added, "I didn't speak Turkish, so I was always falling asleep at my own dinners." This bit of whimsy, like a line from a bad script, carries no conviction.

Mustafa Kemal Atatürk, president of the Republic of Turkey from 1923 until his death in 1938, founded the modern Turkish state, which he seized from the wreckage of the Ottoman Empire. He is also the JFK of Turkey, his legend encrusted with the allure, the errors, the personality cult, the worship and the loathing, the womanizing, and the similar elevation to godlike reverence of the American president.

Zsa Zsa, with her lifelong fetish for powerful older men, invented an Orientalist narrative that costarred her in a Hollywood-tinged romance with Atatürk. That tale is as pretty as an illustrated children's book, as smarmy as some fantoosh version of *The King and I*. Hearing it, one hardly knows whether to laugh or leave the room. Zsa Zsa herself played the scene endlessly as theme and variations. Each performance found her orchestrating with more brass.

Stated in its original form, her yarn goes like this. Burhan and Zsa Zsa, Leman and Yakup are dining at a Russian restaurant in Ankara when Himself enters with an entourage of bodyguards and cohorts. The room is electrified. Zsa Zsa cannot stop staring at Atatürk. "Don't look, don't look," scolds her sister-in-law. But: "I stole a glance at him again. Our eyes met." Minutes later, a presidential aide approaches their table, and bows. "The President would like their Excellencies Burhan Belge and Yakup Kadri and their ladies to join his party."

Zsa Zsa, intimidated by greatness in the room, stammers in response to presidential questions. He invites her to drink raki; she chokes on the Turkish national drink. He offers a cigarette embossed with his initials. One inhale and she coughs and sputters. He asks her to dance, at which she is more adept than at drinking and smoking. When they resume their seats at the table he makes a proclamation. "From now on Turkey and Hungary are brother and sister." For days afterward, young Zsa Zsa remains intoxicated by the fumes of memory that waft Mustafa Kemal Atatürk to her, like jasmine on a summer night. Those French novels she read back in Switzerland were mere nursery rhymes compared to this.

Shortly thereafter, through an intermediary, Zsa Zsa receives a mysterious invitation to drink tea in the old city with a secret admirer. At this point we might imagine a match-up of the Brontë sisters with the Gabor sisters, or more precisely a one-on-one: *When Zsa Zsa Mimed Emily*, for in Zsa Zsa's tale gothic trappings overhang all of Ankara.

In an antiquities shop where she often browsed after dismounting from Fatushka, she is given a key sent by the mysterious admirer. Overcome by curiosity, she locates the address "in a tiny street that wound like a corkscrew through the old city." At the top of a narrow, dark staircase she fits the key in the lock. Behold, there in the gloom of a dim, silent, forlorn chamber she makes out a table, and beyond it an armchair in which someone is sitting, his back to her. "Woman was not made to resist temptation," quoth the voice. "I knew you would come." It is, of course, the voice of Atatürk, to Zsa Zsa's ears as awesome as the voice of Jehovah from the burning bush.

Drunk, and in the later stages of alcoholism (he would die of cirrhosis), Atatürk craves her companionship. Zsa Zsa's faint implication is that he coveted intimacy but suffered from impotence. After tea and conversation, he drops off to sleep and she slips quietly from the room. These chaste assignations, she claimed, continued almost until the day of his death.

Male presidents often consort with at least one girlfriend, or what used to be called a mistress. In the United States, for instance, it became the rage with John F. Kennedy, and has pingponged to the present day. In Turkey, President Atatürk banished the harem while continuing to enjoy its pleasures as of old. Lord Kinross, in his 1965 biography *Atatürk*, almost brings credence to Zsa Zsa's coy narrative. "No woman," he wrote, "was held to be safe at his hands. Turkish mothers might indeed thrust their daughters at him (and Turkish husbands their wives), but diplomatic mothers would hurry their daughters away from a party for fear he would invite them to his table. When he did so he would often merely subject them to a *viva voce* exam. Taking a fancy to a young Polish girl at an embassy party, he was heard asking her for proof of the existence of God. With a married woman the interrogation might be on the more intimate subject of her relations with her husband. He sensed just how far to go with women and was a good judge of husbands, never flirting with the wife of one likely to be jealous. Occasionally, however, a scandal arose when the wife of some diplomat allowed herself to become emotionally too much involved with the President."

Zsa Zsa's Atatürk theme, begun in her 1960 autobiography *My Story*, sounded notes of seduction while remaining in the key of respectability. Whatever accuracy one finds there owes much to her collaborator, Gerold Frank. Frank aided other tempestuous Hollywood women with their life stories, including Diana Barrymore, Lillian Roth, and Sheilah Graham. More scrupulous for detail than any of his subjects, he insisted on as much truth as he could squeeze from his various celebrities. Zsa Zsa's posturing in *My Story* is held to a minimum. Gerold Frank's papers, housed at the New York

Public Library, show his finesse in extracting truth from the deep core of show-business fantasy and invention. Hundreds of pages of outtakes from *My Story* show Zsa Zsa as the willing subject of his subtle probes.

Her second collaborator, the late Wendy Leigh, was almost as off-center as Zsa Zsa. Thus, *One Lifetime Is Not Enough*, which appeared in 1991, slogs along like the tiresome tattle of two over-the-hill drunks in an old-timey bar, viz., Zsa Zsa and Wendy.

In her autobiographical swan song, Zsa Zsa blasted her variations on a Turkish theme in boombox decibels. Earlier, in 1960, many were still alive who might contradict her assertions, including Burhan Belge. The possibility of legal action also restrained authors and publishers. By the 1990s, however, libel laws had relaxed and words, as well as suggestions, that were whispered a few decades earlier could now be broadcast.

Coaxed by Wendy Leigh, a veteran of tabloid British journalism, Zsa Zsa would have us believe that she was Atatürk's concubine. And that countless other powerful men—few of them older, by this point, than Zsa Zsa—wanted to marry her, or at least sample her wares, among them Henry Kissinger. In that same book she claims that Kissinger, after a dinner date, made a move on her virtue and—here we reenter Patrick Dennis territory—"I wasn't married at the time, so I didn't protest when he asked if he could come in for a drink. We started talking, then things got more personal, with Henry showing signs of making an amorous approach to me. I don't know what would have happened had his beeper not suddenly cut into the silence. Nixon wanted him immediately at San Clemente."

Nixon, it seems, like that damn dog back in Turkey, was always cutting in on Zsa Zsa's romantic life. Another time, Kissinger was scheduled to fly to Zsa Zsa's side, perhaps to try again what was foiled by his beeper interruptus. He called to cancel, and when Zsa Zsa asked why, the dutiful secretary of state offered a memorable excuse: "I can't fly down because we are invading Cambodia tomorrow."

Such buffooneries raise questions among readers of Zsa Zsa's pages, among them the immediate one: 1) Finding Zsa Zsa available between husbands number five and six, why did Kissinger soon settle for the decidedly less glamorous Nancy Maginnes; and the historical conundrum: 2) Who was governing Turkey while Atatürk was enveloped in the splendid arms of Madame Belge?

Perhaps Zsa Zsa's close encounters with the likes of Kissinger, Nixon—oh, and John F. Kennedy as well, revealed in 1991 as one of her admirers before Jacqueline Bouvier caught his eye—perhaps these Washington associations gave her greater insight into political matters than she possessed as a young bride in Turkey. Sounding like a Republican fundamentalist, she expressed the thought to Wendy Leigh that "Atatürk was one of those rare men who I believe the Lord sent to save their country." (But then such a man was Nixon, to Zsa Zsa at least; and Ford, and Reagan, and Bush *père et fils,* yet this country remains unsaved.)

Pushed along by Wendy Leigh, Zsa Zsa at last told all . . . We are once more with Madame Belge in the dim, silent, gloomy *chambre de rendez-vous* of President Atatürk. "Just as I was about to speak," Zsa Zsa remembered, "he clapped his hands and dancing girls appeared, their multicolored veils floating suggestively in the coolness of the room. As they danced their slow, sensuous dance, wordlessly Atatürk motioned that I sit on the red velvet and copper-colored cushions next to him. Mesmerized, I complied. He offered me his pipe—and unquestioningly, I took it. Then he passed me a gold-and-emerald-encrusted cup filled with raki. I sipped from the cup.

"Until now, I have never before revealed what happened

next, what happened when Atatürk dismissed the dancing girls and the two of us were alone. Sometimes I think it happened in a dream, sometimes that I was in an opium haze, or a stupor induced by the raki. All I know is that day, Atatürk, the conqueror of Turkey, the idol of a million women and the envy of countless men, took my virginity."

Did she forget, with this thundering revelation, about that damn dog who was bedded down in the kitchen the first—or second, or third—time Zsa Zsa's virginity was snatched from her?

Further along in this heavy-breathing passage, which echoes Omar Khayyam crossed with Maria Montez in *Cobra Woman*, we learn the reason for Zsa Zsa's long marital quest post-Burhan: "Atatürk ruined me for every other man I would ever love, or try to love." During the six months of their liaison, claimed Zsa Zsa, with Wendy Leigh panting beside her on the sofa, "we spent hours together locked in each other's arms, while he dazzled me with his sexual prowess and seduced me with his perversion. Atatürk was very wicked. He knew exactly how to please a young girl. He was a professional lover, a god, and a king."

Given the limited list of perversions available to an alcoholic man in failing health, which Atatürk already was in 1935 when the Belges arrived, one can only surmise. Zsa Zsa's fervid confessions to the highly unreliable Wendy Leigh fail to allow for his weakened physical state and also for the fact that even so, he had a large and difficult country to run; a parliament to sway whenever possible; cabinet ministers to wrangle with and replace. In addition, he often traveled to Istanbul. Moreover, throughout the 1930s on the European horizon loomed the double threat of Hitler and Mussolini. It is unlikely that in his final years Atatürk could escape the presidential office for long afternoons spent sipping sweet liqueurs and lounging on cushions with Zsa Zsa Belge.

A closing note on the late Wendy Leigh, who presumed a friendship with Zsa Zsa's daughter, the late Francesca Hilton. Francesca referred to her as "that S&M creep with her harnesses, rubber suits, and dildoes."

To clear the perfumed air from Zsa Zsa's hallucinatory hideaway, I fling open the windows to Murat Belge, Burhan's son. From one of his emails: "Now, the story of Zsa Zsa's arrival. The word reached Turkey before she did. She was not the international figure then, but somehow news spread to Ankara that Burhan got married to a fabulous woman. It was a real sensation. They came [to Ankara] and rushed to the house of my uncle and aunt. For about a fortnight they stayed in the house. Finally, they gathered courage to attempt to show themselves in public. The main restaurant in Ankara at the time was Karpich, run by a Russian who ran away from the revolution. On a weekday the place was not crowded. However, in about half an hour sirens and sounds of scooters were heard and in came Atatürk and his retinue! Obviously, the message had been transmitted and he came to make his own observations.

"They all acted as if this was a coincidence. The tables were joined and the orchestra of the restaurant started to play waltzes—this was the dance that Atatürk knew best. So he asked Zsa Zsa to dance and off they went.

"I heard the story from both my father and his sister, my aunt. Their accounts agree in general. But now I stick to the version of my aunt. After the waltz with Zsa Zsa, Atatürk asked my aunt to the next one. As they danced, he said, 'Ah, Burhan! Naughty boy.' I never understood what this meant. Apparently my aunt did, because she used to say she started to cry and said, 'My Pasha, please forgive him.' Another mystery for me.

"*After such a start, you might expect a certain development of relations but that did not take place, despite the silly stories Zsa Zsa made her ghost writers to narrate—and they change from one autobiography to the other* [emphasis added]."

These distant memories, the faded, scattered remains of long-ago days, leave us unsettled, like reading an O. Henry story with the last page missing. For that reason, I append my own gloss to the Belge family legends.

It's easy to believe that Zsa Zsa's reputation preceded her. The denizens of Ankara, like those of small towns and minor cities everywhere, were eager for distraction, for variety in their routine lives. Suddenly rumors buzzed: Burhan's wife was Miss Hungary; a star on the Vienna stage; a beauty; and only fifteen . . . sixteen . . . or was it seventeen? In the days before television and social media anesthesized the world, it wasn't hard to arouse rampant curiosity in the bourgeoisie. And let us recall that even then, back in Budapest, the Gabors inhabited a perpetual press release. Nor is there reason to believe that Atatürk himself would have ignored such titillating rumors. With an eye for the ladies, and perhaps foreshadowed by mortality, he, too, wanted a look at Burhan's beauty queen.

As for the president's cryptic remark: "Ah, Burhan! Naughty boy." If we heard it in Turkish, we might interpret it as a sly joke, meaning, Where did he find a dish like that? Or this: on the dance floor, cheeky Zsa Zsa made a suggestive remark; a waggish proposition; an innocent gaffe that the president repeated to Burhan's sister, who, being a sophisticated and very proper lady, found inexcusable on the part of her new sister-in-law. If Mrs. Kadri wept easily, it's conceivable she shed tears of shame on behalf of this Hungarian teenager.

With only enough information to make us wish for more, we must, in *l'affaire Atatürk*, depend forever on scattered hints, uncertain inferences, and conflicting rumors.

* * *

After a detour into Zsa Zsa's fantasy sphere comes the introduction of several genuine alliances from her Turkish years. These friends found her vivacious and delightful to know on her own, apart from her husband's shadow.

Sir Percy Loraine, British ambassador to Turkey from 1933 to 1939, later referred to Ankara's "pathetic bleakness," and Lady Loraine called it "the most godforsaken hole I have ever been in." Sir Percy's posting to Turkey was nevertheless of crucial importance to Great Britain as the prospect of war loomed ever nearer. The ambassador's close friendship with Atatürk helped to cement relations between their two countries. So cordial were the two men that Sir Percy visited Atatürk on his deathbed in 1938.

Although Ankara's population had soared by the mid-1930s, it retained the mores of a sleepy town. The ruling elite, and the foreign diplomatic corps, formed a small nucleus with clearly defined boundaries. Within that perimeter, everyone knew everybody. In Ankara, the theory of six degrees of separation could be reduced to two.

It's not surprising, therefore, that Sir Percy and Lady Loraine befriended the Belges. With Zsa Zsa, they shared a compelling interest: horses. During his years in Turkey, the Ankara Riding Club absorbed Sir Percy whenever he could escape from official duties, and after his retirement from the diplomatic corps he resumed his longtime avocation, the breeding and racing of Thoroughbreds. Zsa Zsa never wavered in her devotion to Fatushka, who was stabled there. A photograph of Zsa Zsa mounted on Fatushka shows her at her smiling prettiest, unlike other pictures taken during her Turkish sojourn in which she looks strained and unhappy. Nor did she have gleaming white teeth until a few years later when she married Conrad Hilton, who paid the dentist's bills.

Only that picture of her on Fatushka, and another one in

which she is swathed in a filmy gown like a sari, suggest young Madame Belge as a sprite. In others, she could have passed for forty-plus while still in her early twenties. But then she and her sisters, and Jolie, as well, aged in reverse, like a quartet of female Benjamin Buttons. At eighty, Zsa Zsa looked not a day over fifty. Eva, a month before her death, could have passed for forty, though in reality she was seventy-six. Wigs and surgery, of course, became synonymous with the family name Gabor.

In some of her Turkish photographs, Zsa Zsa is blonde, while in others her hair looks black, although according to Zsa Zsa herself her natural hair color was red. She spoke of rinsing it in rose water to bring out its reddish highlights. The fact is, however, that Zsa Zsa never looked really young. Always, even in her teen years, her face bore a wolfish expression, slightly mocking, even smug, as though she had not only tasted the forbidden fruit of Eden, but sliced it onto her breakfast cereal.

Zsa Zsa's Turkish chapter reached its apex in London in 1939, when Burhan was invited to lecture on "Modern Turkey" at the Royal Institute of International Affairs. The Belges came with five other Turkish journalists and their wives as guests of the British Council, an international organization for cultural relations and educational opportunities. (It is noteworthy that the *London Times* on May 31, 1939, identified Burhan as "Director of Press, Turkish Foreign Ministry," a title he himself did not claim.)

Burhan's invitation came through the auspices of Sir Percy, for he and Lady Loraine had found much to admire in the oddly matched Belges. Burhan, of course, stood out as an intellectual, capable in international affairs, and a conduit to sources that Sir Percy deemed essential in promoting British interests in Turkey. As for Zsa Zsa, the Loraines responded to her anglophilia. As an older couple—Sir Percy in his fifties, Lady Loraine in her forties when Zsa Zsa arrived in

Ankara—and childless, they found this exotic child-wife an intriguing blend of ingenue and coquette. Then and later, Zsa Zsa had winsome qualities that she herself often obscured behind a self-serving façade.

In Ankara, Burhan and Zsa Zsa sometimes dined with Sir Percy and Lady Loraine, who in turn invited Zsa Zsa to tea during her husband's absences. This sophisticated British couple helped her to gain savoir faire in matters of etiquette and protocol, important attributes for the wife of a highly visible government official. With them, also, she practiced speaking English.

H.G. Wells, the novelist and historian, attended Burhan's lecture in London. Sir Percy had told Wells that he would learn much there, which Wells was eager to do. He knew of Atatürk's great admiration for his writings. Indeed, not long before the president's death in 1938, Atatürk ordered the government printing office to translate and publish Wells's *The Outline of History*. The author had become a hero to Atatürk.

After the lecture, Wells came forward to congratulate Burhan. Owing to his enthusiasm, and to that of Sir Percy, invitations flooded the Belges. They met Prime Minister Neville Chamberlin and Anthony Eden, a former secretary of state for foreign affairs and himself a future prime minister. Zsa Zsa's picture appeared in a number of London newspapers, and H.G. Wells invited her and Burhan to lunch with George Bernard Shaw and his wife. After lunch, Burhan snapped a picture of Zsa Zsa with two of the most famous men in England, Shaw and Wells, a photograph presumed lost until my recent rediscovery.

Chapter 7

Eva and Eric

Eva's first marriage took place on June 3, 1939, at the time of Zsa Zsa's heady visit to London. Several versions exist of the youngest Gabor's introduction to matrimony, the least convincing one being Eva's own as set forth in her evasive autobiography, *Orchids and Salami*. Picturing herself as a teenager awash in romantic fantasies, she claims to have met Dr. Eric Drimmer at one of Magda's parties. Eva said that Magda, as a young divorcée recently returned from life in Poland with her own first husband, considered her sister, at seventeen, too young and unsophisticated for this party. In fact, however, Eva was already either nineteen or twenty, for the time of her meeting with Eric was late 1938 or spring of 1939.

Whatever the circumstances, Eva met him and at some point he proposed. It's unlikely that his proposal issued the night they met, as Eva claimed. Nor did anyone explain what brought Eric to Budapest, for he was a Swede resident in Hollywood and a naturalized U.S. citizen.

Eric Valdemar Drimmer (1910–1967), born in the Swedish village of Järvsjö, has been variously identified as an MD, an osteopath, a chiropractor, a psychologist, a physiotherapist, and a masseur. In one capacity or another, he was said either to massage Greta Garbo's tired muscles during her MGM years, or her mind. Others listed as his clients for services rendered include Clark Gable, Robert Taylor, and Mickey Rooney. Any one of these names, dropped in the presence of the Gabors, would have done much to establish him as a marital catch. From the scant evidence available, however, Drimmer's character bears a shady tint. In apparent violation of doctor-patient confidentiality, he wrote about Garbo in an article published in *Photoplay* in 1942, and again in 1959 in a Swedish women's magazine. And when he and Eva divorced, she made him sound like a villain. "Forced to Act, Wife Testifies" ran the headline in the *Los Angeles Times* on February 25, 1942. Eva told the judge that her husband drove her into the life of a film actress when she preferred to remain a simple housewife. "I wanted to raise a family—to have babies," she informed the court, "but my husband didn't agree with me. He also objected to my having friends of my own."

Asked by the judge to name her husband's profession, Eva replied: "He's a doctor specializing in psychology, and he always treated me like one of his cases." Perhaps, on closer inspection, Dr. Drimmer is no more blameworthy than his wife, for in *Orchids and Salami* her story differs from the court testimony. "I tried to convince myself that in Hollywood my only genuine interest would be my marriage and my home, but deep down I knew I was trying to sell myself a three-dollar bill. I couldn't possibly live in Hollywood and not try to become an actress."

Zsa Zsa's version of Eva's meeting with Eric differs from her sister's. According to Zsa Zsa, their maternal grandmother, Franceska Tillemann, gave a party to which both Eva and Magda were invited. Eva, however, was too tired to attend; perhaps she had been all day on her feet behind the counter of a family shop. She returned home, creamed her face, and went to bed with a plate of salami and scallions. Still licking her chops, she heard the telephone down the hall. Magda on the line, telling her to come at once: "The most beautiful man in the world is here."

It's true that he stood six feet, four inches, he had Scandinavian features—blond hair, blue eyes—and a good profile. In pictures taken a bit later in Hollywood, however, he is not the most beautiful man in the world, though he does resemble the character actor Leif Erickson.

Zsa Zsa added that Eva joined Eric in London and they married there at the Registry Office, where Zsa Zsa, as the closest family member, gave her away. Back in Budapest, Vilmos fumed, although the reason for his displeasure remains unclear. According to Zsa Zsa, she and Burhan saw Eva and Eric off at Victoria Station immediately after the ceremony. From there they went by train to Southampton to board the boat for New York.

Eva, however, wrote that she and Eric spent several months in London while awaiting her entry permit to the United States. In this case, her memory is correct, for after their marriage on June 3, they did not board the SS *Ile de France* until August. Their timing, though coincidental, was extraordinary. Had they waited a few weeks longer, their passage would have been complicated by the Nazi invasion of Poland, and the outbreak of war. In view of Hungary's alliance with Germany, Eva would have been considered an enemy alien in both Britain and the United States and perhaps deported to Hungary.

While in London, the couple were house guests of the writer-translator Ivy Low Litvinov and her husband, Maxim Litvinov. He served as people's commissar of foreign affairs (i.e., foreign minister) of the Soviet Union 1930 to 1939, and as Soviet ambassador to the United States from 1941 to 1943.

It is likely that H.G. Wells, Zsa Zsa's new admirer and a friend of Ivy's father, introduced the two couples.

Eric Drimmer's travels, his ambiguous profession, and his connection of whatever sort with the Litvinovs—taken together, these raise the question of whether his real job was that of foreign agent. The question, intriguing though it is, will remain unanswered, even as one speculates: Was he perhaps an emissary of neutral Sweden, sent to Litvinov to seek Soviet intervention if Hitler violated Swedish neutrality? Lending credibility to this scenario is the fact that one of Litvinov's most trusted friends was Alexandra Kollontai, chargé d'affaires in the Soviet embassy in Stockholm; she later smuggled his writings out of the USSR. Could Drimmer have been part of this nexus? Working against my theory, however, is this: the Litvinovs were in Russia in the summer of 1939. Still, Drimmer could have met with operatives from the Soviet embassy in the Litvinov house.

If not working with the Russians on behalf of Sweden, was he a spy for Washington? Or even a communist sympathizer receiving instructions as war seemed more likely every hour? Drimmer's young wife would have been easily deceived by his clandestine mission. Though Eva later became astute at reading people and situations, at twenty she was an ingenue eager to believe whatever her husband said.

The next version of Eva's marriage comes from her cousin, Mrs. Annette Lantos, whom we met earlier. Mrs. Lantos is certain that Eva and Eric married in Budapest, in the Gabor apartment. A "big reception" followed at the home of Franceska Tillemann, Eva's grandmother. The newlyweds being short of money, it was Sebestyn Tillemann, Mrs. Lantos's father, who bought their plane tickets to London. This report seems credible for several reasons. First of all, Mrs. Lantos, as an intelligent girl of nine or ten, would have been interested in the romance and grown-up activities that swirled around a wedding. Then, too, her father was perhaps the wisest member of the extended family, and the one who, like Burhan Belge, guessed the full, sinister meaning of the swastika.

In 1938, Mrs. Lantos recalled, her father obtained U.S. visas for himself and his family. Both he and his wife felt the impulse to leave, and yet . . . "They stayed on in Hungary," Mrs. Lantos said, "because life in Budapest, they thought, was too comfortable to give it up." Although Sebestyn Tillemann and his family stayed on, he would have been acutely aware of the escape clause that his wedding present provided for his niece. Eva and Eric, happy and in love, thanked him for his generous gift. Promising a return visit to Hungary in a year or so, Eva kissed her uncle repeatedly as they said goodbye; Eric shook his hand and invited him to visit them in Los Angeles.

They never saw him again.

Chapter 8

E.G., Phone Home

If only Eva could have dialed direct! Desperately homesick, she needed to hear Mama's voice, or Magduska's, or Papuska's. But from Los Angeles such a call took hours to place, and cost a small fortune. Before long, war in Europe made phone calls to Hungary virtually impossible. At least, however, Eva soon had the mixed blessing of Zsa Zsa, who arrived in California in June 1941.

After spending several months in Budapest during the winter of 1940, Zsa Zsa returned to Turkey more discontented than ever. Ankara held no new surprises for her. Marriage to Burhan, which for a time had amused her in spite of its lack of love, now seemed stale. He wanted a child, but his mother-in-law back in Hungary was too vain to accept the role of grandmother. "Jolie takes you away from me," he chided. "I have no wife, and because of her no children!" Burhan, and all future Gabor husbands, soon learned that Jolie possessed her daughters body and soul, keeping them under psychological lock and key.

Another reason for Zsa Zsa's wish to leave Turkey was Eva's minor success in Hollywood, for not long after her arrival Paramount Pictures signed her as a contract player. At that time the studios were tossing contracts to all comers, or so it seemed. After making the rounds, Eva found a place at Paramount in the studio's B-movie unit. Blondes with foreign accents were in vogue, although immediately she was told to lose ten pounds. Studio brass disliked the baby fat and Hungarian hips. Thus began Eva's lifelong habit of dieting, so that in later years she stayed trim while Zsa Zsa's weight zoomed—yet another source of sisterly friction.

Other than abundant blonde hair, the accent, and malapropisms that always got a laugh—"I wish to buy a dress for street walking," she told a saleslady; "We sang 'Old Anxiety' on New Year's Eve"—she had no particular silver-screen assets and the studio regarded her as one new face in the swarm of young women and men who landed contracts each year and then vanished. Or rather, many went back where they came from while others took menial jobs and never relinquished their shattered dream. To Zsa Zsa, however, far away in Ankara and bedazzled by the lure of movie stardom, Eva looked already like the new Garbo. Sibling rivalry overspread Zsa Zsa like hives.

Another reason to leave Turkey was the menace of fascism, not only from Germany but from Italy, as well, and from various European countries with fascist leanings: Hungary, Romania, Bulgaria, the pro-German government of Vichy France. In Turkey itself were many who admired Hitler and Mussolini and who lacked sympathy for the beleaguered Jews. Zsa Zsa's Mongolian cheekbones notwithstanding, anyone interested in her ethnicity knew she had Jewish blood.

According to Zsa Zsa in later years, Jolie urged her to leave Burhan and go to comfort Eva, whose marriage to the most beautiful man in the world had devolved from storybook to housework. After their arrival in Los Angeles, she and Eric lived in a small hotel, which suggests that his income did not match that of the average medical doctor. When he went to work each day, Eva lacked occupation. Her English was imperfect; she had little money; she knew no one; and Hollywood, then and now, takes on the bleak lineaments of an Edward Hopper canvas if you're broke or depressed. Eva was both.

"I went back to bed every morning as soon as my husband left for the day, and wept all over the linen," said Eva. Jolie, always the fixer, wrote to Eva that she must look up Ilona Massey, the Hungarian actress then at the peak of her career in Hollywood. Although Jolie and Ilona were acquainted, Eva was not granted an audience. In later years, however, Ilona and the Gabors crossed paths as did all Hungarians in American show business.

Shortly after Eva's arrival at Paramount, the studio sent her on a modeling assignment. Her portfolio comprised only a scattering of print ads for Jolie's shop that had appeared a few years earlier in local papers in Budapest. Despite limited experience, but with shiny new teeth (Jolie claimed she sent two thousand dollars to pay for crowns), Eva posed for a pictorial spread, "Five Steps to Winter Beauty," that ran in several movie magazines in 1940. In the layout, a smiling Eva preps her skin for winter using such products as Palmolive soap, Woodbury face cream, and Yardley hand cream, along with cosmetics by Max Factor.

Zsa Zsa did not so much as throw Burhan a kiss from the train. On her final prewar visit to Budapest, she decided— with Jolie's collusion—not to get off in Ankara but rather to head for Hollywood. When she boarded the train on February 15, 1941, these countries, either all or in part, were under German occupation: Austria, the Baltic states, Belgium, Czechoslovakia, Denmark, France, Greece, the Netherlands, Norway. Bombs were falling on London and across the United Kingdom, and on the very day that Zsa Zsa left Budapest Austria began mass deportation of Jews to Poland.

Despite her diplomatic passport, she could not travel west across occupied countries, so that her sole option was to travel east. Although Bulgaria was still officially neutral, fighting had broken out in the southern part of the country and some railroad tracks had been bombed. As Zsa Zsa's train approached the Turkish frontier, the announcement was made that passengers must detrain and walk across the border. All luggage, including Zsa Zsa's twenty-one suitcases, arrived safely in Istanbul after having been inspected and loaded onto a different train. Passing through Ankara, she almost got off. After all, she had invested six years of her life there, and despite her fatigue with Burhan, she found much to admire in him. He had treated her kindly, and the Turks had welcomed her. But she stayed on the train, eventually changing numerous times as she made her way along the Syrian border and into Iraq.

In Bagdad she waited almost two months to arrange ongoing transportation. Each day she had to report to police headquarters. Her presence in Iraq, everything about her, aroused suspicion. Why was she traveling alone? Where was her husband? How did she obtain a diplomatic passport? Why was she headed to the United States? To the authorities, she was as suspect as a Mata Hari or a Tokyo Rose. Fortunately, she made the acquaintance of a young sheik and lived with him during her Iraqi sojourn. He, like so many who wanted to and the nine who did, wished to marry her. Zsa Zsa liked the sound of the matrimonial title he offered— sheikha—but the gravitational pull of Hollywood won out. Epithets such as "actress" and "movie star" dazzled her like a mirage on the Arabian desert.

Finally cleared to leave the country, she flew to Karachi, then part of India before Partition, and from there to Bombay, where she boarded the SS *President Grant* on April 27, arriving in New York on June 3, 1941, along with her twenty-one battered suitcases. She had traveled from the Indian Ocean across the Pacific, through the Panama Canal, over the Caribbean, around the tip of Florida, and up the Atlantic Coast to New York. Curiosity, and a certain notoriety, awaited her in Manhattan. Although not yet a celebrity, she had accrued a reputation as an exotic adventuress. Someone photographed her on deck before disembarkation, and in that picture she looks as though she has just come from a makeover spa. Blonde, rested, aglow with a confident smile, she was no doubt rejuvenated by ocean air and a new continent to conquer.

Always one to keep her address book up to date, Zsa Zsa had sent a telegram to a retired industrialist in New York whom she and Burhan had entertained in Ankara. He met her at the pier and within hours of touching the Manhattan pavement, she was dining at '21'. The next day several newspapers carried her photograph, announcing "Turkish Beauty Arrives." Eva flew to New York to welcome her. "We fell into each other's arms," Zsa Zsa said, "babbling ecstatically in Hungarian." A day or two after that, they flew to Los Angeles.

One may wonder how a woman of twenty-four, unemployed, a spendthrift, indulged by parents and then by her husband, collected the means to travel halfway around the world, and to do so in style. The only explanation comes from the pen of Jolie, who asked Zsa Zsa in Budapest, before departure, "How will you be for money?"

"I have some from Burhan," she answered. "I also have from Grandmother plus the twelve-carat ring which Grandmother gave me plus some other little bits of jewelry like the ruby necklace Papa gave me for the wedding present." Her perilous journey in wartime across hostile countries and oceans under threat of bombs raises another question: Where did she find such courage? The best answer comes from George Sanders, her third husband, who said, some years after their divorce, "Whatever else could be said about Zsa Zsa, and a great deal could, and is, being said about her, one thing is certain, she has a lot of guts."

Chapter 9

It Was a B-Picture Only to Those Too Lazy to Go Down the Alphabet

Such was Eva's later opinion of *Forced Landing*, her first movie. Before that, she appeared for a few seconds, uncredited, in *New York Town*, filmed late in 1940, and starring Fred MacMurray and Mary Martin. Eva is unlocatable in the picture, meaning that she may appear in a crowd scene or that her bit part was deleted. *Forced Landing*, a war drama shot in ten days during April 1941 and released two months later, is perhaps not so impaired as Eva judged it. Today it might earn a B minus.

Before, during, and after this inauspicious debut, Eva studied acting, first with Florence Enright (1883–1961), a stage actress in the 'teens who appeared in minor film roles in the thirties before becoming a drama coach. Eva called her "a splendid woman who gave me a genuine approach to the art of acting. She worked with me daily from nine to six at Paramount Studios." Since the studio method of teaching young recruits how to act is not well known, I quote Eva's account of it. "When you are new and delivered over for coaching, you work on a miniature stage with a group of actors. In my group were Susan Hayward and Jeanne Cagney (Jimmy's sister). We would rehearse scenes every day, playing before a small audience whom we could not see. Whenever a new lamb was led to pasture he worked with our group, and thus I had constantly to repeat scenes from plays. This was invaluable experience for me."

Eva's next coach was Margaret Webster (1905–1972), a distinguished actress who became one of the earliest female stage directors, notably of Shakespeare, in London and on Broadway, in addition to directing operas in New York at the Met. (She turned down offers to direct pictures.) Webster directed Eva's second screen test, which took place as a sort of midterm exam after her initial six months of acting lessons. They stayed in touch, and Webster later wrote to Eva "expressing her belief that I would become a good actress."

Forced Landing is set on the fictitious Pacific island of Mosaque. Eva plays a refugee from the Netherlands. Victor Varconi (1891–1976), the handsome star of silent pictures in Hungary and Germany before coming to Hollywood, plays Eva's father. These two Hungarians found much to talk about between takes, for he wanted to know how Hungary had changed for better and for worse since he left. Two other stars of silent films, Evelyn Brent and Nils Asther, took small roles in *Forced Landing*. Susan Hayward, Eva's colleague from drama class, was briefly considered for Eva's role.

In one sequence, Eva flies a small prop plane when an emergency on board demands the urgent attention of the pilot, played by Richard Arlen. Under pretext of loading a box of gold cargo, island terrorists slipped in a bomb instead. This is sufficient plot synopsis; in fact, it's difficult to fathom just what is going on in the caffeinated script.

At twenty-two, Eva has long blonde 1940s hair. Her face, while recognizable, differs radically from the dazzling likeness of later decades. Her nose has not yet been surgically reduced, the chin looks more prominent by several millimeters than she later wished it to be, and her teeth are white though one central incisor is slightly crooked. Eva's eyes here look Magyar, meaning faintly Asiatic in shape. When she smiles, they become the vestigal ovals of the Far East that one often sees in Hungarians, Finns, Turks, and others of related ethnicity. (Perhaps the Gabors had a Mongolian progenitor after all.) Eva looks close to thirty, although by the time she reached that age her face had begun to move counterclockwise.

As the most photogenic cast member, Eva gets her share, and more, of close-ups. Her face, even as the mere blueprint of future beauty, is oddly riveting. She would have been a striking screen presence even without the knife of gentrification.

For a negligible product, the film received better reviews than expected. The *Los Angeles Times* called *Forced Landing* "an effective melodrama of aviation," adding that "the writers have cleverly contrived the plot and Gordon Wiles, director, has animated the feature through his direction." As for Eva, the critic found her "interesting, especially in her romantic scenes with Richard Arlen, although one cannot determine all of her qualifications from this production."

Eva's next Paramount assignment was *Pacific Blackout*, shot in late summer 1941 and released a few weeks after the Japanese attack on Pearl Harbor. The title of this story, "ripped from the headlines," refers to the practice of extinguishing all lights, in public and in private homes, to foil enemy aircraft during air raids. "Pacific" in this instance referred to California, even though cities on the Atlantic coast and certain ones inland were also required to go dark.

Robert Preston plays an inventor of military hardware who is wrongly accused of murder by a foreign-born nightclub singer—Eva, forced by threats to her family in Europe into becoming an enemy agent. Eva conveys the character's tortured conflict in a nuanced performance that reflects her many hours of studio acting lessons. In this picture she has made a leap from *Forced Landing* in screen presence and acting ability. Eva has also acquired the face that she will keep, with modifications, for the rest of her life.

Her work found admirers in the press. In the *San Bernardino Sun*, for instance, the reviewer gushed, "Excellent, too, is Eva Gabor, who highlights a splendid performance with a standout rendition of Hoagy Carmichael's torch song, 'I Met Him in Paris.'" (The singing was dubbed by contralto Martha Mears.) Paramount didn't agree with such praise. The studio made her redundant.

And now war fever gripped the country. On December 8, 1941, the day after Pearl Harbor, the United States declared war on Japan. Declaration of war on Germany followed on December 11. As an ally of Germany, however reluctant, Hungary reciprocated on December 13 with a declaration of war on the U.S. The American embassy in Budapest prepared to close. All personnel would soon leave, making direct communication between the two countries virtually impossible for the next four years.

On December 28, 1941, Jolie wrote an eleven-page letter to Eva and Zsa Zsa in Hollywood. It is an extraordinary document for several reasons: 1) It reveals the hidden side of Jolie. Rather than the silly egotist of later publicity, this heartfelt letter testifies to her deep love and concern for her daughters, even as her longwinded, Polonious-like admonitions also make us smile; 2) the frivolous, materialistic Jolie is also there, more involved with fashions, local gossip, and retail profits than with the war that is menacing Hungary; 3) the letter confirms the statements of Jolie's niece, Mrs. Lantos, that even in the dangerous early 1940s, life in Hungary continued almost as normal for those in the middle and upper classes; 4) it is one of the few surviving Gabor family letters. For these reasons, I reproduce a large portion of it.

"My dear, beautiful children in the far away distance, Zsazsika and Evika, my sweet beautiful fairies, I hardly know how to begin this letter which in all likelihood will be the last one I could send you in Hungarian for quite a while to come. This is being sent to you through the good offices of the American Embassy which is departing tomorrow. One of my letters written in Hungarian has already been returned to me; I also sent another in English since I wrote that one." [At some point, Jolie's letter was translated from Hungarian to English as required by the American Embassy in Budapest, where it was no doubt scrutinized for prohibited statements. I quote from the translation, which captures nicely Jolie's various emotions as well as her florid style.]

"For me to communicate in English is like a mute signaling with gestures. How could I be expected to express that undescribable yearning I have for you when I couldn't do justice to that even in the native tongue of my beloved Hungary. I am therefore making the most of this opportunity to describe my feelings for you.

"As long as I have been hearing from you and the news was always better and better it compensated me for the fact that I haven't seen you, Evika, for over two years and you, Zsazsika, for a full year come tomorrow. [Jolie's count was off; Zsa Zsa left Budapest on February 15, 1941, just over ten months prior to Jolie's letter.] You can imagine how depressing it was to hear that all communications had been severed, no more telephone or telegrams. At first I refused to credit this but my optimistic trait soon took over. I am now confident, I simply feel this can't last long and after it is all over I'll take the first clipper to fly to you or perhaps you will to me—what happiness that will be.

"To have the strength to endure all this I must feel confident that you'll behave cleverly and that you will take good care of yourselves and of each other. Needless to say—perish the thought—you must never become estranged or become jealous of each other, grow angry with each other if even momentarily over some triviality. No matter how grave the occasion may appear to you—suppose one of you were to steal the sweetheart of the other, or snitch her nylons, or even flirted with the husband of the other—believe me all of this would be of no consequence compared to the bond existing between sisters, the bond of blood. You must have been aware of that yourselves while you were separated because of the yearning you felt for each other.

"Don't be stingy with each other in money matters either—the one who happens to have more shall unhesitatingly share it with the other. I do not want to preach but I pray to you, if you really love me and want me to retain my good mood, then take very, very, very good care of yourselves!!! For a mother's heart is more sensitive than the finest seismograph and I will detect through the ether everything that affects you, both good or ill, even from a distance of 10,000 kilometers.

"Do not let the tempo of your lives make you careless with cars and planes, do not weaken yourselves with dieting lest your lowered resistance make you an easy victim of pneumonia.

"Be self-assured, clever, strong; laugh and exult in that you exist, that you are alive, that you are beautiful and young, that the sun shines and you can go swimming in the ocean. Do not let even the most serious-appearing fiasco sadden you, skip over annoyances and unpleasantnesses as if they were hurdles and if it saddens you that we are so far apart, skip over that, too. Take solace that all must come to pass and that this war will also end soon.

"One other thought. It is not urgent for either of you to become Greta Garbos in a matter of months. (Apropos: *Ninotchka* is a great hit here.) The longer it takes you to reach your desired goal the better, for as you well know, anticipation is almost better than fulfillment. You have proven yourselves sufficiently to me already. I would not want you to stay entirely idle in this interval for you must keep on learning. You are still very young, other kids of your age are still in school in Switzerland, playing tennis and dreaming about Prince Charming.

"I am worried that your overabundant energies will be even more overstimulated by the rushing American life and that you will be carried away by the tide. Do not be in such a great rush; I fear the inevitable reaction. Come to a halt every once in a while, take each other by the hand, disassociate yourselves for a while from that Hollywood vortex, betake yourselves to some beautiful beach, take a dip in the ocean, recall your childhood when you were playing at Lake Balaton.

[For several pages, Jolie reminds them of childhood pranks and of various boys they chased or who flirted with them.]

"Outside my anxiety over your happiness, I can truthfully assert that I have never led a better and more carefree existence. My stores, thank God, are doing outstandingly well, my personnel is so well trained that managing my stores has become almost play for me. Although the taxes and other impositions on commerce have become fantastically high, the income has also risen in almost the same proportion. I have no financial complaints to make.

"Your father Vilmos is also doing very well and he is most generous with Voros [i.e., Magda]. I often rue the fact that he had been so niggardly with you, but in those days he really didn't have it. Your sister Vörös, who has become one of the most stylish women of Budapest, has really behaved most commendably, spending the last fourteen days before Christmas in the Crystallo working from early morning until the night. Business was excellent there also.

"After fourteen days of rewarding but exhausting work, I am spending all day today, Sunday, in bed, dictating this letter from my bed to Sári [presumably a secretary or salesperson] who is nice enough to sacrifice her Sunday afternoon to type this letter.

"So here I lie in my beautifully decorated neobaroque, rattan-woven and green brocaded chaise longue. My bedding is pink silk, I am wearing a light blue, lacy, seductive silk nightgown embroidered with cyclamen, I have a Karády hairdo with a light blue velvet ribbon in it. [Katalin Karády, 1912–1990, was a top film star, perhaps the Hungarian version of Barbara Stanwyck or Katharine Hepburn. She is revered in Hungary not only for her talent but also for her wartime heroism and for her efforts to save Jewish lives.] I am surrounded by a powerful radio, also an automatic record player, a lot of new records, mostly hot tangoes. I wish I had Zsa Zsa's records from Ankara here.

[She goes on at length about plans for her New Year's Eve party. A few close friends are invited, and of course Magda and "the Minister," meaning Magda's current boyfriend, the Portuguese ambassador to Hungary. More on him presently. Also on Jolie's guest list is "my latest beau, Vilmos de Gabor," whom she divorced the previous year and whom she likes far better as beau than as husband.]

"There will only be fifteen of us for the rest of the family is invited to Grandmother's [i.e., Franceska Tillemann]. Grandmother, thank God, is more beautiful than ever as you can see from the photo and is daily asking for you. She adores you and is very proud of you." [There follows a roundup of family news, viz., Jolie's sisters, her brother, and two nieces, and the latest gossip on friends and acquaintances.]

"Now to tell you something of importance, we finally received a telegram from Burhan that the divorce has been granted, thank God. This was also confirmed by Ali Tevfik by mail. Now be careful, don't rush into some new marriage now that you are free. Duci [another of Magda's nicknames] wrote you in a previous letter the address in Lisbon where you can write and from where it will be forwarded to me.

The letter must be always addressed as follows: On the outside envelope the Lisbon address, inside a second *closed* envelope addressed merely "Ministre de Portugal." The letter should be written in English to pass the censorship quicker. You will find out what other language may be used. Try to make sure that I hear from you by sending more letters for I haven't received all you have sent. You can also write to Ali Tevfik in Istanbul, he'll forward it. Try every means to have your letters reach me for this is indispensable to my existence. The last letter I received was about Eva's return from New Orleans. In contrast to Zsa Zsa's exhaustive account of many pages, Eva wrote only a short page in which she promised to write more the next day. Alas, that longer letter will hardly reach me now.

[The translator added a note: "This is in handwriting from now on."]

"I now say goodbye, I hope I gave you an exhaustive account. Please try everything, everything to communicate with me, for I am yearning for news of you. Million kisses to each of you separately and together. The good Lord bless every step you take. Take good care of yourselves to make the reunion a happy one. Au revoir! Your mummie."

Before Paramount tore up Eva's contract, the studio used her once more in a bit part, and once more she can't be found. The picture was *Star Spangled Rhythm*, a patriotic musical variety show filmed in summer 1942 and starring everyone on the Paramount lot—Bing Crosby, Bob Hope, Dorothy Lamour, Paulette Goddard, Veronica Lake, ad infinitum. After that, Eva dropped out of sight until late 1944, when 20th Century Fox offered her a contract. That one lived up to the familiar complaint, "not worth the paper it's written on."

At first, Eva took it for the big break she had yearned for. What better could a starlet hope for than a role in *A Royal*

Scandal, starring Tallulah Bankhead as Catherine the Great of Russia and directed by the great Ernst Lubitsch? Lubitsch conducted rehearsals, began production in September 1944, then fell ill. Unable to continue, he hired Otto Preminger to finish the picture. Although cast as the Countess Demidow, a fixture in Catherine's court, Eva is once more invisible. Her role seems to have existed at some point, for still pictures show Eva with character actor Charles Coburn. She also started out with dialogue, for Eva recalled that on the first day of filming she was "terribly nervous as Tallulah watched and I prepared to play a sequence with Charles Coburn, who had just won an Academy Award."

Eva and Tallulah bonded, and one day during a lull in shooting Tallulah advised her to leave Hollywood and pursue a career on the New York stage. Eva recalled in her autobiography that since their meeting on *A Royal Scandal*, Tallulah "has provided fun for the entire Gabor family." Which was not quite the case. Zsa Zsa and Tallulah loathed each other and quarreled loudly when Zsa Zsa and George Sanders appeared on the Bankhead radio show. Legend has it, however, that the Gabors picked up their "dahlings" from none other than Tallulah.

Had Lubitsch directed *A Royal Scandal*, Eva's role might have grown rather than shrinking, for they had formed a liaison—Eva called it a "friendship"—even before her arrival at Fox. On July 12, 1943, Hollywood columnist Hugh Dixon wrote, "Ernst Lubitsch and Eva Gabor don't care who knows that they care."

In *Orchids and Salami*, she devotes two pages to him, more than to anyone else other than family. "I was a habitual visitor in his elaborate Spanish villa in Bel Air," she wrote. "He was tiny, shorter than I. He had about him a Panlike quality, as though he had just come out of the woods holding a champagne glass. His conversation was all wit. He teased me mercilessly, pulled my leg, laughed at me, and made me love it and come back for more. I will never forget the pleasant evenings in which he managed to make his huge rooms feel cozy as a well-heated shack in the woods. Since I matched his genuine and natural gaity with a gay front which I supplied for the occasion, I suppose Ernst Lubitsch never fully realized how seriously I took myself. I miss the man."

Born in Berlin in 1892, Lubitsch, twenty-seven years Eva's senior, satisfied the Electra complex common to the three Gabor sisters. His maturity, however, was only one of the reasons Eva loved him. He was urbane, a natural mentor to young women even when they were not his lovers, and according to Eva, "a man who spoke only the truth concerning matters of importance to him." And his old-world manners reminded this homesick young woman of life in Budapest. Their affair lasted from 1943 until his death on November 30, 1947. Until now, the circumstances of that death have been whispered. During Eva's lifetime, no one published the facts for fear of legal action. Biographer Scott Eyman, writing in 1993, two years before Eva's death, veiled the story. "After lunch," Eyman wrote, "[Lubitsch] welcomed the woman he had had dinner with the night before. Shortly after two o'clock in the afternoon, Lubitsch retired to his den with her. They made love. A few minutes later, he felt the familiar tightness in his chest. The constricting pain began to encircle him, possess him. He excused himself and went into the bathroom, probably to get to his angina medicine. Then, a sudden tearing explosion inside his chest overwhelmed and obliterated all that was Ernst Lubitsch."

Lubitsch's chauffeur, "summoned by the terrified woman, picked Lubitsch up and placed him on the couch fifteen feet away." The chauffeur called several of the dead man's friends, telling one of them that he would have to "take the lady out of the house."

Describing the funeral, Eyman continued, "At Forest Lawn, Ernst was laid out in the new suit he had worn to dinner the previous Saturday night. Mary Loos [a platonic friend of the late director] attended with Eva Gabor and Margo [the wife of Eddie Albert, Eva's future costar on *Green Acres*]. Neither of Mary's friends had ever seen a dead body before, let alone that of someone they loved. They were frankly terrified. Loos suggested that they just walk by the open casket and not look. Even so, she kept a firm hold on both their elbows just in case."

For decades, rumor had it that Lubitsch died from the overexertion of sex with a prostitute. In 2014, Scott Eyman clarified for an interviewer on the Hungarian website Magyarnarancs.hu what he wasn't allowed to include in his Lubitsch biography. The woman with Lubitsch during his final hour was Eva Gabor.

Zsa Zsa lived with Eva and Eric Drimmer for five months, from the time of her arrival in Los Angeles in June until Eva's separation from Eric in November 1941. Then the sisters moved to a small bungalow in Hollywood, so modest that they slept in the same bed—even when they weren't speaking. They squabbled just like old times, but each was glad to have the other. Although surrounded by Hollywood glamour, these two now learned the real meaning of fear and anxiety, for after the outbreak of war they had no news of Jolie, Vilmos, and Magda, nor did they learn for a long time the horrendous fate of other family members. Both applied to become U.S. citizens. In Eva's case, a second marriage to a native-born American sped the process: in September of 1943 she married handsome Charles Isaacs, scion of a wealthy Los Angeles family. By this time Zsa Zsa was Mrs. Conrad Hilton, and she arranged for Eva and Charles to marry at the Hilton estate in Bel Air. Zsa Zsa, however, overspent the budget that Hilton had agreed to, and in protest he skipped Eva's wedding.

During the war, Eva's new husband served in the coast guard. "Charles was the most considerate man I have ever known," Eva recalled many years later, saying that he spoiled her and blaming herself for their eventual divorce, in 1949. Her alimony from Isaacs was $1,000 a month for eleven years, to be reduced to $600 a month in the event of his death. That event took place in 1953, when Isaacs was only forty-one years old.

Eva's intermittent affair with Lubitsch, beginning in 1943, ran simultaneously with her second marriage. All parties had ample time for other lovers, and in Eva's case unemployment allowed her and Zsa Zsa to make many attempts to rescue their family from a situation in Hungary that grew more ominous each week. The two sisters in America had a better grasp of wartime reality than their isolated relatives in Hungary, for Jolie and others in the Tillemann and Gabor families danced around the volcano, ignoring its snake-tongue licks of flame and drafts of hot smoke. Their revels resembled the merrymaking of doomed guests in *The Masque of the Red Death*.

Chapter 10

The California Gold Rush

Zsa Zsa hated her role as the poor refugee living with relatives in a new world teeming with rich men and rich opportunities. Here I am in a bungalow, she thought, when a mile away are ten thousand mansions. Surely one of them was destined for her? And an American husband to go with it, since her second desire—or third, after money and fame—was the security of U.S. citizenship. In the aftermath of Pearl Harbor, and the American declaration of war against Axis nations, she risked being declared an enemy alien owing to her Hungarian nationality. Once more, that Turkish diplomatic passport served her well. Still, with divorce from Burhan pending, she could not clutch it indefinitely.

It is unlikely that Zsa Zsa knew the Emma Lazarus poem inscribed at the base of the Statue of Liberty, though certainly its spirit inflamed her. Had she read those words as her ship sailed into New York Harbor—"I lift my lamp beside the golden door"—she might have fancied herself the very one that Lady Liberty had in mind. A sentiment echoed by Oscar Levant, who cracked in 1955, "Zsa Zsa not only worships the Golden Calf, she barbecues it for lunch."

On April 10, 1942, ten months after arriving in the U.S., she married one of the richest men in America, Conrad Hilton. To the public, Zsa Zsa's name is now better known than his. Everyone of course knows the Hilton hotels, and viewers of *Mad Men,* season three, may recall a ruthless character named Conrad Hilton who frustrated and annoyed Don Draper. That character, played by Chelcie Ross, neither looked nor sounded like the actual Conrad Hilton. The producers might as well have cast Meryl Streep. By contrast, compare on youtube.com Conrad Hilton's appearance as a guest on *Art Linkletter's House Party* in 1954. There he exudes bonhomie and sincerity, whether genuine or not. He was sixty-seven years old at the time and as sexy as—well, a senior Don Draper, though minus Draper's tightly wound intensity. Throughout a long career, Hilton used his Southwest accent and easy Western charm, along with the confidence of a super-rich man, to project affability. Unlike today's robber barons, many of them robbing even more efficiently in politics, Hilton was as upright as a multimillionaire capitalist can be. As J. Randy Taraborelli writes in *The Hiltons,* "Generally speaking, he was well liked and had a stellar reputation among his colleagues. He was known as much for his philanthropy as for his hotel empire." It's easy to see how Zsa Zsa, or any woman who liked older men, might go for Conrad Hilton, "Connie" to his friends. What Zsa Zsa didn't realize in 1942 was this: she had met her match.

And so had he. Hilton married her against his better judgment, for he was a devout Roman Catholic who had divorced his first wife, the mother of his sons Nicky, Barron, and Eric. His remarriage meant estrangement from the Church. In his 1957 autobiography, *Be My Guest,* Hilton recalled his sadness at being denied the sacraments. "Sundays when we went to church, for I went as I had always done, and Zsa Zsa went with me, there was this difference: When the congregation rose and made its way toward the altar rail to receive Holy Communion, I stayed on my knees in the pew, chained, as it were, to the side of my beautiful wife."

His better judgment surely told him, too, that beautiful Zsa Zsa, exactly thirty years younger than he, was not unaware of his affluence. Had their marriage lasted longer than five years, she might have depleted the riches of his empire. Turned loose among such bounty, Zsa Zsa toiled not, neither did she spin. But frugal Connie gasped to see her spend.

Before the start-up of her conspicuous consumption, however, she must marry the man, and so she lost no time waiting for him to propose. Zsa Zsa took charge herself. It came about like this. Early in December 1941 she and Eva went to Ciro's, the Sunset Strip nightclub, with their dates. Zsa Zsa's escort that night was Greg Bautzer, a handsome, high-profile Hollywood attorney who had dated every star in town and would continue to do so until his marriage, in 1956, to actress Dana Wynter. As it happened, Conrad Hilton had also come to Ciro's with a date, and during the evening someone pointed him out to Zsa Zsa. She didn't know his exact age—fifty-four—but he reminded her of Vilmos and of the other older men she had swooned over. When she learned that he was in the hotel business, that he had no wife, and that he liked respectable women as long as they didn't carry decency to extremes—she dazzled him with a smile that flashed the signal she meant it to.

He asked her to dance, for he was a good dancer, and as soon as he held her in his arms he realized what an unusual girl he had come across. The accent, the unpronounceable name, the erotic aggression that she, unlike American girls, even in Hollywood, didn't try to cover up. Several times he attempted to wrap his tongue around "Zsa Zsa," but finally gave up. She suggested her stage name from Vienna, and he announced, "I'm going to call you Georgia." And so he did for the next thirty-eight years, for he and "Georgia" Gabor remained friends long after their divorce. He didn't approve of her, and often she irritated him beyond endurance, but that smile like a simultaneous declaration of war and peace, along with the blonde hair and the outrageous wit that really should be censored, Conrad thought, even as he roared at her latest ribald remarks—all of that made her impossible to let go. "She brought more laughter and gaiety than I had ever known in my personal life," he said.

On the dance floor at Ciro's she looked up at him, smiled like an odalisque, and said in her most cunning English, "I think I vill marry you." He had been around, he knew how to play the game, and so he quipped, "Is that what you think, Georgia? Well, why not? I dare you!"

"Our marriage was doomed before it started," Conrad Hilton wrote sixteen years later in his autobiography.

Lest Zsa Zsa appear as a complete mercenary, I quote further from *Be My Guest*. "Zsa Zsa was not always on the receiving end by any means. She herself loved to give. She showered presents and attention on my mother; she would drive halfway across the city to take her a nosegay. Mother was enraptured and, much as she regretted that our church would not welcome Zsa Zsa, referred to her affectionately as 'that dear girl.' Zsa Zsa also bought tennis rackets and fishing poles for Nick and Barron."

Had it not been for Zsa Zsa's inconvenient previous marriage, she might have become a fixture in the Hilton family's place of worship, the Church of the Good Shepherd in Beverly Hills. There Francesca's confirmation took place, and Zsa Zsa herself attended from time to time over the years along with scores of other stars including Eva, Merv Griffin, Loretta Young, Irene Dunne, Gary Cooper, Carmen Miranda, and Rosalind Russell, who dubbed the church "Our Lady of the Cadillacs."

Conrad and Zsa Zsa had more in common than was evident to casual observers of their marriage. Both loved animals, especially dogs and horses, and both thrived on work, although not until her entry into show business did Zsa Zsa begin the grueling agenda that belied her playgirl image. A look at her schedule, and Eva's, makes one wonder how either had time for the occasional rendezvous, let alone fourteen marriages between them. Neither knew the meaning of nine to five. Their days often stretched in the opposite direction—from 5:00 a.m. to 8:00 p.m. or later, with hours of socializing still to come. Zsa Zsa also loved the trappings of Old World romance, and Connie, while courting, sent roses every day.

Even as the roses faded, romance faded. Before long, Zsa Zsa realized that Connie had only two passions in life: his religion, and Hilton hotels. At home on Bellagio Road, in the grandiose Spanish-inspired Hilton estate, he formulated an austere budget for Zsa Zsa to follow. Next, he declared that his wife would have her own bedroom, and he would keep his. He offered two reasons for this: well along in middle age, he had his routines and sleep habits that he did not wish to change. He also disliked witnessing a woman's elaborate beauty rituals—makeup, hair, fussing over this dress versus another one and switching outfits as if in a house of couture. He prayed regularly on his knees at the prie-dieu near his bed, and a sprightly young wife of Zsa Zsa's temperament would surely claim that kneeling bagged her nylons. "Can I stop him from praying?" she wondered, a line that belongs in a Molière comedy. According to members of the Hilton family, separate bedrooms soon precluded conjugal visits.

So the marriage lumbered on, and despite the prestige and financial security of her coveted title, Mrs. Conrad Hilton, Zsa Zsa declined, her self-confidence wavered. Why did her husband no longer find her attractive? Why couldn't she make him laugh? What did the future hold for her? Once she had dreamed of becoming an actress, but here she was in Hollywood and her husband's name and reputation overshadowed her. Zsa Zsa's great consolation, during her empty days in what came to be known as her wing of the vast Hilton house, was Ranger, Conrad's German police dog. "Until I began to lavish love on her, she hid from everyone," Zsa Zsa recalled. "Little by little she grew to have confidence in me and became my constant companion, sleeping on the chaise longue in my room at night. Sometimes when I walked about aimlessly, she would nudge her wet nose into my palm as if she sensed my loneliness."

Zsa Zsa visited Eva almost daily. Bundy Solt, their school friend from Budapest, joined them and "for an hour we were back home again, chattering in Hungarian, our plates piled high with salami and green peppers."

Almost two years into the marriage, on March 19, 1944, Zsa Zsa heard the worst possible news from Hungary. Hitler, losing patience with his lackadaisical ally, Admiral Horthy, had invaded the country. All Jews were to be rounded up and systematically destroyed. Adolf Eichmann arrived in Budapest to supervise the job. Horthy, meanwhile, attempted to negotiate an armistice with any Allied nation not under German control, whether Britain or the United States. Despite his antipathy to communism, he even decided that the Soviet Union was a lesser evil than Germany, and made plans to surrender Hungary to the Red Army. Hitler, learning of Horthy's intent, removed him from office on October 15, 1944. To render Horthy completely impotent, Hitler kidnapped his son to Germany. (These events, and the plight of Hungarian Jews under Hitler, are represented with unusual accuracy in Mark Schmidt's 2014 film, *Walking with the Enemy*, in which Ben Kingsley portrays Admiral Horthy.)

Up to the time of the invasion, most Jews in Hungary, at least those in the middle classes, remained at least dimly optimistic that the war would soon end and normality return. As Mrs. Annette Lantos, Jolie's niece, told me: "From 1940 to 1944, Hungary was a pleasant place to live *if you had money*." Nevertheless, during this time many Jewish men, including Mrs. Lantos's father—Jolie's brother, Sebestyn Tillemann—were inducted into a nonmilitary labor brigade. Mrs. Lantos said that he, unlike some, was treated well "because he was known for his charitable works and giving money to many worthy causes." Since the time had now passed when he, and countless others like him, could leave the country, it seemed wise to face, accept, and let time pass.

Jolie, Vilmos, Magda, and others in the Tillemann and Gabor families, along with thousands of others identified as Jews by Hungarian fascists and German authorities, now wore the yellow star. So shameful was this badge of bigotry and hate that no Gabor ever mentioned it. Mrs. Lantos, on the other hand, like many Holocaust survivors, kept hers as a symbol. I do not presume to speak for anyone who did or did not preserve the yellow star, for each person surely had enormous cause either to remember, or to forget.

Several years prior to the German invasion of Hungary, Magda had joined the anti-Nazi underground. Owing to her marriage to a Pole, and to her time in Warsaw, she spoke passable Polish. When Hitler invaded Poland on September 1, 1939, Magda had already returned to Budapest. Her family gave various accounts of her wartime activities, though Magda herself said almost nothing. For that reason, it is difficult to render a full account.

Zsa Zsa said that her sister volunteered as a Red Cross driver taking medical supplies to Polish soldiers who had escaped to Hungary after the Germans invaded their country. Hungary, however, as an ally of Germany, found itself in a most awkward position vis-à-vis these refugee soldiers. The solution: they were interned in prisoner of war camps some seventy-five miles outside Budapest. Those medical supplies that Magda delivered were sent by the British embassy. Soon, along with medical supplies, Magda also delivered civilian clothes to the soldiers. Once out of uniform, and dressed in the apparel of ordinary Hungarians, many of the soldiers crossed the border into Romania, from there to Bulgaria and on to neutral Turkey, eventually making their way to Egypt where they joined up with British fighting men.

Magda, after delivering civilian clothes, would return to the British embassy in Budapest with a truckload of discarded Polish military uniforms, which were then burned. As the situation became more urgent, she also smuggled men from the prisoner of war camps into Budapest, where they were dispatched with documents forged by the British. One of Magda's few statements about her work is this: "The Embassy gave me directions, telling me when I could bring in men, when I could only transport clothes."

Those activities ceased, however, in December 1941, when the British embassy closed. From then until March 19, 1944, when Hitler at last invaded Hungary, Magda's story resembles a white page sprinkled with cryptic jottings. Based on somewhat sketchy evidence, however, I have pieced together her continued efforts to save lives. To put the situation in context, I quote from Raphael Patai, author of *The Jews of Hungary*.

Patai devotes several pages to what he calls "a relatively unknown chapter of the history of the Jews in Hungary during World War II. It is the story of the Polish Jews who were given refuge in Hungary, and thereby got a brief lease on life until the Nazi fury overtook them." After the German army crushed all Polish resistance in the fall of 1939, many civilian refugees, along with the soldiers already mentioned, streamed into Hungary. They were able to do so because the Soviet Union, in an attempt to stop Hitler, had occupied eastern Poland on September 17, 1939. An estimated 20,000 refugees, Jews and non-Jews, fled eastern Poland, crossed into Soviet Ukraine, and from there into Hungary and Romania. Others took a more direct route through Slovakia, which had achieved brief status as an independent state. The journey was perilous; many did not survive it. According to Patai, "The German Embassy [in Budapest] demanded that the Polish Jews be intercepted at the border and sent back to German-occupied Poland, but the Hungarian border guards were instructed by József Antall, of the Hungarian Ministry of the Interior, to register all Polish refugees as Christians, with the exception of those who insisted on registering their non-Christian religious affiliation."

Roman Catholic clergy in Hungary were also instructed by Cardinal Serédy to issue Christian papers to all Jews applying for them. Printed copies of basic Catholic prayers were distributed to Polish Jews so that they could pass as Christians if tested by Germans attempting to trip them up. Patai concludes his discussion of Polish Jews in Hungary with this melancholy statement: "All these efforts came to naught with the German occupation, after which only a few of the Jews under Christian protection were saved."

Perhaps Magda Gabor's silence had to do with a sense of failure on her part that so many of those she had rescued were soon caught and killed when the Nazis overran Hungary. Then, too, she herself was increasingly under suspicion: Jewish by ethnicity if not by religion; the ex-wife of a Pole who, until his death in May 1944, was a fighter in Britain's Royal Air Force; and not without local enemies whom the Gabors had snubbed or insulted in years past with their high-flown habits, pretensions, and superior airs.

Or perhaps Magda remained silent because the Gabors did not trumpet their good works. While Zsa Zsa and Jolie boasted about their amorous conquests, their jewels, their couturier gowns, their success at every level whether real or imagined, Eva and Magda, by contrast, veered in the opposite direction. Yet the charitable acts of all four remained largely unheralded, and no doubt that was their wish. After all, glamour girls and glamour moms in the public eye of the 1950s worked hard to maintain the image of femme fatales. Neither the studios nor the media wanted nobility; leave that to Eleanor Roosevelt and Helen Keller.

Whatever Magda's level of secrecy, she was observed. The daughter of the jewelry Gabors driving a truck; entering and leaving the British embassy and then after its closure taking a job in the embassy of a neutral country—Portugal—that was perhaps not so neutral after all. Whispers circulated in the Jewish community, then spread across Budapest, reaching the ears of the Arrow Cross Party, Hitler's Hungarian subsidiary. An invisible question hung over Magda's head: Had this un-Jewish Jewess now become a total Jew? She never found out when, but her name appeared on a list.

And then Magda met the ambassador. Her timing could not have been more exquisite, for it was he, and others at the Portuguese embassy, who saved her life, along with the lives of her parents and hundreds of others, as well.

Chapter 11

Inferno

In 1940 Jolie Gabor was approaching fifty, although few people could say from which direction. All three daughters having married and dispersed, Jolie's time to be fabulous had arrived. After long negotiation with Vilmos over furniture, Oriental rugs, gewgaws, and cash settlements, she obtained the divorce she had coveted since her wedding day. From that time forward, in the typical *Alice in Wonderland* trajectory of Gabor lives, Jolie and Vilmos became inseparable. "After the divorce," she said, "we not only had lunch together but Vilmos would take me to the theatre and he would take me to dinner and then he would escort me home and sometimes we would even sleep together. I was happy with him for the first time."

In 1941 Magda took a job as secretary to Carlos Sampaio Garrido, the Portuguese ambassador to Hungary. (Appointed in 1939, he served until 1944.) After Pearl Harbor, when Allied nations closed their embassies in Budapest, their remaining affairs were conducted through the embassies of neutral nations such as Sweden, Switzerland, and Portugal, such procedures being a normal diplomatic function during extraordinary times. The embassy of Portugal handled communications and other minimal business between Hungary and the United States.

Ambassador Garrido, fifty-eight when he met Magda, soon became her lover and, according to some accounts, her fiancé. Given Magda's underground activities, it is possible that her job at the Portuguese embassy served as a front, with the collaboration of the ambassador and other embassy staff. Although Portugal's dictator, António Salazar, ran an authoritarian right-wing government, he seems to have approved the humanitarian efforts of his diplomats in Hungary and elsewhere.

Jolie, leaving aside her usual flightiness, recalled daily life in Hungary from 1942 until March 1944. "We were still relatively unharmed in Budapest," she said, "but everyone knew it was just a matter of time." Once a week during those years, the Tillemann family gathered for a dinner party, sometimes at the home of Franceska, the matriarch, at other times at Jolie's, at one of Jolie's sisters, or at the home of their brother, Sebestyn. "Some of our rapid-fire compulsive talking was from nerves," Jolie admitted, though she delighted to regale her family with every particle of Eva's work in Hollywood and of Zsa Zsa's marital triumph. Many years later Jolie remembered a small detail from the last family dinner before catastrophe. Overcome by nerves to the point of near hysteria, she drank her own champagne, reached for her sisters', then her brother's, until finally someone at the table complained she was acting like a silly child and she slumped in her chair and fell silent. A week later everyone seated at that table wore a yellow star pinned on their clothing each time they went into the street.

The arrival of Nazi invaders turned life upside down for the Tillemanns, the Gabors, and for virtually everyone else in

Hungary. "Everybody was afraid," Jolie said. "Nobody could trust anybody. There was no food, no water. It became apparent that we, too, were in danger. Vilmos because he was known as anti-Nazi, Magda was marked because of her work for the underground." Whether Vilmos had spoken out against the Nazis was really beside the point. Jolie was disingenuous. Whatever else might count against them, the family was in grave danger because they were Jews. Nazis did not distinguish between observant and secular, assimilated or not.

For a time the Jews of Budapest lived on a knife edge of worry, desperation, and near panic. Then they fell over the edge.

In California, no news from Hungary had reached Zsa Zsa and Eva for several months. For a time after the Portuguese embassy took over U.S. interests, Magda sent letters from herself, Jolie, and others in the Gabor and Tillemann families. These letters left Budapest in diplomatic pouches and carried Lisbon postmarks. And then the letters stopped.

Zsa Zsa's imagination ran haywire. Reading newspapers, she broke into sobs at the thought of gunfire in the streets and bombs from the sky dropped by German planes and allied fighters with no thought for those below in Budapest. Conrad offered comfort. "Now, Georgia," he said, "It isn't as bad as you think, it can't be." But Zsa Zsa knew that he knew: it was worse than she thought. She couldn't rest, she couldn't sleep. She chewed her nails to the quick and they bled. Her face was drawn and often she left off the elaborate beauty rituals of earlier days. On some mornings she merely ran a comb through her hair. Zsa Zsa's only comfort was Ranger, who snuggled with her and seemed to understand better than any human the distress of this new friend.

Conrad Hilton worried about her when he had time, but his empire seemed to add a new hotel every week or two, an enterprise that left only time for prayer. Eva, the little sister that the older ones bossed, had turned into a tough young woman despite a faltering career and more lean years than otherwise. She watched as Zsa Zsa's emotions ricocheted from crying spells to hand wringing, then panic that sent her flying from room to room, and speaking faster than an auctioneer.

Never a heavy drinker, Zsa Zsa did not resort to alcohol. In those days no effective tranquilizers existed, and so her condition deteriorated. Eva and Conrad conferred. She announced to Zsa Zsa, "You and I will fly to Washington. Connie has contacts there, you know some people at the Turkish embassy, and we won't leave until we see President Roosevelt!"

In cases of nervous exhaustion, a change of scene often helps. Zsa Zsa had acquaintances from Ankara now on staff at the Turkish embassy; they would offer help, or so she thought. As it turned out, several embassy employees knew people back in Turkey who remembered Zsa Zsa, but these leads produced nothing. Next, she and Eva visited the Portuguese embassy. "We conferred with Dr. Vasco Garin, First Secretary of the embassy," Zsa Zsa recalled two decades later. "Could he not be of help since Portugal represented foreign interests in Hungary? Early in the war I had been able to communicate with my family through the Portuguese embassy in Budapest. Dr. Garin explained that it was a most difficult matter. Portugal accepted war refugees only if the United States guaranteed their admission into this country. But this was impossible in the case of enemy aliens. He shook his head."

For two months in the summer of 1944 Zsa Zsa and Eva knocked on doors in the vast labyrinth of the Capitol. Senators, congressmen, wannabe politicians, con men—anyone who might offer a shred of help. Meanwhile, Conrad seemed to have given up. "Your parents and Magda are enemy aliens," he said. "There's nothing we can do." Charles Isaacs had joined them in Washington, and he and Eva toured the city, sightseeing in the afternoon and in the evening enjoying restaurants and nightclubs. Zsa Zsa recalled Burhan's ominous predictions that everyone in Europe would be killed by Hitler or Stalin. So remote his dark words had seemed; now reality threw them in her face.

One night, having declined Eva's invitation to join her and Charles on the town, Zsa Zsa lay brooding in her hotel room. On the radio, soothing music. Eventually she closed her eyes. A few quiet moments of rest, then abruptly the music stopped.

"We interrupt this broadcast with a news bulletin. A famous Bel Air showplace was gutted by fire tonight. The residence of Mr. and Mrs. Conrad Hilton on Bellagio Road . . ." After a moment of paralyzed shock, she screamed. The news felt like death. Her wing of the estate was completely destroyed: clothes, possessions, family photographs, letters, her diary, the contents of the many suitcases she had brought from Turkey—her past turned to ashes.

The news continued. Zsa Zsa writhed in torment, for Ranger had died in the fire. Gaining a measure of control, she telephoned Ouida Rathbone, wife of the actor Basil Rathbone. The radio announcement had informed that Mrs. Rathbone, a near neighbor, first saw flames and called the firemen.

"Zsa Zsa, it was frightful," Ouida Rathbone said, in tears herself. "I stood in front of your burning house and heard Ranger howling and I couldn't do a thing. She was trapped in your room. I begged the firemen, save the dog! But they were too late."

All night, Zsa Zsa imagined Ranger lost, confused, whimpering. "I could not believe my poor, sensitive, frightened Ranger burned to death. Had she run to my room thinking I would save her?" Throughout that night, visions of the fire blazed in Zsa Zsa's mind. All over America, and across the ocean, the world she saw was on fire, with her mother, her father, her sister, grandmother, uncles, aunts, and cousins howling in the European flames, and she herself trapped and unable to cry out.

Chapter 12

The Hour of Lead

On these grievous days, Zsa Zsa could not imagine that still darker hours lay before her. In advance of that coming debacle, however, her luck shifted, as it did so often throughout her long life. George Sanders said she had guts; he might have added that good luck invariably sought her out.

A few days before she and Eva were scheduled to return in defeat to Los Angeles, a phone call came from the office of Secretary of State Cordell Hull. (Born in 1871, Hull served under President Roosevelt from 1933 to 1944. A year after leaving office, he received the Nobel Peace Prize for his role in establishing the United Nations. Hull died in 1955.) No one left a record of who arranged that interview with the extremely busy wartime secretary, though it is reasonable to assume that calls from Conrad Hilton to influential friends in government helped secure the appointment. In response to an email query to the Library of Congress, where the secretary's papers are stored, I received this information: "I am unable to locate an entry in the index indicating correspondence to or from anyone with the last name 'Gabor' or the name 'Conrad Hilton.'"

"We were escorted into a small office," Zsa Zsa recalled, "and behind a large desk a slender, gray-haired man rose. We begged him to help. I remember that I opened my mouth and for nearly a moment I could not utter a word. Whether it was the courtliness of his manner, the understanding in his deep-set gray eyes, or the knowledge that at last we were in the presence of a man who had the power to help, I do not know, but for the first time in my life I could not speak. Mr. Hull was very kind; he brought a chair, gave me a glass of water, and presently I was myself. Our conversation was brief. He would look into the matter. He could promise nothing. A great deal depended on my parents' papers. He repeated, he would look into the matter."

J. Randy Taraborelli, in *The Hiltons*, adds the important information that Secretary Hull urged Zsa Zsa and Eva to continue on to New York, since Conrad Hilton was there, and to rest. This pointed advice he offered for Zsa Zsa's benefit because "he was alarmed by her appearance; she looked unwell and on the verge of a nervous breakdown."

Eva returned to her husband in Hollywood, and when Zsa Zsa arrived in Manhattan, still highly agitated, she found Connie in bed with the flu in the suite they were to share for a week or so. Zsa Zsa's attempts to wait on her sick husband resembled an operatic mad scene, for she dashed about, running in with glasses of water, then flying to the phone to order cocktails and pungent food from room service, the smell of which made Conrad feel even worse. He buried his head under the bedclothes.

The view outside their windows enthralled her. She would gaze over Central Park, turning to her husband with sad eyes overbrimmed with tears. "Oh Connie, I am trying to see Mamuska. Will Papuska and my darling Magduska—will they come soon? Did the President find them alive? Call the White House now, I demand it!"

Followed by hysterical laughter and snatches of old songs

from the Danube, waltz steps and whirling Gypsy leaps from room to room, then sudden imperatives, "Get up! We are late to tea. They expect us at the Plaza."

"But Georgia, we are at the Plaza."

"Then I must put on more jewelry. Mamuska, hurry with the necklace." Conrad groaned and rubbed his head, which made Zsa Zsa angry. She snatched off her earrings and threw them against the nearest large mirror. "Love me!" she demanded. "You never have, you know. Before dinner, let us go to St. Patrick's and become really married. I am always a Catholic in my heart!"

Days passed, Zsa Zsa's mania calmed and Conrad recovered from the flu, though still he felt weak and hardly knew what treatment to seek for his wife, who assured him she felt brand new after breathing the air of New York and shopping at Saks Fifth Avenue, Henri Bendel, and Hattie Carnegie. They returned to Los Angeles, where Zsa Zsa stared at the charred remains of their uninhabitable home. She looked more than twice her actual age. Conrad took a suite in the Town House, the apartment-hotel on Wilshire Boulevard that he had acquired in 1942. He installed Zsa Zsa in a suite of her own. Summer lapsed into autumn, and after consultations with several doctors, Zsa Zsa fell into the pattern of prescription barbiturates for sleep and amphetamines to energize her when overcome by worry and depression. She read every grim word in every newspaper at hand to learn the situation in Budapest. On December 26, 1944, the Red Army encircled the city. Thousands died—Hungarians, Germans, Russians, Romanians who had joined their Soviet comrades. Zsa Zsa read of block-to-block fighting in the streets where she had spent her youth, but not a word from family. In spite of sleeping pills, "I could not sleep," she said. "At night each time I opened my eyes I saw myself multiplied a hundred times in the mirrored walls. My insomnia took over completely. I stayed awake until my imagination began to play tricks on me. I no longer knew which was dream or reality. I saw Mother and Father killed, I saw Magda struggling in the arms of soldiers—were they Nazis, were they Russians? I saw every member of my family tortured."

All of this in Zsa Zsa's mind, while in Budapest these nightmares, and unspeakable others, struck down thousands, including people that Zsa Zsa knew, although her closest loved ones so far were spared the very worst. With several horrifying exceptions.

In *The Battle for Budapest, 1944–1945*, Anthony Tucker-Jones concludes his text with these staggering statistics: "In June 1944 Budapest had a population of 1.2 million; by April 1945 it had shrunk to 830,000. Some 24,000 civilians perished as a result of starvation and disease and another 13,000 were killed by military action. Allowing for executions and deportation of the Jewish community, the total dead amounted to 76,000 people. Hungarian military losses defending the city totaled 28,500. The damage to Budapest was extensive, with over 13,500 houses destroyed and another 18,800 rendered uninhabitable."

Among the images in Tucker-Jones's book are some that Zsa Zsa would have seen in newspapers and magazines at the time. She would have witnessed similar destruction in newsreels when Conrad, Nicky and Barron Hilton, Eva, Bundy Solt, or other friends coaxed her to the movies: all Danube bridges connecting Buda and Pest blown up by retreating Nazis; Buda Castle reduced to ruins; piles of rubble in the streets on the Pest side of the Danube; abandoned cars riddled with bullet holes; street signs now in Russian as well as Hungarian; dead bodies piled in the snow. From the point of view of Eva and Zsa Zsa, the Red Army's defeat of the

Germans in Hungary offered little comfort. Their family, if alive, had escaped the swastika only to fall captive to the hammer and sickle.

One day in the spring of 1945 Eva banged on the door to Zsa Zsa's suite, ran inside out of breath, grabbed her sister, and burst into tears. A cable had arrived from Lisbon: ALL WELL WE SEND YOU LOVE MOTHER FATHER MAGDA.

Jolie is the only member of the Gabor family who gave a firsthand account of their ordeal in Hungary and their subsequent escape. That account, however, is garbled and also bizarrely frivolous, with gossipy interruptions to tell of in-law squabbles and her typical determination to let the world know that she left Budapest wearing a fur coat. For that reason, I quote from more reliable sources.

The first one is the website of Yad Vashem, the World Holocaust Remembrance Center in Jerusalem. There Ambassador Garrido is honored as one of the Righteous Among the Nations, a designation that refers to non-Jews who risked their lives during the Holocaust to save the lives of Jews. (Throughout this book, I refer to him as Ambassador Garrido. Other citations use his full name in the Portuguest style, Carlos de Almeida Fonseca Sampaio Garrido; on the Yad Vashem website he is Carlos Sampaio Garrido.)

From Yad Vashem: "Because of Allied bombing, some of the embassies chose to move from Budapest to the outskirts of the city, among them the Portuguese. The ambassador rented a house in Galgagyörk some 60 km from Budapest, and moved the embassy offices and his home to the new location. In his new residence he hosted a dozen Hungarian citizens, most of them Jews, so as to protect them from the danger in the city. Among these people were his Jewish secretary, Magda Gabor, and many members of her family. Sampaio Garrido did not inform his government of this fact.

"On 23 April 1944 the Portuguese ruler Salazar decided to order his ambassador to return to Lisbon and leave the Chargé d'Affaires in his place. Five days later, on 28 April 1944, at 5 a.m., the Hungarian political police burst into the ambassador's residence. The ambassador tried to physically stop them from entering his residence, insisting that his home was ex territorial and that they were violating his diplomatic immunity."

At this point, Yad Vashem quotes the testimony of Mrs. Lantos, Jolie's niece. She was thirteen years old at the time, and sheltered there with her parents and other relatives, including the Gabors. "When the ambassador saw them taking Magda," Mrs. Lantos said, "he put his foot in the door and didn't let them leave."

The Yad Vashem narrative continues, "Despite his persistence, the policemen went on and arrested the ambassador and his 'guests' and brought them to Budapest. There Sampaio Garrido continued to argue for his protégés' release, until they were let go. Not deterred by this incident and although he was due to leave Hungary within days, Sampaio Garrido submitted a complaint to the Hungarian government, demanded an investigation and an apology. Several days later the Hungarians declared [him] persona non grata. It was only at this time that the ambassador informed Salazar of the identity of the people he had hosted in his home." (Carl Lutz, the Swiss vice-consul, was similarly harassed and threatened, as were other diplomats from neutral nations.)

According to other sources, such as the International Raoul Wallenberg Foundation, Ambassador Garrido rented other houses and apartments in the Budapest environs in addition to the house in Galgagyörk in order to shelter many more Jews. In May 1944, the ambassador was reposted to Switzerland, and from there he continued to intervene where possible on behalf of Jewish refugees. He is credited with saving the lives of approximately one thousand persons.

After Ambassador Garrido's departure from Budapest, the chargé d'affaires, Carlos de Liz-Teixeira Branquinho, continued to issue Portuguese passports, visas, and safe conduct passes to hundreds of Jews who might otherwise have died in fascist hands. Mrs. Lantos and her mother left Hungary with him, under his protection, "at the very last minute," she said. Her father, Sebestyn Tillemann, stayed behind in Galgagyörk with his mother, Franceska Tillemann and several others who felt they were safe until either the Red Army or the Anglo-American forces liberated Hungary. In Mrs. Lantos's words, "The Arrow Cross [i.e., the Hungarian fascists] broke in. They found the air raid shelter where the elderly people were, including my grandmother. The Arrow Cross herded them out to be shot. My father, in his own hiding place, heard the commotion, ran after the fascists and offered them money if they would let his mother go. Instead, he and his mother died together."

Mrs. Lantos's testimony contradicts the Wikipedia entry on Ambassador Garrido, which states that her father and her grandmother "both were killed during an Allied bombing raid." Mrs. Lantos, of course, is the credible witness. According to Zsa Zsa, her grandmother refused to leave Hungary because so many of her relatives were there, and Sebestyn Tillemann would not depart without her. They were both shot to death.

Jolie learned of these deaths only after arrival in New York. She became hysterical with grief.

Once in the United States, Magda confided to Zsa Zsa some of the horrific sights she had witnessed during her final days in Budapest, where chaos prevailed. "Slaughter in the streets, the yellow badges, the men and women—our family physician, our lawyer, merchants we knew—taken to Tattersall, the famous riding academy, and there machine-gunned to death." Magda saw frantic mothers begging strangers in the streets to take their babies.

In the middle of Magda's narrative, Zsa Zsa stopped her. "No!" she said, trembling and in tears. "Don't tell me any more. I have seen it all in my own nightmares."

Chapter 13

West Hills Sanitarium

"For Magda's Portuguese Ambassador I thank God," said Jolie. "It was this man who saved my life." Even holding Portuguese passports, however, Jolie, Vilmos, and Magda remained under deep suspicion and in grave danger. Suppose a Hungarian border guard asked them to recite a Portuguese poem? Magda, a talented linguist, might convince, but Vilmos? And Jolie's insouciance must have vexed all present, for her account of their escape recalls Aunt Pittypat in *Gone With the Wind* when the Yankees turn up in Atlanta. In the safe house in Galgagyörk, Jolie and her sister-in-law were in love with the same man. When he turned his attention from Jolie, she fumed: "I am a queen in marabou feathers and beautiful hats and perfume. Yet he has left me for that mouse!"

Once in Portugal, the Gabors—three displaced persons among countless others—existed on money that Zsa Zsa and Eva sent each month. Even the Portuguese sunshine did not expel their drab desperation. Magda, thin and drawn, with clumps of hair falling out from anxiety and malnourishment; Vilmos, forlorn, separated from everything he knew and valued; and Jolie behaving like exiled royalty, demanding and inconsiderate, a ludicrous study in refugee chic.

There they remained from April 1945 until the end of that year, when at last they received their entry papers into the United States. Owing to bureaucracy and the vicissitudes of postwar travel, they left Portugal separately: Jolie on December 1 on board a Portuguese freighter, a journey that lasted thirty days; Magda waited a week after receiving her visa, then boarded a plane for New York. Unable to take her French poodle, Canou, on the aircraft, she booked passage for him on a ship. Upon arrival in New York, he was welcomed by a gaggle of Gabors in various states of hysteria. The reason, apart from love of animals, was that Canou's barking had alerted Magda to danger on the day of her arrest. Vilmos, according to Jolie, was delayed until February 1946, though Zsa Zsa contradicted her, swearing that she, Eva, Jolie, Magda, Canou, along with Conrad Hilton and Charles Isaacs, drove to Philadelphia in early January of that year to meet Papuska's boat.

Months before these joyous reunions took place, however, Zsa Zsa suffered a complete nervous breakdown. Many versions found their way into print of how that collapse came on, her suffering while confined, and her eventual release from an institution. I base my account on a few of the more credible ones, along with information from several persons acquainted with retrievable facts, all of whom requested anonymity.

Had Zsa Zsa lived and become sick in an earlier century, she might have been thrown into a literal snake pit. In 1945, she was locked up in a figurative one, despite its high tone and moneyed inmates. (William Faulkner was given electroshock treatments there in 1952 after an alcoholic binge and emotional collapse.) On the outside at least, the place bore scant resemblance to a Hollywood movie asylum such as the one in *The Snake Pit,* a film that won an Oscar nomination for Olivia de Havilland in 1948, or the one eleven years later that earned Elizabeth Taylor a nomination for *Suddenly, Last Summer*. Inside West Hills the nightmare screams followed no script, nor did anyone call "Cut!" If, in later years, someone could have induced Zsa Zsa to re-create onscreen her seven-week nightmare, what a career-changing spectacle!

Readers acquainted with today's *New York Post* as the right-wing mouthpiece of Rupert Murdoch may be surprised to learn 1) that the paper's editorial policies before 1976, when Murdoch acquired it, were to the left of the faint-hearted *New York Times,* and 2) that its publisher, editors, and reporters took seriously the job of journalism. For that reason, I quote the opening lines of an article by Alfred Aronowitz that appeared in the *Post* on November 24, 1958, the seventh article in a revealing eleven-part series on the Gabor family that remains unequaled to the present day for accuracy among such features in the popular press.

"It is late April, 1945. Beneath the overhanging trees on Fieldston Road where the Bronx suddenly becomes countryside, a car, large and expensive, pulls to a stop. A woman emerges. She has reddish blonde hair and she is heavily jeweled. She wears a long mink coat. With quick, graceful steps she hurries down a walk toward a small cottage. A door closes and she steps inside.

"The woman is Mrs. Conrad Hilton. She has just entered West Hills Sanitarium, an institution for the mentally ill."

When did it start, that descent into what was then considered madness? We know that Zsa Zsa suffered from bipolar disorder, and that it appeared in a mild form during her Swiss school days. The excitement of her first years in America—remarriage, travel, Hollywood glamour as close as her sister, plus Zsa Zsa's own ambition to break into movies—steadied her. The occasional tantrum, the high-pitched laughter, the

constant entertaining performance at home and in public—
Conrad attributed it to being a woman, while to Eva it was
all of a piece. Zsa Zsa's personality had always been a vaudeville.

Then, before their eyes, that one-woman show shifted
from comedy to a darker genre. Madness is perhaps the wrong
term. Even in those not suffering from bipolar disorder, extreme and prolonged anxiety can lead to what laypeople, and
many doctors, consider mental illness. Then, too, Zsa Zsa's
disturbance occurred in the 1940s, when women especially—
but men, as well—could easily be locked away for behavior
that today would be looked on as merely unconventional.
Electroconvulsive shock, insulin shock, and other "thera-
pies" were as commonly prescribed then as Prozac in later
decades. Did anyone listen when she told them of unrelenting
worry about her family in Hungary? About her dream marriage turned sour? The loss of her home to fire, and grief for
Ranger? About the galloping panic that overtook her, the
feelings of suffocation, the jelly legs that barely held her up,
the trembling hands and spilled coffee?

Since her return to California in 1944 from Washington
and New York, Zsa Zsa had been under the care of an elderly doctor who believed that prolonged sleep could heal
melancholia, neurasthenia, female problems, and nerves.
Consequently, he prescribed barbiturates for sleep, and also
for times when she felt shaky, or when tense chest muscles
made it difficult to achieve a deep breath, and when she worried that her family would never reach America.

New York! She decided that the cure for some of her troubles, if not all, would take place in that city of endless parties,
nightclubs, and shopping. Conrad agreed, and so did a reluctant Eva. She knew Zsa Zsa's ups and downs, but something
had changed. Nevertheless, she saw Zsa Zsa off at the air-

port. "I carried with me enough sleeping pills for a regiment," Zsa Zsa later recalled. Her doctor's parting words were, "Take those pills anytime you feel the need."

Since Conrad owned the Plaza, she headed there and checked into a two-room suite. A few hours later, exhausted, she took a pill and fell asleep. Up at midnight, out on the town, home at dawn, another pill and ten hours sleep. Zsa Zsa's pattern continued like this for days, but she found New York changed. She had never felt the city so very tiring. Café society and the Manhattan beau monde swarmed around the charming Mrs. Conrad Hilton, and her sparkling glitter made all the columns. "I can't keep it up," she confided to a date who arrived to escort her to El Morocco, one of her favorite night spots. "Why am I so weary?" His advice seemed just the ticket. "Benzedrine! I'll call my doctor tomorrow and make an appointment for you." Soon she skipped meals because she felt too excited to eat. "I swallowed my pills as once, when I was a little girl, I used to swallow chocolate-covered raisins, greedily, guiltily, so that Cuki, my governess, wouldn't see."

Her suite never emptied. New friends, and some of longer duration, called in throughout the day, and many new boyfriends spent the night. Word got around that Mrs. Hilton was behaving more like Miss Gabor. Coded mentions in the columns appeared almost daily: uninhibited ... wild Hungarian ... Gypsy wife ... when the husband's away. ... Then she found a shop on Third Avenue where they sold authentic Turkish charcoal braziers. Perfect for the shish-kebab party she had dreamed of throwing for her new friends. As the meat sizzled, charcoal sparks flew onto the carpet, but Zsa Zsa didn't notice, she was showing them how to dance the *csárdás* and everyone was whirling through the rooms, shouting, clapping, jumping until at last no one could dance another step and so they poured more wine and feasted on Zsa Zsa's home-cooked Plaza meal.

The aroma of roasted meat in the corridor, however, did not please some of the more stolid guests, nor did the wild-party sounds that reverberated off the venerable walls. It sounds like—well, you know, they told the manager, who assured them he would look into the situation.

Next morning, when he requested an interview, a groggy Mrs. Hilton told him to ring back in late afternoon. When finally they met face to face, and he asked tactfully whether she had actually cooked a meal on an open fire in her suite, her nostrils flared and she answered in her most petulant tone: "But that is how we do it in Turkey all the time!"

Nonplussed, he mumbled, "I see."

She added, as though explaining a simple fact to a child, that he certainly could not compare the Plaza's cheap carpeting with "our priceless Oriental rugs." There the matter rested for a time.

A few days later, she spent fifteen thousand dollars on antiques to replace the hotel furniture that to her looked shabby and déclassé. For company, she bought a brindle boxer and a French poodle, who yapped their displeasure when Zsa Zsa failed to provide adequate pet-pet. When she was away, they further stressed the singed carpet.

She bought more jewelry at Van Cleef and Arpels, ordered a new wardrobe from Hattie Carnegie, danced all night and forgot to sleep, occasionally dozing on a bench in Central Park as the dogs ran after squirrels. She screamed at maids, threatened an elevator boy who didn't appear at the push of her button, and talked to everyone she knew in Hollywood at long-distance rates to the tune of six hundred dollars.

Zsa Zsa Hilton became, almost literally, the talk of the town. That talk soon reached Los Angeles. Buzz became a roar when, on April 12, 1945, she filed for divorce from Conrad Hilton.

One night at El Morocco on a date with the actor John Sutton, Zsa Zsa noticed the owner, John Perona, a former lover of Eva's, approaching their table. She disliked Perona, for the previous year when Zsa Zsa was having drinks at the club, he had made an offensive remark about Charles Isaacs, whom Zsa Zsa considered almost as a brother. What Perona said was, "How could you let your sister marry that _____?" The word might have been "Jew," or it might have been something else. Zsa Zsa never repeated it outside the family. (It was far worse than a lovers' quarrel between Eva and Perona. Without revealing the cause, Zsa Zsa claimed that her sister feared Perona would kill her. "He took her jewelry," Zsa Zsa said, "and she went to court to get them back.")

Again, this night, Perona said something that riled Zsa Zsa and she threw champagne in his face. A brawl narrowly averted, he ordered Zsa Zsa and Sutton off the premises and told her she was barred for life. (A few years later, Jolie approached El Morocco's press agent. "My Zsa Zsa is a wonderful woman," she said. "Won't you talk to John?" The answer: "When the Pope visits El Morocco, Zsa Zsa can come in on his arm." After Perona's death in 1961, his son lifted the ban and all the Gabors flocked back. Zsa Zsa had triumphed again.) The El Morocco incident of course made the papers, and since Perona, and his nightclub, were New York institutions, the press took his side against Zsa Zsa, whose behavior was described as outrageous and unladylike.

A few mornings later, while still in bed with the dogs, she heard a knock at the door. Believing it to be housekeeping, Zsa Zsa called, "Come in." She gasped to see Eva and Bundy Solt. "What are you doing here?" she cried out, rushing to embrace the two of them. Their vague answer, to the effect that they happened to be in town, didn't deter Zsa Zsa from an endless stream of questions and chatter. Eva and Bundy sat across the room on the sofa while Zsa Zsa cuddled with her dogs on the bed.

Another knock at the door, Bundy answered, and in stepped a small man in late middle age who might just have landed from Europe had he not arrived in the States years before. Bundy welcomed Mr. Stein, and hurriedly introduced him to Zsa Zsa as a producer from Vienna who thought Zsa Zsa might be just right as the star of his latest play. "Now that I see you," said Mr. Stein, "I am certain of it." Zsa Zsa paced the floor, sitting, then standing, so that this producer could regard her from every angle. Taking her right hand, he said, to Zsa Zsa's puzzlement, "You're a very tired little girl. Why don't you go to bed?" Miffed, she was on the verge of telling him to mind his own business when suddenly she tried to remember the last time she had slept. As best she could recall, it was the previous week. Suddenly she felt a great wave of desire sweep over her, a vast need of rest. She walked into the bedroom, lay down on the bed, and called the dogs to her side. "You are tired," said Mr. Stein. "And you need to eat more. Nothing is really so urgent, you know. The important thing just now is rest. And when you wake up . . ." She hardly felt the needle enter her arm.

Mr. Stein, of course, was no producer but a doctor. He had flown in from California with Eva and Bundy. One look told him of Zsa Zsa's distress, and her jerky movements supplied the rest. The doctor had come at Conrad's behest, as had Eva and Bundy. Although Zsa Zsa had filed for divorce, and Conrad felt that she had made the right decision, still he cared about her welfare and therefore had consulted with her sister and their close friend from childhood, Bundy Solt. To some it might look like revenge on the husband's part, but no one ever accused Conrad Hilton of such an act. On the contrary, after three years of marriage he surely felt relief. For a year or longer, they had been a married couple in name only.

When Zsa Zsa woke up, Eva helped her pick out a flattering new dress, jewelry, and a mink coat. Having filed for divorce, Zsa Zsa considered herself a free woman, and Eva encouraged the notion that an intriguing older man was eager to meet her. Zsa Zsa told the *Post* reporter in 1958,

"When they took me to the sanitarium, I thought I was going to meet a boyfriend. They drove me up to this cottage and inside there were two nurses, and one was a man and one was a woman, and I thought they were going to rob me. I didn't know what it was. I didn't know that it was a nut house. I fought with them and I was knocked down and broke my tooth and was put in a straitjacket. They kept me there weeks and weeks and I didn't think I was ever going to get out. I suppose you can say that this was the worst time of my life."

Speaking to Gerold Frank, her collaborator on *My Story*, Zsa Zsa recalled a scene that he considered too strong for the book; it was omitted: "After breakfast, we went to walk with other people, all terribly broken down—insane people. We walked around the park and that's when we passed by this cage where human people were there without combed hair, those were really the very serious cases. They used to scream at us."

Blanche DuBois, led away at the end of *A Streetcar Named Desire*, depended on the kindness of strangers. For seven long weeks, Zsa Zsa had only herself and the survival instinct that had served her well so far. And then a stranger saved her.

Although inmates were permitted neither radio nor newspapers, the news on May 1, 1945, could not be kept secret. It was the only topic, and so the new night nurse whispered it in Zsa Zsa's ear: "Hitler is dead!" She recounted as much of the story as she knew, Zsa Zsa shed tears of relief, and from that point on the nurse treated her with special attention and kindness. After a couple of weeks, the nurse said, "Sweetheart, you don't belong here. Don't worry. I'm an Irishwoman and I have a heart. I'll help you."

"Pray for me, please pray for me," Zsa Zsa pleaded.

She remembered the telephone number of a Hungarian

friend, whom the nurse called the nex[...] mediately found a lawyer who filed a wr[...] charging wrongful arrest. A court hearing t[...] Bronx, the judge ruled in Zsa Zsa's favor, the [...] tained, and she was released.

The scars of such involuntary incarceration heal slowly[...] at all. How does one spotlight the worst part of it—the isola- tion; the bare walls in a room with only a narrow bed and no personal items; the regimentation of supervised meals and daily walks accompanied by nurses; no visits from Eva, Bundy, or Conrad. Whether the doctors discouraged visits or whether the absences were voluntary never became clear in Zsa Zsa's mind.

Far more dreadful than any of these, however, were the in- sulin shock treatments. The reason for this barbaric therapy in Zsa Zsa's case, rather than the equally barbaric electro- convulsive shock, is now clear: Zsa Zsa had fallen victim to Manfred Sakel, an Austrian psychiatrist who, in the 1920s, pioneered insulin shock. Having washed up on the arrogant shores of American psychiatry, he became the star acquisi- tion of West Hills Sanitarium. Sakel's treatment, widely used internationally in mental institutions, at last fell into disfavor in the 1950s. Untold damage had been done, however, with countless adverse reactions and many fatalities, often unre- ported lest the psychiatric religion be blasphemed.

Let us imagine that you, like a significant percentage of the population, suffer from hypoglycemia, which in everyday language means low blood sugar. If you are otherwise in good health, and not diabetic, you may feel few effects from skipping a meal, or from drinking strong coffee on an empty stomach. If, however, you are especially susceptible to a drop in blood sugar, you may suddenly feel shaky all over, break out in a cold sweat, feel your heart racing, become confused

g. You might be mistaken
nger to yourself and oth-

gnify tenfold all of these
rientation, mental confu-
l the feeling that doom or
eakness, and eventual col-
have a picture of Zsa Zsa
high three times a week for

r day: That friend im-
of habeas corpus
ok place in the
rit was sus-
if

For a long time ... ed that Zsa Zsa suffered not only from bipolar disorder but also from some form of hypoglycemia. This helps to account for the erratic behavior, such as temper tantrums while under stress and sudden mood swings. She exacerbated the problem by excessive coffee drinking, over twenty cups a day! "I know I shouldn't," she said, "but I've been doing it all my life and can't break the habit." She even kept a coffee thermos by the bedside. Less caffeine, more sleep, and fewer Hungarian sweets might have calmed her jumpy nerves and leveled out her blood sugar. In her favor, however, were an unbreakable constitution, moderate alcohol intake, mainly wine, and recreational drugs never. It seems that in Zsa Zsa's case overwork and a dizzying social life contributed to longevity.

In some ways, Zsa Zsa's torture at West Hills Sanitarium parallels the sufferings of concentration camp victims, the last of whom were rescued around the same time as Zsa Zsa. Like them, she was an unwilling participant in medical experimentation. How different, one may well ask, was the work of Manfred Sakel and others like him from that of Josef Mengele, whose experiments at Auschwitz proceeded without regard for the health and safety of his subjects, nor for their physical and emotional pain? The difference between the crimes of the one and those of the other was a matter of degree. Both escaped punishment for their misdeeds.

"I recuperated slowly," Zsa Zsa said. After her release from West Hills in late May 1945, she borrowed money from a Hungarian acquaintance in New York and retreated to a small apartment on Long Island. "A stranger to the world," as she put it, Zsa Zsa emerged from her trauma an emotional displaced person, as damaged and fragile as many who had survived the war.

We have only Zsa Zsa's account of the aftermath of West Hills, and that in bits and pieces. Her sketchy narrative raises many questions: Was she in touch with Eva, Conrad, or anyone else from her Los Angeles circle? Neighbors on Long Island treated her kindly, unaware of exactly who she was, for she used the name Sári Gabor. Somehow she retrieved her two dogs—surely Eva placed them in safekeeping with New York friends pending Zsa Zsa's release—and she spent the summer days of 1945 walking, resting, painting, and lingering over meals at a seaside lobster bar owned by a couple from Poland. They became friendly with one another, and one busy Saturday night when the husband was ill the wife asked Sári to help her wait on tables. This routine work, which continued for a time, proved therapeutic. Although Zsa Zsa never breathed a word of it, it is reasonable to assume that she had mentioned to the Polish woman, as they became friends, that back in Budapest she worked behind the counter in her family's jewelry shops.

Zsa Zsa's days and nights in the unnamed town on Long Island resemble an Impressionist painting, in particular a misty work by Monet or Whistler, of a distant lady, her back to the viewer, who gazes over ocean fog and whose identity, if ever it was known, has now merged with the elements.

Chapter 14

The World Was All Before Them

"All the silly, wonderful nonsense began again the moment Mother arrived from Lisbon," said Zsa Zsa fifteen years later, having not only survived but prospered as an international movie star, a Hollywood glamour queen, a devil-may-care comedienne on TV talk shows—call it sit-down comedy—and almost daily in the press, where her antics were reported with the regularity of White House briefings. Anyone trying to pinpoint the day or the year when that phenomenon known as "the Gabor sisters" first took shape faces a paradox. It was neither Eva's arrival in 1939, nor Zsa Zsa's in 1941, but rather Jolie's alighting on American soil on December 31, 1945, that acted as yeast for their rise into celebrity and notoriety. She resumed immediate control of the two daughters who had languished outside her dominance for six years and four years, respectively. Magda she had never relinquished, and now all three regressed to some juvenile state where the only voice to be heeded was that of Nyuszi, Nyuszika, Mamuska—in other words, Jolie the Total Mother. Her mere presence, however, was not sufficient to trigger the blast-off that Jolie demanded and that her girls desired for themselves. She reminded them of their granny's favorite saying: "It's not enough to be Hungarian—you also have to work."

Although Eva's career had languished since 1941, she at least had a toehold in the movies and so, Mama said, she must toil even harder at her calling. Jolie reminded her that since childhood she had dreamed of nothing but acting in theatre and cinema. "Make Nyuszi proud" was the ongoing subliminal directive.

For a week or so in late summer 1945, and while Zsa Zsa was waiting tables on Long Island, Eva worked with director Edgar G. Ulmer in *The Wife of Monte Cristo,* an enjoyable costume drama released the following year. When not on call for the picture, she appeared in minor plays, popular in their day, at small Los Angeles venues. On her meager resumé were Arthur Schnitzler's comedy-drama *The Affairs of Anatol* at the Las Palmas Theater and Molnar's *The Play's the Thing* in Sherman Oaks.

In the midst of her professional drought, Eva accepted an invitation from comedian Phil Foster to appear in his nightclub act at El Rancho Vegas just when the desert town had hit upon the combination of gambling and glitz that would draw the world to Las Vegas. Eva's comic timing got big laughs. For instance, when Foster, during the act, asked her favorite perfume, Eva answered, in a foreshadowing of Lisa Douglas on *Green Acres,* "I prefer Chanel 9 to 5." She appeared with him several times.

The publicity of Zsa Zsa's divorce from Conrad Hilton might almost have served as her screen test, for in every newspaper photo it was obvious that the camera loved her. That divorce remains the most full-bodied of them all in a family total of some two dozen if you throw in the occasional annulment, Francesca's one or two marital mishaps, and at least one marriage over so quickly that no Gabor bothered to count it. The Hilton divorce involved heaps of money, lawyers, court hearings, tears, whispers of adultery, witty insults from a fully recovered Zsa Zsa, a mysterious pregnancy, and a background chorus line of big names, small names, gossiping servants, in-laws, and barking dogs. A film version of these bewildering arabesques would have been titled *My Favorite Divorce*.

It could only be a screwball comedy. Over the course of 1946, with all Gabors present and accounted for, Zsa Zsa and Conrad rekindled their early passion. That, at least, remained her version of the year's events. They maintained separate residences, and divorce proceedings continued, although at a somnolent pace. Both traveled constantly, so that when they met up it seemed more like a romance than marriage ever could.

A bit later, Conrad fronted the money for Jolie's first jewelry shop, called simply "Jolie Gabor," which opened in the West Forties near Broadway in the spring of 1946. No one in the family ever mentioned this location, which was decidedly less chic than her later one at 699 Madison Avenue between East Sixty-second and East Sixty-third streets, where the "Jolie Gabor Pearl Salon" opened in fall 1948 and remained for decades. A newspaper photo of Jolie in that first Manhattan location shows her still carrying a few too many pounds, along with a matronly visage that has been hacked, and none too smoothly, by a surgeon's scalpel. Or was it a putty knife that gave her the spackled look? She even retained half of a superfluous chin. Soon, however, that botched face vanished like April snow, along with her West Side shop. Thanks to the eponymous salon on the East Side, Jolie became an institution—the Queen of Costume Jewelry.

On November 8, 1948, the *Times-Herald* reported that "the three glamorous Gabor sisters" were seen hanging magenta satin in the windows of their mother's new Madison Avenue jewelry shop. "Wearing overalls and bandannas, and using hammers and stepladders, Magda, Sari, and Eva caused quite a stir among pedestrians on the street." This is probably the first notice in print of that phenomenon known from that day to this as "the Gabor sisters."

In winter of 1949 Eva worked on *Song of Surrender*, directed by Mitchell Leisen. In her small role she received ninth billing. Still, this might be considered her most important early picture owing to Leisen's prestige as an outstanding director of actresses (among them Stanwyck, Dietrich, and Joan Fontaine) and to the elegance of his films. Having begun his career as a costume designer and art director, Leisen had a keen eye for accuracy in dress. While planning *Song of Surrender* he acquired the wardrobe of a wealthy elderly lady who had just died. Since the picture is set in 1906 in a small New England town, these outmoded fashions were perfect. "They were originals from the great French couturiers of the period," Leisen said. "We didn't change a thing. We just altered them to fit the actresses. Eva Gabor had a black net dress studded with real turquoises." It was perfect for her role as Countess Marina, a piano-playing, *csárdás*-dancing vixen calculated to rattle the local puritans.

When the picture wrapped, Eva at last heeded Tallulah Bankhead's advice and went east. There she appeared in the early TV dramatic series *Your Show Time* (later syndicated under the title *Short Story Theater*). This small-screen exposure gave Eva a boost in the early 1950s as she established herself in summer stock. Audiences on the straw-hat circuit flocked to see this fledgling star of stage, screen, and television.

In late summer 1949 Eva made her first East Coast stage appearance in Samson Raphaelson's *Accent on Youth*, costarring fellow Hungarian Paul Lukas. A few months later she made her Broadway debut in *The Happy Time*. Eva had finally burst from her starlet cocoon into the dazzling brightness of show business acclaim. All too soon, however, at least from Eva's point of view, a new cocoon, vast and inescapable, enveloped her. Spun by Jolie, this silken prison yoked Eva to Zsa Zsa, and forever after she was mistaken for her older, more outrée sister. Magda, also one of Mama's brood, acted as peacekeeper and referee. But Jolie, spinner of fates, held illimitable dominion over all.

Sometime in the late forties Eva made a picture called *Love Island*, a Poverty Row turkey that was shelved until 1952, when its release caused her great embarrassment. By then, Eva really was a star of early television. In 1951 she made more than fifty appearances on network and local shows. In addition, during the 1950–'51 season *The Eva Gabor Show* was a hit in the New York metro area, followed later in 1951 by another, this one called *Famous Women of History*, in which Eva portrayed the likes of Marie Antoinette (or "the cake lady," as Eva called her). During that same period, while still appearing nightly in *The Happy Time*, she hosted two radio shows and still found time for summer theatre productions and countless appearances at charity events and fashion shows. This nonstop chronology disproves the silly clichés about the Gabors as famous for being famous. They were famous because they never stopped working at it. Eva's last TV appearance, for example, took place exactly one month before she died.

In *Love Island* Eva wears a black wig, with a succession of orchids and hibiscuses over one ear. The plot: male lead Paul Valentine parachutes onto a tropical island and falls in love with native girl Sarna and her ebony hair. About one-fourth of this sixty-two-minute picture is intercut footage from a 1935 quasi-documentary called *Legong: Dance of the Virgins*, which was actually filmed in Bali by Henri de la Falaise, ex-husband of Gloria Swanson. Along with the louche dances and temple ceremonies of *Legong*, Eva's hapless performance seems snatched from a cautionary training film for tight-lipped missionaries.

* * *

On September 17, 1946, a year and a half after proceedings began, Zsa Zsa's divorce from Conrad Hilton at last became final. None of the parties involved could have known that in a sense the matter would never reach resolution. The reason: in mid-June of that year Zsa Zsa became pregnant, and nine months later—on March 10, 1947—her daughter, Constance Francesca Hilton, was born. "When they brought my child to me, I think really it was the happiest moment of my life," she said. Zsa Zsa never wavered in her claim that Conrad was the baby's father. According to many accounts, however, Zsa Zsa's sexual activity in those warm summer months amounted to a cottage industry. If such reports were accurate, then in a game of Gabor roulette neither Zsa Zsa nor anyone else would know the father's identity. Many years later, when I became friends with Francesca, I occasionally studied her face in search of genetic clues. Yes, there were Hilton traits, although none strong enough to convince a casual observer. Nor did she look very much like the Gabors.

The person who suffered long and poignantly from this paternal blank was Francesca. All her life she yearned for a father who might add stability to counteract Zsa Zsa's emotional fluctuations and the frequent absences demanded by a Hollywood career. As we will see in a later chapter, Francesca pleaded for Conrad Hilton's affection, which he doled out in small measures throughout her childhood and into her adult years. Ultimately, however, he rejected her as if she were a needy stray who would find a home elsewhere. She told me of visiting his grave at Calvary Hill Cemetery in Dallas. On that pilgrimage she took along a female friend. Francesca said no more, but I wondered whether she feared emotional catastrophe if unattended at the gravesite.

These are gothic images out of Emily Brontë. The next belongs to a silent movie melodrama of heart-tugging pathos and a black-caped villain. For years, Francesca clung to each new husband or long-term lover that Zsa Zsa brought home. Until the final one. Some were kind to her, others indifferent, but all eventually vanished. By 1986, when Zsa Zsa married the pantomime prince, Frederic von Anhalt, Francesca had grown tough and abrasive—on the outside. Inside she remained that lost little girl looking for a daddy.

She disliked von Anhalt on sight, as did Eva. Francesca's verbal dagger was soon unsheathed and pointed toward Frederic, whose own psychological armaments exceeded those of the war-mongering Krupps. The job required years, but he struck the final blow by throwing up a latter-day Berlin Wall to separate Zsa Zsa from her daughter. "My mother used to call me ten times a day," Francesca told me, "and now he has disconnected her phone."

Not once in his autobiography, *Be My Guest,* does Conrad Hilton mention Francesca. By 1957, when the book was published, he had convinced himself that she was not his daughter, a suspicion held from the time of her birth. And yet, after Francesca's confirmation into the Roman Catholic Church in 1960, which he attended, Conrad took her and Zsa Zsa to lunch at the Beverly Hilton Hotel, which he owned. Zsa Zsa included a happy photo of the three of them in her first autobiography, published that same year.

How does one account for such switchback behavior? I can offer only meager clues. Patricia (Trish) McClintock Hilton, the widow of Conrad's son Nicky Hilton, married into the family several years after Zsa Zsa and Conrad were divorced. Yet, according to her and many others, Zsa Zsa was always considered part of the Hilton family. (Years in the future, Paris Hilton and her little siblings would splash in Zsa Zsa's pool.) In a recent phone conversation, Trish Hilton had only good things to say about Zsa Zsa and about Francesca, and in general she admired Conrad, although she told biographer Jerry Oppenheimer, in *The House of Hilton*:

"In many ways, Connie was a very naive man. He ran from problems even though they involved his own flesh and blood. His thing was business and that's all." She added that in effect he abandoned her husband—his oldest son, Nicky Hilton, who suffered from severe alcoholism and who died in 1969 at age forty-two. Nicky—Conrad Hilton Jr.—is best remembered as the first husband of Elizabeth Taylor.

When I asked Trish Hilton, "Was Francesca the biological daughter of Conrad?" she paused for a long moment. At last came her enigmatic reply: "I can't even answer that." Since she was a Hilton insider, and privy to family secrets, I take this to mean that neither she, nor anyone else, held more than shifting opinions.

Insofar as he was capable, Conrad treated Francesca well. When she asked to borrow money, however, he balked. But so did he with the three sons born from his first marriage. His traditional American capitalist belief never wavered: Make your own fortune and don't ask me for handouts. Yet he was a philanthropist.

In his autobiography, Hilton mentions prayer so often that he sounds like a televangelist. Mixing Roman Catholic piety with Protestant work ethic, he believed that prayer, hard work, enthusiasm, and dreams could make anyone rich and successful. In his case, the formula worked. To his credit, Conrad's genius for business deals and the resulting millions did not corrode his heart. Like the Gabors, he also revered his mother. He claimed that after his first divorce, she "took over my social life." Before his marriage to Zsa Zsa, he would decline unwelcome invitations with the tongue-in-cheek reply, "My mother won't let me."

Hilton disliked firing employees, and his disinclination to banish anyone helps to explain his ambivalence toward Francesca. He wanted her as a distant relative, but no nearer. In this regard, he and Zsa Zsa were alike. "I believe in large families," she said. "Every girl should have at least three husbands." True to her witty precept, she remained on good terms not only with Conrad but with all ex-husbands except one. Zsa Zsa never forgot a kindness, but woe to anyone who dared abuse her or anyone close to her.

Given these two quicksilver personalities—both of whom loved the almighty dollar—it's understandable that Zsa Zsa's divorce from Conrad Hilton resembled a surreal cross of *Judge Judy* with Jarndyce and Jarndyce, the court case in *Bleak House* that dragged on for generations. In April 1945, shortly before she was locked away in West Hills Sanitarium, Zsa Zsa filed for divorce with a price tag of ten million dollars as settlement. The *Los Angeles Times* quoted her as saying, "I don't want that money for myself. I wouldn't take it. I would give it for relief of European refugees, particularly Jewish refugees who have suffered so much." Even in the throes of a breakdown, as she then was, Zsa Zsa surely realized the impossibility of such a sum.

A year and a half later, when the divorce was finally granted, Zsa Zsa received $275,000, along with other favorable considerations such as stock in two Hilton hotels. Jolie berated her for not getting a Plaza suite for life. "How stupid of my daughter," she said. "Not even a ten percent discount in the Hilton hotels. She, the wife, even the ex-wife, should never be charged for one of his rooms." In later years Zsa Zsa said on television, to the great amusement of Jack Paar and the studio audience, "When I divorced Conrad Hilton, I got six thousand Gideon Bibles." She repeated this line in one of her Las Vegas nightclub appearances when Conrad was in the audience. He shouted back, "Why don't you read one of them!"

That made Zsa Zsa laugh, though usually it was Conrad who roared at her bon mots. "Zsa Zsa and I are very good friends," he told the *New York Post* in 1958. "There is no bitterness between us."

"I can always call up Conrad and ask him for a favor," Zsa Zsa told the same reporter. "We have lunch together very often." They were obviously better suited as pals than spouses.

During the divorce hearing, Zsa Zsa never mentioned that she was pregnant. J. Randy Taraborelli, in *The Hiltons*, devotes many pages to the divorce and to the lingering question of who fathered Francesca. "The big question," he writes, "was whether or not Conrad Hilton had sexual relations with Zsa Zsa Gabor during the time that they were separated, and in this case it would have been sometime in the summer of 1946. She claimed that they saw each other just one time between April and August of that summer, and that is when they were intimate. He said he did see her once, but that they most certainly did not have sex. They weren't even having sex when they lived together, he argued. Why would he fly all the way to New York to be intimate with her? Zsa Zsa listed Conrad as the child's father on the birth certificate. He didn't contest it."

Taraborelli suggests that Conrad did not repudiate his name on the birth certificate because he did not want an innocent child to bear the label of bastard, which in those days could mar a life. Nor did he want any breath of scandal that might affect the reputation of his family and of his company. For these reasons, he did the gentlemanly thing.

Certainly a convincing argument, and yet . . . the Gabor-Hilton chronology for 1946 raises still another question. Why did Conrad finance Jolie's first jewelry shop if she was soon to become his ex-mother-in-law? He set her up in business in spring 1946, quite near the time when Zsa Zsa conceived. Given Conrad's frugality with blood relatives, it seems uncharacteristically generous on his part to shell out thousands for a woman he had met for the first time in January of that year. One possibility is Catholic guilt: after a night in the arms of the seductive wife who has estranged him from his religion, he presents a benefaction to Zsa Zsa's blessèd mother. To Jolie it was a mitzvah, for Conrad a plenary indulgence.

But still another plot twist. Taraborelli reveals that in a 1947 codicil to his will, Conrad stated, "It is my express purpose to leave nothing to the child born on or about March 10, 1947, to my former wife, Sari Gabor Hilton." Only after Conrad Hilton's death did this codicil come to light, contradicted by the fact that he left Francesca $100,000 in a subsequent will. Zsa Zsa felt irritated and betrayed by the paltry amount. As for Francesca, the great mischief it caused her included still another tidal wave of rejection.

Chapter 15

We Were Both in Love with George

What a shame Noël Coward didn't script Zsa Zsa's marriage to George Sanders. Imagine the witty dialogue, the arch innuendoes . . . Herewith, a sketch for the comedy that Coward never wrote.

Curtain up on a cocktail party in a Manhattan penthouse. Act II is then set in Bel Air, Act III in Las Vegas, and the final act plays out in a Hilton hotel on the Riviera. The revelations draw laughter and blood. Finally, after waspish aspersions, highly civilized insults, and roguish asides, all is resolved as George sweeps his irrepressible wife into a stage embrace at curtain fall. But the next instant he parts that very curtain to deliver a coup de théâtre: "My dear, I want a divorce."

Reality began as comedy. During Christmas week 1946, Zsa Zsa saw George in a movie and whispered to Mama in the darkened Manhattan cinema, "There is my next husband." The picture, as Zsa Zsa recalled, was *The Moon and Sixpence*, which had been released four years earlier. She remained resolute in that memory, despite his having starred in some half-dozen pictures in the last year or so that might also have been showing around town.

Even Jolie was nonplussed. "This is no time for you to think of a next husband," she hissed. Jolie's reluctance sprang from the fact that Zsa Zsa was seven months pregnant. For once, Mama's opinion fell by the wayside. Zsa Zsa made it her mission to meet the irresistible Mr. Sanders. Baby Francesca Hilton was born March 10, and five weeks later, on April 19, 1947, mission accomplished. Since the next best thing to Coward dialogue is Gabor-Sanders repartee, as recorded over many years in books and newspapers and on television, I have distilled it to the form of a playlet. With apologies to Sir Noël.

ACT I, Scene I—A penthouse apartment, Manhattan, 1946

George Sanders: I never really met Zsa Zsa. We collided in New York at a party given by Serge Simonenko, the banker.

Zsa Zsa Gabor: Serge, I must meet Mr. Sanders. Please bring him to me.

Serge Simonenko: Mrs. Gabor Hilton,* Mr. George Sanders.

ZZG: Oh, Mr. Sanders, I have been wanting to meet you for so long. I have such a crush on you.

GS: Indeed. How very understandable.

ZZG: I'm such a fan of yours. I saw *The Moon and Sixpence* and I cried in all the right places.

GS: You're a very pretty girl.

Scene II—Later that evening, Zsa Zsa's East Side brownstone

Enter Zsa Zsa, George, and another gentleman from the party.

---

* In society at the time, a divorced woman with a child would often use her maiden name followed by the name of the child's father.

ZZG: Won't you both come up for a drink? You must see my baby. (*George ignores baby, looks distastefully at growling dog. The other gentleman pets the dog and coos to the baby.*)

Scene III—The same, much later that evening
The other gentleman: It's late, George. I think we must go and let Zsa Zsa get some rest.
GS: You go, old boy. I'm staying.
(*Zsa Zsa feigns astonishment.*)
GS: There was really nothing fit to eat at that dreadful party. Have you any vodka and caviar? Afterwards, you might bring me a glass of milk, my dear. Just be sure to take the chill off it.

ACT II—Bel Air, the early 1950s
GS: We have been married two years and I haven't spoken to Zsa Zsa since she said yes.
ZZG: All during my marriage to George Sanders, we had one thing in common. We were both in love with George.
GS: A man has to be married at least twice to appreciate being a bachelor.
ZZG: George was always unfaithful. Once I heard him on the telephone, and I picked up the extension in my bedroom. A woman said to him, "What are you doing with that Hilton woman? You know that I love you . . ."
GS: Being married to Zsa Zsa was like living on the slope of a volcano. Satisfactory between eruptions.
ZZG: . . . and that woman on the telephone was Lucille Ball.
GS: During the five years I was married to Zsa Zsa, I lived in her sumptuous Bel Air mansion as a sort of paying guest. I was allotted a small room in which I was permitted to keep my personal effects until such time as more space was needed to store her ever-mounting stacks of press clippings and photographs.

ZZG: The trouble with George was that he never knew who or what he wanted to be—an English duke, a beachcomber in the tropics, or the greatest woman-hater of his time. In his indecision he gave me some of the most wretched—and happiest—hours of my life.

GS: Zsa Zsa urged me for some time to see her own analyst. Her taste in psychiatrists, as in other spheres, turned out to be examplary. In due course he not only cured me of my obsessional impulses and my periodic backaches. He also cured me of Zsa Zsa.

ZZG: We were two of a kind. We both lived in a special world. In time I was to discover that I saw things not as they were but as a play within a play, in which I was always the heroine.

ACT III—*Las Vegas, 1953*

ZZG: Our marriage could never survive the threat to George presented by my success in the movies.

GS: I never see my wife—only when she washes my socks.

ZZG: George read Schopenhauer in bed while I was reading scripts.

GS: Zsa Zsa said I was the best of all her husbands. I was.

ZZG: I loved that guy. Like no husband I ever had.

GS: I must get out of this ridiculous marriage in which I have got myself involved.

ZZG: A reporter asked George, "Are you still friendly with Zsa Zsa?" He said, "Not very." That's not true, dahling. George just never learned to show his true feelings.

ACT IV—*A Hilton hotel on the Riviera, 1954*

GS: Zsa Zsa becomes angry when I fail to catch her TV appearances. And angrier still when I explain that I am too sensitive an artist to watch her.

ZZG: He was ashamed of being an actor.

GS: In our profession the papers are always full of something or other. And, on occasion, I think that Zsa Zsa is, too.

ZZG: George's pet name for me was Cokiline, pronounced "cookie-line." "It's a Russian term of endearment," he said. "It means my little sweet cookie, my cookie with a little spice."

GS: I arrived in Cannes. Zsa Zsa flew down from Paris where she had been the house guest of His Excellency Don Porfirio Rubirosa, Dominican Ambassador to the Republic of France. After two weeks in Cannes where we went to parties and generally had a very good time, I took off for Hollywood and Zsa Zsa returned to Paris to assist in the promotion of, ahem, good will between the Dominican Republic and France.

ZZG: I was addicted to Rubirosa. He was in my blood and he possessed my soul. He was renowned for his machismo and above all for his sexual prowess.

GS: Every age has its Madame Pompadour, its Queen of Sheba, its Cleopatra, and I wouldn't be surprised if history singles out Zsa Zsa as the twentieth-century prototype of this exclusive coterie.

ZZG: George dropped a bombshell. He filed for divorce.

GS (*reading aloud his farewell letter to Zsa Zsa*): Don't be unhappy. I am really much too old for you. You need someone closer to your own age, someone who can respond to your admirable effervescence, someone who has more vitality. I shall always love you, and yield to no one in my admiration for your many qualities.

ZZ: You never really know a man until you divorce him.

GS (*continues reading letter*): A big kiss for Francesca, and a hug for you. George.

ZZG: We always lived happily ever after—before the marriage, during the marriage, and after the marriage.

GS (*some years later*): I might remarry you. I find your money a great aphrodisiac.

Chapter 16

Backstage at . . . *We Were Both in Love with George*

All of the above is true, as far as it goes. The question lingers, however, whether theirs was a match predestined by the gods or tailored by Lucifer himself. Perhaps, like all marriages, it had patches of perfection surrounded by brimstone and pitch.

When they met in New York in 1947, it's likely that Zsa Zsa imagined George Sanders as a duplicate of the characters he often played onscreen. Many others thought the same, and no wonder. That's the image that George wished the world to have. Dorothy Parker, reviewing his *Memoirs of a Professional Cad* for *Esquire* in 1960, took him literally. "As shown by this book," she wrote, "George Sanders off the screen is just like George Sanders on it—the curled lip, the look down the nose, the rigid stance, the high, icy detachment from the herd." She should have known that autobiographies always lie.

Zsa Zsa said many times that she liked a man who would slap her around. She also liked to slap back, to scream and rant and throw things and then make up with her man like panthers mating. In this regard, George disappointed her: he was too phlegmatic for fisticuffs. He was happiest when left alone in his workshop with his inventions, for he was an amateur scientist who held patents on several Rube Goldberg contraptions. Among them, the one that he called "the greatest work of my career."

As reported by columnist Sidney Skolsky in 1951, "Sanders was inspired to his greatest work by his bride, Zsa Zsa Gabor. Day after day, hotel managers would come screaming that the bathtub was running over and guests below were wet."

"My wife," said Sanders, "has the habit of turning on the water full force and then going off to write a letter. So I invented this gadget, which consists of a rubber ball with an electric connection inside. The bather puts the rubber ball at the height she wants the water. When the water reaches that mark, it turns the ball over, setting off an electric discharge which rings a three-fire alarm bell." Whatever George's helpful intentions, it sounds like a scheme to electrocute Zsa Zsa! Nor will you find this useful, though risky, tool at the Home Depot.

Not only did Zsa Zsa find controlling, dominant wife beaters alluring, she could not resist the challenge of an indifferent, unapproachable man. Spotting passive-aggressive George, she recognized her ideal target. And for him, a big turn-on was an audacious woman in pursuit. The more brazen that woman, the more he savored keeping her desire unassuaged. For both, it was a high-stakes gamble when he moved in with Zsa Zsa.

For a time, both were winners. She discovered that he listened to her, as no previous husband had. Even Jolie, Magda, and Eva felt uncomfortable when she tried to unburden herself and talk about the horrors of West Hills Sanitarium, the attacks of nerves that plagued her before and since that confinement, her hopes for little Francesca, the uncertain future ahead and whether she would succeed in show business, even if someone in Hollywood decided to hire her. Jolie's pat answer to everything was, "It wouldn't have happened if I had been here" or "If you're ever *verklempt* again, Zsazsika, I'll take you on an ocean cruise."

George found Zsa Zsa highly amusing, and she him, though he soon realized that their fun would have remained unspoiled if only they had not married. "No one is a better date than Zsa Zsa," he said, "and no one is a better companion on a trip, even if it involves roughing it." Their travels resembled a continuous honeymoon.

In those happy days of 1947, Zsa Zsa lived in a remodeled brownstone at 8 East Eighty-third Street, between Fifth Avenue and Madison. Whether she bought it with money earned from Hilton hotel stocks, or whether another Gabor bought it for forty thousand dollars, depends on whose real estate prospectus you read. Whoever held the deed, that house was filled with Gabors. Vilmos, still in the United States pending his return to Hungary; Jolie, now the insouciant Manhattan jewelry entrepreneur and matron-about-town; Eva, when in New York between Hollywood assignments and West Coast stage appearances; Magda, recently remarried to William Rankin, a minor screenwriter, and a part-time resident on East Eighty-third Street when not on speaking terms with her groom; and Zsa Zsa and baby Francesca in the penthouse apartment. Soon George Sanders took up residence with Zsa Zsa.

Such libertine behavior scandalized Vilmos, who walked into Zsa Zsa's apartment one morning to visit his granddaughter and found the bed occupied by an extremely tall man eating fried eggs and drinking milk, and Zsa Zsa caroling from the kitchen, "Georgie, dahling, what can I make for you now, my love?"

"*Jó napot, drága Papuska,*" she managed to say in a language he understood. "*Éhes vagy?*" A stony silence from Vilmos conveyed that he had no interest in eating the same food she was serving to that long foreigner. As she tried to explain that her friend was very lazy, that he followed the adage, Never stand when you can sit, never sit when you can recline, Vilmos stormed out and slammed the door, waking up the baby, whose vociferous screams quite ruined the remainder of George's meal.

A month later, Zsa Zsa put Francesca in a wee basket and, along with the baby's nanny and the dog, flew to Hollywood to be with George. A month after that, suspecting that he had two-timed her, she reversed course to New York.

And so they were married, on April Fool's Day 1949. Zsa Zsa was partial to the month of April for her weddings, having married Conrad on April 10 and before that, Burhan in May, which, she reasoned, in Hungary was not so different from April.

This new wedding was delayed by George's divorce from his first wife, Susan Larson. Little is known of her except that she worked at a studio where George was filming and that they married in 1940. Although Zsa Zsa never met the first Mrs. Sanders, she had this to say: "He had a miserable marriage with that woman. He treated her badly, like a peasant, and she was mentally not very strong. She was in a mental home for quite a while."

In April 1950, one year after their marriage, George and Zsa Zsa arrived in San Francisco where he was to join Bette Davis, Gary Merrill, Celeste Holm, Thelma Ritter, Marilyn Monroe, and the rest of the cast of *All About Eve*. In it George played Addison DeWitt, the role for which he is best known and for which he won an Oscar as Best Supporting Actor. Since I have covered this period of George's life, and of Zsa Zsa's, in a previous book—*All About "All About Eve"*— I will avoid repeating myself. Throughout those weeks of filming, in San Francisco and later back in Hollywood at 20th Century Fox, George faced the professional task of long hours before the camera, squabbles with Bette Davis both scripted and otherwise, and, at the end of the work day, tussles with Zsa Zsa over her myriad concerns and frustrations.

Famished for a career of her own, she badgered George to persuade Joe Mankiewicz, the director, and Darryl Zanuck, the producer, to let her play the role of Phoebe, a teenage fan who appears for a minute or two in the film's final sequence. So persistent was she in that quest that Mankiewicz eventually banished her from the set. Adding to George's woes was Zsa Zsa's intense dislike of Marilyn Monroe, who, she imagined, was trying to steal George from her—despite the fact that Marilyn had more suitors than anyone in town. When Zsa Zsa learned that George and Marilyn often had lunch together in the commissary, she forbade him even to speak to her unless required to do so by the script.

On Oscar night—March 29, 1951—Zsa Zsa's emotions soared to heights undreamed of even by the evening's nominees. She was delirious with pride on George's behalf; despondent because she had no career and could only loiter in the shadows of his fame and Eva's; ravaged by jealousy when she imagined all the actresses backstage who might be flirting with George—and his Oscar—while she sat alone in a seat at the RKO Pantages Theatre on Hollywood Boulevard. No one took her picture. And who would want the autograph of a mere wife, a hausfrau?

Cecil B. DeMille, to Gloria Swanson in *Sunset Boulevard*: "You know, crazy things happen in this business, Norma. I hope you haven't lost your sense of humor." The crazy thing that happened to Zsa Zsa in that business was this: not quite a year later—on March 20, 1952—she swept onto the stage at the RKO Pantages Theatre on Hollywood Boulevard to present the Oscar for Black and White Costume Design to Edith Head for *A Streetcar Named Desire*.

1951 was Zsa Zsa's annus mirabilis, for as we saw in the opening pages she became famous overnight after her first appearance on the TV show *Bachelor's Haven*. Soon after that she made two pictures, and by Oscar night 1952 she had appeared in three more. She had just been signed for *Moulin Rouge*, John Huston's expensive, prestigious new film to be shot in Paris and London in summer and fall of that year. Zsa Zsa was now every-other-inch the movie star, for despite her newfound fame her work so far guaranteed only this: that in her next picture she must prove she had real star talent. Otherwise she would remain just another wife, although a wife who had presented an Oscar to Edith Head.

For Zsa Zsa, the remainder of 1952 loomed like a precarious cliff. She must not only survive as a movie actress, she must also zoom past those previous five performances in small roles and convince Hollywood that she could do a lot more. Failing that, she saw her next role as recurrent hausfrau: cooking eggs and washing socks for an ungrateful husband who barely bothered with a thank you. The sole membrane between Zsa Zsa Gabor movie star, and a has-been blonde with an accent, was John Huston.

Chapter 17

An Actress Prepares

Zsa Zsa didn't scare easily, one reason being that she never thought too far ahead. She rushed into each day's adventures, expecting the world to do her bidding, and if those biddings went awry she vented her emotions and whizzed straight ahead. Although rarely intimidated, in 1944 she briefly lost her voice from nerves in the office of Secretary of State Cordell Hull. Not until late September 1951 was she again so petrified. That was the day she reported for work at MGM and her first day on the set of *Lovely to Look At*. Mervyn LeRoy, the director, had seen her on *Bachelor's Haven* after her sensational debut on the show, and one night when he spotted Zsa Zsa and her brother-in-law Tom Conway dancing at the Mocambo, he tapped her on the shoulder and introduced himself. "I'm doing a new picture and there's a part that's just right for you. A cute French model. Would you like to do it?"

She thought he was joking.

"No," he said. "I mean it. You're so right I won't even bother with a test."

George was still filming *Ivanhoe* in England, but his agent gladly accompanied Zsa Zsa to LeRoy's office at MGM. To her astonishment, no one argued when the agent named her price as a thousand dollars a week. The following days found her at the studio for drama lessons, photo shoots, and fittings with Adrian, one of Hollywood's premier costume designers. Then a phone call came from Russell Birdwell, press agent to countless stars and the inventor of the hunt-for-a-star format. It was Birdwell who made *Gone With the Wind* the most talked-about movie in history before its release by extending the search for Scarlett O'Hara over three years.

Zsa Zsa had now joined the big leagues, and Birdwell wanted in on it. "I'm laying out a campaign for you," he said at their first meeting. "Our aim is not to impress the whole country. You're already doing that. We want to impress the ten top picture makers." He began taking Zsa Zsa to premieres in a chauffeured limousine. Her own expertise in fashion, jewelry, and makeup gave her the look of a movie star before she even stepped in front of a camera.

Looking like a star, however, is easier than becoming one. This Zsa Zsa realized that first day of filming. Her nerves froze. The excitement overwhelmed her. Early that first morning she was directed to makeup and told to sit at a long table in front of a gigantic lighted mirror. Looking to her left she saw Lana Turner and Grace Kelly. Down the table, on her right, Ava Gardner, Elizabeth Taylor, and Kathryn Grayson.

Everyone nodded, said good morning, then Ava Gardner leaned over to Zsa Zsa and said, "Sydney will make his entrance any minute now." Sydney, of course, being Sydney Guilaroff, coiffeur to everyone who mattered at MGM. When he swept in, he commanded, "Girls, put your lipstick on. I don't fix up dogs." Zsa Zsa loved his campy joke, and she immediately felt at home with Ava Gardner, who told her that girls at this studio did their own lipstick, the theory being that no makeup artist could apply it to a woman's lips as well as the woman herself.

"I arrived on the set practically speechless," Zsa Zsa recalled. "I was given my cue, but I was so scared I couldn't even open my mouth." Kathryn Grayson, the leading lady and an established star with over a dozen roles to her credit, sized up Zsa Zsa's predicament after a quick look. "Hey, Merv," she called out to the director. "Can we take a break? I've got a run in my stocking and I need to go and change."

Zsa Zsa, on her mark but bereft of that steel-jaw self-confidence that had carried her through many a crisis, stood rooted to the floor. At first she didn't comprehend why Kathryn walked toward her. Looking into Zsa Zsa's terrified eyes, she smiled and said, "Come with me, honey. Let's go to my dressing room." She put her arm around Zsa Zsa's shoulders and led her away.

Zsa Zsa never forgot what happened next. "I followed her, grateful for the reprieve, yet still feeling crestfallen and inept. Once in the dressing room, Katie invited me to sit down, made a certain amount of small talk to give me time to compose myself, then poured me a stiff shot of vodka, telling me, 'Drink up.' When we went back onto the set, my performance was virtually flawless. And Kathryn Grayson became my best friend." The friendship endured, although by the time of Kathryn's death in 2010, Zsa Zsa was unable fully to comprehend her friend's passing.

Everyone knew Zsa Zsa from *Bachelor's Haven*, and on her second day at MGM the cast and crew played a joke on her. Several weeks earlier, she had said on the show, "I hate how American men dress—all those Honolulu shirts." Arriving on the set, she saw a dozen men done up in "Honolulu shirts."

Kathryn Grayson's daughter, Patricia, was one year younger

than Francesca, so the two girls often played together. Francesca had happy memories of those times, and her most endearing childhood story was this one. A year or so after filming Lovely to Look At, Kathryn and Zsa Zsa took their little daughters trick-or-treating in Beverly Hills in costumes borrowed from MGM's wardrobe department.

Seven years into their friendship, Kathryn spoke about Zsa Zsa to the New York Post for that paper's series on the Gabors. "This Zsa Zsa in the newspapers is not the real Zsa Zsa. It's just a façade. Inwardly, she is a frightened, nervous person. When she sees a horde of newspaper reporters descending on her, she says she just doesn't know what to do, so she talks. Then she's shocked when they print what she says. I tell her, 'Hide, like I do.' But she says, 'I cannot hide. They expect me to say something.'" Over the years, Kathryn was the rare person who saw Zsa Zsa weep.

Marge Champion was the one cast member that Zsa Zsa didn't like. Without going into detail, Zsa Zsa claimed that Marge was not nice to her. Again, Kathryn Grayson took Zsa Zsa's part. "I will not allow such behavior," she snapped after Marge directed a catty remark to Zsa Zsa.

For Zsa Zsa, Lovely to Look At proved an inauspicious debut, though in it she was indeed lovely and poised. Adrian, the costume designer, thought Zsa Zsa was mad when she insisted on wearing a black cocktail dress. "It's just not done," he declared. But Zsa Zsa's insistence paid off. She walked away with fashion honors while the other female stars in their pastel gowns—Kathryn Grayson, Ann Miller, Marge Champion—resembled scoops of sherbet at Baskin-Robbins. It's a miracle, however, that Zsa Zsa received future film offers, given this deadly musical that foreshadowed the demise of MGM and its famous genre. She does nothing but giggle and chatter in French like a francophone monkey.

Even those in the cast who often did better work—Howard

Keel, Ann Miller, Marge and Gower Champion—sink under the dull script and hackneyed direction. The Jerome Kern songs fare badly when rendered in Grayson's piercing soprano. (A trivia note: When Kathryn Grayson speaks a few lines of French, they're dubbed by Zsa Zsa.)

In his memoir, *Take One*, Mervyn LeRoy recalled not Zsa Zsa's nerves but "the quantity of flowers that were delivered to the set for her" that first day. "There were baskets of flowers, bouquets of flowers, vases of flowers. The stage smelled like a florist's shop, and so did she." And of the female cast members: "This was one film where the problem wasn't that they didn't get along, but that they got along too well. The girls—Kathryn, Ann, and Zsa Zsa—became an instant sorority. They were always off in some corner, giggling like schoolgirls. I like a happy set, but I also like a quiet set when there is work to be done. I had a devil of a time trying to get those girls to simmer down."

Typical of Zsa Zsa's reviews in her first screen appearance are these, from *Time* ("blonde Zsa Zsa Gabor just flounces around") and the *New York Times* ("Kurt Kasznar and Zsa Zsa Gabor make a couple of noisy appearances as a Broadway producer and his giggling Gallic girlfriend.")

After her short stay at MGM, Zsa Zsa moved to 20th Century Fox in December 1951 for *We're Not Married*. What should have been a fluffy little anthology film ended up heavy and indigestible. That's owing to Edmund Goulding's sluggish direction and to editing that loiters when it should dance and skip.

Five couples—among them Ginger Rogers and Fred Allen, Eve Arden and Paul Douglas, Marilyn Monroe and David Wayne—find out they're not legally hitched because the justice of the peace who performed their respective ceremonies was not yet qualified to do so. Nunnally Johnson, who wrote the script, created a segment for Zsa Zsa and character actor

Louis Calhern that starts as an in-joke and becomes a miniature operetta without music. In her first scene, Zsa Zsa is eating breakfast in bed in a finely appointed bedroom, with a
poodle beside her. (It was probably her own.) She's the trophy wife of a Texas oil millionaire.

Sound familiar? Conrad Hilton's money didn't come from
oil, though he did try drilling for it en route to his hotel empire. Like Calhern in the picture, he was the older husband of
a petted young wife. Zsa Zsa's split from Calhern in the
movie follows the same track as her divorce from Hilton a
few years earlier: schemes, detectives following one or both
parties, an attempt to take half the husband's wealth which,
onscreen as in real time of 1946–'47, goes awry for the plot-
ting wife. Calhern outfoxes Mrs. Melrose—Zsa Zsa's character—just as Conrad outsmarted Mrs. Hilton. At the moment
when Mrs. Melrose is about to take her husband to the
cleaners, he gets the letter informing him: you're not married.

Gorgeous Zsa Zsa plays what was to become her usual
role—hard-boiled, cynical fortune hunter swathed in top-
notch couture. She was as photogenic as Marilyn Monroe,
though in a very different way. The camera dotes on vulnerable Marilyn, eager to come closer. Zsa Zsa's impenetrable
porcelain face rivets the camera eye. It wants to pull away,
but can't: she has taken a mortgage on it.

Zsa Zsa returned to MGM in early 1952 for *The Story of
Three Loves,* another anthology film with two segments di-
rected by Gottfried Reinhardt and Zsa Zsa's by Vincente
Minnelli. What a cast: costarring with Zsa Zsa in the episode
titled "Mademoiselle" are Leslie Caron, Farley Granger,
Ethel Barrymore, and eleven-year-old Ricky Nelson. In the
other episodes are James Mason, Agnes Moorehead, Moira
Shearer, Kirk Douglas, and Pier Angeli.

Leslie Caron plays Mademoiselle, Ricky's governess, with
damp whimsy. He chafes under her tutelage because she re-

quires him to memorize endless French verb conjugations. By chance the lad encounters a hammy sorceress—Ethel Barrymore—who grants his wish to be a man, not a little boy. Voilà! He's Farley Granger. During the boy's two late-night hours as a grown-up, he goes to a bar, orders his first drink, and encounters a beautiful flirt, played by Zsa Zsa.

In her one brief scene she coos to this naive boy-man, counsels him on what to drink, and how. Minnelli must have seen her potential, for she and Granger give the best performances in the picture. Zsa Zsa weaves a spell around him, like the good fairy in a tale. Her work here is a sad reminder of the career she might have had. Instead, heedless, careless, undisciplined Zsa Zsa wrecked that career without giving it a chance to grow.

During her short time on the set, she recalled that "I would look up at the boom and see this tiny little girl with enormous brown eyes staring down at me." That girl was six-year-old Liza Minnelli, as reluctant to leave her father's side as he to return her to his ex-wife, Judy Garland, at the end of the day's shoot.

Zsa Zsa remained at MGM for her next picture, *Lili*, which filmed during March and April 1952. Fourth billed after Leslie Caron, Mel Ferrer, and Jean-Pierre Aumont, she gives a performance that suggests diligent work with her acting coach. As Aumont's wife/assistant in a magic act with a provincial carnival in France, Zsa Zsa is a knockout. As part of the act, she loses her dress and is left standing onstage in black lace halter and matching panties, a scene that caused Zsa Zsa considerable discomfort. The Gabors avoided cheesecake for two reasons: their figures were not conducive, and showing skin would outrage Papa if he ever learned about it. They maintained that in public, ladies kept their clothes on. Zsa Zsa owned the most confident walk in Hollywood, and in *Lili* she moves like the leader of a fine-posture parade. Unlike Marilyn Monroe's wiggle, Zsa Zsa's gait is less seductive than militaristic.

In later years Zsa Zsa sometimes quarreled with female costars, but during her apprenticeship she valued their regard for her. Leslie Caron, in her memoir *Thank Heaven*, had this to say: "Dear Zsa Zsa Gabor was a generous colleague. One day I admired the blouse she was wearing; the next day she brought it to me, washed and ironed. She was fun and believed in getting the best out of life—and men. She played the role in *Lili* with the discipline of a pro."

Chapter 18

Pink Danube

While Zsa Zsa was building a career in Hollywood, Eva, Magda, and Jolie were doing the same in New York. We left Jolie at 699 Madison Avenue, superivising her daughters as they draped magenta satin in the windows of her new shop, the Jolie Gabor Pearl Salon. A name more reflective of the brains and labor behind that enterprise might have been Magda Gabor Costume Jewelry, Inc. Evidence points to Magda as the maven who kept everything on track while Mama cavorted in Manhattan nightclubs and prowled for husband number three.

In 1947, Jolie had married number two, Peter Howard Christman, a man she met during her brief tenure in the West Forties before her ascent to Madison Avenue. Christman worked at a nearby eatery called Hamburger Heaven, and although in later years Jolie billed him as manager of several such establishments, in truth he manned the cash register. The marriage, as both parties realized from the start, was one of convenience: an American husband guaranteed a fast and easy route to citizenship for Mrs. Christman. "I told him my problem of an expiring visitor's visa," Jolie said.

It seems likely that Christman made a profit from the marriage. After all, Jolie's three daughters had married into money and were in a position to chase the immigration wolf from Mama's door. "Imagine the headlines," Zsa Zsa warned Conrad, "if your mother-in-law is deported. How much easier to buy her a husband."

Jolie proposed to Christman with these words: "I want desperately my citizenship and secondly I want you." Is it possible that he found himself addled by Gabors and drink? For according to Jolie, Christman had suffered a bout of pneumonia some years earlier and a doctor prescribed a daily bottle of whiskey to prevent recurrence. Christman never deviated from this prophylactic regimen, while the doctor no doubt attracted hordes of thirsty patients. "Each morning," said disingenuous Jolie, "he would start with a few sips in the bathroom before breakfast, but always he was gentlemanly and nice to me." In 1948, however, he inherited a small house in Arizona, whose dry air and cheaper whiskey proved too tempting a situation to refuse. (Or did he buy the house with uxorious cash?) Then, too, Jolie's chaotic bookkeeping, and her enlistment of Christman to help her in the shop after a long day at Hamburger Heaven, surely persuaded him to choose the West over the West Side. "I cannot add," Jolie stated, "but I can take one glance and estimate correctly. I am not so good either with multiplying or subtracting or dividing but I can look at a pile of merchandise and guess how much it is to the last rhinestone." Realizing the dangers of this marital morass—as legal spouse, Christman might be liable for Jolie's debts to suppliers and to the IRS—he filed for divorce.

Jolie lost two husbands almost at once. Peter Christman fled to Arizona, and Vilmos, unable to speak English and not eager to learn, prepared for a return to Hungary. Saturated by cajoleries from his ex-wife and three daughters, with all such pleas accompanied by *geschrei* and wet tears, he decided that war-ravaged Budapest looked calmer than the battles raging in Gaborland.

Zsa Zsa, casting aspersions on Eva during one of their frequent blowups, implied that her sister was partially responsible for their father's unhappiness in the U.S. "He stayed for a while with Eva in California," she said. "He was miserable because she gave him a room with a tiny little bed to sleep in. I don't know why unless she's so stupid—she's always so very cheap and I don't like that."

A more likely reason for his telling Zsa Zsa one day in 1948 that he wanted to go back was owing to a new government ruling. "If you returned to Hungary," she said, "you got back everything you previously owned. So he got his shop and also furnishings that relatives had hidden for him. He had a villa again and everything was fine." His other objective was to marry the woman Zsa Zsa called "his adoring secretary who had doted on him for twenty-five years, even when he was still married to Mother. His second wife was not like my mother, who is always the grande dame."

Not long after Vilmos arrived in Budapest, while still occupied with rebuilding his former business, a new government ruling came down. Zsa Zsa explained that "the communists confiscated everything except five pounds of one's belongings, and began deporting people. They deported Father to a peasant house where he lived with his wife and three other people."

That "peasant house" was in the drab suburb of Budakeszi. In 1950, the repressive communist government labeled Vilmos and his second wife as "undesirables" and banished them from Budapest. Reasons for this banishment were perhaps his former bourgeois status and prosperity, or his rumored support of the quasi-fascist interwar regime of Admiral Horthy. De facto anti-Semitism, along with his original Germanic

family name—Grün—may also have accounted for his disfavor, for many ethnic Germans and others with Germanic
names were deported after the war, even those whose ancestors had lived for several centuries in Hungary. (For a time in
the nineteenth century, Jewish families could buy Hungarian
surnames. This is perhaps how Vilmos Grün became a
Gabor.)

When Vilmos approached Zsa Zsa about a return to Budapest, she realized that "he somehow didn't belong any
more to our life." Without discussing the matter with Eva
and Magda, she bought him a ticket, gave him several thousand dollars, and saw him off on a transatlantic ship. He left
behind his walking cane, which Zsa Zsa kept by her bedside
for the rest of her life.

No doubt Vilmos came to regret his decision. He had returned to a democratic parliamentary government officially
called the Second Hungarian Republic, which lasted from
1946 until the communist takeover in 1949, at which time
the country became the People's Republic of Hungary with a
constitution patterned on that of the Soviet Union. Almost
overnight, Vilmos found himself behind the Iron Curtain.

Throughout much of the 1950s, communication was spo-
radic between Vilmos and his family in the United States. Virtually all letters entering or leaving Hungary were subject to
censorship or confiscation. Telephone connections, even
when possible to make, took hours or days to arrange, and
then were listened to in communist Hungary and probably in
McCarthyite America, as well. The Gabors, knowing his vulnerability, rarely spoke of Vilmos in public. Asked by a reporter in 1957 about his welfare, Eva gave this laconic reply:
"Yes, we hear from him. He is fine." They were well advised
never to criticize the Hungarian government, for the safety of
Vilmos and other relatives in Hungary. Not until the late
1960s was Zsa Zsa able to obtain a visa to visit the country.

*   *   *

During Jolie's entrepreneurial early days, Magda had joined the marital merry-go-round that enriched her sisters. From 1946 until 1947, her husband was the writer William Rankin. In midsummer 1949 she married attorney Sidney Robert Warren and remained his wife until the next year. When not honeymooning or divorcing, Magda helped her mother, though she despaired of Jolie's cockamamie business methods.

Even in childhood, one of Magda's nicknames was "the General." Her dangerous work in wartime and her success in escaping to Portugal with members of her family proved her sangfroid and steely determination. As Jolie fiddled and floundered in her first shop on the outskirts of Hell's Kitchen, Magda decided that she must fill the power vacuum.

For details of Magda's expertise and her accomplishment, I summoned Tony Turtu, my good friend to whom this book is dedicated. Tony, author of the visually stunning *Gaborabilia*, published in 2001, is an authority on all things Gabor. He owns the world's most extensive collection of photos and documents relating to them, and in addition he is a fashion designer with a profound appreciation of costume jewelry, its design and merchandising. Recently, I asked him to explain why Magda and Jolie, working as a team, succeeded where many colleagues and competitors failed.

This is what he said. "Jolie guided and nurtured her jewelry business, but it was Magda who provided the initial foundation. While Jolie acted as the amusingly daft figurehead, Magda piloted the ship during those early New York years, keeping flamboyant Mama in line.

"The costume jewelry business in the 1940s, '50s, and beyond was crowded with companies such as Dior, Scaasi, Laguna, and Corocraft, to name only a few. Enter Magda Gabor who, despite a limited grasp of English and even smaller knowledge of American business practices, knew how to

conceptualize and execute her own and Jolie's costume jewelry designs. That, however, was only step one. What came
next after their designs were turned into actual jewelry?

"That is, how to sell the lovely brooches, rings, necklaces,
and earrings when they arrived at 699 Madison Avenue from
the manufacturer? Magda sold them to department stores
and drew attention to them with her own high-kilowatt
glamour, exotic charm, and a family name that, by 1950, had
already gained a coveted place in American media. Magda
often oversaw lighting, music, program notes, and selection
of models in venues where Jolie Gabor jewelry was featured.
She pushed it on radio and television, and in personal appearances at major department stores such as Bonwit Teller
and in fashion showcases. Early on, for instance—in March
1949—Magda made one of her first in-store appearances at
a trunk-show display in the Don Loper Studio on Sunset
Boulevard. Quite the publicity master stroke! And little sister
Eva was on hand for the big event, as well.

"Magda and Jolie did their own best advertising. 'Magda
is publicity minded,' cooed Jolie, but so was Jolie herself. No
Gabor ever spoke in private if they could say it for publication. They understood that wearing their own creations at
the Stork Club, '21', and Sardi's cost less, and seduced a better clientele, than an ad in the *New York Times*. Nor did
Magda overlook well-publicized showcases at the Waldorf
(owned by former brother-in-law Conrad Hilton), the War-
wick, Philadelphia's Bellevue-Stratford, and other high-end
hotels. And of course, Zsa Zsa and Eva never left home without a full complement of diamonds, emeralds, and rubies—
most from Mama's inventory, although in interviews they
shamelessly upped the price tag from seventy-five dollars to
seventy-five thousand."

Removing a newspaper clipping from one of his file folders, Tony said, "Here is a typical print feature: *Own Family
Designs Eva's Jewels*. This syndicated photo layout pictured

Eva wearing a three-piece ensemble designed by Mama and Magda. Based on copies of Empress Maria Theresa's crown jewels, the pieces were made of cultured pearls, simulated emeralds, and rhinestones."

He continued, "Magda pioneered the art of group concepts, which is the background of any good design business. For example, when Jolie designed a beautiful three-strand faux-pearl choker, it was Magda who added a matching bracelet and earrings to the line. Providing the customer with additional options is a shrewd marketing strategy that can lead to exponential sales volume.

"In their philosophy of nonstop jewelry, Magda and Jolie also taught their customers never to neglect daytime jewelry. Sportswear and casual clothing? Try a chic necklace and button-earrings paired with a simple sweater. A pearl ring on the smallest finger? *Dahling, it's perfection! It vill drive your man crazy*.

"Then along came Jolie's newly launched line of cosmetics, with the ritzy-tawdry brand name Pink Danube."

I interrupted to ask, "Was the pun intentional? After all, pink is in the family of *red*, and the Red Scare was still up and running."

After jokes about Pink Danube's possible hidden meanings, Tony went further with specifics of a business model that might save almost any company from failure. "Magda," he said, "engineered cross-promotions between those two lucrative product lines, jewelry and cosmetics. Other family-endorsed products that debuted around this time were the Gabor Foundation Cream, the Madame Jolie Gabor Makeup Base, and, best of all, Pearl de Jolie perfume, in a bottle mounted with 'pearls.' I have one, and there's neither a pearl nor a 'pearl' in sight.

"Now, remember that in the early fifties there was not the deluge of perfumes that exists today, when every pop princess with a tin ear and any reality-show nobody can have

The Gabor family, circa 1922, in Budapest. From left: Jolie, Zsa Zsa, Eva, Vilmos, Magda.
(Collection of the late Francesca Hilton)

Jolie Gabor and her girls
at Lake Balaton, circa 1926.
From left: Eva, Zsa Zsa, Magda, Jolie
(Collection of the late Francesca Hilton)

Zsa Zsa's birthplace, Múzeum körút 31, Budapest.
The Gabors lived in many locations and rarely
told the address or the dates of habitation.
Everyone agreed, however, that this was the site
of Zsa Zsa's birth on February 6, 1917.
The building, constructed circa 1900, was
destroyed in World War II.
(Collection of the author)

The famous Gabor features begin to take shape in a family snapshot from circa 1929. Magda, nicknamed "The General," was always the most independent daughter. Unlike her sisters and her mother, she did not bob her hair in the style of the Roaring Twenties. From left: Eva, Zsa Zsa, Magda, Jolie.
(Collection of the late Francesca Hilton)

Contrary to Gabor family mythology, Zsa Zsa was never elected Miss Hungary. She was, however, a runner-up in the 1933 pageant. Pictured here, left to right: Lily Radó, runner-up; Júlia Gál, winner; and fifteen-year-old Zsa Zsa. *(Filmhíradók/Magyar Nemzeti Filmarchivum)*

Zsa Zsa and her first husband, Burhan Belge, Ankara, Turkey, 1939.
The marriage lasted from 1935 to 1941. Zsa Zsa disliked this photograph
because it made her look middle-aged when, in reality, she was twenty-two. *(Photofest)*

A family photograph taken circa 1940. Front row: Jolie, in the most unflattering photograph ever taken of her, is convalescing from an illness, possibly pneumonia. Beside her is Zsa Zsa, on a visit to Budapest from Turkey shortly before her departure for the U.S. Magda is in back row, left. Beside her, the elderly woman is perhaps Francesca Tillemann, mother of Jolie and grandmother of the Gabor sisters. The woman beside her is unidentified. *(Courtesy of the Lantos and Tillemann-Dick families)*

Zsa Zsa, at 22, begins her conquest of the world. Photographed in London in 1939 with two famous admirers: H.G. Wells (center) and George Bernard Shaw.
(Photography Collection, Harry Ransom Center, The University of Texas at Austin)

Eva, with costar Richard Arlen, in her first film, *Forced Landing*,
released by Paramount in 1941. *(Photofest)*

Eva in *Pacific Blackout* (1942), with costars Robert Preston and Martha Drisco
As the dedicated actress in the family, she worked hard to perfect her craf
yet the accent always stood between Eva and the roles she coveted. *(Photofes*

Eva and Zsa Zsa in Hollwood in the early 1940s. Eva was a film starlet, but Zsa Zsa's career lay ten years in the future. Neither sister had yet undergone cosmetic surgery to obtain a more svelte nose.
(Photofest)

Eva in *Song of Surrender*, 1949.
Director Mitchell Leisen made sure
her wardrobe outshone the
costumes of other cast members.
(Photofest)

Zsa Zsa and costar Leslie Caron
in *Lili*, 1953. In Caron's words,
"Dear Zsa Zsa Gabor was
a generous colleague.
She played the role in *Lili*
with the discipline of a pro."
(Photofest)

Zsa Zsa in *Moulin Rouge*, 1953. On the set, director John Huston yelled at her, "You can't act, you can't sing, you can't dance. At least show your face to the camera." In later years they became friends, and Zsa Zsa credited him with making her a star. *(Photofest)*

Zsa Zsa and Porfirio Rubirosa, the lover she never married. "I was addicted to him," she said when their affair was over. "He was in my blood and he possessed my soul. He was renowned for his machismo and above all for his sexual prowess." *(Photofest)*

Zsa Zsa and George Sanders in the 1956 television comedy-drama *Autumn Fever*.
They costarred that same year on the large screen in *Death of a Scoundrel*.
George was Zsa Zsa's third husband, and the one she always called her favorite and
the great love of her life. They remained close until George's suicide in 1972. *(Photofest)*

In *The Girl in the Kremlin* (1957), Zsa Zsa plays twin sisters caught up in a Stalinist plot. Asked by a reporter about taking on a dual role, Zsa Zsa replied, "I have to be careful not to steal scenes from myself." *(Photofest)*

Francesca Hilton, 1947-2015. This photograph was taken circa 1968.
Francesca bore very little resemblance to her mother or her aunts. *(Photofest)*

Francesca Hilton, in the late 1960s, in drama school. Her career did not progress, one reason being that she preferred photography to acting. *(Photofest)*

Eva and Mrs. Mary Smith, in Texas in the 1970s. Good-natured Eva had countless friends in all walks of life. *(Courtesy of Mrs. Mary Smith)*

Zsa Zsa, on trial in 1989 for slapping a Beverly Hills cop. The circus-like atmosphere of the trial made Zsa Zsa more notorious than ever before. Here she displays a sketch she made in court of the plaintiff, Officer Paul Kramer. At trial's end, the judge sentenced Zsa Zsa to four days in jail.
(Courtesy of Heritage Auctions, HA.com)

The grave of Eva Gabor, Westwood Village Memorial Park, Los Angeles
(Courtesy of Rousselle)

a fragrance. Fashion icons—Helena Rubenstein, Elizabeth Arden, Chanel—each had a signature scent. This was the rarified world that Jolie entered, or should I say elbowed her way into? Magda no doubt had a hand in it. And Pearl de Jolie meant that Jolie Gabor had arrived.

"When loyal customers asked for advice, Magda said, 'My suggestions are general. Learn to experiment.' Since she, and the other Gabor women, lived their philosophy of jewelry every day, her clever retorts to customer questions carried conviction. They are part of her legend. Among Magda's best quotes are these:

- More than one stunning ring on one hand is unchic.
- Never wear gold jewelry with an evening dress.
- Jewelry does not have to be flamboyant to be beautiful.
- Pearls offer a softness and a glow that no other stone imparts.

"And," he concluded, "she meant every word. The Gabor family lived by those precepts. Remember, too, that owing to Magda and Jolie's complete design control over their product, and the superior workmanship of Jolie Gabor costume jewelry, even today pieces from Jolie's collection are highly sought after."

Chapter 19

Husbands Get in the Way

Or so Eva seemed to believe, for after divorcing Charles Isaacs in 1949 she remained single until 1956. Her abstention from marriage, however, did not equal celibacy. During this seven-year sabbatical, Eva dated scores of eligible men—some for publicity, others because they caught her fancy.

Leading the parade was Ned Magowan, a wealthy New York broker with the investment firm Merrill Lynch. Magowan, although in his forties at the time of World War II and therefore beyond draft age, enlisted in the Navy and served with distinction. Another beau with a similar wartime record was theatre producer Richard Aldrich (1902–1986). When he and Eva met in 1953 he was the widower of London and New York stage star Gertrude Lawrence, who had died the previous year. Eva and Kirk Douglas, according to a gossip columnist, "turned heads when they showed up for drinks at the Stork Club." Eva also had romances with Charles Luckman, a wealthy rancher; playboy Ernie Byfield Jr.; Stewart Barthelmess, adopted son of silent screen star Richard Barthelmess; and Robert Merrill, of the Metropolitan Opera.

*   *   *

Looking at Eva's chronology for those years, one wonders when she found time to sleep, eat regular meals, and to show up in public as the very picture of glamorous perfection. She appeared almost daily on radio or television, among the shows many of which are known only to archeologists of early TV. Among the more obscure: *Answer Yes or No, Leave It to the Girls, The Kate Smith Hour, The Name's the Same*. She rushed from game show to talk show, sat on guest panels, lit up variety shows and celebrity showcases, taped or appeared live in TV dramas and comedies, and still found time for myriad charity telethons and money-raising events, both televised and in person.

Since one of the Gabor stereotypes that this book seeks to disprove—at least in part—is that of selfish and self-centered gold diggers, I include here a sample list of Eva's work on be-half of the less fortunate. In 1951, the Sister Kenny Founda-tion telethon; the same year, during the run of *The Happy Time*, the cast gave a benefit performance in the Bronx at Kingsbridge Veterans Hospital for grateful patients and staff. Throughout the fifties, Eva appeared in March of Dimes telethons and personal appearances at money-raising events such as fashion shows at the Waldorf for the Polio Fund; in 1953, the City of Hope All-Star telethon found her joined by Zsa Zsa in support of a charity to which both devoted time and money for decades. Also in 1953, Eva participated in the Salute to the Bravest and Finest at Madison Square Garden, a fund-raising event for the widows and children of police offi-cers and firemen. And in 1954 and again in 1955, the Annual Celebrity Parade for Cerebral Palsy, a seventeen-hour tele-thon with appearances by many stars.

Eva, no doubt realizing that she would not become a per-manent fixture on Broadway, built a stage career on the road. During the first half of the 1950s, she toured much of the country in regional and summer theatre productions of half-a-dozen comedies, among them *Bell, Book, and Candle; Her Cardboard Lover; The Happy Time* (after its Broadway run); and *Blithe Spirit*. Eva became such a fixture in the latter that Noël Coward, who admired her in his play and became a close friend, joked that "whenever you're broke you do *Blithe Spirit*." During a performance in summer 1956 at Ephrata, Pennsylvania, a deafening thunderclap rattled the theatre. Eva screamed and hurled herself on a settee. The play resumed when she picked up her lines.

Around the same time, playing a mermaid in *Sailor's Delight*, she earned praise from Elliot Norton, a respected theatre critic in Boston. "Miss Gabor's performance," he wrote, "was a notable surprise in the summer theatre season. She emerged as a comedienne of very comparable quality to Gertrude Lawrence in light comedy, deft and delightful." Groucho Marx, attending the play in Los Angeles, had a different opinion. Enjoying a drink between the acts, he famously told the bartender, "This production needs a longer intermission and a much shorter play."

Sometimes Eva's linguistic mishaps came off funnier than her dialogue. In 1952, appearing in *Strike a Match* at the Alcazar Theatre in San Francisco, Eva confused the local press by insisting that she was playing at the *Alcatraz*. (The producers rushed into damage control mode.) Most of the time, however, she knew exactly what to say for a laugh. When someone asked which Gabor was the oldest, Eva said, "Mama."

Always serious about her work, Eva attended the Actors Studio for a short period in 1955. A photograph of Eva with Lee Strasberg shows her deglamourized in a simple sweater and string of pearls. Her plain-Jane makeup is so minimal that she seems just to have rolled out of bed and dashed off to acting class. According to press reports, she was to participate in a staged reading of *Uncle Vanya* for the student body and faculty. Five years earlier, during the run of *The Happy Time*, Eva had appeared with Boris Karloff in a TV production of the Chekhov play. Another costar in that production was Leora Dana, also in the cast of *The Happy Time*. Eva played Yelena, the young, restless wife of a retired professor (Karloff). She recalled that "we rehearsed *Uncle Vanya* for ten days, Leora and I going over our material between acts at the theatre. On the night we played it, the entire cast of *The Happy Time* gathered before the television set in my house to watch Leora and me perform."

While promoting her autobiography during 1954, Eva made the usual rounds of bookstores and interview shows. Its title, *Orchids and Salami*, supposedly came from the sole contents of her fridge when someone opened it looking for a snack. But since *Champagne and Goulash* was also in the running as a title, that refrigerator could have morphed from one of Eva's stage comedies. Either title is more evocative than the book itself, whose ghostwriter seems to have grabbed a few fuzzy facts from Eva as she dashed from stage to screen to wardrobe fitting. The *New York Times* review began, "This is the autobiography, in a manner of speaking, of a highly publicized actress of Hungarian birth."

In addition to everything else, Eva appeared in five films in the early fifties. *Paris Model* (1953), shot in just ten days, is a sly little comedy that should be better known. The "Paris Model" is not a woman but a dress from a famous couturière. Despite French laws that protect against copying such originals, a version of one dress from the fashion house turns up in New York. It is called "Nude at Midnight," copied from an $890 original. This anthology film follows several additional copies of the original "Nude at Midnight" through a series of adventures on the backs of their various owners.

Eva, in the first episode, is Gogo Montaine, a Parisian

mantrap who sets out to seduce a beturbanned maharajah, played by Tom Conway (brother of George Sanders, and thus still Zsa Zsa's brother-in-law when *Paris Model* was filmed in summer of 1953). Stunning in the eponymous gown, and decked out in jewelry (Mama's, no doubt), Eva almost nets the maharajah and his millions. But he spies a younger woman in a restaurant and ditches Gogo for her. Next, Paulette Goddard, playing secretary to businessman Leif Erickson, vamps him in her prêt-à-porter version—until his wife turns up, in her own illegal copy. Then effervescent Marilyn Maxwell almost steals the movie, and finally Barbara Lawrence, as a rather plain girl, catches her man thanks to the "Paris Model" she found in a thrift shop for nineteen dollars.

This under-the-radar movie—a funny, well-crafted vehicle for actresses past their first youth—is more entertaining than many a big-budget behemoth of the era. It surprises with underplayed comedy and witty touches along the way, e.g., when Paulette Goddard in an *I Love Lucy* moment snags her own copy of the dress on a chair in a restaurant and it rips apart, leaving her stranded in a slip.

Seeing Eva at her best, as she is here, you realize that she was the real beauty of the family and, especially in sexy comedies, an accomplished actress. Here she makes theatricality work in her favor: the wide eyes, sweeping gestures, head swerving, and coquettish half-turns as she speaks her lines. She commands a certain kind of non-naturalistic acting acquired from years on the stage. Zsa Zsa, on the other hand, being by nature overly theatrical, couldn't tone it down before the camera. The result is that she caricatured herself. Debbie Reynolds in a wicked imitation of Zsa Zsa on *The Joan Rivers Show* is not very different from Zsa Zsa's imitation of herself, or should I say, Zsa Zsa imitating the alter ego she wanted to be.

*   *   *

In *Captain Kidd and the Slave Girl* (1954):

- See Eva covered by bubbles in a scalloped tub that no Carnival Cruise fantasy could duplicate.
- Watch her row a boat from ship to shore, and capsize it.
- Hold your breath as she draws a seventeenth-century musket and fires.
- Witness her desolation on the beach of a desert isle after a near drowning, though with perfect piled-up hairdo and voluminous robe dry and intact.
- Peer at Eva as she disrobes down to her bloomers and jumps into the Caribbean.
- Hear Eva scream in defense of her virtue, not once but twice, as pirate galoots try to sample her charms.

She plays Judith Duval, a treacherous femme fatale on the high seas aboard a British ship. Although betrothed to the Earl of Bellamont, she switches her affections mid-voyage to the pirate Captain Kidd after a bit of bodice ripping. Though made on the cheap, this energetic swashbuckler sprints from one high-drama moment to the next. It must have been great fun for kiddies who considered themselves too sophisticated for *Howdy Doody* and that uncool TV Captain, viz., *Kangaroo*. The picture's great set piece is the rollicking cat fight between Eva and Sonia Sorrell as Anne Bonny, the legendary eighteenth-century female pirate. Eva lunges, attacks, pulls hair, and the two women roll on the ground in a knockdown, drag-out fight that won't stop until Captain Kidd picks up Eva and carries her off into the tropical underbrush as she shrieks, "Let me go! I'll murder her!" (Stuntwomen did the actual clawing and scratching; we see Eva and Sonia in only a few shots.)

The Mad Magician (1954), a cult favorite set in the late 1800s, is imitation Hitchcock. Eva has little to do but wear fancy gowns and furs up to the moment when Vincent Price, as the magician of the title, strangles her.

The Last Time I Saw Paris (1954), based on the short story "Babylon Revisited" by F. Scott Fitzgerald, droops under Richard Brooks's dull direction and the phlegmatic screenplay. Tired, also, even in 1954, was the self-pitying myth of Scott and Zelda, the Lost Generation, and their long American hangover in Paris.

MGM was drooping, also, and the big-name cast seems worn-out: Elizabeth Taylor, Van Johnson, Walter Pidgeon, Donna Reed, and Roger Moore. Eva, however, sparkles in the gloom. She plays Lorraine Quarl, a jaded butterfly of café society and the international set in the high-fashion costumes designed for her by the studio's Helen Rose. In two scenes with Elizabeth Taylor, Eva is equally striking, which cannot be said of many other stars. Two of Eva's scenes stand out. In one, she lets the camera reveal her stripped of glamour, violating the Gabor code that you only accept roles where you look better than anyone else. When she's caught in a downpour, Eva's hair is mussed and makeup dribbles down her waterlogged face.

Her next stand-out scene occurs in a nightclub. Eva's character is having an affair with Van Johnson. In a drunken brawl, Johnson starts a fight with another man. His wife, played by Elizabeth Taylor, stalks off in a huff, leaving Eva alone at the table to witness the fistfight. The camera moves to Eva in a five-second reaction shot that may be the best acting of her career. An expression of total despair crosses her beautiful face, which seems to age five years in an instant. She lowers her eyes, then her head, in complete dejection, as if her character's hedonistic, empty life had flashed before her to reveal the darkness of the world.

Speaking of Elizabeth Taylor in later years, Eva said, "She wasn't very friendly back then. We get along better now."

Elizabeth's reserve surely had to do with Zsa Zsa, who, owing to Taylor's marriage to Nicky Hilton, narrowly missed becoming her mother-in-law. In later decades, Zsa Zsa and Elizabeth became friends, although wary ones. Taylor liked to needle Zsa Zsa by calling her "Mother." Zsa Zsa was quick to point out on talk shows that "this is ridiculous, since we are the same age." Except that "Mother" was born in 1917, and Elizabeth in 1932.

If you must watch a Dean Martin-Jerry Lewis comedy, *Artists and Models* (1955) is perhaps the least unbearable. Directed by Frank Tashlin as a long cartoon, it offers Dorothy Malone, who was such a pro that she manages to act a bit even here; Garboesque Anita Ekberg, who can steal any scene just by standing still; Shirley MacLaine; and Eva as a Russian spy who vamps Jerry Lewis.

Here, Eva lowers her voice to a throaty chest register and speaks in slow, seductive whispers. Owing to such careful line readings, her accent recedes. This is how she should have spoken in all her performances. Unfortunately, in many scenes she is shot in profile so that, owing to a weak jawline, she looks matronly and a bit staid. Eva required full-face cinematography in order to glow.

Chapter 20

Moulin Rouge

Films about artists and their lives usually go astray. Two examples: *Lust for Life*, starring Kirk Douglas as Van Gogh, and *The Agony and the Ecstasy*, with Charlton Heston as Michelangelo. One reason for the failure of such biopics is the difficulty of showing an artist at work: it's seldom engrossing onscreen or off, just as movies about writers must rely on everything *but* what a writer does. In the movies, a painter at the easel or an author at a keyboard holds as much interest as a dentist filling teeth.

John Huston poured much love into *Moulin Rouge*, since Henri de Toulouse-Lautrec was one of his favorite painters. The director owned several of his works. Watching the movie is like seeing the Lautrec catalogue raisonné come to life across the screen, for Huston's color palette matches the painter's own. The result is that Huston's re-creation of the paintings, and of fin-de-siècle Paris, succeeds better than his scripted biography of Toulouse-Lautrec. Therein lay the aesthetic challenge, which Huston met head-on. To a great extent, his visual accomplishment hides the picture's flaws, so that *Moulin Rouge* stands among the iconic films of the 1950s.

"From the first," Zsa Zsa recalled, "John Huston had a paralyzing effect on me. He was the kind of dour man who makes me feel that he thinks everything I say to him is a lie."

Huston didn't want her for the part of the dancer and singer Jane Avril in *Moulin Rouge*, and he was hostile to her during much of the shoot. According to Stuart M. Kaminsky, author of *John Huston: Maker of Magic*, "Huston was unmerciful to Gabor, who had trouble with her lines. He had her repeat scenes over and over and sing [i.e., lip-synch] the film's theme song dozens of times. He criticized her for dropping words at the ends of sentences, and she replied that this was her natural Hungarian inflection." (Anyone studying Hungarian soon learns that this is indeed the case.)

How, then, did Zsa Zsa land the most important role of her career, the role for which she is best remembered? Huston had nothing to do with it, although he was a producer of the film, along with Jack Clayton, who is best remembered as director of such pictures as *Room at the Top* (1959) and *The Great Gatsby* (1974). The other producers were the British founders of Romulus Films, John Woolf and his brother, James Woolf. It was the latter who chose Zsa Zsa and stuck by his choice. In Hollywood scouting for an actress to play Jane Avril, Woolf met Zsa Zsa and realized immediately what she might bring to the part. "You're more like Jane Avril than anyone I can imagine," he told her. As a gay man, Woolf perhaps valued the oddball quality of Zsa Zsa's screen presence: the high-gloss mannerisms, along with the petulant, voluptuous ego of a drag queen, plus the camp accent of a Moon Goddess—all of this, plus eye-popping beauty, made her as indelible as a Dietrich or a Mae West. It was perhaps Woolf also who acceded to demands from Zsa Zsa's agent that she receive star billing, even though she appears in a mere handful of scenes and her total screen time amounts to no more than eight or ten minutes. But her name comes second in the credits, under that of José Ferrer, who plays Toulouse-Lautrec.

"Almost from the day the script arrived," Zsa Zsa remembered, "I began learning my lines. In Jane Avril I saw myself—or the self I wanted to be." Zsa Zsa was no dummy, though sometimes she might appear so. Reading the script, she grasped the melancholy subtext that ultimately turns the film, for some viewers, into a Technicolor nightmare. On page after page she found what she considered "lovely, heartbreaking scenes, as if my own heart were speaking the words."

John Huston surely knew that if he made *Moulin Rouge* in Hollywood it would end up as Dore Schary's picture, or Darryl Zanuck's, or Jack Warner's. Meaning a big beached whale of an enterprise, chopped by censors, with no doubt a tacked-on happy ending to qualify as family entertainment. Huston was having none of it. The Huston of *Moulin Rouge* is a European director, literally and figuratively. He shot *Moulin Rouge* in Paris and London, with an international cast that included no native-born Americans in leading roles except for José Ferrer, whose Hispanic heritage qualified him as quasi-European although he was born in Puerto Rico and thus a U.S. citizen. (Two later Huston films, *Reflections in a Golden Eye* and *The Dead*, have the look and feel of European works.)

"I want this film to look as though Toulouse-Lautrec himself directed it," Huston told his director of photography, Oswald Morris. Together they devised a system of running the film past a specialized light to fog it before it was loaded into the camera. Their next step was to produce the desired effect with the help of gauzes. Huston also hired Eliot Elisofon, a photographer employed by *Life* magazine, to experiment with new techniques and special filters in the use of Technicolor. In collaboration with consultants from the Technicolor laboratories—or in spite of them, according to some reports—Huston, Morris, and Elisofon created a muted palette of soft, flattened tones that contradicted the usual saturated colors of the Technicolor process. Going further still, Huston wanted his actors photographed under blue lights. Zsa Zsa recalled yet another special effect: "All about us were prop men with machines puffing blue smoke. John wanted everything to appear as Toulouse-Lautrec saw the world around him, in shadows of blue and green—the colors that haunt his paintings and express the sadness of his spirit." These mood-colors functioned somewhat like motifs in music and literature. As in the paintings and posters, so in the film: vivid colors in the foreground, blue-green shadows behind. Zsa Zsa's costumes, designed by Schiaparelli in crimson and regal purple, are the best example of Huston's technique in re-creating Toulouse-Lautrec's palette on celluloid. In one scene, she blazes in a red gown, with even redder jewelry—ruby tiara, ruby necklace and earrings. In another, gowned in black with a long boa of warmest sunflower yellow and matching plumed hat, she looks like a ravishing bumblebee.

The happy result of such extraordinary attention to detail is a film that seems to recapture the light, the smoke, the very air of nighttime Paris as savored by habitués of the Moulin Rouge. But also the narrow, cobblestoned streets and the cluttered apartment of the afflicted artist, whose growth stopped in childhood owing to a fall that stunted both legs. Toulouse-Lautrec reached a height of only four and a half feet. Owing to his tortured sense of inadequacy, and to the impossibility of finding a woman to return his love, he died in 1901 as a result of severe alcoholism and other ailments. He was thirty-seven years old. During his lifetime, and ever since, Toulouse-Lautrec and the famous cabaret with the red windmill on its roof have seemed conjoined, even though the original Moulin Rouge burned in 1915. (Soon rebuilt, it still packs in tourists by the busload.) According to Gerstle Mack in his 1938 biography of Toulouse-Lautrec, "Among the picturesque cabarets, dance halls, cafés-concerts, restaurants of every sort, hole-in-the-wall dives, and every sort of establishment catering to macabre, fantastic, or hilarious tastes, none ranked higher during the painter's prime than Le Moulin Rouge."

Huston wished to show all of that and more, but to ward off the howls of offended puritans he and co-author of the screenplay Anthony Veiller sanitized the Lautrec story. Even so, illicit suggestions jostle one another in the final cut: cancan dancers in lacy pantaloons flinging up skirts to show front side and back; streetwalkers; seedy taverns where the consumption of absinthe resembles an opium den; brothels; and a hint of lesbianism as two women, pressed together, twirl around the dance floor of the Moulin Rouge. Huston's only significant clash with the Hollywood production code had to do with an advertising poster that showed a cancan dancer's exposed thigh. The leg was soon edited, *Moulin Rouge* opened in late December 1952 in Los Angeles to qualify for Oscar consideration, and Zsa Zsa's hour of triumph came in February 1953 at the New York premiere.

No one, however, was immune to right-wing tyranny at the height of the Red Scare, and so a phalanx of American Legion protesters showed up on December 27, 1952, at the Fox Wilshire Theater in Los Angeles for the *Moulin Rouge* premiere. "American Legion Bans José Ferrer" was a typical sign held aloft. Another was "Communist Press Praises John Huston." The protesters were disgruntled because Huston, in 1947, had helped to form the Committee for the First Amendment, an action group in support of the Hollywood Ten and others affected by the black list. Members of the group included Lucille Ball, Humphrey Bogart, Lauren Bacall, Myrna Loy, Bette Davis, Groucho Marx, Lena Horne, Gene Kelly, and many others.

Ferrer, a liberal Democrat, was tarred as a communist sympathizer. Zsa Zsa, considered a refugee from communist

Hungary even though she had not seen her native country since 1941, remained above suspicion. During the witch hunt of the early fifties, with Hollywood fogged in by fear, José Ferrer was taking no chances. He wired the American Legion that he would be glad to join the veterans in their "fight against communism." A few days later, he denounced his fellow actor Paul Robeson for accepting the Stalin Peace Prize. Among Huston's reasons for moving to Ireland a bit later was his dislike of American political paranoia.

"She moved like a tank," said Oswald Morris, referring to Zsa Zsa. It is doubtful, of course, that Zsa Zsa ever moved like a tank, though Huston's intimidation may have temporarily stiffened her spine. One thing she did extremely well onscreen and off was to walk with confidence and grace, and in ballroom scenes throughout her career she glides across the floor with swan-like ease. Morris, as Huston's crony and director of photography on *Moulin Rouge*, no doubt absorbed the director's prejudice against her. Morris added that he and Huston asked Colette Marchand, another star of the picture, to show Zsa Zsa how to move. If so, the instruction seems misguided because Marchand had trained as a ballet dancer and Zsa Zsa's character, Jane Avril, was a self-taught dancer who, in her youth, was treated for the movement disorder known as St. Vitus dance. The dance style she invented, captured only in a few photographs and in Lautrec's work, evokes a spidery grace that verges on the grotesque. Nor is Zsa Zsa called upon to dance. The script—and Huston—portrayed Jane Avril only as a singer, and whatever Oswald Morris's reservations, he made Zsa Zsa the most dazzling woman in the film.

She first appears ten minutes into the opening sequence in long shot at the top of a flight of stairs at the Moulin Rouge. She is singing what became known as "The Song from *Moulin Rouge*" (dubbed by Muriel Smith, who appears in the film as Aicha, the fiery Algerian cancan dancer). The camera glides up the stairs to meet her, then pulls back and back to show her long descent of the staircase. With each step she makes Lautrec's Jane Avril come to life. Zsa Zsa's willowy arm movements replicate exactly Lautrec's posters and tableaux of Jane Avril. Pauline Kael's comment on those movements—"her gestures while she pretends to sing are idiotic"—couldn't be more wrongheaded. Zsa Zsa uses not only her arms but her entire body to capture the wavy, art nouveau undulations of Jane Avril through the eyes of Toulouse-Lautrec.

At the end of the picture, the artist lies on his deathbed. Unshaven, distraught, he looks—perhaps intentionally on the part of Huston—like Proust as photographed in his own final hours. Hallucinating as he dies, Lautrec sees the characters he has sketched at the Moulin Rouge materialize through the wall and, in feverish montage, dance wraith-like to his bedside. The cancan dancers; Chocolat, the young black dancer; double-jointed Valentin, of the exaggerated nose and prominent Adam's apple; and finally Jane Avril, in a haunting valedictory that Zsa Zsa claimed to have invented: "Henri, my dear, we just heard you were dying. We simply *had* to say goodbye. It was *divine* knowing you. We will see you later, of course. But now, if you forgive me, I must fly. There is the most beautiful creature waiting for me at Maxim's. Goodbye, Henri. Goodbye!"

She blows a kiss and vanishes into air.

Fast-forward to 1983. Zsa Zsa, looking years younger than she did in 1953, stood before a stellar audience in Los Angeles and spoke with affection about the director who hadn't wanted her at all in his picture. By the end of *Moulin Rouge*, however, they had become friends owing to their mutual love of horses. Addressing her old nemesis at the American Film Institute Salute to John Huston, she said, "John dahling, you didn't want me for the movie *Moulin Rouge*. Before seven hundred extras, you screamed into the loud-speakers, 'Miss Gabor, you can't act, you can't sing, and you can't dance! At least show your face to the camera!'

"You put a big red heart on it and you said, 'Make love to the camera.' John dahling, you made me what I am today—rich and famous—but you never married me!"

She might have added that owing to her role in the film, forever after when she entered a nightclub or a restaurant, the orchestra would play "The Song from *Moulin Rouge*." In a sense, John Huston not only made her famous, but immortal. When she died, every obituary named *Moulin Rouge* as the high point of her career. One of the better elegies echoed her final lines from the picture. Writing in *Time* magazine, Richard Corliss concluded: "Mademoiselle Gabor, you silly delight, it was divine knowing you."

Chapter 21

The Destroyer

Moulin Rouge made Zsa Zsa the movie star she wanted to be. That success, however, left her vulnerable to forfeiture. Having almost reached the top, she faced a crisis: either to climb higher, or else to fall back into a great passion. Had she not met Porfirio Rubirosa, and spent the night of February 10, 1953, with him after the New York premiere of *Moulin Rouge*, she might at least have held her position. It would have been difficult for her to move beyond second-tier stardom because of her heavy accent and her basic lack of interest in acting as opposed to starring. Hollywood liked her, and studio brass considered that whatever it was she did, she did well enough. Besides, the studios could always use a new blonde.

As Marilyn Monroe's career zoomed at 20th Century Fox, the other studios—and Fox itself—stockpiled sexy blondes to compete with, and, should need arise, to replace M.M. The plan was that if Marilyn became uppity, they would bring in Jayne Mansfield, Cleo Moore, Anita Ekberg, Sheree North, Diana Dors, Zsa Zsa, or any one of a dozen others. None of these, however, outshone Marilyn, who survived by a couple of years the very studios that created her and later tried to sabotage their creation. But the threat remained, and a morals clause was part of the boilerplate in every contract. The studio system required sluts onscreen, while Hollywood hypocrisy demanded middle-class respectability, or its semblance, to please moralistic America. Some of these actresses made unwise career choices; others failed to play by Hollywood rules and so found themselves left out.

In Zsa Zsa's case, she mistook libido for love. After an in-the-headlines romance with Rubirosa throughout 1953 and after, during which she neglected career and all else, she returned to Hollywood to find the front gates closed. From then on, she was directed to the service entrance. All was not lost, however, for she did her best screen work later, although in Europe, not Hollywood. But Zsa Zsa's reputation was ruined. Even so, she might have made a comeback, like Ingrid Bergman. For an actress, a few divorces never hurt, and everyone carried on extramarital affairs, but the rules stated unequivocally: Discretion Above All. Survival could be arranged if justified by box office grosses, as in the case of Lana Turner after her daughter stabbed Lana's gangster lover to death. *Imitation of Life*, a moneymaker, kept Lana afloat. And Elizabeth Taylor triumphed despite breaking up the marriage of Eddie Fisher and Debbie Reynolds and then scandalizing several continents before settling down with Richard Burton.

Zsa Zsa's margin for error, however, was microscopic. In the eyes of Hollywood, she had a small but visible talent, though no one was able to define it precisely. Even worse, every day brought her closer to forty, yet Zsa Zsa had no intention of playing someone's mother. When she sliced off a decade, she believed it really gone. Oscar Levant on television said what everyone knew: "Zsa Zsa has discovered the secret of perpetual middle age." A big dose of sanctimony would have worked in her favor, but Hungarians lack skill in that game. Their culture values candor; bluntness is the done thing. It's part of their sophisticated earthiness.

Copius tears could often resurrect a fallen star, especially if photographed for the papers. Zsa Zsa's eyes stayed dry. An afternoon of repentence with Hedda Hopper or Louella Parsons, supplemented with expensive Christmas gifts to those ladies, might have labeled her an outstanding mother of the year, along with Joan Crawford. And if only Zsa Zsa had dragged little Francesca to midnight Mass at Church of the Good Shepherd, she could have been Hollywood's newest Mary Magdalene. (Not as farfetched an idea as some might think. She was mentioned for a biblical drama titled *Joseph and the Wife of Potiphar*, to be filmed in Egypt with Errol Flynn beginning in January 1954. A significant role, it might have elevated both career and reputation. But the picture was not made.)

Zsa Zsa, however, would not, or could not, relinquish her adulterous passion for Rubirosa. Adulterous because she was still married to George Sanders. Although Rubirosa married twice after the climax of their affair, he and Zsa Zsa were unable to stay apart. Their flames rekindled again and again until 1958, when she saw him for the last time.

Porfirio Rubirosa was, above all else, the dark secret love in the erotic fantasies of many women and not a few men. Described as the "Caribbean Casanova" in the tabloid press of the fifties, Rubirosa had a great secret that remained only guessed at and whispered about until later decades when it was revealed by a man who stood beside him at a urinal, and peeked. "I thought I was seeing Yul Brynner in a turtleneck," he said. This macrophallic report flashed across the celebrity network, finding its way into print only after Rubirosa's death in 1965. Other witnesses compared the famous appendage to the large brown peppermills used in some restaurants, a comparison that led Parisian waiters to nickname their pepper dispensers *les rubirosas*. Delighted with his reputation as a male sex object, Rubirosa smiled when a French journalist described him as "*toujours prêt*" (always ready).

He was born in 1909 into a bourgeois family in the Dominican Republic. In a country that serves as a case study in corruption and political vice, Rubirosa grew up a scion of privilege in a typical banana republic setting: dictators, revolutions, torture, murders, and endless strong-arm meddling by the United States. In 1915, his father was appointed chargé d'affaires in the Dominican Republic's embassy in France, so that young Rubi, as he was called, ripened in Paris and acquired the sophistication of an *homme du monde*. Not until 1926 did he return to the Dominican Republic. In 1930, a rigged election brought Rafael Trujillo to power. Almost overnight Trujillo became the country's immovable dictator, a position he held until his assassination in 1961. His long tenure was one of terror and cruelty matched by such dictatorships as those of Saddam Hussein in Iraq, Pol Pot in Cambodia, and the Kim dynasty of North Korea.

In 1931 Rubirosa met Trujillo, who became the younger man's patron. Their relationship endured, although at times the dictator became so enraged at his protegé that Rubirosa fled the country. Generalissimo Trujillo, as he styled himself, was a bumpkin in general's garb covered with spurious medals. Rubirosa's erudition and savoir faire charmed the old vulgarian, who appointed him to the diplomatic corps. His first posting was to Berlin at the time of the 1936 Olympic Games, with later assignments to Buenos Aires, Havana, Rome, and Brussels. He served for many years in the Dominican embassy in France, where his chief duties were ceremonial and amatory. In later years, press reports named him as ambassador; this was never the case. Asked by a reporter about his specific duties, Rubirosa replied, "Work?

But I have no time for work." To another such query, he answered, "Women are my full-time job."

The perfunctory demands of his office left ample time for love, and for polo and race cars. Owing to his handsome face, trim athletic build, and requisite social grace, café society welcomed him. His first marriage, to Flor de Oro Trujillo, the dictator's daughter, lasted from 1932 to 1938. During World War II, he was the husband of French film star Danielle Darrieux, and after her the trophy spouse of Doris Duke for just over a year. It was a year well spent, for Rubirosa's bounty from the woman said to be the world's richest included a check for $500,000 as a wedding present; several sports cars and as many polo ponies; a converted B-25 aircraft; and a seventeenth-century mansion in Paris, at 46 rue de Bellechasse, a house the size of a small chateau.

Some of his history and accomplishments Zsa Zsa knew when they met on that winter night in Manhattan in 1953, others she would learn in time. It surely belies her reputation as a gold digger, however, that she didn't marry him. She herself said it on *Bachelor's Haven*: "I'm a wonderful housekeeper. Every time I get a divorce, I keep the house." A Parisian chateau would be quite a house to keep, along with a chunk of his bulging bank account.

"Rubi was a sickness to me," she said, meaning that the man himself intoxicated her and would have done so had he been a pauper or a ploughman. To illustrate Zsa Zsa's erotic affliction, and its metaphorical source, I quote a poem from the eighteenth century, William Blake's "The Sick Rose":

> *O Rose thou are sick.*
> *The invisible worm,*
> *That flies in the night*
> *In the howling storm:*

Has found out thy bed
Of crimson joy:
And his dark secret love
Does thy life destroy.

Change the word "life" in that final line to "career" and it describes the gaping professional wound that Zsa Zsa never recovered from. That damage wasn't caused by sex, or infatuation, or high living—all of these a top-energy woman like Zsa Zsa could have incorporated into her schedule. Rubirosa, however, insisted, for the two years they spent together, on her full attention, which she found herself unable to withhold. Even so, had he been a reputable lover, they might have compromised. But beneath his seductive charm— the low-hung baritone and the perfect grooming, the roomful of roses he delivered to her suite at the Plaza after their first night together, his warm maleness in bed even when not aroused, the Continental manners of an aristocrat, except when angered—Rubirosa might have sprung from the pen of Edgar Allan Poe, if Blake had not already imagined his dangerous type. Zsa Zsa didn't guess, until much too late, that the real Rubirosa flew by night in a howling storm.

Who hasn't encountered the type? If survived, they leave a festering bite mark. Aristotle Onassis was also such a one; he maimed Maria Callas. Benumbed by the sexual power of that rustic billionaire, she neglected her career, lost her magnificent voice and ultimately her will to live because of unrequited love when he ditched her for Jacqueline Kennedy.

If Rubirosa had not existed, a novelist would have invented him, or a script writer, as the charismatic demon lover in a film noir. Although never convicted of a crime, Rubi was a frequent suspect. As far back as the 1930s, he aroused the suspicion of New York police who believed him complicit in the murder of a Dominican dissident working to overthrow Trujillo. On other occasions Rubirosa happened to appear, with payoff money, in the city where one of the dictator's enemies was to be rubbed out. And stayed just long enough . . .

In later years, his associates included the notorious mobster Sam Giancana. Around the same time, Rubi's friendship with Frank Sinatra included flights on Sinatra's private jet with questionable fellow passengers and introductions to useful third parties. Rubirosa became an intimate of John F. Kennedy, who shared his interest in women and whose incautious pursuits while president endangered the United States more than once. The dots have never been entirely connected; they may never be. The point here, however, is the nexus between Washington, the Dominican Republic, organized crime in the U.S. and throughout the Caribbean, the Cuban Revolution, the Mafia and its fellow travelers such as Sinatra and the Kennedys, Trujillo's assassination of political enemies with the aid of his government's employee, viz., Rubirosa—shadowy figures and their dark connections cast Rubirosa as the real-life player in a drama that is at best unsavory, at worst soaked in blood.

Shawn Levy, in his biography *The Last Playboy: The High Life of Porfirio Rubirosa,* delved into all aspects of that life, with emphasis on the playboy's associations with Trujillo and with Zsa Zsa. Among the many books that chronicle Trujillo's atrocities, the most succinct is *The Changing Sky*, a collection of essays by Norman Lewis. The following passage comes from those pages.

"The best known of Trujillo's resoluteness of purpose occurred when in 1937 he decided to stop the illegal entry of Haitian sugar-cutters from across the border, and a number estimated at a minimum of 7,000 and at a maximum as 20,000 of these defenseless people were bayoneted by his troops." (Other writers upped the total to 30,000 or more, of men, women, and children.) Among Trujillo's other methods for keeping order was to drop his enemies into vats of boiling water while alive. Others he fed to sharks.

He ruled every facet of Dominican life. From Shawn Levy: "Santo Domingo would be renamed Ciudad Trujillo; calendars would all be dated according to the Era of Trujillo, with 1930 as Year One. In the course of time, every home in the country would boast a sign reading *God and Trujillo*—often right out on the roof in large letters." Any house that omitted the obligatory homage risked destruction.

This was the world that Zsa Zsa entered, probably unwittingly. Her romance with Rubi, gaudy and all-consuming, obscured the background of fear and bloodshed. Many times she said, "I know nothing about politics." Indeed, no one ever accused her of reading *U.S. News and World Report*. In her ignorance she resembles those wives and mothers in *The Godfather* who ask no questions and have no wish for answers.

Although Rubirosa cannot be called the defining man in her life, he stands at the fork in her road. With him, she took the off-ramp that led in the opposite direction from MGM and Fox, away from name directors like John Huston and Vincente Minnelli, and from Oscar night at the Pantages Theatre, from cover stories in *Photoplay* and *Life*. Like figures in mythology, and in Kafka, she didn't recognize her metamorphosis until it had taken place. Afterward, she remained in many ways the same Zsa Zsa across the decades, from the late 1950s until her final appearances in the twentieth century's dying days. But a change occurred as she traveled on twisting, shadowy Rubirosa Road. After a few years, she found herself on a one-way street with turn-offs to cheapo pictures like *Country Music Holiday* in 1958, and a long, narrow trail of depressing TV game shows, weekly dramas, daytime programs aimed at housewives, variety specials, and finally Jack Paar's late-night talk show, where she became a regular for several years. When Paar retired, Zsa

Zsa talked the same talk for thirty years more as she drifted into self-parody.

Onscreen, she devolved to such embarrassments as *Frankenstein's Great Aunt Tillie* in 1984, punctuated by a long string of cameos in sad endeavors until her final two minutes in *A Very Brady Sequel*, in 1996, as herself—the only character, finally, that she knew how to play.

Chapter 22

Honky-tonk Gabor

Throughout 1953, Zsa Zsa's euphoria resembled the delirious effects of nitrous oxide, or laughing gas. If Rubi wasn't on a plane from Paris or South America to see her in New York or Hollywood, she was flying to him. Telegrams arrived daily; if no telegram then an intercontinental phone call. The lyric of every love song had come true for Zsa Zsa, their limerence embodied in Rubirosa.

And yet she loved her husband, difficult, sardonic, lazy-bones George Sanders. Extreme, giddy happiness with Rubi notwithstanding, Zsa Zsa found herself in a state of cognitive dissonance, defined as a person's unease in a situation where two or more emotions or judgments compete for dominance. Zsa Zsa's heart stretched in opposite directions. At the erotic end of the spectrum, Rubirosa and orgasmic ecstasy. A hundred and eighty degrees distant, laughter and fun with George, and deep love, for he understood her and kept her always a bit off kilter, which she liked. With George, she could linger at breakfast in a robe and no makeup, hair uncombed, looking every day of thirty-three, thirty-four, thirty-five . . . He helped with bathing the dogs: he handed her the soap. George was the old one, he often said so himself, and to him she was always Sari the kid, and Cokiline, his spicy little cookie.

But for Rubi, she must outdo even the Jane Avril that had earned her such plaudits. He demanded a Zsa Zsa raised to the tenth power. Or else. After all, as she well knew, any woman in the world would come if he beckoned. Rubi's lifted eyebrow meant conquest. At times, she felt herself on a swinging bridge high in the air, rocked by Rubi's assurance that no other woman mattered but unsettled by the vertigo. And always a high-pitched little question wafted on those lofty breezes, as if chirped by a skittish greenfinch, What if? What if?

What if Rubi ran short of money, not an impossible scenario in view of his spending. Women owed him a living, this Zsa Zsa recognized as his moral and financial credo, even as she tried to push away that insight. At least she had the distraction of work, and in mid-April 1953 she began filming, in Paris, *L'Ennemi public numéro un* (aka *The Most Wanted Man*), with French superstar comedian Fernandel.

His trademark was a long, expressive horse face, which made his good-natured, blunderbuss goofiness irresistibly funny. Fernandel was the Woody Allen of France, or more specifically the Allen of *Take the Money and Run* and *Everything You Always Wanted to Know About Sex*—that is, before Allen mistook himself for a matinee idol. Fernandel wanted Zsa Zsa, and no other, to costar in his next picture. Watching it, you can see why. In French, she's not only a deadpan comedienne but also an impeccable, disciplined comic actress. For once, her onscreen vanity doesn't trip her up.

Fernandel's character is a friendly beast of a man who works in a department store. Fired after a series of mishaps, he goes to the movies, where he seats himself beside a man who turns out to be a dangerous gangster. The gangster inadvertently takes Fernandel's overcoat; a bit later, unsuspecting Fernandel leaves the theatre wearing the gangster's. In the subway, he reaches into a pocket and, to his astonishment and the shrieking panic of fellow riders, pulls out a handgun. He is arrested, the police announce the capture of Public Enemy Number One, and local mob boss Lola—played by Zsa Zsa—plots his escape from jail. (Since the shadowy real boss is unknown to his syndicate, she takes wimpy Fernandel for the capo. After all, the headlines called him that. It adds to the comedy that she's much tougher and smarter than he.)

When, in her first scene, a mobster underling dares to address her as Lola, she glowers like Gale Sondergaard and snaps: "*Mademoiselle* Lola!" Masterminding the jailbreak and subsequent hideout, Zsa Zsa commands her every scene with timing and movement. Nor is glamour sacrificed. She's as chic as Audrey Hepburn, especially in a scene where she wears slacks and a white shirt with rolled-up sleeves, and another where a turban covers her hair and she foils the police chief with designer glasses.

Another revelation: her voice. Under control, it sounds an octave lower than her usual shrill nasality. Zsa Zsa speaks French with a slight accent, though it doesn't take over as so often in English. Directed by Henri Verneuil, she underplays. Zsa Zsa Gabor is nowhere in sight; she's entirely *Mademoiselle* Lola.

For two months, during the filming of *L'Ennemi public*, Zsa Zsa's official residence was the luxurious Plaza Athénée on the Right Bank. In reality, her suite saw little use, since Rubirosa collected her at the end of each day's shoot and drove her in his Ferrari or another car from his fleet to his house on the Left Bank, in the rue de Bellechasse. From time to time, little Francesca came to visit, for she liked Uncle Rubi enormously.

The house was run by a staff of half a dozen, including

concierge, chef, maids, and Rubi's valet. "Within," Zsa Zsa recalled, "all was perfect and in exquisite taste: the paintings, the Aubusson rugs, the furnishings, polished and gleaming, even the scents I loved: leather, tobacco, sandalwood." On her first visit, Rubi gave her a tour. They began in the kitchen, continued "to his dining room with apple-green and gold paneling identical to that at Versailles, and wall cabinets holding his collection of china and porcelain. We mounted to the upper floors. On the third floor was a gymnasium complete with boxing ring, rubbing table, and a steam bath." In another room, he showed her "saddles and riding equipment of every kind, and to my surprise bullfighting costumes and paraphernalia. On the walls were photographs of his favorite polo ponies, the standard of his team which had won the world's championship in Deauville the year before, and his helmets. Everywhere in the house—in the bathrooms, the library, the kitchen, the concierge's rooms, the maids' rooms—trophies, trophies, trophies, the gold and silver loving cups awarded him in polo, or for racing his Ferraris and Mercedes-Benzes on courses in Europe and South America."

Like France and like Paris, Rubi's world, whatever its flaws, seemed for a time more real and more attractive to Zsa Zsa than the world of Hollywood. Had she pursued a career in France, she might now occupy a place in cinema history alongside Martine Carol, Geneviève Page, and Michèle Morgan. Nor would *l'affaire Rubirosa* have sullied her reputation; quite the contrary.

During her protracted stay in Paris, Zsa Zsa geared up for a visit to the Hungarian embassy on behalf of her father. "The young chargé d'affaires received me," she recalled. "The picture with Fernandel was a huge success behind the Iron Curtain. Father wrote how proud he was of me—'Our Zsa Zsa is on all the marquees.' At the embassy, the young man said, 'Miss Gabor, it's so nice to see you and talk to you. We all love you in Hungary. Why don't you come back to your own country and become our national actress?' He said I would receive a villa and an allowance from the government."

Rubirosa accompanied her to the embassy and, owing to his jealousy, waited until she finished her interview. The chargé d'affaires invited her to a later café rendezvous, which she dared not accept because of watchdog Rubi. She did consider how she might arrange an assignation with the young man if her charms could secure the release of Vilmos. Such a meeting did not take place, however, but her request was partially granted all the same. Eight months later Vilmos and his wife were allowed to leave the peasant house in Budakeszi and return to Budapest. There they lived first in a government apartment, then in a somewhat better one that his daughters secured for him. Soon it also became easier to reach him by telephone.

George Sanders: "The Las Vegas act of the three Gabor Sisters—Zsa Zsa, Eva, and Magda—is the greatest agricultural achievement of all time. Never before have three hens laid a single egg."

Eva agreed. She had misgivings from the start, but under pressure from Zsa Zsa, Magda, and of course Jolie, she finally agreed to the nightclub act called "The Gabors: This Is Our Life." Opening on December 28, 1953, at the Last Frontier Hotel, they did two shows nightly during a two-week engagement. "Men," a specialty number from the act, was singled out by the reviewer in *Billboard* magazine as proving that "the girls can't sing, either." But given this sample lyric from the act, who could: "Our mother told us we should have the skin that men love to touch—MINK!"

Owing to generally poor reviews and the circus-like atmosphere that surrounded their Las Vegas engagement, Eva refused to continue in the show after their initial commitment. The resulting loss of a hundred thousand dollars in future bookings caused many an abrupt hang-up and slammed door in Gaborland. Perhaps to spite Zsa Zsa, Eva spoke out. "It was horrible!" she told a reporter. "The lines were bad and the act was bad and yet everybody came to see all three Gabor sisters in one place."

It might have turned out worse. A fourth hen—Jolie—flapped her wings and squawked to join the act, but the girls were having none of it despite Mama's claims that the hotel wanted her onstage, as well. "You are not an actress!" they scolded. Her snarky rejoinder: "Such actresses like you are, *I am*!"

Not onstage, but stage managing her daughters—this became Jolie's role during the final week of December 1953. Before their noisy descent on the desert city, however, all the Gabors had assembled at Zsa Zsa's house for Christmas. Unlike the little town of Bethlehem, no stillness lay over Bel Air. George had recently filed for divorce, and Zsa Zsa was shattered. In her confusion, she clutched Rubirosa like a life raft. Believing that because they loved each other, she and George could stray but always retrace their steps to the marriage bed, she had misjudged his limit. Had she conducted her affair with Rubirosa with discretion, meaning a minimum of headlines, George might have busied himself elsewhere for a time. His mother-in-law advised precisely that. He spoke frankly to her in his distress, telling her that Zsa Zsa had embarrassed and humiliated him with her scandalous behavior.

"Don't you see," said Jolie, looking up from a pearl necklace she had been examining through a magnifying glass, "it is only *pour passer le temps*." More bewildered than ever by Hungarians, he soon decided that the time had passed when he could excuse Zsa Zsa's Dominican pastime.

On Christmas Eve, presents having been exchanged, they all sat down to dinner—Zsa Zsa, Rubi, Eva, Magda, Jolie, and six-year-old Francesca. Unrestrainable, the little girl jumped up and ran to the Christmas tree to play with her gift from Rubi: an elaborate electric train that he had set up himself and that tooted and squealed as it whizzed along the track. "Oh, Uncle Rubi," she exclaimed when she saw it, running to kiss him.

But cheer was absent. Rubi seemed preoccupied, even depressed. Jolie resented her exclusion from the Las Vegas engagement, and Eva's intuition urged her to run away, but of course it was too late. Magda, always the most serious, didn't care for the too-muchness of this holiday, nor for Rubirosa and his drinking, and she had agreed to Las Vegas only for the money. Since the war, Magda made an effort at gaiety, but for a Holocaust survivor merriment verged on sacrilege. She remembered the suffering, she remembered the dead.

And stage fright gripped them all. Despite attempts at cheer, this was neither a Merry Christmas nor a *Boldog Karácsonyt* like those of old back in Budapest. The Gabors sipped Tokay and champagne, while Rubirosa, whose alcoholic excess rankled Jolie in particular, barely touched his food. Empty cocktail glasses encircled his plate. Holiday fatigue sent everyone to bed early.

Zsa Zsa and Rubi in bed, the conversation resumed, or more precisely the debate.

"Why won't you marry me?" he demanded, as he had done dozens of times in recent days.

"Because I love George," was her standard answer.

"But he is divorcing you! How can you be so stupid?"

"He is always my husband. You don't understand what we have."

On and on, past midnight, into the small hours, as Rubi drank from the bottle he kept nearby.

"I ran into Barbara Hutton in Deauville recently," he said, and his words hung in the air. "At the Casino. And we went out together."

"Rubi, why are you telling me these things? I know that when we are not together you—"

"She wants to marry me, but I love only you."

"Marry you? And do you want to marry her?"

"What you won't do, she will. And her millions . . ."

George, having filed for divorce, learned from his lawyer the financial consequences to a husband in California: heavy alimony directed to the wife. If caught *in flagrante*, however, the court might find more favorably for the aggrieved party.

Several years after George's death, his close friend, British actor Brian Aherne, published a book about their friendship. The title: *A Dreadful Man*, which Aherne used ironically since he knew George's good points as well as the less attractive ones. Aherne's account of the remainder of that Christmas night seems the most accurate, since he heard George's version, then Zsa Zsa's, and even Rubirosa's. As a disinterested third party, Aherne recounted events with dry understatement not available to the participants themselves.

"Late at night on Christmas Eve," he wrote, "wearing dirty blue jeans, a sweatshirt and a beard, accompanied by two detectives and carrying a brick that he had carefully gift-wrapped, George stealthily crossed the lawn of Zsa Zsa's house and placed a ladder against the wall." What followed recalls a prank from any one of a thousand Hollywood comedy-mysteries, for George and the detectives climbed to the balcony outside Zsa Zsa's window and, after a quiet moment of coordination, George shattered the window and stepped like a younger, more trim, and unbearded Santa Claus into her boudoir. Well acquainted with the layout, he switched on the light, held out his holiday offering, and said, "Merry Christmas, my dear!" Zsa Zsa's companion sprang up and rushed into the bathroom—too late, for the detectives had got their incriminating photos before the sleepers could realize what was happening.

"Zsa Zsa behaved with perfect aplomb. Smiling and putting on a lacy dressing gown, she said, 'George dahling, how lovely to see you! You are just in time to get your Christmas present, which is under the tree. Let's go down and have a glass of champagne and I will give it to you.' She led the way downstairs, laughing gaily, gave George his present, gift-wrapped, and poured champagne for the detectives, who were enchanted with her." George, not really surprised at anything Zsa Zsa did, joined the merriment as though auditioning for a remake of *Miracle on 34th Street*. Zsa Zsa was sorry that George and his *vonderful* detectives couldn't stay for breakfast.

Francesca, dreaming of Father Christmas, learned a few years later that he, or rather Uncle Christmas, took chilly refuge in her mother's en suite bathroom. As for other members of the family—had their breakfast-table repartee the next morning been transcribed, the Ortonesque comedy might still be playing off-Broadway or in the West End. It was decided, however, that what happens in Gaborland stays in Gaborland. The same was not the case in Vegas. What happened there remained private for less than a day.

For Rubirosa, that Christmas Eve gathering, despite its Agatha Christie possibilities, ended not with murder but a bang and a hangover. Late on December 25, a caravan of limousines arrived to convey everyone to the airport, along with voluminous luggage. They were off to Vegas, where *the actresses*, Jolie sniffed, were to open at the Last Frontier on December 28.

Dress rehearsals for the Gabor opening were arduous, Zsa Zsa said, "for when I am with my sisters, each of us has her own will." Rubi, still drinking heavily, telephoned constantly with his same question, "Are you going to marry me?"

Newspapers coast to coast, with their many gossip and entertainment columns, buzzed with news of the Gabors in Las

Vegas, but even more with wild speculation: Will Zsa Zsa marry Rubirosa? Then, on December 27, the day before the Gabor opening, a trusted columnist tipped her off: he is planning to marry Barbara Hutton.

At last she knew the truth. Zsa Zsa flung open the door of her suite. "Now, Rubi," she commanded, "get out of this room and as long as I live I never want to see you again."

"No!" he said. "Say you'll marry me or I go back to New York and marry Barbara."

"Now get out," Zsa Zsa repeated.

"Why not? Tell me why not!"

"Because I love George, I've always loved him, and I'll always love him! Now get out of here and marry that woman."

Zsa Zsa piled into him and shoved. He slapped her, she fell against the door and banged her forehead. Screaming at him, she landed another punch and Rubirosa was gone.

From nearby suites, they flew to her side, Eva, Magda, Jolie, and Russell Birdwell, Zsa Zsa's publicist and the mastermind of the Las Vegas show. Birdwell called a doctor, who applied ice packs and administered a sedative to hysterical Zsa Zsa. Everyone knew by evening, less than twenty-four hours before the first show, that she would have an enormous shiner.

Sometime after nightfall, she woke up to a suite full of red roses. Rubi strikes again! Full of liquor and remorse, he had roamed around Vegas, taking in Marlene Dietrich's show at the Sahara and Lena Horne's at the Sands. He had lost thousands at the gambling tables. He cared nothing for Barbara Hutton, but he was determined to marry her.

When he knocked, Zsa Zsa let him in. The Q and A recommenced. He bent over her bed of woe and kissed her. "Darling, I love you," he said as he left for the airport. At the time, Rubi denied having struck Zsa Zsa. Some years later, however, he confessed that "once, during a tiff, she received a black eye," adding, "then she gave a party to show it off and have it photographed."

A party indeed, with everyone invited. In the early afternoon of December 28, just hours before Zsa Zsa, Eva, and Magda were to go onstage for their first show, Marlene Dietrich knocked on Zsa Zsa's door. Although she and Zsa Zsa were not fond of each other, Dietrich and Eva had formed a liaison and now, in the interest of damage control, Eva enlisted Marlene's help. "I've brought you some panstick to cover that eye," said Dietrich. She sat down on the bed. "He's a beast," she opined, "but he must love you very much to strike you like that." Zsa Zsa claimed that Dietrich, from the bedside, phoned gossip columnist Dorothy Kilgallen with the scoop.

Was Zsa Zsa properly grateful for such ministrations? Unfortunately not. "Next day Marlene turned against me," she said. "When she saw all those headlines, it was too much for her. She even denied she saw the black eye." Denial or not, it is true that Dietrich did not like being overshadowed by someone she considered an upstart.

Russell Birdwell spotted gold in Zsa Zsa's purple bruise. "Tell everybody!" he ordered. "And cover it with a black eye patch." After convincing her that such patches were not limited to pirates and the male models in Hathaway shirt advertisements, Birdwell called a press conference. "Make a lark out of the whole thing," he whispered as Zsa Zsa entered like a giddy buccaneer to flashbulbs and whistles.

Chapter 23

It Didn't Stay in Vegas

In a matter of hours Zsa Zsa and her eye patch became an iconic image, as famous as the picture of Marilyn Monroe's skirt blowing up on a New York sidewalk. The next night, dancers in Dietrich's show appeared in eye patches. At New Year's Eve parties around the country, black patches were the *dernier cri*, especially those encrusted with rhinestones. After the Vegas show closed and Zsa Zsa flew to New York, every reporter who met her plane had on a patch. Eva, Magda, and Jolie didn't find it funny: she had stolen the show. "Thank God, I only have one of you," chided Jolie. Eva especially resented being caught up in Zsa Zsa's exhibitionism. She guessed, and with reason, that her sister's ongoing sideshow diminished the chances that producers and casting directors would take her seriously as an actress. Who could gainsay her apprehension, for Eva would always be a Gabor, with all the perks and liabilities of the name.

Surely the most interesting feature of the Rubirosa-Hutton nuptials was the headlines. A typical one, from the *New York*

Daily News on December 29, 1953: RUBIROSA, SPURNED BY ZSA ZSA, TO WED BABS HUTTON TOMORROW. The marriage, such as it was, took place on December 30. A writer for the *Milwaukee Sentinel* captured the funereal atmosphere of the ceremony with this line: "The bride, for her fifth wedding, wore black and carried a scotch-and-soda." The coupling lasted fifty-three days, until February 20, 1954. Hutton was forty-one at the time, and owing to prescription drugs, alcohol, and myriad illnesses, could have passed for sixty. The quid pro quo of the marriage was always clear: sex for her, money for him. Whether the Woolworth heiress was really the world's second-richest woman or not, she paid well. In this case, two and a half million in cash, along with miscellaneous gifts including a coffee plantation back home in the Dominican Republic.

A week after the Las Vegas engagement, Zsa Zsa was in New York to emcee a fashion show. Early one morning the phone rang in her room at the Plaza. It was, of course, Rubirosa, bored and annoyed by the new wife he could barely tolerate. He was nearby; he begged to come up. Zsa Zsa refused, he hung up in a fury, but a few days later he telephoned from Palm Beach, where reporters swarmed day and night around the newlyweds. He bombarded Zsa Zsa with calls wherever she went. If the concept of stalking had existed at the time, Rubirosa might have been judged guilty.

The headlines would not go away, nor the feeding frenzy, and for a time newspaper stories about the pair—Zsa Zsa and Rubi, since Barbara Hutton, after fifty-three days as Mrs. Rubi, was both gone and forgotten—eclipsed the first issue of *Playboy* with its pictures of a nude Marilyn Monroe; the coronation in London; and the threat of nuclear war. From 1953 until 1955 and beyond, Zsa Zsa and Rubirosa's media avalanche foreshadowed that of Taylor and Burton in the early sixties and the much later downmarket one of Brad Pitt and Angelina Jolie.

Zsa Zsa, determined to forget him, signed for a Dean Martin-Jerry Lewis picture, *3 Ring Circus*. The shoot began in the middle of February 1954 at Paramount, then moved to Phoenix in April for several weeks of exteriors. While still at the studio, Zsa Zsa left the set to testify in George's divorce suit. "In spite of myself I cried on the stand," she said. "It was the first time I had ever shown my true feelings in public."

Accustomed to actressy tears on the witness stand, several costars and others at Paramount turned Zsa Zsa's distress into a comedy. "Lucky girl, you're free again," someone called out. This time it wasn't Kathryn Grayson who came to her rescue, but Grace Kelly, on break from a nearby set where she was filming *The Country Girl*. "Why don't you stop teasing her," she admonished the jokesters. "She's unhappier than you think." Remembering Grace's kindness, Zsa Zsa said, "I have always been grateful for her friendship that terrible day."

3 Ring Circus belongs, of course, to Martin and Lewis. Zsa Zsa and the other female costar, Joanne Dru, serve as accessories, each with a few brief scenes scattered through the picture. They did not like each other, and clashed often. After one dispute in which Joanne came out the winner, Zsa Zsa threatened, "I'll get even with you if it takes forever." Her adversary shot back, "It probably will, but aren't you rather old to talk about a future?"

To continue Zsa Zsa's Rubirosa-as-sickness metaphor . . . he trailed her to Phoenix, and she could find no antidote to his viral obsession, nor her own. In reality, if a cure existed she didn't want to find it. Even so, the world grew tired of Zsa Zsa and Rubi. Newspapers and magazines, however, must fill pages, and so paparazzi and reporters kept at it, famished for any new detail. Rubirosa, like Zsa Zsa, had a keen wit. He flew to Arizona in the private plane that Barbara Hutton had given him to replace the one from Doris Duke. Reporters surrounded him, demanding, "Where is Zsa Zsa?" and "What are you doing in Phoenix?"

"I was headed for Nicaragua," he answered, "but I was blown off course."

In spring, with Barbara Hutton divorced and Rubi a free man, he and Zsa Zsa announced their engagement. In June 1954 came an even more amazing announcement: they would costar in a film for Republic Pictures to be called *Western Affair*, with a script by Bundy Solt. Other working titles included *Zsa Zsa Goes West*, *Zsa Zsa the Kid*, and *Rubi Rides Again*. Fortunately for moviegoers, and for the shreds of Zsa Zsa's career, Rubi was denied a work permit by the U.S. State Department.

Ironic, and sadly indicative of Zsa Zsa's future trajectory, was her fall from MGM, Fox, and Paramount to Poverty Row and Republic Pictures. Even though the bizarre horse opera didn't materialize, from 1954 onwards she would be thought of as a trash actress, and often named as such along with Vera Hruba Ralston, wife of Herbert Yates, founder of Republic Pictures and studio head for many years. Anyone familiar with the word "camp" is likely to name Vera Hruba Ralston as the concept's leading lady, even in such a crowded field. (The authors of *The Golden Turkey Awards*, a 1980 book, nominated her, along with Candice Bergen and Mamie Van Doren, as "Worst Actress of All Time." All three lost to Raquel Welch.)

Like a summer cold that lingers with low-grade fever, Rubirosa was unshakable. The precise reason that he and Zsa Zsa never married was her refusal to abandon her career. In 1956, he found a woman who would, the nineteen-year-old minor French actress and model Odile Rodin. Their marriage lasted until his death nine years later.

He telephoned Zsa Zsa from Paris the day before the wedding so that she would hear it first from him. On the verge of great tears, she could say only, "I wish you all happiness." When nine-year-old Francesca heard the news, she said, "Mother, is it true that Uncle Rubi got married?"

"Yes, darling."

"But I thought he loved only us." She had lost two fathers already, Conrad Hilton and George Sanders, and now Uncle Rubi was gone. Francesca's quest would go on and on, until at last no fathers remained.

Even at the eleventh hour, hope was not lost for Zsa Zsa's career. Before the final break with Rubi, she and George costarred twice, first in a TV drama and then in the feature film, *Death of a Scoundrel*. On television in April 1956, the comedy-drama *Autumn Fever* shows Zsa Zsa in the afterglow of her good performance in *L'Ennemi public*. Again she lowers her voice to a breathy whisper. As Countess Dara Szabo, she almost succeeds in breaking up the marriage of a middle-aged grandfather, played by George. He is one reason for Zsa Zsa's good performance. She was still in love with him, and together they effervesce. When they kiss, we see what drew them together onscreen and off. They dance the mambo and it's their entire relationship in miniature: Zsa Zsa the aggressor, and George passively willing. We're like voyeurs peeping into the marriage, now defunct, of Zsa Zsa and George.

In *Death of a Scoundrel*, we ascertain more clearly the eccentric chemistry of their match. The scoundrel, of course, is George Sanders as Clementi Sabourin, a Czech refugee who arrives in New York after World War II and amasses a fortune through a nexus of corrupt deals. The character is based on Serge Rubinstein, whose millions came from currency manipulations and other shady schemes. In 1955 he was found murdered in his Fifth Avenue town house. The murderer was never found, but *Time* magazine quoted a reporter as saying, "They've narrowed the list of suspects to 10,000."

Described as "the most hated man on earth" and "an evil genius," Sabourin in *Death of a Scoundrel* engages in nothing that every crooked politician in Washington isn't guilty of: financial chicanery, insider trading, money funneled to mistresses, fraud of every sort. But because this is a noirish morality play, the title's prediction must come true.

Zsa Zsa, a wealthy widow who plays the stock market, falls in with Sabourin's scheme to get richer quick. She also falls for him, but so does Yvonne De Carlo. Others in the cast include Victor Jory and Sanders's brother, Tom Conway. Photographed by the legendary James Wong Howe, the picture should have turned out better. It was doomed from the start, however, by the inexpert and inexperienced Charles Martin as writer-producer-director.

In her scenes with Sanders, Zsa Zsa the coquette seems as amused by the challenge of George as when they were home alone and inventing their own Albee-esque scripts. "Don't play with me," she warns. "I'm a tigress. I'll bite you."

"I accept the offer," he purrs.

Her militant flirtation, and his effete response, suggest a parallel universe: a home movie of Zsa Zsa and George as they were just a few years earlier, so happy to be unhappily wed. His campy line in the movie—to Colleen Gray, at an intimate dinner—should have been delivered to Zsa Zsa: "I flew the lobster in from Maine and the onions from Bermuda."

Yvonne De Carlo and Zsa Zsa have one scene together. De Carlo plays a wiggling tart from the New York waterfront, and Zsa Zsa snubs her when they meet in Sanders's office. This is how Zsa Zsa sometimes reacted in real life to women she instinctively disliked or who made her feel insecure. (A psychological graph might show fifty percent Zsa Zsa and the other fifty percent insecurity.) Not deigning to speak, she lifts her head like a Persian cat in a Disney film—so high that her nose nears the ceiling. With a slight grimace, as if catching a whiff of soiled laundry, she sashays out of the room. A famous photograph of Rubirosa introducing his new wife, Odile Rodin, to Zsa Zsa captured the very same look.

Chapter 24

Mama, Don't Cry at My Wedding

In the early 1950s Eva bought a five-story, one-family town-house at 1033 Fifth Avenue, between Eighty-fourth and Eighty-fifth streets, and one block north of the Metropolitan Museum of Art. Owing to the long run of *The Happy Time* and to her radio and TV appearances, she felt financially secure. Eva daydreamed of a gilded life in her spacious multi-story, with herself as chatelaine and vassals at her side. Before applying for a mortgage, however, she sought Jolie's opinion. "Mama dashed over to look at the building and deliver final judgment," Eva recalled. "She told me I am not her smartest daughter, since it was evident to anyone with eyes that ten apartments could be made in the building." Eva swapped vassals for leases.

A year and a half later, there were exactly ten apartments in the 9,752-square-foot building, with a doctor's office on the ground floor and Eva's floor-through apartment on the second. In 1956, in the high-ceilinged, mahogany-paneled drawing room of that apartment, Eva took husband number three, but not for long.

The magistrate who performed the ceremony on April 8,

1956, was careful to follow's Eva's instruction that he omit the word "obey." Whether or not the phrase "till death do us part" was also omitted, the parting of ways took place a few months later and their divorce became final in March 1957. In public, Eva said nothing about the match. In 2007, however, her abbreviated husband, John Williams, MD, devoted a chapter to it in his self-published memoir, *Chasing Pig's Ears: Memoirs of a Hollywood Plastic Surgeon.*

He must have seemed, to every Gabor, dropped like the gentle rain from heaven. And, should Dr. John be unable to cut and lift and sew with expert craft, he had a twin brother, also a plastic surgeon. Eva and John met in Los Angeles. After a few dates, she returned to New York for rehearsals of *The Little Glass Clock*, which opened on Broadway on March 26, 1956. Ebullient at the prospect of another theatrical triumph, Eva invited John to come for opening night of what she predicted would be "a hit play."

"After the final curtain," he recalled, "a party was held at mother Jolie's home to await the early morning editions of newspapers and to read reviews of the play. They were all bad. The mood of the party changed to resemble a wake."

A few days later, having recovered from the depression of failure, Eva phoned her new friend. "Dahling, since the play failed I don't have anything to do. Why don't we get married?" If that's really what Eva said, perhaps it was a recycled line from her recent flop, or from a better play she had done last summer.

All the Gabors attended the nuptials, along with thirty or so friends, most of them Eva's. Reginald Gardner, her costar from the hit manqué, gave the bride away. Zsa Zsa served in her recurring role as matron of honor, with John's twin brother as best man.

After a honeymoon spent at Jolie's weekend house in Connecticut, the couple settled for a time in Beverly Hills. Williams joined the practice of an elderly surgeon, and almost immediately Eva left on tour with *Blithe Spirit*. John's companions after office hours were a Cockney maid whose dentures clicked when she talked, and two dogs. He soon gauged his importance in Eva's hierarchy as somewhere between the click and the bark. The tour ended, Eva returned to Beverly Hills, but to her chagrin she learned that doctors often receive late-night calls from patients. "*Sveetheart*," she cajoled, as her smile congealed, "can't you move that goddamn phone out of our bedroom?"

Remembering the manners of his Texas boyhood, he tried to explain that if the phone left the bedroom, he must remove himself with it. And so they met over coffee at breakfast, but rarely in the evenings. As tax time approached, and year-end forms showed that Eva had made four times as much as John, the real reasons for the marriage emerged. He wanted a Gabor in his life. She wanted a doctor, but a *rich* doctor. "Dahling," she said, her voice now less friendly with him than with her dogs, "the man should take care of all his wife's expenses, including the taxes."

And then someone called him "Doctor Gabor." As the moving van departed, Eva's valediction struck him as terribly wise. Now why didn't we think of that before, he wondered. "Dahling," she said, with genuine affection, as if expecting a slow curtain and waves of applause, "we should never have married, we should just have lived together."

"Eva was a lesbian. Did you know that?" So said Francesca one afternoon over coffee at her favorite Starbucks in Hollywood. I had heard the rumor years before, but a more accurate term for a woman who married five times is surely bisexual. All the same, I listened as Francesca reeled off the names of some, but not all, of the usual suspects.

In a previous chapter I said that Eva and Marlene Dietrich had formed a liaison. In contemporary parlance, they were friends with benefits. This Jolie must have known, for she told a revealing story about Eva, Marlene, and John Williams, a story with a loud subtext. According to Jolie, Eva telephoned to tell her, "We're getting a divorce. We had a terrific fight."

Eva continued, "Thank God for Marlene Dietrich! She is such a good friend. I called Marlene and she came rushing over and you know how Germans are. With such strength she shouted to him, '*Out!*' She all but threw him out bodily." Whether Marlene stayed on to console her young friend is not recorded in any book . . . but it's well known how friendly *this* German could be.

Behind these versions of the marriage, however, lurks a sinister scenario. What if *Confidential* or another scandal magazine had a tip-off about Eva's bisexuality? So feared were these publications, especially by gays, lesbians, and bi-sexuals, that stars considered vulnerable were either ordered by their studio to marry fast, or, if not under contract, their agents and managers issued similar orders.

Eva, a freelancer at the time, lacked studio protection. Moreover, she had been single since her divorce from Charles Isaacs in 1949—a condition looked upon with suspicion in the conformist fifties. Then, too, among her close friends were Marlene, Tallulah Bankhead, and other women they whispered about. The last thing Eva needed was a suggestive magazine cover line: "When Dietrich Gave Eva Gabor's Man the Boot," or, even worse, "The Night Dietrich Spent with Eva Gabor."

Marry a doctor, problem solved. Even if the marriage lasted hardly longer than an office visit.

By the mid-1950s, Eva had reluctantly accepted her status as perpetual supporting player in the movies. Only on televi-sion and in regional theatre would she be first or second billed. From 1956 to the end of the decade, however, she sel-dom had a day off. While still in California prior to re-hearsals for *The Little Glass Clock*, she costarred with June

Allyson and David Niven in *My Man Godfrey*. Also in the cast was Martha Hyer, who, ten years later, turned down the role of Lisa Douglas in *Green Acres* over a salary dispute. In so doing, she inadvertently gave Eva one of the best opportunities of her career.

In 1957 Eva traveled to London for *The Truth About Women*, in which she costarred with Laurence Harvey and Julie Harris. The sex-comedy genre, to which this film belongs, is one of limited possibilities, but this British example outshines anything that prudish Hollywood dared at the time. *The Truth About Women* could pass for a naughty French farce, since it makes no moralistic apologies for the various characters' adulterous relationships. Just about every man has a mistress and every woman a lover. This in contrast with Eva's sophomoric American movies of the same period, *It Started with a Kiss* and *Don't Go Near the Water*.

Like so many pictures of the time, these two depend on tiresome titillation. In *Don't Go Near the Water* Eva plays a correspondent for *Madame* magazine who is sent to a remote Pacific island in the closing days of World War II. She's the feistiest presence in this puerile comedy as she flutters in like an unwitting canary to a taxidermy shop. As the only female on a carrier with a thousand sailors, she creates horny pandemonium by hoisting her black lace panties to dry high up on the ship's cordage near the main mast. Glenn Ford, star of the picture, was Eva's boyfriend before and during the shoot. Attempting to escape the "Glamorous Gabor" stereotype, Eva told an interviewer, "I refused to wear anything but a very unchic uniform of military khaki. I was very drab. Not even *one* basic diamond!" Appearing on *What's My Line?* in 1957, shortly after the film's release, Eva said, "I spent three days on a battleship with the boys." Jim Backus, a member of the panel, mentioned that Eva was his landlady; he was subletting her apartment at 1033 Fifth Avenue. "Do you like sleeping in my bed?" she asked with her particular brand of wide-eyed innocence. (Zsa Zsa once described Eva as "the little innocent one, but she's not that innocent.")

Although Glenn Ford was Eva's costar once more in *It Started with a Kiss*, it was Debbie Reynolds who claimed her attention. On location in Spain in 1959, they met for the first time. "I was prepared not to like Debbie," Eva told Louella Parsons. "That's because in the split from Eddie Fisher she seemed goody-goody. On the contrary, from the minute we reported for work, I found her to be a girl who can stand on her own two feet. She is strong, courageous, and she doesn't ask for sympathy. We became good friends from the very beginning. I encouraged her to make the most of her beauty and to go out with other men and to forget the past." Debbie's much publicized friendship with Eva helped her shed that goody-goody image for a more sophisticated one. And, as one of the best mimics in show business, Debbie did hilarious Gabor imitations for the next forty years.

It Started with a Kiss belongs to Debbie, who makes a mediocre story come alive with tomboy energy and comic timing. Eva, as the Marquesa del Rey, has little to do except smile and wear fetching outfits designed by Helen Rose. She seems undirected, but unlike Zsa Zsa she knew how to direct herself. Instinct told her to move with the grace and hauteur of a real marquesa, at least the kind imagined by MGM. Again in contrast with Zsa Zsa, who was poised in person but seldom seemed at ease with herself onscreen, Eva uses face, body, and costumes to avoid going rigid as the film plods along.

Eva's last picture of the decade, *Gigi*, is an MGM behemoth, loved by audiences from its release in 1958 to the present, smothered in Oscars, and the apotheosis of what a studio musical might have been. Instead, it's a Vincente Minnelli picture that runs out of steam, and Leslie Caron in the title role is an unconvincing gamine on the verge of womanhood. (At twenty-seven, she was a decade late.) Eva, as the

courtesan Liane d'Exelmans, gives a champagne performance—
light, pale gold, and sparkling.

One week before Eva married John Williams, Magda married her fourth husband. Arthur Gallucci was his name,
though everyone called him Tony. They met in 1950 at a
cocktail party on Long Island, where his family's business
was located and where he lived in a seven-bedroom mansion
in Southampton. That business was variously reported as a
contracting firm, a manufacturing concern, and a plumbing
corporation. There were rumors, also, of underworld connections, which Francesca vehemently denied. Whatever his
dealings, three facts are inarguable: he was wealthy, a volatile
alcoholic, and he treated young Francesca with kindness.

After their first meeting in 1950, Magda and Tony became
inseparable and eventually lived together in Magda's town
house at 13 East Seventy-first Street and in Tony's estate on
Long Island. Tony's amorous inclinations, however, matched
the Gabors' in complexity. Jolie spotted trouble early on:
womanizing and drink. Whatever his charms, the following
story shows him as a sometime louse.

At the end of a long afternoon in 1955, Magda's little dog,
Coco, began yapping to remind them it was time for his
walk. Tony volunteered to take him out, and an hour later
they had not returned. Two hours, three, then four. Imagin-
ing the worst, Magda paced. Should she call the police? The
nearest hospital?

Then Coco barked at the door. He raced in without leash
or collar. At this point the narrative grows bizarre, whether
recounted by Jolie or reported obliquely in the press. While
on the walk, Tony ran into a former girlfriend who invited
him to join her for a drink at a nearby bar on the East Side,
not far from Magda's house. He became inebriated and at
some point noticed that Coco had wriggled out of his collar
and escaped. Tony did not go in pursuit.

Although Magda and Tony had recently become engaged, he didn't return to her that night. Instead, he shacked up with the girlfriend and, a few days later, married her. Magda, distraught even with Coco safely home that night, and without waiting to find out what had happened, swallowed an overdose of sleeping pills. As the bottle contained either four, or ten, depending on Jolie's wavering memory, the overdose was not fatal. Always the woman of the hour, Jolie sensed that something was wrong at Magda's. She raced over, found Magda passed out on a bed, called a doctor who induced vomiting, and except for a terrible headache Magda returned to normal. That precipitous overdose, taken before she learned of Tony's flight, suggests an unstable relationship riddled with doubts. It also belies Magda's reputation as the strong, dominant sister. Then, too, Jolie's chronology no doubt omits significant details.

Months later, Magda heard that Tony's brief marriage had ended. She invited him to her house. Once she had him inside, she beat him with a whip. "Magda didn't hurt him too badly," Jolie reasoned, "because he managed to stay alive for another twenty years." (Her math was off; he lived twelve years longer and endured several other beatings from his wife. Jolie did not divulge his level of pleasure.)

Although Magda, unlike her mother and her sisters, did not chase publicity, her marriages made news. The romantic details of Magda and Tony's wedding day, however, remained largely untold for sixty years, appearing at last in 2017 in the *New Jersey Herald*, a paper published in Sussex County. By then, all the adults who attended were dead, and youngsters who recalled the day were in their seventies. Events were reconstructed for the newspaper from their childhood memories and from local press coverage of the wedding, which took place on April 1, 1956.

Neither Tony's betrayal nor Magda's use of the whip was mentioned on the happy wedding day. They were married at the home of Dr. and Mrs. Leslie Vermes on Rutherford Avenue in Franklin, New Jersey, with the town's mayor, Alfred B. Littell, officiating. Dr. and Mrs. Vermes, members of the local Hungarian community, had met Eva a few years earlier. Their son, Bob Vermes, recalled that "my parents were flying back from a vacation in Mexico, and they were seated next to Eva Gabor. The three of them struck up a conversation in Hungarian and they quickly became fast friends."

It is unclear why Magda and Tony chose this location rather than Manhattan or Southampton. Perhaps it was because a New Jersey wedding was something no Gabor had tried before. After the ceremony, which was attended by family and close friends, the hosts opened the front door and invited the many onlookers gathered in the street and on the lawn to meet the Gabors and to share the traditional Hungarian feast prepared by members of the local Hungarian Reformed Church, including six wedding cakes.

Up until the marriage, Magda remained active in regional theatre, appearing in such light entertainments as Molnár's *The Play's the Thing* and the French farce *Pajama Tops*. Like Jolie, Eva, and Zsa Zsa, she turned up frequently on television and at charity events, though she seemed abstracted from the sparkle created by her mother and sisters. Magda and Tony loved and fought until his death in 1967. And beyond.

Believing that she was Tony's primary legatee, Magda learned otherwise when his will was filed for probate. Less than two months before he died, her husband added a codicil that removed her as beneficiary of his personal jewelry, art objects, automobile, and other holdings. From his estate in excess of a million dollars, Magda received a bequest of twenty-five thousand, plus the income for life of a trust fund. All else went to Tony's brother and a nephew. Later that year, Magda was ordered to appear in court to answer questions about the disappearance of valuables including a check for ten thousand dollars, jewelry, and other personal possessions of the deceased worth in excess of a hundred thousand dollars.

Magda won the bitter, protracted court battle with Tony's family and emerged not only a merry widow but a rich one as well, with two husbands yet to come. For the last thirty years of her life, however, she would need more than money could buy. While the unbreakable fibers that brought her through the war and its terrors sustained her through years of hardship, at times that strength wavered. But whenever Magda foundered, the other Gabors, never failing, united to form her bulwark.

Chapter 25

Ruszkik Haza!
(Russians Go Home!)

When the Hungarian Revolution erupted on October 23, 1956, the non-communist world reacted with an outpouring of sympathy and support for the courageous Hungarians who dared rise up against the brutality of their Soviet-imposed government. The revolt began as a student demonstration in Budapest. Soon it spread to all levels of the population and to every part of Hungary. For a brief time it seemed that the Hungarians had triumphed, but on November 4 hundreds of tanks crossed the border from the Soviet Union to suppress the uprising and to mete out horrific punishments for anyone suspected of taking part.

While Radio Free Europe and the Voice of America long urged people living behind the Iron Curtain to fight communist oppression, 1956 was an American presidential election year and Dwight D. Eisenhower, running for a second term, did not want to risk a confrontion with the Soviet Union. It was believed, also, that any such confrontation might lead to all-out nuclear war. In Hungary, therefore, freedom fighters waited for help from the West, but none was forthcoming.

Before the borders were resealed after the Soviet invasion, some 200,000 Hungarians fled the country, creating a need for emergency relief funds and resettlement in other lands. A number of Hollywood stars at the time, as well as directors and others behind the camera, were Hungarian either by birth or descent, among them Tony Curtis, Cornel Wilde, George Cukor, Michael Curtiz, and Adolf Zukor, founder of Paramount Pictures. While many of these joined their show business colleagues to raise money for refugee relief, no one drew more attention to the cause than Ilona Massey (1910–1974). Billed upon arrival in Hollywood in 1937 as "the new Dietrich," she made only a dozen films in a career that lasted two decades. Today she is best remembered for *Frankenstein Meets the Wolf Man* (1943) and for her angry protests in 1956 outside the Russian mission to the UN and the Russian embassy in Washington. Nor did her hatred of Russian barbarism abate after the Hungarian Revolution. In 1959 she led pickets in Hollywood when Soviet Premier Nikita Khrushchev's visit to the United States included a luncheon at 20th Century Fox.

In 1956, dramatic photographs appeared in the press of Ilona Massey standing on platforms, or sometimes on the hood of a car, fist upraised, blonde hair blowing and tears streaming down her cheeks, as she denounced the Soviet Union and pleaded for United States intervention to stop the carnage in Hungary. From the beginning of the uprising, she urged the Gabors to join her. Owing to their celebrity, she believed they could raise vast amounts of money.

The Gabors were as distraught as Ilona Massey at the events in Hungary. They hesitated, however, to take such a confrontational approach as their countrywoman. At the time, their refusal was not well understood. They joined no protest demonstrations, and their fund-raising efforts received only such random mention in gossip columns as, "Zsa Zsa Gabor really shelled out for Hungarian relief, even though she hates to part with money," and this from Hedda Hopper: "Zsa Zsa is out raising money for the Hungarian war relief; says she can't think of anything else. 'All our relatives are there,' she told me."

It was true, many relatives remained in Hungary, on the Gabor side and the Tillemann. The Gabors' main concern, however, was Vilmos, who had been in disfavor with the communist regime for years. Now he was old and in poor health, and therefore less subject to official harassment. It was no secret, however, that persecution of ordinary Hungarians resulted from criticism of the government made by relatives abroad.

Before the revolution, and after, the Gabors maintained regular contact with Vilmos. How they managed to do so is not entirely clear, because several factors militated against such communication. No communist government welcomed attention from flashy capitalists, which the Gabors had become as soon as possible after arrival in the United States. Then, too, as previously noted, Vilmos in the early fifties had been labeled an "undesirable," stripped of his real estate holdings and all else, and forced to live with his second wife in a cramped suburb of Budapest. Old and infirm, he offered no threat to the government, but neither did communist officials have a reason to treat him favorably.

A partial explanation for the ease of communication between Vilmos and his family is this: in 1953, at the height of the Cold War, Imre Nagy was appointed prime minister of the Hungarian People's Republic. Attempting to steer Hungary away from Stalinism and the heavy hand of Moscow, Nagy sought to usher in limited press freedom, openness to the West, and economic reforms. His agenda earned the name "the New Course in Socialism." Such innovative thinking displeased the Kremlin. The Soviet Union considered Nagy's Hungarian brand of communism not only weak but untenable, setting a dangerous example for other Iron Curtain countries. He was therefore removed in 1955, and the country returned to its former lockdown. This renewed despotism helped to spark the revolution.

During Nagy's brief rule, however, Vilmos benefited. For a time, his daughters were able to telephone him almost at will, a freedom unheard of before Imre Nagy. Perhaps he was even singled out by the regime as an example of the beneficent new face of communism.

And so it happened that in 1954, one of the most frigid years of the Cold War, Vilmos was permitted to give an interview to a visiting Hungarian-speaking journalist for the Associated Press. With tears in his eyes, he spoke openly about his famous offspring, calling them "the best daughters in the world" and adding that "all three are angels to me." Of Jolie, he said that after their divorce they remained good friends, adding that "she is a kind-hearted woman." At the end of the interview, Vilmos pulled from his pocket a stack of postcards to show his visitor. Sent by his loved ones from various countries, they were said to be "couched in warm, loving words." And possibly in prearranged code to tell Vilmos things not otherwise permitted. Since letters were subject to censorship and confiscation, postcards were considered the safest medium. (As late as 1987 I was cautioned by a friend in Czechoslovakia not to mention certain topics in my letters lest he face retribution.)

During this period of slight relaxation, an outbreak of polio threatened countless Hungarians. The country was ill equipped to cope with routine medical troubles, let alone a crippling epidemic. The mother of József Gabor, Zsa Zsa's cousin, wrote asking for any help available from the United States. Upon receipt of the letter, Zsa Zsa set to work via contacts in Washington and elsewhere. According to József Gabor, "a plane load of polio vaccine from Switzerland arrived in Budapest." Speaking after Zsa Zsa's death, he added, "She was a very good person. She claimed she wanted only understanding and love, but couldn't get that from people, only from animals."

Returning to 1956, it seems obvious that the Gabors' hesitation to take part in overt protests against the Soviet invasion of Hungary had to do with the safety of Vilmos and other relatives. To do so would likely have guaranteed the end of all contact. Instead, they worked tirelessly behind the scenes, raising thousands of dollars in the weeks and months immediately after the revolution. These included:

- Making a personal appearance in Kansas City, Eva signed autographs in exchange for donations to the Hungarian Relief Fund. Total amount raised: $500. She made similar appearances in San Francisco, Houston, and Pittsburgh.
- In Philadelphia, Zsa Zsa, Ginger Rogers, and Anna Maria Alberghetti each got a $10,000 contribution for the Relief Fund in exchange for a single dance.
- Magda, working closely with the International Rescue Committee, headlined a five-hour pledge drive for the Relief Fund at a theatre on Long Island, raising an impressive $7,000.

In 1958, Eva was reported helping Hungarian refugees to find jobs. And in 2016, after Zsa Zsa's death, it was revealed that she donated half a million dollars of her own money to the refugee cause. One source even said that she had joined Ilona Massey's picket line outside the Russian consulate in New York, though I have found no further confirmation.

Before the decade ended, Zsa Zsa and Nikita Khrushchev found themselves in the same room, although, as far as anyone knows, they did not speak nor even nod to each other. This bizarre near-encounter took place on September 19, 1959, in the commissary at 20th Century Fox. Incongruously

named the Café de Paris, the commissary could accommo-
date four hundred people, while at least twice that number
clamored for invitations. The Soviet premier had come to the
United States at the invitation of President Eisenhower, who
apparently soon regretted the presence of such a rowdy guest.
Diplomacy and suave talk were not Khrushchev's strong
points; he spoke his mind even if his words offended his hosts.

Le tout Hollywood clamored for an invitation to the luncheon for Khrushchev and his entourage, the only exceptions
being those on the political far right. Among the refuseniks
were Bing Crosby and Ronald Reagan. Otherwise, Eisenhower Republicans—not to be confused with the latter-day
brand—probably outnumbered Democrats that day.

The story of this event is delicious, and Peter Carlson has
covered it in detail in his book, *K Blows Top: A Cold War
Comic Interlude, Starring Nikita Khrushchev, America's
Most Unlikely Tourist*. An excerpt from the book appeared
in *Smithsonian* magazine, July 2009, and is available online.
Since Carlson has done such an admirable job, I limit my
focus to Zsa Zsa and the names of a few other glittering
guests, among them Judy Garland, Debbie Reynolds, Elizabeth Taylor and Eddie Fisher, Tony Curtis and Janet Leigh,
Marilyn Monroe—on time for once. Surveying the crowd, director Mark Robson quipped, "This is the nearest thing to a
major Hollywood funeral that I've attended in years."

Ilona Massey, of course, did not show up. As for another
unlikely Hungarian, viz., Zsa Zsa—why was she there? Her
opinion of Khrushchev and of Soviet brutality matched Ilona
Massey's. The question teased me for years, without resolution. Nor did Peter Carlson have an answer. In an email, he
said, "I have no idea why they invited Zsa Zsa, considering
her Hungarian background. It does seem odd, doesn't it?
Tickets to the Fox lunch were hard to get; Zsa Zsa must really
have wanted to go and she must have had good connections."

Finally, however, her probable reason for attending the

event occurred to me. She did it to benefit Vilmos and others still in Hungary. The guest list would, of course, be scrutinized in the Kremlin, and the fact that a lone native Hungarian turned out to honor the Soviet leader would carry incalculable weight. No doubt it eased communications between the Gabors and their father, and made it easier for Zsa Zsa in future years to obtain a visa for visits to communist Hungary.

Francesca, age thirteen, writing from California to Zsa Zsa in Paris in 1960, inquired, "Were you able to telephone Granddaddy?" Thanks to her mother's shrewd diplomacy, the answer was yes.

A decade after the Hungarian Revolution, Eva divulged to syndicated columnist Hal Humphrey that she had flown to Austria in 1956 at the height of the uprising. Her mission: to bring Vilmos out of Hungary among the floods of refugees crossing the Austrian border.

Disguised in black wig and nondescript coat, she slipped into Vienna unrecognized and from there to a point near the Hungarian border. Through friends and other connections, she found a peasant who told her that for a thousand dollars he would conceal her father under straw in a wagon, along with other refugees, and deliver him into Austria. As battles raged in Budapest and across the country, the border had become porous.

The peasant told Eva that the last mile or so would be risky. "I called my father on the phone," Eva said, "and told him we were planning to take him to the hospital, which was our code word." Vilmos, old, infirm, and forgetful, spilled the beans. He said, "Oh, it will be wonderful to fly to America and all of us be together again."

"I was petrified," Eva said. "I was sure someone must be listening."

There were delays, and Eva made several more trips to the

border where she spoke with arriving refugees. The more she heard from them about the horrific gunfire in Budapest, the more nervous and frightened she became at the daring plan. She conferred with Jolie, Magda, and Zsa Zsa by phone. The consensus was that Vilmos would be safer to remain in Budapest.

Eva left Austria. Not until two years later, in October 1958, did the family see Vilmos. Speaking in 1967, five years after her father's death, Eva said that in Vienna, at that reunion, they tried to persuade him to come back to America with them. "No," he said, "I am too old a tree to replant."

Zsa Zsa expanded further on their week in Vienna with Vilmos. "When we heard Father talk about his ugly little apartment, we all started to cry. He spoke with such enthusiasm. After his stroke in 1954 he lost much of his hearing and I bought him a hearing aid. He would rather die than wear it. He was too vain to admit he couldn't hear."

Jolie was less bothered by her former husband's circumstances. At the reunion in Vienna, she whispered to Zsa Zsa, "Now he is really happy for the first time in his life." Later on, Zsa Zsa came to believe that her mother had a point. Jolie continued, "He was never happy in the big apartments, in the big houses. He was always worried about expenses, about taxes, about his businesses."

Although Zsa Zsa, her sisters, and her mother betrayed no annoyance with the invasive cameras and intrusive reporters in Vienna—on the contrary, they smiled for the whole world— in private, Zsa Zsa was furious. "The press insulted me," she said off the record to her ghostwriter, Gerold Frank, in 1960. "They wrote that I made a grand exit from the plane. They even said I repeated it four times for photographers!" (Newsreel footage contradicts this outrageous claim.) "And," she continued, "they hounded us for interviews, didn't give us a minute to be alone with Father."

By 1968, when Zsa Zsa returned to Hungary for the first

time since 1941, the country had changed. Although still communist, still repressive to political dissidents, for the average Hungarian daily life now more closely resembled the milder totalitarianism of Yugoslavia than the severity of East Germany or Bulgaria. In Budapest, Zsa Zsa received a royal welcome. She was photographed endlessly, for instance, at a fitting in the salon of couturière Klára Rothschild in Vaci Street.

She returned several times in later years, always to acclaim and always doing more or less as she pleased. In the early 1990s, Eva returned and her nostalgic visit in Budapest to sites from her childhood formed the basis for a teary episode of Robin Leach's television show. Around the same time, Zsa Zsa, still in the afterglow of her cop-slapping publicity, appeared on the popular Hungarian talk show hosted by Sándor Friderikusz.

She and her ninth husband, Frederic von Anhalt, roll onstage in a small automobile. The host, dressed in cowboy gear, opens the door and, playing western sheriff, demands her driver's license and registration. "I have it right here," she says, "but do not look at my birth date because I am ten years younger." Zsa Zsa is, of course, elegantly begowned and bejeweled. She is unusually relaxed speaking Hungarian with a host who, unlike the Phil Donahues and Maury Poviches of American tabloid TV, treats her with respect even while spoofing her recent exploits. Zsa Zsa also makes sport of herself. The youngish audience, too, finds her unlike anything homegrown they have encountered.

"So you were born in 1948?" asks the sheriff.

"Yes," she answers. "Nowadays I'm younger than my daughter."

"You must blow into a breathalyzer," he says, hauling one out.

"And now I slap you," she informs him, and does exactly that, as the audience peals with laughter.

"I must now arrest you," he rejoins, "and incidentally I have diamond handcuffs."

"Very pretty," she exclaims. "With that you can arrest me."

"The verdict is that you must sit and talk with me," and from there Zsa Zsa's more or less standard talk-show spiel unfolds.

It was on this visit that Zsa Zsa obtained a souvenir that she kept on a coffee table in her salon for the rest of her life: a five-inch piece of the barbed wire barrier that had been a part of the Iron Curtain.

Chapter 26

If Mama Was Married

Jolie Gabor, having passed beyond middle age into a state of not-young, not-old, imagined herself permanently girlish, like her menopausal daughters. By the mid-1950s, however, when she had reached her sixties, Jolie acknowledged that her time for great love, and a third marriage, had probably lapsed. But—"the heart has no winter," she said, as if quoting a Harlequin romance.

She had become sensitized not only to wrinkles but to the extra pounds that refused concealment under tailleur or ball gown. Always zaftig, but unable to lower her calorie intake, Jolie went to comic extremes to hide her embonpoint. During one of Zsa Zsa's many solo appearances in Las Vegas, Jolie joined her at the Flamingo Hotel for opening night. "She was overweight at the time," Zsa Zsa confided off the record to Gerold Frank, "but she wanted to swim in the hotel pool. So she draped herself in a large terry cloth robe but hesitated to take it off. She said, 'I shouldn't look too fat—after all, I am the mother of the glamorous star who is appearing tonight.'

"This was her big dilemma, how she could swim before sundown and not be criticized for the little tire around the waist. Finally we agreed that I would walk with her to the edge of the pool and just as she jumped I would pull the terry cloth robe off her. At the last minute she was in mid-air when I pulled the robe and then she swam like a little duck. When she was ready to come out, I had to walk into the pool up to my knees holding the robe and throw it quickly around her before anybody could see."

Nor did Jolie relish the role of grandmother. "You don't know what sacrifices I make for your daughter," she groused to Zsa Zsa.

"This is your only grandchild!"

"She ages me."

And so, in December 1956, feeling past her romantic prime, Jolie busied herself with activities in aid of the 30,000 Hungarian refugees temporarily housed in army barracks at Camp Kilmer, New Jersey. At a holiday party for seventy of these displaced Hungarians that Jolie gave in her Manhattan town house, she chatted briefly with a man two decades younger than herself. He seemed shy, or was he merely reserved? She made inquiries, and learned that his name was Edmond de Szigethy.

Excited by the "de," which suggested a pedigree, Jolie inquired further. She learned, from reliable sources or otherwise, that he was an aristocrat from a landowning family. After the communists seized their lands, Edmond earned his living in the textile business. Jolie found out also that although Edmond was a Catholic, he had sheltered several Jews in his apartment when the Nazis invaded Hungary. During the recent revolution, he escaped to Vienna with twenty-seven dollars in his pocket and the clothes he was wearing.

Edmond wrote Jolie a thank-you note after the party. Its proper phrasing, neither flowery nor stilted, helped capture her unwintered heart. So elegant, so handsome was he that she did not hold poverty against him.

Jolie's account of their courtship echoes romance novels and *Cosmopolitan* raciness. In her town house was an apartment seldom occupied, although rented to Harry Karl, the future second husband of Debbie Reynolds. Jolie's description of the apartment perhaps explains why the tenant avoided it, for she had decorated it "not for a businessman but for a French madam, with gilt chairs and a round red velvet bed." Becoming fonder of Edmond, she rang up her absentee renter to ask whether she might use his apartment "for a beautiful Hungarian who is broke and good-looking."

"Okay," Harry chuckled, "but only if you promise to sleep with him in my round red velvet bed."

For the sake of propriety, Jolie would traipse upstairs late at night in her pajamas, or Edmond would descend to her. Head over heels in love, she nonetheless hesitated. He was so much younger, and really, how well did she know him? Jolie was able to reach her sister Dora in Budapest, who sent a cable with distressing news: "He is a heavy drinker. He beat up his former wife. He is impulsive, throws money away but is smart and can make life even on an iceberg." When Edmond explained that this report came from the divorce papers of his angry ex-wife, Jolie's anxiety eased. She would marry him and put him to work in her jewelry store.

During the period from 1955–1958, Jolie was at the peak of her creativity in the world of costume jewelry. A columnist called her the Queen of Madison Avenue, and with reason: she would not have survived in that high-end location if she merely sold jewelry. She had become an institution: a Hungarian Auntie Mame. Everybody went to Jolie's—to her shop came wealthy matrons, movie stars, and ladies of the stage, and at night these and others partied in her town house with husbands and escorts. They laughed at her outrageous pronouncements as they shelled out hundreds of dollars, and an invitation to her soirées meant more than tea with Mrs. Vanderbilt. Jolie was madcap fun, nutty, wacky, and only too eager to tell you whether you looked good, or lousy.

Her wedding to Edmond took place on March 3, 1957, in the Gallucci town house. Zsa Zsa and Magda gave their mother away, years too late they joked, and everyone lamented that Eva could not be present. She was dealing with the opposite end of marriage, viz., her divorce from that Dr. Williams whose ringing telephone disgruntled her sleep.

Soon the family chronicles anointed Edmond as "Count de Szigethy," and Jolie as a consequent countess. But a counternarrative reached American shores. Some who knew him in Hungary claimed that he purchased the title and that he never had more money in his pocket than those twenty-seven dollars that were in it when he left Hungary. Whatever the illusions, their marriage endured as perhaps the family's happiest. It ended with Edmond's death in an automobile accident in 1989.

Although the protracted Rubirosa affair had tarnished Zsa Zsa's reputation, she did some of her best screen work—and some of her most errant—post-Rubi. While *Death of a Scoundrel* qualified as a solid noirish B-picture, her next one, *The Girl in the Kremlin*, almost demanded a laugh track. Or so moviegoers imagined, without bothering to see it. The gaudy title kept all but the desperate out of theatres. Directed by Russell Birdwell, Zsa Zsa's sometime publicist, in a wet-cement style, it's a Cold War exploitation movie that's creepy despite its cheap sluggishness.

Zsa Zsa plays twins, Lili and Greta Grishenko. Lithuanian by birth, they were separated by the war. Lili went to the U.S., Greta to Russia, where she became a nurse who, in the opening sequence, assists a plastic surgeon doing a makeover on none other than the old monster, Joseph Stalin. The reason: coup plotters in the Kremlin plan to assassinate the mega-assassin himself. The writers should have brushed up on surgical procedures: Stalin is given only a local anaes- thetic, as though for removal of a skin tag. In an anticipatory scene Zsa Zsa slaps costar Lex Barker, as she was to slap the Beverly Hills cop thirty-two years later.

Asked by a reporter about taking on a dual role, Zsa Zsa replied, "I have to be careful not to steal scenes from my- self."

Albert Zugsmith produced *The Girl in the Kremlin* in 1957. Filming at Universal lasted a mere two and a half weeks, from February 4 to 22. On February 18, Zugsmith's production of *Touch of Evil* began shooting, also at Univer- sal, with Orson Welles as director. Since Zsa Zsa was still on hand at the studio, Zugsmith put her into one of the most prestigious films of her career, although for less than a minute and with two brief lines of dialogue. Zugsmith liked the Gabors; in 1953 he had chosen Eva for a lead in *Paris Model*.

Marlene Dietrich and Zsa Zsa, in that order, are listed as "guest stars" in *Touch of Evil*. Among the collection of grotesques in this Dickensian film noir, Zsa Zsa stands out as almost wholesome. Playing the madam of a bordello in a Mexican border town in a story that oozes corruption, Zsa Zsa descends a staircase to answer questions for the sheriff, played by Welles, about one of the strippers.

"Zita? I didn't know her. She only joined the show a few days ago." That's all we hear from Zsa Zsa, a silvery pres- ence, slightly tarnished, floating above this slimy firmament.

According to Universal-International production notes, Zsa Zsa was paid a thousand dollars plus an additional eighty dollars under her day player agreement with the stu- dio, meaning of course that she worked for a single day. Zsa Zsa's contract stipulated that "if the name of any other guest star is accorded credit so must she [be credited] as a guest star. The name of no other guest star shall be in size of type larger than that used to display her name." Dietrich, on the other hand, demanded contractually that "no other guest star may precede her name."

Another Gabor made an even briefer appearance in *Touch of Evil*. Or did she? For the first time around 2015, on IMDb.com, the name of Eva Gabor appeared near the bottom of the film's complete cast list. My first thought was, "Not again! Why do they always confuse Zsa Zsa and Eva?" But according to this reliable website, Eva is a stripper sitting at the bar. And uncredited onscreen. To be sure, there is a woman seated at the bar who looks like Eva. She appears for a split second in one shot, as the camera tracks toward Zsa Zsa descending the staircase. But is it Eva? I have scrutinized the shot on DVD and Blu-Ray, both the release version from 1958 and the 1990s restoration. Just when I'm certain that it's Eva on the bar stool, I become equally convinced that it isn't. (The American Film Institute's online Catalog of Feature Films does not list Eva Gabor in the *Touch of Evil* credits.) Given Orson Welles's playfulness in casting the picture, however, it fits that Eva, in profile, might be half hidden under makeup. After all, several other stars appear uncredited, unrecognizable, or both. When I contacted the University of Iowa Libraries, where Zugsmith's papers are housed, I learned that neither Gabor is named in the producer's documents for *Touch of Evil*.

My theory is this: Eva and Marlene being friends, and Eva in town and available—she was filming *Don't Go Near the Water* at MGM in February 1957—she and Dietrich decided to have a bit of fun with Zsa Zsa. Imagine their glee when Zsa Zsa glides down the staircase, all ready to speak her two lines to Welles, and glimpses Eva twenty feet away. And, in Zsa Zsa's heated imagination, stealing her scene.

My speculation is based in part on this paragraph from Frank Brady's biography, *Citizen Welles*: "So eager were they to be in a film directed by Orson Welles that Joseph Cotten, Marlene Dietrich, Mercedes McCambridge, and Keenan Wynn agreed to work for union scale wages, simply to be included. Perhaps out of jealousy over the fact that Welles was hiring so many friends, Zugsmith insisted that *his* friend, Zsa Zsa Gabor, be given a cameo role. Ultimately, Cotten, Dietrich, and Gabor were given slight salary increases over the union scale." Since Zugsmith was friends with Eva, as well, he would probably have agreed to the in-joke cooked up by her, Dietrich, and Welles. Or maybe not. The film's production notes list two starlets, June McCall and Betty Uitti, as "1st girl" and "2nd girl" in the scene.

Whatever the circumstances, Zsa Zsa said at the time, "When Orson beckons, I come. He's a dear. He once held my baby in his lap all the way from Paris to America on the plane."

Later in 1957, Zsa Zsa traveled to London to appear in *The Man Who Wouldn't Talk*. Her costars, Anthony Quayle and Anna Neagle, both highly regarded for their films and he for his Shakespeare roles onstage, as well, must surely have found much to admire in her work or they would not have accepted her, especially since Neagle's husband, Herbert Wilcox, was the director. In her 1974 autobiography Anna Neagle wrote, "For some reason the combination of Zsa Zsa and myself met with a sceptical reaction, but we ignored it. I found her a first-class actress, very beautiful and extremely witty."

The film is a Hitchcockian thriller with a Cold War plot. It opens with Zsa Zsa and Quayle, newlyweds, boarding a plane in New York for their flight to London. She is as frothy as ever, chirpy and oblivious to all except hair and makeup as she primps on the plane. When the door closes behind them in their honeymoon suite in a London hotel, they drop the façade. They are not married at all. She is a Hungarian-born undercover agent for British intelligence. The fake marriage served as a deceptive way to bring Quayle, a virologist, to England.

There he meets in secret with a famous Hungarian virologist who is in London for an international conference. This man knows of a deadly killer virus developed by the Russians and intended for horrific use. He gives Quayle the formula for an antidote to counteract the virus, which he describes as a hundred times more virulent than any other.

A bit later, Zsa Zsa's character is killed by Soviet agents and her murder pinned on Quayle, who must remain silent during his trial in order to maintain his cover and deliver the vaccine formula to Washington. In unusually advanced casting for the fifties, Neagle plays the queen's counsel who defends Quayle in court. This she does with the deadpan aplomb of Charles Laughton in *Witness for the Prosecution*, which Billy Wilder was shooting around the same time.

Here Zsa Zsa gives her best dramatic performance, her finest comic role having been in *Public Enemy Number One* with Fernandel. It's obvious once more that if she had remained in Europe, her career would no doubt have assumed more respectable lineaments. By the late fifties, however, she had become rigidly self-important, a star clutching at diminished stardom. Lacking judgment in the selection of roles, she jumbled good work on film with ubiquitous one-note TV performances.

By 1958, Zsa Zsa had done irreparable damage to career and reputation. Whether she herself at the time recognized the harm, or whether she believed the public still clamored for her as they had at the premiere of *Moulin Rouge*, no one knows. (Years later, she was clear on what happened, though she claimed to have no regrets. "Professionally, I missed my moment," she said in 1990. "I followed my heart and to this day I still don't care.") At the very time when she should have sought a "mature" supporting role like that of Joan

Crawford in *The Best of Everything* or Claire Trevor in *Marjorie Morningstar*, she grabbed the starring role in *Queen of Outer Space*. It made her immortal, of course, but for all the wrong reasons—and she didn't even play the queen.

Before that celluloid *succès de scandale* was released, however, Zsa Zsa entangled herself in a personal scandal that dropped her reputation even lower and labeled her, in public opinion, as a teammate of Polly Adler and the Mayflower Madam.

Chapter 27

The Trujillo Stink

Ionce heard someone call Zsa Zsa "the world's most brilliant stupid person," and her judgment in the late fifties confirms the epithet. This time the career vandal was not Rubirosa but his amigo and former brother-in-law from the Dominican Republic, Rafael "Ramfis" Trujillo, rancid son of the foul dictator.

Born in 1929, Ramfis was awarded the rank of colonel at age five. From then on, he appeared often with his father at state occasions in full military regalia. Adding to the child's grotesque costume was a chest covered with fake medals. Shawn Levy, in *The Last Playboy*, his biography of Rubirosa, portrays Ramfis as "a pouty brat" who was "weak, uncertain, childish." Despite such liabilities, he remained the apple of his father's evil eye. Trujillo *père* promoted him to brigadier general at age nine. In his twenty-second year, Ramfis was named commander of the Dominican Republic's midget air force, even though, as Levy points out, "he couldn't pilot so much as a crop duster." Beginning in his teens, Ramfis learned torture and massacre from his father, who intended this first-born son to carry on the dynasty.

In 1957, Trujillo enrolled his heir at the U.S. Army's Command and General Staff College at Fort Leavenworth, Kansas. If Robert Altman had filmed this story rather than *M*A*S*H,* the comedy might have been not only dark but stygian, for Ramfis the cadet possessed all the diligence and character of a Donald Trump, had that future commander-in-chief not received five deferments to avoid the draft. As politicians-in-waiting, however, both fought similar battles. Trump told Howard Stern in 1997 that his own "personal Vietnam" was avoiding sexually transmitted diseases. "I feel like a great and very brave soldier," he crowed, implying Napoleonic battles minus a genital Waterloo. Such was Ramfis's own field of battle. He waged his venereal campaigns with such vigor that he often lacked time and energy to show up for class.

Upon arrival in Kansas at age twenty-eight, Ramfis deposited a million dollars in various bank accounts. He also received a monthly allowance from the dictator of $50,000, while the majority of Dominicans struggled in poverty. After weekday classes, Ramfis and his sizable entourage occupied a ranch house in the town of Leavenworth and on weekends they drove to Kansas City, Missouri, where the heavily guarded ninth floor of the Ambassador Hotel was theirs for the entire nine-month course of study. At both locations, some three dozen detectives and bodyguards patrolled around the clock, for the Trujillos were hated throughout the world.

Having been prodigiously indulged all his life, Ramfis quickly grew bored in Kansas. Along with sloth, he suffered from depression, anxiety, insomnia, and excessive drinking. Doctors prescribed pioneering tranquilizers and antidepressants, but no drug listed in the *PDR* was effective in treating a sociopathic personality. Nor did he find comfort in his wife, Octavia, and their six children, five of whom had accompanied their parents to the American Midwest.

Ramfis, Octavia, and their youngsters returned to the Dominican Republic for the Christmas holidays in 1957. While there, he explained to the dictator that responsibility for a wife and children made study difficult, not to mention their hindrance to pleasure after long hours of instruction. A divorce would be so convenient, he whined. Exit family.

During the spring term Ramfis welcomed his mentor, Rubirosa. Learning of his friend's boredom, Rubi called Zsa Zsa.

"Do you remember young Ramfis?" he asked.

"Of course," Zsa Zsa giggled. "He's my favorite Dominican after you." She had met him twice, once when she visited the Dominican Republic with Rubirosa and another time in New York.

"If I send him out, can you show him around?" He told her that Ramfis loved movies and the beautiful stars, like herself, who starred in them.

"Perfect timing," Zsa Zsa purred. Her latest picture had just wrapped, and she was thrilled because *Queen of Outer Space* offered one of the biggest parts of her career.

Learning that Ramfis was famished for blondes, and that he had a burning crush on Kim Novak, Zsa Zsa told Rubi that she and Kim were good friends. "Any friend of mine is a friend of Kim's," she assured him. "It's happened before. Did I tell you about the time—well, you remember."

When he put down the receiver, Rubi smiled at Ramfis. Whatever his actual words in Spanish, the gist of it was, She will make you glad you're not in Kansas anymore. "Nobody gives a party like Zsa Zsa," Rubi assured his protégé. "The things I could tell you."

Before Zsa Zsa could set to work on her welcome-to-Hollywood soirée for Ramfis, she had to meet several professional obligations. So grateful was he for the promised event, however, that he began phoning her several times a week to drool about movie stars and to remind her obsessively of his eagerness to meet Kim Novak. "Yes, dahling,"

Zsa Zsa said as she rushed off to rehearsal for an episode of *The George Gobel Show*. During a break, she got a message to step outside and see the present that had just been delivered for her. Parked at the door was a red Mercedes-Benz convertible that Ramfis had sent by chartered plane.

She called him in ecstasy. "But you shouldn't have," she gurgled unconvincingly. "How can I thank you?"

"Your friendship is thanks enough."

Zsa Zsa drove the car home and parked it in the garage beside her several others. Since a chauffered limousine usually picked her up for television shows, she had no need of yet another fancy car. Her hectic pace continued. In January 1958 she appeared on the popular afternoon drama series, *NBC Matinee Theater*. In February she flew to Palm Beach for the annual Heart Fund Ball, of which she was honorary chairwoman. While there, she heard from Ramfis again. "I'm in New Orleans for Mardi Gras," he informed her. He had sailed across the Gulf of Mexico on the presidential yacht and wanted Zsa Zsa to come on board as his guest. "I have the consul general of the Dominican Republic and his wife aboard, and several other friends. You'll be well chaperoned." So Zsa Zsa recalled, though it's doubtful that the word "chaperone" entered his mind or issued from his mouth in any language.

She arrived in New Orleans at night. Her low-light description sounds like the opening sequence in a film noir. "At the airport three of his aides waited to whisk me in an enormous black limousine through the city to the dark, black docks. It was like a murder mystery—squads of police on guard, secret-service agents in the shadows, and there, looming like a great trans-Atlantic liner, the magnificent *Angelita*. It was the longest yacht in the world. I saw dark sailors in white uniforms peering out. I heard, floating across the water to me, the soft Caribbean music of the orchestra."

On board the yacht, she wallowed in banana-republic luxury for several days in the company of shady fellow guests whom she named only as "six or seven men and three or four lovely women." She hardly recognized Ramfis when he greeted her. Gone were whatever youthful looks he once had. Zsa Zsa tried not to notice his swollen face, puffy from drink and drugs, the piled-up hair that gave him the look of a swarthy cockatoo, and the banal, imbecilic eyes.

She focused on the overdone sumptuousness of her Louis Quinze suite and its golden bed, the Aubusson carpet, the pink marble bath with gold taps. Like the aimless rich in an Antonioni film, the Trujillo party and his entourage of goons moved off the sultry waters and into the sweaty town, joining the Mardi Gras revels and elevating Zsa Zsa, their quixotic star, to elegance concocted of tinsel and paste, which to her looked like Versailles. And like Marie Antoinette, she gave no thought to the poor peasants across the water in the Dominican Republic.

In the powder room of a nightclub a woman claiming to be a fan took Zsa Zsa's picture. At the time it seemed harmless enough. Next day, the mayor of New Orleans came on board the *Angelita* with his wife. He brought along the morning paper, which headlined: ZSA ZSA IS HERE; BUT WHERE? IS SHE VISITING THE TRUJILLO YACHT? Illustrating the story was the powder-room photo of Zsa Zsa. "They love to make scandal wherever I go," Zsa Zsa groused. The mayor soothed her feelings. "You'll come with me to city hall and I'll present the keys to the city and name you an honorary citizen of New Orleans."

Humid mist and gray shadows hung not only over the yacht and above the entire city; the murky damp closed in quietly on Zsa Zsa herself, whose nervous merriment among the masked faces of Mardi Gras could not dispel the stealthy whisperings in the *Angelita*'s corridors and the curious cries in the night. Whatever her pleasures, she could not linger on in the fantastic dream, and so her revels ended.

The sunshine of Los Angeles, draped in webs of haze, did not relieve Zsa Zsa's vague foreboding. What was the gnawing that refused to state its scheme? But work, always work, pushed it away. Jack Benny's *Shower of Stars* in March, another appearance on *NBC Matinee Theater* in April, and her first invitation to Jack Paar's late-night talk show, which would take her to New York in early May.

But before departure, two conspicuous events.

If one listed the ten most assiduous party givers of the twentieth century—in the U.S., at least—the names would include Elsa Maxwell, Perle Mesta, Truman Capote, and Zsa Zsa. By the late fifties, her parties routinely earned photo spreads in big-city newspapers and occasionally in *Life* and other national magazines.

In that spring of 1958, Zsa Zsa's house seldom quieted. She was either planning two big occasions, attending to every detail as expert party givers do, or else the events were taking place. First came Francesca's eleventh birthday celebration on March 10. For this annual event Zsa Zsa wanted more than cake, sweet drinks, and kiddie games. She hoped Francesca would remember the day forever. This year Zsa Zsa decided that the children would dress as grown-ups. She counted on their behavior matching their outfits. In previous years mayhem had erupted, leaving her house a shambles. Invitations specified long evening gowns for girls, tuxedos and black ties for boys. Zsa Zsa's canny sense of how dress affects behavior worked as she predicted with the assembled guests, who loved the pretense of adulthood. They sipped ginger ale from martini glasses and parroted the latest talk in "the industry."

Conrad Hilton gave Francesca a gold and pearl necklace. Ramfis sent a bouffant ball gown from New Orleans. (In future years Francesca would not speak his name.) Other gifts included Nancy Drew mystery novels and a gold watch. On that Monday afternoon the house filled with young sophisticates: Kathryn Grayson's daughter Patricia, Van Johnson's daughter Schuyler, Dick Powell and June Allyson's Pamela, Keenan Wynn's son Tracy, Deborah Kerr's Melanie, and the two sons of Franchot Tone, Jeff and Pat. There were eighteen guests in all.

Carrie Fisher, not yet two, didn't attend, but her father did. A picture in *Life* shows him hugging Francesca. Like many young girls across the country, Francesca had a crush on Pat Boone, who was then at the height of his cloying fame. Unlike other little girls, however, Francesca was called to the phone to hear her absolute idol sing "Happy Birthday, dear Franci." After much ribbing from the youngsters, Eddie Fisher sang "April Love"—Pat Boone's big hit. Then Johnny Mathis sang, accompanied at the piano by Jolie.

Well-mannered children, like obedient dogs, are never one hundred percent house trained. As afternoon faded to evening, little ladies and gents regressed. Tired; out of sorts; tears—Zsa Zsa witnessed the entire palette of childhood disgruntlement, as fisticuffs broke out among the boys and minor hair snatching among the girls. Yet no one wanted to leave, even as annoyed parents threatened dire detentions.

"But for my sweet daughter," Zsa Zsa said with great satisfaction, "it was the night of nights. And also for me, her proud mother."

A few weeks later, in April, Zsa Zsa gave her party of the year. She determined to invite everyone in Hollywood that Ramfis wanted to meet, and then some. One hundred and ten invitations went out, with only a few regrets from those filming on location. For Zsa Zsa, any party was an ordeal because of her exacting arrangements. "Every flower must be in place," she said, as if writing a manual, "an ashtray cannot be awry, house, food, help, decorations, program, music—all must be perfection."

Lending respectability to the occasion were cohostesses

Jolie and Eva. Who could criticize a lady whose mother and sister were in attendance, even if the guest of honor was a squalid reprobate? Arriving guests also towered above the unseemly: Mr. and Mrs. James Stewart, Mr. and Mrs. Robert Taylor, Mr. and Mrs. Robert Mitchum (his jail term for marijuana almost forgotten), Zsa Zsa's close friends James and Pamela Mason, her very best friend Kathryn Grayson, Louella Parsons, Mr. and Mrs. Kirk Douglas, Bea Lillie, Ginger Rogers, Rhonda Fleming, Shirley MacLaine, Maureen O'Hara, Ann Miller, George Sanders ("Dearest Cokiline," he whispered as he kissed her cheek, "this is a party to end all parties"), Kim Novak, who was already intimately acquainted with Ramfis since his arrival in town a week earlier. And Rubirosa and his young wife, Odile. Ramfis had flown them in from Paris just for tonight.

"Mr. George Sanders," Zsa Zsa said, hooking her arm through his, "may I introduce Mr. Porfirio Rubirosa." Then she recalled: they had met unforgettably on Christmas Eve a few years back, when attire was considerably less formal than tonight's black tie. Mr. Sanders and Mr. Rubirosa shook hands and smiled as if for a dental X-ray. The encounter was one of perfect aplomb, except that a moment later George's left hand quivered and he spilled a flute of champagne on Zsa Zsa's party frock.

Zsa Zsa dreaded the encounter with Odile, but the younger woman won her over with a question, posed in French: "Rubi stays out all night in *les boîtes de nuit*, drinking and—well, what shall I do?"

"*Chérie*, that is Rubi. There is nothing at all to be done. *Rien du tout!*"

Ramfis flitted from star to star. Among the guests, the savvy Masons, James and Pamela, would have been aware of the Trujillos and their reign of terror, and a few other guests also. But Hollywood was still a company town, as insular in some ways as a medieval walled city. Then, too, since the

United States government and the largely subservient American media favored bloody dictators placed strategically in Latin America, so long as they were anti-communist, real information about Trujillo and his offspring would have required searching beyond the *Los Angeles Times* or the trade papers, which constituted most of Hollywood's reading.

The party cost $10,000, which Zsa Zsa said came from her pocket. Given Ramfis's bank accounts, however, it's more likely that he picked up the tab. The consensus among departing guests around 4:00 a.m., and among the wide-awake Gabors who swapped gossip and bon mots for another hour, was that Zsa Zsa's party was the social event of the season.

Two days later, her furrier telephoned. Could she drop by his store in Beverly Hills to choose the style chinchilla coat she preferred? One had been ordered for her just that morning.

Astounded, she asked who ordered it.

"Mr. Ramfis Trujillo, with his compliments."

In 1956, Zsa Zsa had formed a professional alliance with Joey Adams, the Borscht Belt comedian and *New York Post* columnist. Their initial act, which ran for a month in Las Vegas at the Riviera Hotel, proved a lucrative outlet for Zsa Zsa's talents. Now, with film offers becoming less frequent, she approached Adams and they landed a ten-day engagement at the Cafe de Paris in Washington, D.C. Zsa Zsa's take was said to be a thousand dollars a night.

Despite its elegant name, the Cafe de Paris was the kind of glitzy front where you might glimpse money laundering in the kitchen and payoffs in the parking lot. Audiences there being less demanding than in, say, New York, they laughed when Adams greeted them: "Good evening, ladies and germs. Here's a story I just heard—a Jew and a parrot walk into a bar . . ."

Eventually Zsa Zsa came onstage in a sequined low-cut dress and costume jewelry from Mama's shop. Gazing at her chest with goggle eyes, Adams said, "It's thrilling to be here with the three of you." Billed as the Professor of Love, she took questions from the audience: "Zsa Zsa, how many husbands have you had?"

"Do you mean apart from my own?"

"What's the best way to keep a man from straying?"

"Shoot him in ze legs."

This shtick, of course, was old and gray even then, but Zsa Zsa recycled it in every venue and continued to do so for the next forty years on television. At some point she must have faced the wretched fact that she had become a cartoon, but given her guts and determination, plus the indomitable Gabor genes, she never stopped playing the star. And it worked, to a point. Even those who dubbed her a has-been prefaced it with the words "celebrity" and "glamorous."

The grimness of her professional situation had not yet dawned, but with Hollywood studios on the verge of collapse, and contracts cancelled rather than renewed, she and other famous blondes were about to become passé. In six years she had gone from John Huston and *Moulin Rouge* to this vulgarian and his tit jokes.

In proportion as her claim diminished—her claim to consideration as a diva—Zsa Zsa counterclaimed prima donna rights. She grew more temperamental, demanding, mercenary, headstrong. Deeper into her forties, but claiming twenty-five, she became a parody of the earlier Zsa Zsa. Added to her miseries was deepening bipolar disorder, for which no foolproof treatment existed. As a comedienne, she covered humiliation and heartbreak with witty comebacks, even if that meant coasting on lines exhausted and moldy from overuse. All the same, she might still have rescued her career had she chosen her friends more judiciously.

While appearing with Joey Adams in Washington, Zsa Zsa received a telephone call. "Miss Gabor, this is United Press

International calling. Is it true that General Trujillo gave you a Mercedes-Benz roadster?" Standing at a wall telephone outside her cramped, unadorned dressing room at the Cafe de Paris, and caught off guard, Zsa Zsa answered, "Yes, of course it's true. Why?" Since the gift had arrived months earlier, she couldn't imagine why anyone was interested now.

"Is it true that Miss Kim Novak also received a Mercedes from the general?"

"I don't know anything about that," she snapped.

Next day's headline: KIM NOVAK AND ZSA ZSA GABOR RECEIVE GIFT AUTOS FROM TRUJILLO.

When the press got wind of the chinchilla evening jacket— a confection of the thickest pelts—they called again for a statement. Even if Russell Birdwell had been there for damage control, it was too late. The scandal flamed and scorched like wildfire. It didn't help her case that Zsa Zsa told a reporter, in flippant tones, "He gave me a lovely chinchilla coat because I worked so hard to make his visit to Hollywood pleasant. I gave a terrific party for him and he is not the kind of man who says thank you with a bouquet of flowers."

Headlines roared on and on, even in small-town newspapers. *Time* and *Newsweek* had their fun, and *Life* ran a photo spread: in one picture, Zsa Zsa, Kim, Ramfis, Rubi, and Odile; in another, Ramfis's children and their nurse. According to the story in the issue of May 26, 1958, Zsa Zsa's Mercedes 190 SL cost $5,800 and the chinchilla $17,000. Kim's Mercedes 220 S convertible cost $8,700, and her suitor's generosity extended to $5,000 worth of jewelry. Zsa Zsa claimed she had tried to sell her gift car because it lacked automatic transmission and was therefore difficult for her to drive. All the same, she posed for *Life* seated under the steering wheel. In the photo, her expression was that of the proverbial cat who has lapped up the cream. Elsewhere, she posed in the chinchilla as if the little animals had grown it especially for her.

Soon *Confidential, Whisper,* and the other scandal magazines ran cover stories on Zsa Zsa, Kim, Ramfis, and his
largesse. On television and in night spots comedians made
lurid jokes about Zsa Zsa's party giving secrets. One columnist even suggested that she be deported for moral turpitude.
Zsa Zsa later admitted that Eva was "terribly upset" by the
scandal. "She is much more practical minded than I am,"
said Zsa Zsa, as if the Trujillo episode were no more than a
parking ticket stuck on her windshield.

Then the coup de grâce. A reporter phoned the Cafe de
Paris to ask Zsa Zsa whether she had a response to the congressman. She had no idea what he was talking about until
he explained in detail. "Congressman Wayne Hays of Ohio.
What do you think about his statement in the House of Representatives that you are the most expensive courtesan since
Madame de Pompadour?"

The reference was to the Marquise de Pompadour, chief
mistress to Louis XV of France in the eighteenth century. Behind the congressional podium, Hays had this to say: "If this
scarlet woman continues her tricks with this Latin American
playboy of hers, foreign aid as we know it today may come
tumbling down around our feet."

Hays was known as the meanest man in the House. Peter
H. Brown, in his biography *Such Devoted Sisters: Those Fabulous Gabors*, sets the indelible scene: "A gigantic color ban-
ner of Zsa Zsa Gabor striking a seductive pose from the film
Lili was unfurled before the men in the U.S. House of Representatives. Congressman Hays, a big man with a thundering
voice, looked around to see if his words were having the
proper effect. A silence had settled over his peers. He let the
hush play its course before he pulled out his ace in the hole.

"'And here,' said Hays, unfurling still another photo of
Zsa Zsa, 'is the most expensive courtesan since Madame de
Pompadour. And I have seen evidence that direct American
aid to the Dominican Republic is being sent right back to our

own shores in the form of expensive gifts to Miss Zsa Zsa Gabor and her friends. If we want to give foreign aid to movie stars, let's pass a special bill and get rid of the middleman. Hell, let's pass a bill and send the money straight to Zsa Zsa out there in Beverly Hills.'

"There was a strong reaction. The congressmen rose to their feet, clapped, whistled, and cheered."

Zsa Zsa's response in the press sounded weak. "If Mr. Hays comes from behind his congressional wall of immunity and repeats this statement, I will sue him for slander." Rage as she might, there was nothing she could do. She should have listened to those friends who warned her not to get involved with anyone named Trujillo. She never named them, but the warnings may well have come from James and Pamela Mason, from Eva, from Tony Gallucci. He, perhaps more than anyone else in her circle, could smell taint from afar. And unlike his impetuous sister-in-law, Gallucci knew what to do when an odor grew noxious.

The U.S. Congress had not finished with Zsa Zsa. Representative Charles Porter of Oregon, echoing his Ohio colleague, suggested that since Ramfis "spends a million dollars a year, the $1.3 million in U.S. aid to the Dominican Republic be given directly to the taxable movie stars instead of going through the Trujillos."

Zsa Zsa's heedless behavior caused this embarrassment, as it would trigger disputes and scandals for the rest of her life. In this case, however, she had the last laugh, although it took eighteen years. In 1976, Wayne Hays resigned his seat in the House of Representatives after a sex scandal involving his former secretary, Elizabeth Ray. The *Washington Post* quoted Ray as saying that while she was ostensibly hired for office work, "I can't type, I can't file, I can't even answer the phone." But disgraced congressmen, like old soldiers, don't die; they just fade away. Three years after his own scandal, Hays was elected to the Ohio House of Representatives and served one term.

Zsa Zsa holds the distinction of being one of the very few film stars to be censured in the U.S. Congress. The other is Ingrid Bergman, who became pregnant by Italian director Roberto Rossellini while still married to her first husband. When the story broke, a senator condemned her as "an assault upon the institution of marriage" and "a powerful influence of evil." The irony of such pronouncements is glaring. The sexism, the hypocrisy, and the pestilential wrongs of the U.S. Senate, the House, and the presidency are as enduring as the republic for which they stand.

After the assassination of Trujillo the dictator in 1961, Ramfis briefly took over the country. He continued the former policies of murder, torture, and repression until later that year, when he was deposed. He and all the remaining Trujillos fled to Europe aboard the luxurious *Angelita*. Also on board was Trujillo's casket, which was said to be lined with four million dollars in cash as well as jewels and incriminating documents.

In 1962 Ramfis and others of the Trujillo family settled in Spain under the protection of another bloody dictator, Francisco Franco. Ramfis died in Madrid in 1969 of injuries sustained in the crash of his blue Ferrari sports car.

Chapter 28

The Queen of Negative Space

Some movies emit fumes of testosterone, others clouds of estrogen. *Queen of Outer Space* gives off bursts of egotism, thanks to Zsa Zsa's performance. In every frame she dares you not to acknowledge her magnificence. Playing Talleah (and not the queen, as is often assumed), she *is* big; it's the universe that got small.

If *Moulin Rouge* counts as the high-class apex of Zsa Zsa's career, then *Queen of Outer Space* demands separate but equal recognition. A favorite among cultists, it's famous for low camp and fifties weirdness. All that is true, but what sets it apart is Zsa Zsa's one-woman celebration of herself. Rearrange the scenery, change a couple of dates, and finally she has won the beauty contest. Not Miss Magyarország 1933, but twenty-five years later she crowns herself with the diadem of vainglory. Set on the Female Planet, the picture could have been titled *The Gabor Who Conquered Venus*.

She never fully recovered from her grandiose coup. Arsenio Hall, interviewing Zsa Zsa in 1994, held up the VHS package of *Queen of Outer Space*. "How old were you when you made that movie?"

"Twenty-one. It was the beginning of my career."

He accepted her answer with a gentlemanly nod.

Once the picture had reached the heights of cult status, Zsa Zsa couldn't decide whether to bask or to hide. Eventually she claimed it as her own. By the time of its reissue in a fully restored CinemaScope print in 1995, she was expected at the Film Forum in New York to preside over the event. Rumors circulated that she might make similar appearances across the country. Still grief-stricken over Eva's recent death, however, she was not up to the travel and levity involved. She did consent to a telephone interview with the *San Francisco Chronicle* when the Castro Theatre screened the film. "To tell you the truth, we never even thought it would get released," she said, a doubt not voiced by anyone else connected with the picture.

After its release in September 1958, *Queen of Outer Space* took some dozen years to reach immortality. After Stonewall, when revival houses in New York, Los Angeles, and San Francisco began screening florid favorites from previous decades, hip audiences made it a gay emblem along with some of its betters, such as *The Wizard of Oz*, *All About Eve*, and *What Ever Happened to Baby Jane?* Once lodged in the consciousness of connoisseurs, the picture—and Zsa Zsa's immortal line, "I hate zat qveen"—never left. Endlessly quoted, the line has worn thin with use, like stairs at a place of pilgrimage.

Despite its reputation, *Queen of Outer Space* is not really all that hilarious. (Pictures like *Attack of the 50 Foot Woman* are more over the top.) It has many static sequences, and low-budget cheesiness pervades the picture from the start, when the spaceship crew recline for takeoff in seats like Barcaloungers, and a blonde starlet on the ground—Joi Lansing—waves and blows kisses to her flight engineer boyfriend as though he were on board a Cessna.

Captain of the spaceship is Eric Fleming, whose face, like

that of a Gabor, had been reconstructed by plastic surgery owing to a disfiguring accident while in the navy in the 1940s. The surgical procedure worked well, for by the time of *Queen of Outer Space*, and then the TV western *Rawhide*, he looked like an aging Dolce & Gabbana model.

Diverted from its intended course, the spaceship crash-lands on Venus, a planet ruled by gun-totin' women who hate men, along with a few subversives who long for knowledge of the strange opposite sex. *Variety*'s review in 1958 noted that "most of the female characters look like they would be more at home on a Minsky runway than the Cape Canaveral launching pad." More obvious today is the lesbian subtext that pervades the planet.

In a plot that's slow in thickening, Zsa Zsa appears thirty-one minutes into the film. With her dazzling face, as tight and Mongolian as any one of her supposed Asian forebears', she looks all set to play Turandot. She's not a queen, not an empress—not yet. That role went to Laurie Mitchell. At the end of the picture, however, *zat qveen* gets incinerated and Zsa Zsa, in gold lamé, ruby earrings, and tiara, ascends the throne, which resembles a chair in a dentist's waiting room.

The queen's face is horribly scarred from radiation burns, and so she wears a mask. "Men did this to me!" she cries out when finally Eric Fleming unmasks her. She wants to destroy Earth before it can attack her planet. The politics of this picture could be read from the left as an allegory of U.S. imperialism, from the right a condemnation of Soviet Cold War policies.

Zsa Zsa, who seems to be an eminent Venusian scientist, wears a parade of evening gowns to the lab. When captive earthmen elude their female guards and a melee breaks out in Zsa Zsa's workspace, she screams, "Get out! You are disturbing my vork!" And petulantly pulls her filmy shawl tighter across her shoulders. Eventually she sides with the earthmen, whom the queen considers responsible for wars and planetary mayhem. While the film's sexism was funny in 1958, today it is jeered at screenings. The queen and her battalion of strong women get the applause.

Tom Weaver, author of *Interviews with B Science Fiction and Horror Movie Makers*, joined Laurie Mitchell for the DVD audio commentary on *Queen of Outer Space* in 2008. Fifty years after filming, she recalled much of interest. "Edward Bernds, the director, shot one-fifth of the picture in a day. He explained to the cast that Zsa Zsa was a very *sensitive* actress. During the several weeks of filming, she wanted me to hang out with her. I don't know why. The gossip columns ran items that we were not getting along, but that was baloney." Mitchell recalled that Rubirosa would phone Zsa Zsa from France when she was on the set. He also sent champagne, which she kept in her dressing room.

"Do you want to drink some?" she asked Laurie.

"That's very sweet," Mitchell replied, "but I don't drink while I'm working."

"Okay, you come back later."

Several years after filming, Laurie Mitchell was collecting her luggage at Heathrow Airport in London when she saw Zsa Zsa at the same carousel.

> LM: *"Hello, Zsa Zsa. I'm Laurie."*
> ZZG *(nonchalant): "Hello."*
> LM: *"Do you know who I am?"*
> ZZG: *"No, I do not."*
> LM: *"I did* Queen of Outer Space *with you."*
> ZZG: *"That's nice."* (Pause) *"I'm so terribly upset. They will not let my dog sit next to me in the plane."*

It was a puppy, Laurie recalled, and Zsa Zsa was afraid he would die in the compartment where animals travel. Laurie tried to reassure her that he would be all right. Zsa Zsa's last words were, "I am going to make a big fuss over this. I want him to sit next to me."

For his book, published in 1988, Weaver interviewed Edward Bernds. The director told him how the picture came to be made. At the time, no one dreamed that *Queen of Outer Space* would transcend its low origins to soar into the kitsch stratosphere, taking Zsa Zsa with it. The producer Walter Wanger, husband of Joan Bennett, shot his wife's lover and went to jail. Needing work after serving a four-month sentence, he came to Allied Artists. He brought with him a ten-page story outline by Ben Hecht titled *Queen of the Universe*, which Bernds recalled as "not a motion picture story at all. It was just a satirical look at a planet ineptly ruled by women."

Eventually Ben Schwalb, rather than Wanger, produced the picture from a screenplay by Charles Beaumont. There being very little of use in the Ben Hecht outline, the screenplay, according to Bernds, turned into "pretty much an original." After extended rewriting by Bernds and other hands, the shooting script incorporated virtually everything that later made it unforgettable.

Asked about directing Laurie Mitchell, Eric Fleming, and Zsa Zsa, Bernds said that he had used Mitchell in several previous films and liked her work. Fleming, he recalled, was "a model of professionalism, always prepared, dialogue solidly memorized, all business despite Zsa Zsa's flightiness."

Questioned further about Zsa Zsa, Bernds said that "she was not thoroughly professional, she didn't have her lines well prepared, she had a kind of giddy attitude toward things." During wardrobe wrangles before filming began, Bernds complained to the producer about her demands. He told Schwalb, "This is our chance to dump her. If she wants to walk, let her walk." The producer demurred. "No, we need a star. Without a star we haven't got a picture. Humor her."

According to Bernds, "Ben Schwalb went to the hospital with ulcers halfway through the picture," the implication being that Zsa Zsa caused them. "I was left to cope with her alone," Bernds added, "and she damn near gave *me* ulcers. If the picture's shown on TV, I won't watch it, because Zsa Zsa Gabor still gives me a swift pain."

Eventually, Bernds softened somewhat toward Zsa Zsa. Interviewed in 1998 by *Scary Monsters* magazine, he said, "When Zsa Zsa and I went to choose her costume, she was much too picky and wouldn't wear anything they had to offer. This became at the time quite irritating to me. Looking back, however, I can agree because she was indeed a beautiful woman but also she was our star with the power of drawing people into theatres to see *Queen of Outer Space*. Her appearance was our future. If she had allowed us to put something on her just because it was available that would not have been in her best interest. I respect her for this. She had to protect her image."

Laurie Mitchell added that Zsa Zsa "wanted to know what I was wearing and where did I get it. The wardrobe woman made sure none of us in the cast had the same hair color as Zsa Zsa, nor similar costumes." Mitchell said she believed that Zsa Zsa had a special designer for her clothes, one not affiliated with Allied Artists, the Poverty Row production company.

By the time of Zsa Zsa's collaboration with Wendy Leigh on *One Lifetime Is Not Enough*, a highly fictionalized memoir published in 1991, she had convinced herself that Ben Hecht wrote *Queen of Outer Space*. She added, "I adored my costumes, designed by Edith Head and costing a staggering $15,000 apiece." Since by her own admission she received $10,000 for her work in the picture, one suspects that her own brand of creative accounting added several zeros to the dressmaker's tab. And while no one disputes the graffito,

"Edith Head gives good wardrobe," she didn't give Zsa Zsa any of it for *Queen of Outer Space*.

In October 1958 Zsa Zsa flew to Italy to film *For the First Time*, with Mario Lanza. Directed by Rudolf Maté, whose career as cinematographer includes such classics as *The Passion of Joan of Arc* (1928), *Foreign Correspondent* (1940), and *Gilda* (1946), the picture promised more than it delivered. As a director, Maté lacked the artistry that he often achieved with the camera. Zsa Zsa plays a Continental playgirl whose line—"When I first came to Capri, I used to fall in love every other day"—predicts her next forty years of TV chitchat. For several in the cast, it was a valediction. Lanza died shortly after the picture's release; the ingenue, Johanna von Koczian, had a low-grade career confined to German-language films and TV; and this was Zsa Zsa's last costarring appearance in a respectable, though mediocre, movie. Her role fits the image the public had now formed of her: a publicity-seeking playgirl. When Mario Lanza complains about so many reporters at what was supposed to be an intimate party, Zsa Zsa replies: "But dahling, these are my most intimate friends—United Press, Associated Press, and Mister Reuters."

Next came an obscure Italian picture, *La Contessa Azzurra*, released in 1960, followed by *Pepe* the following year. In it, Zsa Zsa begins her devolution into meaningless cameo roles. (Her first one, in *Touch of Evil*, had a purpose thanks to Orson Welles.) Neither she, nor the two dozen other stars who make cameo appearances in *Pepe*, adds anything to George Sidney's long, lumpish bore. Her next humiliation came when she happened to be in England in 1961. Hearing that Bob Hope and Bing Crosby had reunited for another of their popular "Road" pictures, she turned up at their location shoot thirty miles outside London. "Bob dahling," she said, "I understand there is the most wonderful part in your picture for me."

"Sure is, honey," he replied. "We'll have it written tomorrow." According to Bob Hope's memoir, *The Road to Hollywood*, the writers devised a scene in which Zsa Zsa played a nurse attempting to cure Hope of amnesia. This hurried-up scene, along with Hope and Crosby's burned-out shtick, plus pervasive Hollywood mediocrity in the early sixties—throw them all together and what you get is Zsa Zsa's brief scene deleted and Zsa Zsa left to television: *Make Room for Daddy, Mister Ed, General Electric Theater, Burke's Law, Gilligan's Island.* Despite the eventual rerun popularity of some of these shows among viewers who weren't subjected to the original telecasts, those titles and dozens in the same key add up to a sad legacy for someone of Zsa Zsa's earlier possibilities.

It's hard to realize today that just over fifty years ago Hollywood made sophomoric movies about horny adults. The Doris Day virgin role in *Boys Night Out* (1962) went to Kim Novak, who perhaps put in a good word for Zsa Zsa and got her a wee part at the end of the picture. In a ten-second shot, she glides in, swathed in chinchilla. This one, however, was not the Trujillo jacket that caused the uproar four years earlier but another one from her closet. The tepid filmography continued through the sixties, with Zsa Zsa in the kind of movies that made people stay home and watch TV: *Picture Mommy Dead; Arrivederci, Baby; Jack of Diamonds.* And throughout the seventies as well, with *Up the Front, Every Girl Should Have One,* and *Won Ton Ton: The Dog Who Saved Hollywood.*

The bleak cavalcade seemed endless, like a ghost train circling the world. In the eighties, *Frankenstein's Great Aunt Tillie; Smart Alec; A Nightmare on Elm Street 3: Dream Warriors; Johann Strauss: The King without a Crown;* and into the nineties: *The Naked Gun 2 1/2: The Smell of Fear; The Naked Truth; The Beverly Hillbillies;* up to her finale, a cameo with Rosie O'Donnell in *A Very Brady Sequel* in 1996.

The period known as the fifties did not necessarily finish at midnight on December 31, 1959. Some say the spirit of that decade only ended with the election of JFK in 1960; others move the date to November 22, 1963. In Hollywood, distant rumblings became more ominous, and on August 5, 1962, catastrophe struck: the death of Marilyn Monroe, a terrible event in itself but also a convenient symbol to mark the demise of old-fashioned glamour, in Hollywood and else-where. For the legions of blonde actresses who claimed the 1950s as their decade, the following years turned barren and bitter. Those who survived had to undergo a metamorphosis. Even so, few emerged from the ordeal with wings; the change more likely took them backward, into a cocoon of ruptured dreams. Zsa Zsa and Eva at least kept their own wings, which by the early sixties were showing battle fatigue.

An apocryphal story: at a Hollywood party in the early sixties, two iconic fifties blondes are sitting together on a patio, looking up at the stars and commiserating. Their talk is about the difficulty of maintaining any semblance of a career in the post-studio era, when their kind of glamour and hijinks have become passé and they now must grab any job they can get, whether cheap TV or dinner theatre or summer stock in bottom-feeder plays.

"You know," says Jayne Mansfield to Mamie Van Doren, "Marilyn was the lucky one."

Chapter 29

Shatterproof

Magda Gabor viewed life through a darker lens than others in her family. If Eva was the optimist, and Zsa Zsa the absurdist, then Magda might be called the realist. As such, if history had not decreed otherwise, Magda might eventually have taken over the family businesses in Budapest, for she had the mind of a CEO. In the gender-role terminology of last century, Magda did a man's work: as an underground operative and Red Cross volunteer in Hungary, she drove trucks and ambulances at a time when many women could not imagine their hands on a steering wheel. Without stouthearted Magda, Jolie and Vilmos would surely have perished at the hands of the Nazis.

We have seen how, later in New York, she masterminded Jolie's success in the jewelry business and drove it forward. At times, Magda functioned as her mother's keeper, especially when irrepressible Jolie played the scatterbrain. Scolded by her elder daughter, giggling Jolie would say, "Oh Magduska, you are always anxious and worried about me. It is like you are the mother and I am your daughter."

"You do stupid things. That's when I feel I must take care of you."

Magda, having absorbed her father's no-nonsense business acumen, perhaps comprehended herself in masculine terms. Once when the columnist Earl Wilson expressed doubt over some gossipy tidbit she confided to him, Magda's comeback was, "You know I tell the truth. After all, I am a gentleman."

Genteel exterior notwithstanding, she could fight like a bruiser. In the mid-fifties, Magda and Eva had a huge quarrel. ("I don't know why," she said later, "and anyway it's unimportant.") The sisters did not speak for months. Then one evening Magda and Tony Gallucci went to El Morocco. No sooner were they seated than who should enter but Eva and her husband of the moment, John Williams.

"If you call her to our table," Magda said to Tony in a steel-blade voice, "I will never talk to you again." He demolished a drink and quickly ordered another.

After studiously avoiding Eva's glances, Magda excused herself to the powder room. She returned to find her sister and brother-in-law seated at *her* table, chatting merrily with Tony. In Hungarian, Magda spat out, "You fool!"

To which Eva replied, in English, "I think you are so bitchy." Eva's linguistic sucker punch infuriated Magda even further.

"Why did you say it in English? We fight in Hungarian, not English. Get away!"

Eva and John left. A bit later, a family friend stopped by to greet Magda and Tony. Magda's sullen face prompted him to ask, "What has upset you?" Eyes flashing, she gave a terse account.

"Why do you lower yourself to her standards?" was his tactless query.

"How dare you speak of my sister like that!" Magda exploded. And never spoke to him again. The point of her story was one that every Gabor made sooner or later: "I don't think that any of us alone could really stand. Even when I re-sent my sisters, we stick together."

Tough, moody, a no-nonsense businesswoman with a get-on-with-it attitude towards life and work, she spent many years in struggle, first to distance herself from her family's an-tics, then to regain her damaged health. For in 1962, Magda suffered a debilitating stroke. She was forty-seven years old at the time.

This massive stroke was foreshadowed by what appears to have been a ministroke, or transient ischemic attack (TIA). Five years earlier, during a heated quarrel with Jolie, Magda temporarily lost the ability to speak.

Then, in the fall of 1962, Jolie and her husband, Edmond de Szigethy, came to the Gallucci estate in Southampton for a long weekend with Magda and Tony and to take in the Horse Show Ball, a traditional event that ended the summer social season in the Hamptons. In the early hours of Friday morn-ing, Magda got up from her bed. Not wanting to wake Tony, she didn't turn on a light. Although she always warned visit-ing family and other guests not to trip over Maxim, her black poodle who slept on the staircase, this time she herself for-got. The dog didn't move. Magda tripped and banged her head on the stair rail. Tony heard the crash, turned on the light, and rushed to help his wife. Other than the immediate pain of the bump on her head, she seemed all right. He rang for the maid, who applied cold compresses for an hour or two, and then everyone went back to sleep.

On Friday afternoon, Magda was restless. She seemed un-reasonably annoyed with Tony because he was drinking with the butler and watching a baseball game on TV rather than keeping watch by her bedside. Jolie took Tony's part. "He is good and generous with you," she said. "Be a little under-standing with him and don't excite yourself."

By Saturday afternoon Magda was herself once more, and that evening, according to Jolie, she was the belle of the Horse

Show Ball. Toasted by friends and looking her high-toned best, she was photographed atop a wooden horse and seemed to enjoy every moment of the long evening. But if Magda, Tony, Edmond, and Jolie had paused to recall the Trojan Horse of mythology and the calamity it brought with it, superstition might have made them flee and seek all possible help.

On Sunday morning a panicked Tony summoned Jolie, who occupied the guest house. "Come quick," he panted. "Magda cannot speak. I think she's in a coma." Arriving at the main house, Jolie and Edmond knew immediately that Magda was gravely ill. An ambulance took her to the local hospital, and in the afternoon she was transferred to Mount Sinai, in Manhattan.

Zsa Zsa happened to be in New York. As soon as she got word of Magda's condition, she telephoned Eva, who had arrived that very morning in Palm Beach. Eva took the next plane to New York, and by late Sunday evening the family had gathered in Magda's hospital room.

After four months of hospitalization and rehabilitation, Magda at last was able to return home to Southampton. Speech therapists at the Rusk Clinic in New York told her she would never speak again. Jolie recalled that "Magda became bitter and it broke my heart. She kept trying to tell me something but she couldn't. She could manage a word or two but she couldn't connect phrases." She sank into a depression. One evening she said to Jolie, "No speech . . . die."

Stunned, Jolie said to her in grave tones, "If you die then I will die, too." Even at this nadir, gloom did not stay. Like a titanium alloy of strength and toughness, these two women began the rigorous journey that would eventually return Magda to functional health. In her future was a new home in Palm Springs, new friends, several lovers, and two additional husbands.

*   *   *

That journey toward healing required alpine effort. Although Magda never reached the top, she did achieve a lower plateau that confounded the negative prognosis of the Rusk Clinic. The young Helen Keller comes to mind: the high-pressure drive to speak, the angry frustration when words would not come, the despair and then the joy when at last sound, any sound, broke through the tongue-tied barrier. In the case of the deaf, blind, and mute girl, the first sentence was "I am not dumb now." For Magda, the open-sesame phrase became "Believe you me."

No doubt her flair for languages served her well, for she knew that in Hungarian (as in English and other languages) certain inflections and intonations not only convey nuance but also change the meaning of words. Although Magda did not know a tonal language such as Chinese, she eventually turned "Believe you me" into a palette of tones and timbres that could mean, according to tonality, emphasis, facial expression, and volume, everything from "Yes, it's exactly that way" to "If you don't like it, shut up."

A similar multipurpose phrase was "You better believe it." Family and close friends learned to follow her modulations, almost as if she were playing a musical theme and variations on the piano. Eventually Magda's glossary of shortcuts became an entire thesaurus. "I am able to understand her," Zsa Zsa said. Francesca explained further that "my aunt Magda can't speak, but she has all her brain power. By now we can all understand her." Magda remained as much a Gabor sister as always, meaning that she attended Jolie's parties, also Zsa Zsa's and Eva's, turned up at nightclubs and society soirées, and proved herself an actress after all: so clever was she in hiding her challenges that press and public soon forgot. Perhaps she had Garbo in mind, who left the screen in 1941 and for the next fifty years was seen but not heard.

In 1966, when Magda's efforts to recover sometimes threatened to overwhelm her, Tony Gallucci developed cancer and died the following year. Again, Magda was devastated. She almost gave up. Jolie, seeing her smoke two packs of cigarettes a day and drink too much coffee, couldn't bring herself to say, Stop. Nor had Magda yet developed her later idiosyncratic vocabulary and syntax. After Tony's death, for instance, if she wanted to tell Jolie that friends had visited, she would say on the telephone, "Couple." When Jolie asked who had paid a call, Magda would fumble: "Man. Woman." At last, unable to go further, she would snap, "Forget. It."

An earlier chapter chronicled Magda's bitter fight with Tony's family over the codicil to his will. By the late sixties, when this probate war took place, she was advised to settle out of court. This Magda refused to do. In furs and jewels, she made her entrance in court with the aplomb of a Vanderbilt or an Astor. No one guessed that the words she whispered to her lawyers amounted to "yes," "no," "fight," and a few other monosyllables.

Zsa Zsa, within the Gabor family and out, was said to be tightfisted. In the matter of distributing ex-husbands, however, she had grown philanthropic. Happy was she when they found new wives—except in the case of George Sanders. Even so, she befriended his third spouse, Benita Hume, whom he married in 1959 and with whom he lived in great contentment until her death in 1967. Zsa Zsa visited them in England, and Benita wrote regular letters telling Zsa Zsa of their travels and of George's health. After Benita's death, George sank into depression and drink. At times he seemed unhinged, the aftermath perhaps of a light stroke that left him shaken both physically and emotionally.

Benita Hume and Tony Gallucci died the same year. Zsa Zsa, increasingly concerned for widow and widower, invited

George to come and live with her. "He's lonely, and I have plenty of room," she said. (Marriage and divorce being so fluid under Zsa Zsa's roof, George's homecoming resembled that of a prodigal welcomed once more into the parental nest.) George, although loath to admit it, found a measure of contentment with his wacky in-laws. When Zsa Zsa was away, he consoled himself with Jolie and Magda in Palm Springs, and now that Francesca no longer required kiddie games and baby minding, he enjoyed hearing of her volatile adventures. He also encouraged her independence from draconian Grandmother Gabor. As ironic connoisseur of the absurd, George occasionally wondered why he hadn't stuck around.

Zsa Zsa, having disburdened herself in 1967 of husband number five, found George the perfect male to live with. Their "dates" involved watching television, walking dogs, refereeing cat fights—between actual felines as well as Gabor sister-cats—and settling into middle age, though woe betide anyone who applied the term within Zsa Zsa's hearing.

It was almost like being in love—until George, in a moment of candor, let Zsa Zsa in on a secret. A rich society lady had suggested that he marry her (for money being understood) but also for security, companionship, villas on tropical islands and spacious apartments in New York and Europe. This announcement formed icicles on Zsa Zsa's heart. Always a quick thinker, she countered with, "Magda is also rich. She is terribly lonely, and so are you. You need each other, you can help each other. Besides, you always said I talk too much. Magda can barely speak. She always loved your movies, now she will listen to you all the day and night."

George, only in his early sixties but feeling much older, considered the proposition. While he shopped marital possibilities in his mind, Zsa Zsa flew to Jolie's side. "Nyuszika," she gurgled, "I want to keep George in the family. We have all loved him, even you. He didn't mean it the time he called you a fucking Hungarian. Let's give him to Magda, then they will have each other to lean on."

A few days later, George told Zsa Zsa, "Cokiline, I've thought it over and for once you make sense." Meanwhile, Jolie informed Magda of the latest marital plans afoot. "Unbelievable. Beautiful," Magda said.

Decision made, George acted like a young groom-to-be. He bought forty red roses in Los Angeles and rushed them to Palm Springs into the hands of his former sister-in-law, now his betrothed. "Let's have vodka and caviar," he said, "and get married immediately." Like a hurry-up wedding in an RKO western circa 1940, they rushed off not to a grizzled frontier preacher but to a judge in the small town of Indio, a few miles out of Palm Springs. There they exchanged their vows on December 4, 1970. At the reception, held in the Palm Springs Racquet Club, Jolie said, "It's always nice to welcome a son-in-law back into the family."

For a brief moment, generosity flooded George's heart. He bought Magda a television set and paid $300 to repair her Cadillac. Then the flood receded; after all, the new Mrs. Sanders was rich—why should he unglue his banknotes?

The wedding shocked the world, or at least that fragment of the world who still remembered George Sanders. As for Magda, many mistook her for Zsa Zsa and Eva's mother. The revolution had happened—the sixties—and now the seventies swept away the few remnants of studio-era stars and glamour. The likes of Ali MacGraw and Carrie Snodgress became icons of antiglamour, and few movie fans in the younger set knew such names as Sanders or Gabor. These grotesque nuptials struck them, if at all, as belonging to a firmament wedged between *Hollywood Babylon* and the Motion Picture Country Home.

Less than six weeks later, the marriage was annulled. George, who perhaps believed that Magda was a quieter Zsa

Zsa, awoke to the realization that his new wife was a semi-invalid. Since the stroke, her right arm was paralyzed, meaning she did everything with her left. According to Jolie, she learned to adjust her wigs, apply makeup, even attach false eyelashes. But Palm Springs, for the unsocial like George, might just as well be Bakersfield. What does one do all day after a quick morning look at mountains and palm trees? How many hours can anyone splash in an azure pool? One day George drove away and never returned. Magda didn't grieve. The end of a marriage had become as routine as tax day on April 15 or a dental checkup twice a year.

George's health continued to decline and he suffered another stroke and showed signs of dementia. Zsa Zsa went to him in Europe and tried to help, but he had decided his fate. On April 25, 1972, he died from an overdose of sleeping pills in a hotel in Spain, where he had lived after leaving Magda. His suicide note echoed the cynical, world-weary characters he often played onscreen: "Dear World, I am leaving because I am bored. I feel I have lived long enough. I am leaving you with your worries in this sweet cesspool. Good luck."

George's death saddened every Gabor. Each one, and Francesca, as well, absorbed the grief in her own way.

Other suitors came calling, for Magda was known as a rich, lonely widow. Anyone mistaking her for vulnerable soon found out the opposite, for in addition to her own powerful will, any hint of exploitation locked the Gabor testudo into place—testudo being a Roman military formation in which soldiers turned their shields into protective cover like a tortoiseshell against enemy projectiles.

Then in August 1972 Magda married Tibor Heltai, a Manhattan real estate broker born in Hungary in 1918. They separated ten months later and divorced in 1975.

Chapter 30

Dahling, I Love You,
but Give Me Park Avenue

Eva Gabor had two marital mottoes. The first was, "Marriage is too interesting an experiment to be tried only once or twice." The second, "I will tolerate many things from a husband but I will not tolerate a husband who cheats." Richard Brown, whom she married in 1959, met both conditions. Husband number four was blatant in his infidelities. When Eva found out, he joined the exes.

They met in 1957. The press described Brown, divorced with two teenage sons, as a retired, at thirty-seven, textile manufacturer and also as a millionaire stockbroker. Whatever his profession, Eva made sure this time that the husband would pay at least more than his share of the bills. After dating for a year, they were in Las Vegas to see Betty Grable's show at the Flamingo Hotel. Between sets, Brown whispered in Eva's ear, "Will you marry me?" Speaking to reporters after the ceremony, she said, "I played hard to get and said yes."

Like two kids fleeing a paternal shotgun, Eva and Dick decided the wedding must take place the next day. The following afternoon, she assembled a trousseau from the hotel dress shop, then rounded up comedian Red Buttons to give the bride away and his wife as matron of honor. The marriage took place with such speed that no other Gabors had time to fly in. Jolie and Zsa Zsa telephoned congratulations. When reporters called Zsa Zsa in New York, she said, "I'm sorry I can't be there but I'm giving her away by approximately— oh, that's not right, but you know what I mean." The press helpfully supplied the word "proxy."

"This time is for real," Eva said, as if that ominous phrase had never before been spoken.

Six months before the wedding, scandal had touched Eva. She, unlike Zsa Zsa, was not accustomed to it and disliked its effects. A typical tabloid headline: EVA GABOR CALLED LOVE PIRATE. JILTED MODEL TAKES HER LIFE. The model was Venita Ratcliffe, who committed suicide with an overdose of sleeping pills in her Park Avenue apartment. Her note addressed to Dick Brown ended with the words, "I love you more than life itself."

Eva learned of these headlines at MGM, where she was filming *It Started with a Kiss*. Extremely upset, she left the soundstage and went to her dressing room accompanied by several costars. A studio publicist issued a statement from Eva: "I am very, very sorry that this beautiful girl took her life. But I am really an innocent bystander in all this. The romance between Richard and me began long after he left Venita."

Eva, falsely accused, grew angry once she recovered from the initial shock. An Associated Press story reported her fury. "I do not go around taking anyone's man," she declared. "*I am no love pirate!* Besides, if a man is truly in love, the most beautiful woman in the world couldn't take him away."

Eva was indeed innocent. The Gabors didn't break up homes—except their own.

*   *   *

Eva's career in the 1960s did not nosedive as Zsa Zsa's did. She made only two films, in both of which she gave a pleasing performance. In *A New Kind of Love* (1963), four good actors—Paul Newman, Joanne Woodward, Thelma Ritter, and Eva—are humiliated by the stultifying script and the coy direction of this sex comedy that's at least ten years over the hill.

Eva is the best thing in it. As feisty French sophisticate Félicienne Courbeau, she outshines the provincial Americans in Paris who behave like clichés. Resplendent in Edith Head gowns, she has effervescent comic moments when she does the twist (not very well) with George Tobias, and then with Thelma Ritter.

In 1963, Eva was forty-four. Her latest face surgery had begun to wear off, and you see lines and a hint of sag, neither of which detracts from her beauty. Eva's softer face, with its touch of wistful vulnerability, made her more winsome than Zsa Zsa.

In *Youngblood Hawke* (1964), Eva plays the wife of a New York publisher. Youngblood Hawke (James Franciscus) is the naive young novelist from Kentucky that Eva's husband takes advantage of. Eva, in a small role, seems in her element as a social arbiter and party giver in the New York literary world, mass market division.

In retrospect, Eva's attempts during the early sixties to be taken seriously as a stage actress draw admiration for effort over result. She herself realized this disparity. Asked near the end of her life, "Do you have any regrets?" Eva gave a melancholy answer: "Oh yes! If I had been born English, I could have done Shakespeare, such wonderful plays I could have done if I didn't have this accent." Even so, she could always crack a joke. Appearing on Liberace's television show, she chirped, "I went to the same school in New York as Marlon Brando—I studied at the school of Methodist acting."

(At the Actors Studio in 1955, she did indeed attend classes in *Method* acting.)

Eva always took herself seriously as an actress, despite mountainous obstacles. She never stopped polishing her craft. In 1967 she studied for a time with Agnes Moorehead, who was highly regarded as both actress and drama teacher. Nor did she ever lose the desire for thoughtful audiences and perceptive critics. Several colleagues in New York theatre must have seen promise beyond the accent and Eva's reputation for theatre-lite on the summer circuit, among them David Ross, a respected producer and director of off-Broadway modern classics in the fifties and sixties. Ross cast Eva in 1958 as the eponymous *Lulu* in Frank Wedekind's controversial erotic tragedy. The play documents the strange story of a young woman whose sexuality and innocence lead her from risky lovers in Germany and Paris to the streets of London and Jack the Ripper. Wedekind's play is still performed, though its later adaptation by Alban Berg as the opera *Lulu* is more widely seen today. Eva accepted a salary of seventy-five dollars a week. Neither the play nor the production, however, was liked by playgoers or reviewers. *Lulu* ended its run at the Fourth Street Theater after sixteen performances.

Surely Eva's bravest attempt at classic theatre took place around 1961 before an audience of only forty or fifty. Gene Gill was there that night, when Eva played the title role in Ibsen's *Hedda Gabler*. Gill is probably the only remnant of that vanished evening. For that reason, and also because she has been an avid theatregoer since her earliest years, I quote at length from her unique recollections.

"I remember Eva Gabor's performance in *Hedda Gabler* quite well, though I can't be certain of the year. My mother was in New York, and we went somewhere off, off, off-Broadway and walked up at least one flight of stairs into what seemed an apartment that had been gutted for use as a tiny theatre. When we got out of the taxi, the driver was worried about our safety. A scary neighborhood, someplace on the Lower East Side.

"We sat in a U-shape, not a complete circle, and we happened to be in the front row. Eva Gabor was the most beautiful creature I've ever seen. She was a foot or two away from me, and her skin looked like porcelain. She had provided her own costumes. I only remember one, a garnet shade of velvet. Of course it had a bustle for period detail. Her blonde hair was piled high.

"Lester Rawlins played Tesman, Hedda's husband. He was quite a credible actor. I don't remember anyone else in the cast. I attended the performance because I'm an Ibsen freak and I really wanted to see it. I didn't go because of Eva, but I became her fan. I thought she acquitted herself with professionalism. It was not the best Hedda I had seen before, nor since. But she did not embarrass herself in any way. No, it wasn't a staged reading. The cast had memorized the script. There were several pieces of furniture in that small space—a love seat and a couple of other pieces."

Asked whether this was a backers' audition, Gene Gill said, "I believe it was more of a vanity production. In fact, Eva herself may have put money into it." And was the one-time performance more flamboyant or subdued? "I considered it subdued."

Since Eva's costar Lester Rawlins had appeared in David Ross's production of *Hedda Gabler* at the Fourth Street Theater in 1960, it seems plausible that both Rawlins and Ross had Eva in mind for a more visible production. Eva's bravery in attempting this daunting role suggests her dissatisfaction with standard-issue stock comedies and predictable TV dramas. Hedda is a role that many an actress wants to play. Before Eva, and after, legends performed it, including Eleonora Duse, Alla Nazimova, Ingrid Bergman, Diana Rigg, Claire Bloom, Maggie Smith, and Glenda Jackson.

*   *   *

Next Eva turned to musical comedy. While it is true that many ad hoc singers in Broadway musicals can't sing, in Eva's case the term "vocal shortcomings" is an understatement. Hers could have inspired the phrase, "can't carry a tune in a bucket." (In the *Green Acres* opening montage, she veers off-key with the line, "Dahling I love you, but give me Park Avenue.") Certain nonsingers know enough tricks to fool an audience; for instance, Rex Harrison in *My Fair Lady* talk-sings his way through the picture, as he did through the play. Marlene Dietrich sang for years without really singing— her triumph had to do with style, illusion, and the Dietrich legend.

When Eva replaced the ailing Vivien Leigh in *Tovarich* on Broadway in 1963, eyebrows raised. Not that Leigh was really a singer, but she could *act* a song. The show's producers must have concluded that Eva had the same ability, since they could have chosen from a battalion of other candidates. Eva took over on October 21; the play ended its eight-month run on November 9. The following summer, she had a longer success with the play on tour.

Jean-Pierre Aumont, male lead for the run of the play, recalled Eva as costar in *Tovarich*: "I knew the Gabor sisters well, since I had already filmed *Lili* with Zsa Zsa. Eva proved to be charming, both on and off the stage. Though she didn't have Vivien's royal bearing, she compensated for this by her good humor and her communicative warmth. The play wavered a little. Instead of the story of a grand duchess who is transformed into a maid, it became the story of a lovely young thing who disguises herself as a grand duchess."

Tovarich did not end Eva's work in musicals. In 1973 she toured in *Applause*, the Charles Strouse and Lee Adams musical based on *All About Eve*. The tour, a financial and critical disaster, cost the producers some $200,000 in losses. One

cruel reviewer wrote, "No applause, Eva Gabor is dreadful."
Another misfortune: during a performance at the Valley
Forge Music Fair outside Philadelphia, Eva fractured her
thigh bone. She missed only two performances, resuming the
tour in a cast from hip to ankle. According to an audience
member, "They wheeled her down the aisle and sort of
dumped her onstage." Chorus boys immediately scooped her
up and hoisted her as necessary up to the finale.

Always a pro, Eva performed in the cumbersome cast for
six weeks, during which time she suffered migraines and a
mild case of pneumonia. Incidentally, Lauren Bacall, who originated the role of Margo Channing in *Applause* on Broadway,
was also an unconvincing singer and dancer.

During that painful summer, Eva quietly divorced Richard
Brown. Later she talked about his infidelity. "I know how
men are—strange creatures, and being what they are I don't
mind maybe if they have a one-night stand. But at least they
must be discreet. When everybody in the studio knows but
me, then I say it's too much. Even so, I stayed with him three
years more even after I found out, so you must say I tried."

A few years after *Applause*, Eva appeared in a dozen performances of *A Little Night Music*. These took place in Warren, Ohio, far from Broadway and Stephen Sondheim, who
might have required CPR had he heard Eva's rendition of
"Send in the Clowns."

Why, given Eva's musical challenges, did producers continue to cast her in roles beyond her reach? The main reason:
audience likeability. In show-biz lingo, she put asses in the
seats. Then, too, except for *Tovarich*, her musicals took place
after *Green Acres* left the air, meaning that the series had
made her a household name. It was thought, therefore, that
out-of-town playgoers, considered less demanding than New
York audiences, wouldn't notice if she flitted through a song
with the giddy effervescence of Lisa Douglas. Such audiences
came for the name, not for the notes. Another reason pro-

ducers liked casting Eva: she was always the pro. Unlike Zsa Zsa, whose high maintenance, lack of dedication, and fits of pique made her the bottom choice instead of the top, Eva toiled as a team member. After all, she adored her *Green Acres* colleague Arnold the pig.

It was in 1965 that Eva landed the role for which she is remembered by legions of TV viewers, Lisa Douglas. Although not the legacy Eva would have chosen, *Green Acres* made her a bigger star than ever before. Its 170 episodes also provided steady work and a large income for six seasons, until 1971.

Given the many oddities of network television, it's risky to single out one show as especially bizarre. Even so, *Green Acres* belongs among the more indelibly flaky. It deconstructs the archetypal myth of happy rural America by mixing elements of a surreal fever dream with the frantic action of Hollywood animated cartoons, the paintings of Grant Wood and Grandma Moses, and chaotic set pieces from the silent films of Charlie Chaplin and Buster Keaton. Perhaps with a nod to the Marx Brothers, language turns somersaults: endless puns, malapropisms, figures of speech taken literally, meanings turned inside out. The alphabet has gone mad. The result, when these visual and verbal elements are chopped up and reassembled as a goofy collage, is a work of American Dada.

Like the original European Dadaists from roughly 1915 to 1925, the creators of *Green Acres* rejected reason and logic in favor of chaos and irrationality. Whether the producers and writers of *Green Acres* also intended their work as antiwar protest and a rejection of bourgeois capitalist society, as their European predecessors had done, is a topic for academic seminars. (To start that discussion: Paul Henning, creator/writer/producer at various times of *The Beverly Hillbillies, Petticoat Junction,* and *Green Acres,* came from Missouri, like Mark Twain, whose writings no doubt influenced these sitcoms. David Marc, in his book *Demographic Vistas: Televison in American Culture*, depicts Henning as "unabashed and hyperbolic in his idealization of backwoods life.")

Although Henning is often called the creator of *Green Acres*, he neither desired nor accepted such credit. He insisted that Jay Sommers be given full acclaim as the show's creator. Henning was executive producer only. Nor did he write any of the scripts. One might say that while *The Beverly Hillbillies* and *Petticoat Junction* were Henning's progeny, to *Green Acres* he was godfather. Nevertheless, his semblance hovers around every episode. For one thing, *Green Acres* is the mirror image of *The Beverly Hillbillies*. In the latter, country comes to town; in the former, city slickers Oliver and Lisa Douglas try farm living. Then, too, Henning had written for George Burns and Gracie Allen in the early days of television. So memorable was Gracie's gaga shtick that the writers of *Green Acres* updated it for Eva's Lisa Douglas.

Eva, however, was no one's first choice for the role. According to Stephen Cox, in *The Hooterville Handbook: A Viewer's Guide to Green Acres*, Jay Sommers wanted Martha Hyer for the part, but she demanded too much money—$100,000 per show. Next, Sommers tested Marsha Hunt and Janet Blair, followed by some two dozen other actresses. Neither he nor CBS thought Eva right for the part, one reason being her accent. But Eva was Henning's choice from the start. He and his wife remembered her from fifteen years earlier on Broadway in *The Happy Time*, and to them she was the only viable candidate for Lisa Douglas. Unlike Sommers and CBS, they liked the incongruity of her accent. Another point in her favor with the Hennings was the lingering foreignness that she (like the other Gabors) retained even after decades in the U.S. Eventually Henning overruled his producing partner and the network: "I'm going to use Eva Gabor!"

FINDING ZSA ZSA   295

Henning's choice delighted Eddie Albert. He and his wife, Margo, had met Eva and Zsa Zsa in the 1940s at a party given by Ernst Lubitsch, when he and Eva were lovers. During the *Green Acres* years, Eddie, Margo, and Eva often socialized in the evenings after work. "Margo was one of my best friends ever," Eva told Stephen Cox in 1993. "I loved her. And I love Eddie very much also." (Margo retired from acting in 1965 after a twenty-year career. She died in 1985. Eddie Albert died, age ninety-nine, in 2005.)

Despite Eva's congeniality, she had Gabor nerves and during the first season she tangled with Richard L. Bare, who directed virtually every episode of *Green Acres*. Interviewed by Stephen Cox, Bare said, "When Eva got on the show she must have thought, I'm going to be a television superstar. She immediately started to dominate the set."

Eventually Jay Sommers intervened. He called Bare and Eva together and said, "Now what's all this about, Miss Gabor?"

"He keeps me in a box," she answered vaguely. "He won't let me do anything."

Bare's version of the conflict was more pointed: "Miss Gabor tends to overact and I've been trying to restrict her hand movements. I'm trying to get her into what I think is an acceptable mode."

Eva argued, "I just cannot do that. It's either him or me."

Whereupon Jay Sommers turned to her and said, "Miss Gabor, if anyone leaves the show, it's going to be you."

Years later, Bare clarified Sommers's bluff. "If Eva had taken her complaint to CBS, I would have been expendable." She didn't, and from then on she and Bare were friends. "I never had a day's trouble with Eva after that," he said. In his office hung a photograph of him directing Eva in a *Green Acres* bathtub scene. Eva's inscription, in green ink: "To dear Richard. Believe it or not, I love you. Eva."

* * *

The grind of a long-running TV series means boredom and hardship no matter how grateful the actors are to have work, and no matter how seriously they take the job. Penny Stallings, in her exposé *Forbidden Channels: The Truth They Hide from TV Guide,* recounts the grueling process that Eva underwent to remain ageless and beautiful, from age forty-six when the show began to fifty-two, when it ended: "Eva insisted on bringing along the well-known makeup man Gene Hibbs [who] devised a mechanical, as opposed to surgical, face lift for her based on a technique that had been used earlier for Lucille Ball and Barbara Stanwyck.

"The procedure began with the affixing of several discreet adhesive patches to the top of Eva's forehead and above her ears. Tiny silver hooks embedded in the tape were attached to elastic cords which encircled her scalp and were hidden under the elaborate bouffants and wigs she wore as Lisa Douglas. With the bands pulled tight, Eva's face remained supernaturally taut—even when she got allergic smelling hay."

Eva's devotion to Hibbs and his facial necromancy led to a rumor that persists to this day. According to Stallings, Hibbs's work was so crucial that Eva refused to give him a two-day leave in June 1969 to do the makeup on Judy Garland's corpse "even though Liza Minnelli had made a special request."

Eva denied being so imperious. "He and Judy were good friends," she said, "and she wanted him to do her hair when her time came. Gene told me he did not want to do that. But he could have gone if he'd wanted."

Those who write about Hollywood glamour seldom mention the underside: the tape and hooks holding up a face, the hot wigs, and, in Eva's case at least, getting up 5:00 a.m., working until after six in the evening, then going home to memorize "about thirty-eight pages of script every week," as she recalled.

Was it worth it? Eva's Lisa Douglas looked so ethereal, so unworldly that she seemed like Titania among the rustics, and in every episode she met the requirements for a fairy queen. One reason that Eva in *Green Acres* is remembered so vividly is because of her ravishing costumes. And not just one or two per episode, but many. In the first season, the eminent Hollywood designer Jean Louis did her lavish outfits. During contract negotiations, Eva demanded that he be hired. She would not settle for anyone else. Her further demands almost cost her the role, for she insisted on Peggy Shannon for her hairdresser and Gene Hibbs for makeup. Eventually the producers realized that Eva was right: lacking her dazzle, the show might not have survived its laugh track. (One reviewer counted 161 annoying hee-haws in just thirty minutes.) Eva made sure the producers saw a batch of fan letters that arrived after she appeared in a certain Jean Louis gown that she had worn in an episode a few weeks earlier. "What happened?" these viewers demanded. "Can't you afford a new dress?"

Jean Louis was nearing the end of his career, however, and his taste in materials far exceeded television budgets. Eva's costumes for subsequent seasons were almost entirely the work of Nolan Miller, in his early thirties and so new to film and TV fashion that Eva considered him her discovery. Everything she wore—dresses, negligees, evening gowns (often worn in the barn or in the kitchen while preparing inedible meals), boas, furs—were either Miller originals or else redesigned by him using prêt-à-porter from department stores and boutiques. In some episodes, Eva's costumes are elaborate to the point of excess, often so garish they put your eyes out.

Long after the series ended, a TV interviewer asked Eva, "What is it like to look beautiful and glamorous all the time?" A look of perplexity shadowed her face, as if she were about to reveal something momentous. "It is exhausting," she sighed, and for a moment she seemed ready to deflate.

Her colleagues on the show liked her, though in a few cases it took a while for Eva to warm up. Mary Grace Canfield, who played the inept carpenter Ralph Monroe, noted "a lot of insecurity, and maybe a certain amount of delicate fear. I have a feeling that what we saw on the outside was not what was on the inside." Eddie Albert said, "She isn't harebrained, no matter what you may hear. The Gabors have gotten that reputation mainly from Zsa Zsa. But Eva is very responsible." If Arnold the pig (and his two stand-ins) could have spoken in reality as in the show's Disneyesque scenes, they might have praised her above all humans, for she said, "I loved Arnold. I always made sure they treated him safely. One day they bound him inside a baby cradle and I refused to work until they stopped." Eulogizing Eva after her death in 1995, one of her friends said, "There is a special place in heaven for animal lovers, and especially for those who adore their porcine fellow-creatures."

On the set and off, the Gabor wit seldom waned. One of the show's dialogue coaches, Phil Gordon, told Stephen Cox about the time when he chatted with Eddie and Eva as they were being made up for the day's shoot. Eddie asked whether he had heard any new jokes, and when Gordon started telling one, Eva interrupted. "Please, dahling, I do not like dirty jokes." Then she turned and said, "Now where's my fucking comb?"

Another time, Gordon drove Eva home after work. "I was nervous because she's the star of the show, so I was driving slower than usual. A man was in the crosswalk and I stopped far ahead. Eva said to me, 'Dahling, what are you doing? You drive the way an old man fucks.'"

Gordon's retort: "Well, you ought to know." They laughed all the way to her front door.

During the first season of *Green Acres*, Richard Brown

flew from New York to Los Angeles on weekends to be with Eva. After the show became a hit, he moved to California and became a vice president of Filmways, the company that produced the series.

According to David Marc in *Demographic Vistas,* "both *The Beverly Hillbillies* and *Green Acres* were still in Nielsen's Top 20 in 1970." Their days were numbered, however, as networks and ad agencies panted after younger audiences— the eighteen-to-thirty-four age group—that they considered hip and more likely to buy products promoted on hip shows. These youths, in Madison Avenue-speak, comprised the "quality audience." Enter *All in the Family, Maude, The Mary Tyler Moore Show, Good Times,* et al. (As for so-called quality in sitcom programming, one size fits all, then and now, with only rare exceptions.) After the 1970–71 season, no more rural comedies. And, as David Marc points out, "The 1971 television season found the prime-time network schedules without a new Paul Henning work for virtually the first time in television history."

Nineteen years after *Green Acres* left the air, someone concocted a follow-up. *Return to Green Acres,* with a familiar cast sadly slowed by age, resembles a pageant staged in a care home. The exception is Eva, who, seventy-one but looking forty, with her svelte figure and dazzling wardrobe, could pass for Eddie Albert's granddaughter rather than his wife.

To distract myself while watching this misbegotten sequel, I looked for an unusual angle—and found it. Nostradamus-like, *Return to Green Acres* predicted the rise of Donald Trump!

Hooterville is threatened with destruction. A villainous New York real estate developer (played by Henry Gibson) and his obedient, cowardly son—Eric? Donald Jr.? Jared Kushner?—trick the inhabitants into selling their property for an environment-destroying industrial park and mall. Meanwhile, just when they are most needed in Hooterville, Oliver and Lisa have moved back to Park Avenue. Finding the city unendurable after their long absence, they heed the call of their friends who beg them for help.

Back in Hooterville, the naive rural folk had at first believed the villain to be on their side with his offers of money and commerce. By the time they realize his heartless plan to destroy their homes, it's almost too late. Oliver and Lisa organize a huge protest, the New York destroyer brings in state troopers armed with rifles, and the Douglases end up in jail. All is lost until . . .

The tyrant is defeated. Hooterville's citizens stage a fake earthquake that scares the despot, convincing him that his land lies over a dangerous fault line. Poltroon that he is, he jumps into his limo and hightails it out of town. The parable is uncannily prescient: the New York mega-crook at first seems a shrewd businessman. In the end, however, he's exposed as an evil dunce easily outwitted by the innocents he set out to fleece.

Sic semper tyrannis. *

In 1992, when Stephen Cox was writing *The Hooterville Handbook*, he interviewed members of the cast. In a recent telephone conversation, he talked about his afternoon with Eva at her mansion in Holmby Hills. I wondered whether she greeted him in full Gabor grandeur—wig, makeup, diamonds.

"No," he said. "A little makeup, and if she wore a wig it

---

* Were the writers, Craig Heller and Guy Shulman, clairvoyant? *Return to Green Acres* aired on May 18, 1990. In that year's March issue of *Playboy*, loudmouth Trump said, "I know politicians who love women who don't even want to be known for that—because they might lose the gay vote. OK? If this is the kind of extreme we're heading toward, we're really in trouble." He offered this as just one of the reasons why he would one day like to be known as Senator Trump or even President Trump.

was one of her less showy ones. She was dressed down, if you can imagine a Gabor dressing down. She wore jeans and a white shirt, the collar up a bit, and white tennis shoes."

The interview proceeded well, according to Cox, who had brought along a stack of publicity pictures from the show. Having interviewed many TV actors, he found that such photos prompted them to recall details. "I handed Eva a stack of pictures that I planned to use in my book. She started looking through them and making a pile. She put aside half a dozen or so, and handed back the rest. She didn't even ask, 'Are these for me?' I did not know what to say; it put me in a difficult position. I didn't want the interview to veer off course, so I let her keep the pictures."

At the end of the interview, which lasted a couple of hours: "She asked if I would help her move some lawn furniture!" At that, we paused the phone conversation for laughter. "Well," he continued, "we went to her guesthouse, which was lined with huge enlargements of *TV Guide* covers beautifully framed, along with other memorabilia.

"Eva said, 'I want to move this lounge chair over here, so you get in back and help me.' Which I did."

I suggested to Cox that when an older Hungarian asks you to do that sort of thing, which no one in Britain or Scandinavia, for instance, would dream of asking, it translates as, I like you, I trust you, and that's why I'm asking for your help. That Old Country custom, added to the Gabor sense of entitlement, meant that Eva would not have thought it at all strange. And since Stephen Cox was in his twenties at the time, and Eva had commented on his rosy cheeks, calling him an "Irish boy" though in fact he was Canadian, he took it as a compliment.

Their interview at an end, he asked Eva to sign one of his remaining photos. "Would you please write on this one, 'Give me Park Avenue'? She said, 'Oh no, dahling, I'm just going to write "Love, Love." ' And that's what she wrote."

* * *

A year or so after his convivial afternoon at Eva's, Cox encountered her again. "That's when it got weird," he said. "At almost the same time that my book came out, a publisher had contacted Eva through her agent to float the idea of an *Eva Gabor Green Acres Cookbook*. The publisher, learning of *The Hooterville Handbook*, rescinded Eva's offer. They believed that one *Green Acres* book was enough. She got wind of it, and it made her angry."

Movie stars, like others unfamiliar with publishing, imagine that any book they "write"—meaning a book that bears their name although written by someone else—will earn millions and garner endless publicity. They will become *authors*, even *auteurs*.

Around the time of Eva's disappointment, the 1993 feature film *The Beverly Hillbillies* was released. CBS also produced a special called *The Legend of the Beverly Hillbillies*—a "mockumentary" based on the anniversary of the TV show, and Cox, who in 1988 had published a book on that phenomenal series, was hired as a consultant. This pseudo-documentary included archival clips and new interviews having to do with the Clampett family. Eva and Eddie Albert, in character as Lisa and Oliver Douglas, were included in the special. A small set was built for them to reminisce about the Clampetts, recalling their zany arrival in Beverly Hills from the backwoods.

On the day that Eva and Eddie filmed their scene, sitting on a sofa in front of a mantel, Cox happened to be at the CBS studio in Hollywood. "I was taking pictures of the set," he said. "I noticed *Green Acres* photographs on their mantel, which turned out to be photographs the CBS prop department had borrowed from me and then put in frames. At the end of the day, Eva gathered up those framed pictures—mine—and started to leave with them. I called aside one of the producers and asked him to make sure they were not re-moved from the set.

"He conveyed the message to Eva, who became upset. In front of Eddie Albert and everyone, she started yelling at me—I'm in the shadows at the edge of the set—'You ruined my life! I need these photographs!' She started to rant that I didn't tell her our interview was for my book. Eddie came to my rescue. 'Yes, he did,' Eddie told her. 'You know he did.' I realized that he was the only one who could stick up for me. He was her equal. He calmed her down. I don't even remember how it got resolved. Maybe I said, 'Oh, whatever, let her take them.'"

Cox phoned Rogers and Cowan, Eva's PR firm at the time, telling them how she embarrassed him in front of a number of people at CBS. The gist of their response, according to Cox, was, She gets a little batty at times. Now you know what we have to deal with. In twenty minutes it's gone from her head and from everyone else's.

Although this incident shows Eva in an unflattering light, it is important to fathom the desperation behind it. At seventy-four, though still beautiful and full of energy, she qualified for that dreaded category: a has-been. She had done nothing of significance for years. Her last picture was *The Princess Academy*, released in 1987. On TV, she turned up sporadically on sitcoms, and she lived alone, having divorced Frank Jameson, her fifth husband, in 1983. Merv Griffin, for years considered her great romance, was a friend. He was gay, she was his beard, and her own low-key lesbianism satisfied only the occasional longing. Nothing remained for Eva but mediocre and repetitive talk shows. She did have her highly successful wig business, but that spotlight shone too dim. Like so many stars of the studio era, now lost and wandering, Eva craved acting assignments. For most of her life, the camera had been more present, and more faithful, than her husbands. Nor did she ever quarrel with a camera as she did with her sisters, her niece, even the indomitable Jolie. Given Eva's desolation at this time, the notion of a *Green Acres* cookbook with her name on it must have seemed momentous, like a return to those busy years of summer theatre, personal appearances, so many offers from TV and Hollywood that her agent stayed busy turning them down. Now she felt she must grab any morsel dragged to her doorstep, and growl at the hand reaching to snatch it away. When she snarled at Stephen Cox, it covered a wailing cry of pain.

The *Beverly Hillbillies* movie came out in October 1993, and Cox was invited to the wrap party. Zsa Zsa was there, since she played herself in a cameo in the picture, and Cox met her. "It was a quick encounter," he said, "nothing more than hello, good to see you." Paul Henning told him, however, of his own encounter with Zsa Zsa a year or so after *Green Acres* ended. She said, "You should have hired me, dahling, instead of Eva."

Had Zsa Zsa forgotten that midway through the run of *Green Acres*, she had a crack at her own show? In 1969, KCOP-TV in Los Angeles aired the pilot episode of *The Zsa Zsa Gabor Show*—a trainwreck of epic proportions, mercifully short-lived. It was obvious from the opening moments that the show would flop. A talk-show host must appear interested in the guests, but Zsa Zsa was glued to herself. Among the many duties of the host is to keep guests in place both literally and figuratively while avoiding lags in the conversation, and to steer the show along in what seems an effortless direction. Poor Zsa Zsa looked like a YouTube amateur facing the camera: thrilled but strained.

Her first guests were Adam West, of TV's *Batman*, and Marty Allen, the comedian. After a stretch of lame, rhythmless repartee with them, Zsa Zsa introduced "my dear, dear friend, Miss Lucille Ball." The problem with this big-name guest, here and elsewhere, was that everyone wished for hilarious Lucy Ricardo rather than staid Lucille Ball. Even such pros as Johnny Carson and Joan Rivers labored to squeeze a funny line from her.

Upon entry, each guest stood about for several minutes as if waiting to hail a taxi; they probably wished they could. Zsa Zsa, so confident as a talk-show guest and so much in control as hostess at her own parties, lacked all sense of traffic control. And the script, if one existed, was abominable.

Zsa Zsa: "Who was the most fascinating man in your life?"

Lucille Ball: "Are we on that subject already? I've met some fascinating men. I think you married some of them." After a long pause, she came up with Bernard Baruch, the financier, statesman, and political advisor to Presidents Woodrow Wilson and Franklin D. Roosevelt.

Zsa Zsa: "I love gray-haired men."

Lucille: "He had a lot more than gray hair. He had a lot of gray matter. FDR was another fascinating man."

Zsa Zsa: "I used to date him." No one even chuckled at her preposterous joke.

Lucille: "I thought it was Kennedy." She grew visibly ill at ease with this surreal conversation.

To make matters worse, the set looked like a funeral parlor: off-white walls, tight floral arrangements, possibly artificial—and then Marty Allen presented Zsa Zsa with flowers in the shape of a casket wreath. You can almost smell the sickly-sweet odor of mortuary carnations.

As if to quadruple the show's awfulness, the final guest was a lounge lizard vocalist. Ostensibly from Hawaii, he revealed that he came from the Bronx.

Okay then, a Bronx cheer for the show and everyone on it.

Chapter 31

Another One Gone, and Another One Bites the Dust

Whether Zsa Zsa guessed it or not, post-Rubi and après Trujillo, her long-running future role would require no memorizing of lines, no study with drama coaches, no auditions or screen tests. She had learned the character by heart, having played her already for four decades. Hereafter, she would act the part of Zsa Zsa Gabor, and her evolution as actress-personality would take place as slowly as that of Little Orphan Annie in the comics. Unlike that famous ragamuffin, however, who wore the same dress for eighty years, Zsa Zsa's appearances on TV and elsewhere resembled an haute couture runway that stretched to the vanishing point. And so well did she know her craft that even when audiences thinned and applause grew anemic, she played her part upon that long, narrow stage to the last syllable of her allotted time.

One of Zsa Zsa's smartest moves in her transition from big screen to small was to accept an invitation for *The Jack Paar Tonight Show*. Making her most significant debut on late-night TV (earlier, she had been Steve Allen's guest in the same time slot), she sashayed into camera view on May 9, 1958, in the first of dozens of appearances with Paar. As Paar's guest, she was everything she wasn't in that disastrous pilot for *The Zsa Zsa Gabor Show* eleven years later.

Her host, who in retrospect seems unattractively sentimental and mercurial, as well as deficient in the sincerity he worked so hard to project, nevertheless put together a sophisticated lineup of talk and variety that showcased talent from New York, Hollywood, and elsewhere. He invited actors, writers, politicians, comedians, musicians, and eccentrics, among them the established as well as newcomers who, in Paar's opinion, deserved nationwide exposure. Conversation occupied over half of each *Tonight Show*, and the talk ranged from serious discussions to witty, even goofy, repartee, from barbs to bonhomie. Considering the time and place—late fifties into early sixties on American TV—Paar's conversations with such guests as JFK, Richard Nixon, Eleanor Roosevelt, and Fidel Castro set a gold standard matched by few subsequent shows. In later years, some television historians named Paar as an *auteur* of early TV. Egos were not absent, of course, but neither did guests parrot only preapproved, manager-scripted plugs for their latest endeavors. Controversy also shadowed the Paar show. He and his guests made headlines, most famously when Paar himself, angered by network censorship of an opening monologue, quit the show after an on-air tirade.

Writing about Zsa Zsa in *I Kid You Not*, the first of his several books, Paar echoed the tone of his nightly opening monologues: "Zsa Zsa is like the girl next door—if you live next door to Tiffany's. The first time she came on the show I thought she was carrying a flashlight; her engagement ring looked so heavy I suspect she had to starch her finger to support it. Just before coming on, Zsa Zsa asked me what I wanted her to do.

"'Just be yourself,' I told her."

"That was my first mistake. She burbled on about her romances, interrupted the commercials and otherwise confused
the National Broadcasting Company. Her performance was
unbelievable, and, as Earl Wilson said, I unbelieved.

"Mama Gabor is a friend of mine, too, as are her other
daughters, Magda and Eva. Once on the show Eva reported
that Mama planned to sell her jewelry store in New York and
move to Palm Springs but there were so many protests that
she changed her mind. Eva didn't clarify whether the protests
were from New York or Palm Springs."

During the 1960s and thereafter, Zsa Zsa was unstoppable, everywhere at once: premieres, nightclub acts, dinner
theatre, summer stock, personal appearances, TV specials,
and if you name a network show from the period, it's likely
that she made at least one appearance on it. Overexposure
led to surfeit, at least to TV viewers who had heard it all before. The wisecracks began to seem older than Zsa Zsa herself, while the tales of her marriage at "fifteen" to a Turkish
diplomat, the miserliness of Conrad Hilton, the lazy vanity
of George Sanders, came to sound as hollow as a politician's
promise to make America great again.

In November 1961, seventeen years after fire destroyed
Zsa Zsa's wing of the Hilton estate, she lost another home.
This time the conflagration swept through Bel Air and Brent-
wood, destroying 484 residences. Zsa Zsa, in New York at
the time, flew back to Los Angeles to find nothing standing
of her house on Bellagio Road except three forlorn chimneys.
"The whole house went," she said, "furs, jewelry, silver,
everything." The fire also destroyed her personal memorabilia. She was photographed in skirt and blouse, hair mussed,
with shovel in hand as she dug through ashes in search of
jewelry.

*   *   *

Love, marriage, and remarriage became her logo and her leitmotif, on TV and in the few hours of private life remaining to a celebrity of Zsa Zsa's exposure. In 1970 an editor at Doubleday, working with a ghost-for-hire, cobbled together 155 pages of her wit and wisdom, giving it the gaudy title *How to Catch a Man, How to Keep a Man, How to Get Rid of a Man*. Ultimately, she proved so adept at all three maneuvers that the book title became her de facto trademark. Keeping that Gabor trademark burnished, however, required periodic rebranding (translation: preowned husband swapped for newer model), so that during the sixties, seventies, and eighties, she was quick to propose if her intended moved too slow. Or to divorce him if he tarried too long. In the end, she kept one husband for thirty years—probably twenty-nine years too long.

Her romances outnumbered her offers of work, or so it seemed. Work, that is, of any substance, work that might require—what? After all, what could she do? Her creditable performances from the fifties were forgotten, and no one dared bring her a script with the message, "They want you for the mother."

For she had grown sequins on her soul. Occasionally they flashed a brilliant idea, as when she went to visit Mae West. Her mission: to obtain rights for a revival of Mae's 1928 play, *Diamond Lil*. ("When I'm good I'm very good, but when I'm bad I'm better.") If a transcript of that meeting existed, it would be a camp playlet in its own right. Alas, we have only Zsa Zsa's report: "She said to me, 'Oh honey, you're far too young!'"

Trapped in her celebrity cocoon like a scarab in amber, she no longer tried to emerge. Zsa Zsa's situation gave a new spin to the question of vocation vs. marriage: How many husbands will it take to indemnify my career?

After her divorce from George Sanders in 1954, she took an eight-year sabbatical from the marriage bed. Then, in

1962, she married the best one of the lot, Herbert Loeb Hutner. "He was an angel," Zsa Zsa said. And he bored her. Everything about him was good, but had she quoted her new friend, Mae West, Zsa Zsa's lament might have been "Goodness had nothing to do with it." "I loved him as a human being," she said, "but I was not in love with him." After enduring three years of unbearable benevolence, Zsa Zsa realized that her grounds for divorce were unique and "completely unacceptable to any judicial system in the world: divorce on the grounds of mental kindness." Eva accompanied Zsa Zsa to Mexico for the happy divorce.

The couple's parting presents to each other sound like suggestions for divorce gifts from the Harrods catalogue: from Hutner to Zsa Zsa, two strings of pearls. She reciprocated with a Rolls-Royce, slightly used, and a silver whistle in case he should want to summon her back.

In 1969, Hutner married the actress Juli Reding, who has a smallish cult for her 1960 film, *Tormented*, in which she plays a ghost. In a recent conversation, Juli Reding Hutner spoke of her own friendship with Zsa Zsa. "We went to many parties at her home, and she was always very cordial," Juli said, "and constantly witty. I'll give you an example. I had a male friend who held an important position in Los Angeles, and one day I took him to lunch at the Bistro Gardens. By coincidence, he and I were seated near Zsa Zsa and her entourage. Spotting me, she came over and whispered in my ear, 'Dahling, are you cheating on *our husband*?' "

Juli and Eva also became friends. The Hutners were neighbors of Eva and Frank Jameson, her fifth husband. "We often went out with them," Juli said, "especially because Herbert and Frank knew each other through business. Eva would say to me, 'Don't let Zsa Zsa find out we're friends. She would be very jealous.' "

"Does that mean Zsa Zsa was the boss of the family?" I asked.

"I think she probably was. I used to say to Herbert that the only reason Zsa Zsa is better known than Eva is that silly name. I think that had a lot to do with her fame, her notoriety."

Although Juli was fond of Zsa Zsa, she had greater affection for Eva. "When I heard the news of her death," she said, "I couldn't stop crying. I attended her funeral at Church of the Good Shepherd. I had gone there to services with her. She loved going to church, and wanted to be involved with the Catholic faith."

Zsa Zsa's fifth husband, Joshua S. Cosden Jr., came from Texas oil wealth. Most of it, however, had disappeared when she met him in 1966, leaving him a thirty-thousand-dollar millionaire. Contrary to Gabor repute, *he* married Zsa Zsa for *her* money. It turned into a marriage for the birds—literally. She bought a new house in Bel Air, and just prior to moving in she arrived one Monday morning to find a bird lying dead on the drawing room floor. It had flown into the house before the workmen left on Friday and starved to death. "With tears in my eyes," Zsa Zsa recalled, "I picked up the body of the bird and buried it in the garden, knowing that now I could never live in the house." Such an ill omen was it that Zsa Zsa sold the house at a loss.

Soon another bird entered the marriage. While shopping at Neiman Marcus on a trip to Dallas, Zsa Zsa bought a large macaw. She named him Caesar, and followed the store's care instructions: a piece of orange every morning in addition to his other food. For months Zsa Zsa did not fail, until . . . the morning that she forgot the slice of orange. "On my way to the kitchen I passed Caesar's cage. Our eyes met and he fixed me with what, at the time, seemed to be an evil eye. In the clearest voice possible, he pronounced the words, 'Fuck you!'

"Totally unnerved and remembering my omission, I fetched the piece of orange for Caesar, careful to avoid his eyes. In silence he ate it. I breathed a sigh of relief. Prematurely. Because from that moment on, all Caesar would say to me, to Joshua, or to anyone who crossed the threshold of our house, was 'Fuck you!' "

Whether Zsa Zsa's ears were more offended by the horrendous language, or whether she feared the evil menace of that ornithological eye, she did not elaborate. Neiman Marcus, tops in customer service, accepted Caesar's return with a full refund to Zsa Zsa, plus shipping charges. For once, however, she did not have the last word. Caesar did. As if channeling another bird of vocal renown—the one made immortal by Edgar Allan Poe—Caesar took leave of his mistress with the unfriendly adieu, "Fuck you!"

After a six-month marriage, the Cosdens also bid each other farewell. Their divorce was almost as effortless as returning a purchase to a department store, nor was the marriage more memorable. If their goodbyes included that frightful macaw malediction, Zsa Zsa didn't mention it.

In simplest terms, the reason for Zsa Zsa's serial marriages was this: she could not bear to live alone. And although a strong woman, she firmly believed that without a man she was incomplete. As she aged, not to be married, or at least in the market for a consort, came to be as unthinkable as wearing only one shoe. Or revealing her date of birth.

One can safely assume, also, that from about 1960, when Zsa Zsa was forty-three years old, her mental state was not in the category usually considered normal, meaning reasonably sane. Plagued by bipolar disorder, she often seemed not fully aware of what she did. Then and later, according to Francesca, Zsa Zsa often skipped her medications because "they made her fat." Unlike many in Hollywood, however, she avoided other pills and alcohol. And while she spoke the word "menopause" only to her doctors and within the Gabor circle, that phenomenon added to her behavioral anomalies.

*   *   *

Jack Ryan, husband number six, also suffered from bipolar disorder, along with alcoholism, drug abuse, and a compendium of bad traits. Born in 1926, and thus nine years Zsa Zsa's junior, he became well known, while employed by the toy manufacturing company Mattel, as the creator of the Barbie doll. (Ryan's claim was later disputed by a female colleague at Mattel. His biographer, Jerry Oppenheimer, nevertheless credits Ryan with the doll's invention.) A few years afterward, in a reversal of the biblical creation story, Ryan formed Ken as Barbie's companion, although not from Barbie's rib.

His Bel Air mansion stood not far from Zsa Zsa's, and they became acquainted when she complained about loud music from his parties. He invited her to the next one and others after that. She should have fled the vulgarity of his over-elaborate estate, which he called the Castle; instead, she accepted the proposal which, Oppenheimer believes, Ryan made while off lithium and atop a bipolar crescendo.

They lived together less as spouses than the neighbor husband to the wife next door. He had no intention of forsaking his swinger habits, and Zsa Zsa demanded fealty, at least on the surface. When not fighting, they sometimes had fun. Jack Ryan was a Groucho Marx kind of cutup, Zsa Zsa his Margaret Dumont. When Zsa Zsa and Eva appeared together in a production of *Arsenic and Old Lace* in 1975 in a Chicago suburb, Ryan was there—but not in the audience.

In the play, the murderous sisters, Abby and Martha Brewster, who have poisoned a man, hide the body in a window seat. When Zsa Zsa, speaking her lines, bent over the rectangular seat to open it, she broke out in hysterical laughter, for instead of the imagined body of the text it was her husband, Jack Ryan, curled up inside and making funny faces at her.

Before that, however, the management faced an explosive

quandary: Which one of these prima donna stars would get top billing? With the wisdom of Solomon, the theatre printed a playbill that credited only "GABOR." Regarding her costar, Eva said, "It's so difficult to appear with your own family. Zsa Zsa kept saying, 'You do this' and I kept saying, 'Don't you tell me what to do.'"

The laughter in Zsa Zsa's marriage to Jack Ryan soon died away, and in 1976, the year after their vows, they divorced. In 1989, he suffered a stroke that left one side of his body paralyzed. Two years later, he committed suicide by firing a .45 caliber pistol into his mouth. Zsa Zsa, saddened by his death, attended his funeral, for they had remained friends. Long after the divorce, Jack and his next wife sometimes went to Zsa Zsa's for dinner.

When Zsa Zsa married her next husband, this joke went 'round: "Now she's Zsa Zsa O'Hara, just like Scarlett." But Scarlett stopped at three, and Michael O'Hara was Zsa Zsa's seventh. He happened to be the lawyer who had finalized divorce number six. "I almost feel like characterizing my marriage to Michael O'Hara by just writing his name and leaving a blank page," said Zsa Zsa to her collaborator Wendy Leigh. To Zsa Zsa, however, more was more, and so she continued. "I should have listened to the words of my friend Merle Oberon, who cautioned, 'Be careful. I wouldn't marry a lawyer because it can only cost you.'

"My marriage to Michael O'Hara did, indeed, cost me. Emotionally, that is. We were married for five years and, at first, things were wonderful." But then Zsa Zsa discovered that while he looked like a gorgeous Irishman, six feet four with green eyes and tanned skin, he was in fact of Yugoslavian extraction. She did not explain where he picked up the Celtic cognomen.

Nor did she include in *One Lifetime Is Not Enough* any reason for their marital dissonance other than her husband's moodiness. For once, words failed her. "I am still not sure what really happened. Only that Michael and I don't—to this day—ever exchange a word. And that he is the only ex-husband who is not still my friend." Indeed, Zsa Zsa could have been chairperson of the Hollywood Ex-husband's Club.

Magda, on the other hand, was the opposite. When one of her marriages went belly-up, the locks were changed, his belongings thrown on the curb, and his aftershave poured down the drain. Eva, though not vindictive, remained close-mouthed. When David Letterman asked, "How many ex-husbands have there been?" a streak of irritation crossed her face. "Oh, three or four. Vy do you vant to know such a thing?"

Did Merle Oberon, perhaps, or some other well-meaning friend, hand Zsa Zsa a Syllabus of Undesirable Traits to look out for in future mates? And if so, did Zsa Zsa read it upside down, or mistake it for desiderata? For the worst was yet to come.

Before the bitter end—husband number nine—came a farcical interlude. Zsa Zsa called it marriage number eight and a half, perhaps alluding to Fellini's great film. In reality, it merits a lesser fraction than one-half. Call it minus eight.

The nuptials took place in April 1982 on the yacht belonging to Frank Jameson, Eva's husband and the bride's brother-in-law, with the Jamesons present. The place: the Pacific Ocean, a dozen or so miles from Puerto Vallarta, Mexico, and therefore thought to be in international waters. The yacht's captain performed the brief ceremony that united Zsa Zsa with the Spanish aristocrat, Felipe, Duke of Alba.

Felipe, however, was a duke only in the sense that John Wayne was called "Duke" by his friends; he was a citizen of Mexico. The yacht's captain possessed nothing other than a marine license, which did not entitle him to perform a marriage ceremony, and besides, the yacht apparently remained in Mexican waters without reaching the high seas. A storm blew up during the ersatz wedding and resulted in several guests hanging over the boat's rails while others clung to ropes in order not to be swept overboard. Among the guests were John Huston, who thirty years earlier on the set of *Moulin Rouge* had berated Zsa Zsa for lack of talent, and Zsa Zsa's long-suffering daughter, Francesca. The bride, who had recently given her age as fifty-four, was in reality sixty-five and still the wife of Michael O'Hara. On her calendar she had marked the wrong date, for instead of gaining her freedom on April 4 she would remain legally Mrs. O'Hara until the fourth of July. And the sham marriage almost caused an international incident. When King Juan Carlos of Spain heard of it, he commanded the Spanish embassy in Washington to enlighten the American press: there was no duke of Alba, but rather a duchess. That lady had no intention of ceding her title to Señora Gabor.

Upon discovering that they were not man and wife and never had been, each party issued a snarky statement about the other. "We were planning to legalize our status in July," said Zsa Zsa, "but I called it off. He bored me. He was nothing but a playboy, and I am a hard-working actress." Her recent paramour struck below the belt: "Zsa Zsa told me she was fifty-four. When I learned that she is nearly seventy, well—"

The marriage, which had never existed, was annulled the day after it didn't take place.

Chapter 32

Don't Cry for Me, Philadelphia

In 1970, Zsa Zsa took time off from marriage to appear in *Forty Carats*, her only Broadway appearance. Julie Harris having opened the show, her replacements were June Allyson, Joan Fontaine, and Zsa Zsa, who took over the lead on July 6 and gave 180 performances until the show closed on November 7. New York audiences, along with out-of-towners, turned her four-month engagement into a personal triumph. They found Zsa Zsa effervescent in the comedy, and they applauded loudly with standing ovations. After performances, crowds gathered at the stage door to take pictures and clamor for autographs. On Zsa Zsa's opening night, Eva sent an elaborate floral arrangement with forty *carrots* peeking from the blossoms. Zsa Zsa roared at the joke. Two months later, George Sanders attended a performance and afterwards invited his favorite ex-wife to a champagne supper.

In her suite at the Waldorf Towers, Zsa Zsa's companions were Miss Pussycat, a silky white Persian, and Ruby Red, a Lhasa apso. These two, unlike her eight cats at home and several other dogs, were deemed suitable traveling companions for a star reborn.

After Broadway, Zsa Zsa traveled with *Forty Carats* to several regional theatres. A dozen years later, she signed to do the play for a month at the City Line Dinner Theater in Philadelphia. There, in 1983, she became embroiled in another damaging scandal when she was accused of insulting the handicapped.

The Philadelphia engagement opened on May 25 and was scheduled to run through June 26. From the start, Zsa Zsa locked horns with the management. She arrived for rehearsals to discover that her leading man lacked what she considered the requisite virility for the part. (Her character is a middle-aged New York businesswoman on vacation in Greece who meets a twenty-two-year-old man. After a summer fling, he turns up in Manhattan and they rekindle the romance. And yes, for once she did play someone's mother; her character has a teenage daughter.) Zsa Zsa demanded, and got, a more manly costar. Others in the cast and crew were outraged by her highhandedness; the stage manager quit the show in protest.

She perceived growing hostility. "A lot of people with the theatre were out to get me after that," she said, "but that first actor just wasn't believable as anyone my character would be in love with." She further irritated the management by complaining when dinner was brought to her dressing room by a waiter instead of a bell captain, as she had stipulated. As if to blacken the gathering stormclouds even further, Zsa Zsa's two dogs ran loose, snarled and yapped, and soiled the executive offices.

Such unprofessional behavior was deemed inexcusable, although Zsa Zsa wasn't the first performer to act like a diva. By any measure, hers was a sad comedown from Hollywood studios to a provincial theatre where cooking odors eclipsed the smell of greasepaint. The very term "dinner theatre" implies food service over thespian talent. Like it or not, however, actors must often accept such assignments if they are to work at all. Zsa Zsa believed herself too chic for Philly; and perhaps she was.

On the night of May 31, a group of sixteen handicapped people from the Woods School in suburban Langhorne attended the performance of *Forty Carats*. According to Deborah Missanelli, a supervisor at the school who escorted the group to the theatre, "These were all patients who were normal until a certain point when a car accident left them brain-damaged."

According to several members of the group, during the intermission a waiter told them that Zsa Zsa Gabor had instructed him to move six people in wheelchairs from their front-row seats to the back of the theatre. The waiter's stated reason to the group was that by laughing out of turn they had disturbed the star and interrupted the performance.

Shocked by the accusation and by the request that their seats be changed, the group discussed a course of action. Missanelli, their escort, said later that she looked around the theatre for several minutes in search of alternate seating. By that point, however, the entire group of sixteen had decided to leave.

Two days later, with the incident gathering momentum in newspapers and on television, the management fired Zsa Zsa. The media, underttstandably, along with their readers and viewers, took the part of the handicapped. Although Zsa Zsa's side was reported, her difficult reputation had preceded her. Headlines portrayed her as a shrew crossed with the Wicked Witch of the West (and her little dogs, too).

My purpose is not to cast doubt on statements made by the group of handicapped persons, for in my opinion they were part of an unfortunate misunderstanding. Rather, I have tried to marshal facts overlooked at the time and to show that Zsa Zsa, blameworthy on various other points, was innocent of any deliberate affront to those in her audience who were physically challenged.

Let us imagine that we are onstage that night, with bright lights in our eyes yet unable to see clearly those audience members seated in pervasive shadows. The men and women from the Woods School, according to their escort, had dressed up for the occasion—"women in formals and the guys in coats and jackets." Their attire would have blended with that of others in the audience who had also dressed up, and would have further obscured wheelchairs and prosthetics.

Zsa Zsa, in her own defense, said that the theatre had been too dark for her to tell that handicapped people were in the audience. As far as she could see, everyone was able-bodied. In the *New York Daily News*, a photograph of nine of the sixteen people from the Woods School suggests that even in daylight, when the picture was made, they might be taken for nonhandicapped. Only two wheelchairs are evident in the photo, and those partially.

Years earlier on Broadway, Zsa Zsa had surely become adept at making quick entrances and exits for her sixteen costume changes. Now, however, she was a dozen years older and a dozen years more nervous. At sixty-six, she had to work harder and pay closer attention to every cue. Any distraction might make her go blank. And by Deborah Missanelli's own admission, some of those from the Woods School "tended to laugh loudly or a little later than nonhandicapped people might. But no one laughed at an inappropriate moment."

Zsa Zsa said that she *and other actors on the stage* heard noise in the audience on that evening of May 31 and thought that some theatregoers were intoxicated, since dinner theatres routinely serve alcoholic drinks. She pointed out that with so many costume changes, she barely had time to enter and exit on cue, far less to scrutinize the audience. Zsa Zsa denied that she asked for anyone's removal. Even if she did complain to theatre employees, she might well have done so without realizing the actual source of noise. "If I had known the handicapped people were there," she said, "I would have sent them cake and champagne." She stated that she was unaware of the incident until the owner of the theatre called her the following day to demand that she make a public apology. According to Zsa Zsa, he said, "Tell the press you requested that they sit at the back of the auditorium, otherwise the pickets will close this theatre."

It is important to note that *a waiter* brought a message to the group, saying that Zsa Zsa had instructed him to remove them to the back of the theatre. Was it perhaps the same waiter who served Zsa Zsa's dinner and whom she insulted by demanding a bell captain instead? Silly snobbery on her part, and very unwise: one should never antagonize those who serve one's food. The consequences can be fatal.

Although theatre management denied any involvement in the order to move audience members, it is possible to doubt their word. Fed up with Zsa Zsa, they nevertheless required order in the house. Clues enumerated above suggest a management decision that boomeranged to the difficult diva. How could Zsa Zsa, backstage at intermission adjusting costumes and makeup, have located a waiter to deliver her ultimatum? A stage manager or headwaiter, on the other hand, would have ready access to waitstaff.

The night after the incident, some hundred handicapped people and their supporters demonstrated outside the theatre. Zsa Zsa came out and spoke with them. Along with her denials, she said she hoped to perform free at the Woods School. This suggests good intentions, though it's likely that Zsa Zsa, nervous and defensive, lacked the apologetic skills of an oily politician. No doubt she sounded shrill in maintaining that she had nothing to apologize for. Nor did anyone among the demonstrators, or in the media, know of Zsa Zsa's longstanding efforts on behalf of many charities. Later that year, while starring in *Forty Carats* in Dallas, Zsa Zsa appeared at a charity brunch for the city's Society for Crippled Children. Her presence raised $1,500 for the local chapter.

Unfortunately for Zsa Zsa's reputation, she never made it to the Woods School. Her agent phoned the institution with news that she had left town owing to harassment by theatre management and the media. Callers also left death threats at her hotel and at her agent's office in Los Angeles. After her departure, performances were canceled until further notice. The theatre claimed losses in excess of $100,000. Eventually Terry Moore came in as replacement, playing to a nearly empty house.

Zsa Zsa hired a New York attorney to file an arbitration suit with Philadelphia's Commission on Human Relations. His statement carried weight in the commission's deliberation. He said, "Actors have no authority in respect to their audience. All they're supposed to do is put on a show. The dinner theatre has control over patrons and it was obviously the theatre's decision [to move those patrons]." Leaving aside the question of whether Zsa Zsa or the theatre management wanted the handicapped people moved, the commission ruled two years later that the theatre was guilty of discrimination because Zsa Zsa was its employee at the time.

After Actors' Equity entered the ruckus, two outcomes were reported: a decision against Zsa Zsa, or else a ruling not made public. Inquiries to the actors' union went unanswered owing to its privacy policies.

A few months after Zsa Zsa's fiasco at the dinner theatre, Eva returned to Broadway as the Grand Duchess Olga Katrina in *You Can't Take It with You*. Her character is kitchen-sink glamourous, for the grand duchess fled the Russian Revolution only to end up waiting tables in a Childs' Restaurant. This was Eva's fifth, and final, Broadway appearance. She filled in for a vacationing Colleen Dewhurst, and one of her costars was Eddie Albert. By nostalgic coincidence this play ran at the Plymouth Theatre, where Eva had made her debut thirty-three years earlier.

In a small role, Eva entered only in the third act. As usual, she was popular with cast and crew. Sandy Faison, a cast member who was also in *The Edge of Night* on daytime television, persuaded Eva to do a guest spot on the show. In the only soap opera appearance of her career, she played—Eva Gabor.

You Can't Take It with You was Eva's second time to replace a star more critically acclaimed than she herself. In 1963, she briefly took over Vivien Leigh's role in *Tovarich*. In that instance, audiences had come to see a double legend—Vivien Leigh, and Scarlett O'Hara. Many, no doubt, felt disappointed to see Eva's name on the marquee. As Dewhurst's replacement, however, Eva's presence perhaps delighted more than it chagrined. She and Eddie Albert together again, a dozen years after *Green Acres*, created something of an event. Then, too, Dewhurst was not at home in light comedy. Outside of the O'Neill roles that made her famous, she could become a lumbering presence onstage. For that reason, Eva's down-at-the-heels duchess struck many playgoers as a better fit. She was Lisa Douglas à la russe (though the accent was echt Budapest, never Moscow).

Chapter 33

The Ninth Circle

Onlookers—and there were many—to Zsa Zsa's final marriage found themselves as polarized as Democrats vs. Republicans. Was the groom, who projected a vague distinction and who called himself Prince Frederic von Anhalt, really the aristocrat he claimed to be, or had Zsa Zsa hooked the Faux Prince of Bel Air? Later, she herself claimed that this marriage was among her happiest, and indeed it lasted thirty years, four months, and four days—from August 14, 1986 until her death on December 18, 2016. Her previous marriages combined totaled less than this stretch of time.

When one is a faded star crashing into seventy, is it wise to take on a forty-three-year-old German with a dodgy past, a questionable present, and a blank future? This cockeyed coupling with self-styled royalty presented itself to Zsa Zsa as the culmination of a long quest, a quest not so much for marital happiness as for a title. Perhaps the secret *rosebud* in Zsa Zsa's century-long life, the great desire never fulfilled until Frederic came along, was to be addressed as Miss Magyarország, or even better as countess, duchess, sultana, principessa, or Lady Zsa Zsa. Any title at all to fill the aching void created by that prodding mother who spurred little Sári toward fame and greatness, the mother whose own neurotic frustrations trapped her daughters, and Zsa Zsa most of all, in a twisting labyrinth of ambition.

Recall how Jolie taunted young Zsa Zsa at the circus as an Indian fakir swallowed fire while climbing a ladder of razor-sharp swords on naked feet. "Now," Jolie hissed in the darkness, "when will you be able to do that?" Any child would suffer from such an absurd and abusive challenge, and this taunt no doubt represents a lone example from a pattern of impossible demands.

It would take an Orson Welles, and a *Citizen Gabor*, to unpeel the petals . . . Imagine a snowy scene in wintertime Budapest, and Jolie promising trustful Zsa Zsa the world and its kingdoms, if only: "You must be a princess, and then Mamuska will love you most of all." Eventually Zsa Zsa became that princess, at least in her own fevered fantasy. The title was a joke to everyone else, but with those fabulous words, "Princess Zsa Zsa," ringing in her ears like golden bells, she dismissed the stark fact that the prince had paid a California photographer $5,000 for an introduction to her. He brought as tribute a pedigree written in vanishing ink. As this fairy-tale script played before an audience of one, Princess Zsa Zsa preferred not to question the tenability of the fairyland from whence came her liege.

From Cindy Adams's column in the *New York Post* on August 14, 1986: "Jolie, the mother of the bride, won't attend the wedding. She's unhappy about it. 'But you told me last week you were giving Zsa Zsa a diamond ring as a present,' I said. 'Yes, but that was last week,' Jolie said. 'This week we are not speaking.'"

Jolie recognized Zsa Zsa's piece of royalty as a piece of work. She warned her silly daughter that this was a frog who, even when kissed, would remain a reptile. Although

Jolie specialized in imitation jewels, hers carried the stamp of expert craftsmanship. Her hard, practiced eye could distinguish, from any distance, a real diamond from a rhinestone, or a gob of paste parading as a pearl, and as with jewels, so with people. Even when Zsa Zsa's dream came true, Mamuska remained unpleased. Her daughter created a circus, but the Indian fakir had morphed into a German faker, and instead of flames what Zsa Zsa swallowed was a line of bull. The marriage was a circus that featured too many clowns.

Celebrity media—*People* magazine, tabloid dailies, *Entertainment Tonight*—found the match of passing interest, and Zsa Zsa was still quotable. "I've only had three real husbands—Conrad Hilton, George Sanders, and my first, Burhan Belge. The others were only legalized love affairs." She also told anyone who would listen that she was fifty-five, and therefore—"It's time to settle down."

"I know he's no good," Zsa Zsa confessed to Alan Richman, a reporter from *People*. Echoing Judith Anderson's line in *Laura*—"He's no good but he's what I want"—Zsa Zsa was referring to her new husband, Frederic von Anhalt, soi-disant prince, soi-disant duke of Saxony, holder of a sheaf of unlikely titles. You will not find him in the *Almanach de Gotha*, though he did make regular appearances in police files back in Germany. As reported in *People* on September 1, 1986, "according to various published reports Prince Frederic is a con man, a shoplifter, and a brawler. He denies all but the scrapes."

The *People* article detailed the wedding with tongue-in-cheek thoroughness: Zsa Zsa's Ruben Panis gown, pale glacial ice-blue with embroidered satin flowers; the groom's Graustarkian medals strung across his ruffled shirt; the congratulatory telegram from Ronald and Nancy Reagan, read aloud for all to hear; the hundred-plus guests in formal attire; and the bridal bouquet, which Zsa Zsa, breaking with tradition, tossed before the ceremony. She pitched the bouquet to

Francesca, who dropped it—a dark omen to the romantic and the superstitious.

For Francesca, the omen proved deadly. At first she planned to boycott the nuptials. Having attended so many maternal weddings, she considered this latest a mere summer rerun. A week before the ceremony, she told Cindy Adams, "I hope Mother will be happy, but I'm afraid." Adams added, in her next column, that neither Eva nor Francesca would attend. Two days later, Adams reported that "Francesca answers her phone: 'Royal Wedding Information.'" Perhaps to please Zsa Zsa, Francesca had decided not only to attend but also to act as official photographer, even though she considered the whole affair as frivolous as a skit on *Saturday Night Live*. Zsa Zsa was miffed at Eva not only for her refusal to attend but also for her sister's harsh words about the groom-to-be. "She is so jealous of me," Zsa Zsa informed the press. "If Eva married a murderer, I'd still go to her wedding."

It was reported that Zsa Zsa had hoped for a Catholic ceremony. Defying canon law, church teachings, and social protocol, she asked for a priest to marry her and Frederic in a lavish barn owned by her friend, the horsewoman Elizabeth Whitney Tippett in Saratoga, a small town south of San Francisco. Her reasoning sounded unassailable: since none of her previous marriages, nor Frederic's, had been recognized by the Church, this would be their first. The request was denied nonetheless. As for the venue, Zsa Zsa said, "I love animals. I'm not so fond of people."

Was she really more audacious than Henry VIII, or did the bridegroom float this silly prank for publicity? Almost certainly the latter. Except for an article in the *New York Daily News*, however, the gimmick failed. Zsa Zsa, no doubt enraptured by her forthcoming title, would have supplied the witty quote when a reporter phoned. Without Frederic's prodding, however, she would never have committed this minor sacrilege against an institution that she held in awe.

* * *

"I always marry bad men," Zsa Zsa told the writer from *People*. "It's a sickness, my sickness. The more bad they tell me they are, the more I am attracted." Zsa Zsa did not define her meaning of the adjective "bad," but in this case she surely got worse than she bargained for.

During the next thirty years, plot and characters resembled a Danielle Steel novel or a bad TV drama: A rich dowager, slightly off in the head, meets a much younger European man who lets it slip that he belongs to the nobility. Having found what she has always wanted, the lady takes him in, finds him compatible, and soon marries him. While she is up and running, he remains discreetly in the background. Some years after the marriage, however, she falls ill. Her condition worsens. The crafty husband now takes over her elaborate home, her millions, indeed her very life, for she has vested all power in him. He alienates her family and friends, barring them from his wife's bedside, until at last all have either died or disappeared, so that he, left in command, mistakes himself for a real celebrity and engineers one tacky publicity trick after another while his elderly wife languishes in semiconsciousness. His final moment in the spotlight comes at her funeral, after which he retreats to his shady pastimes in the hilltop mansion that he has inherited, along with her fortune. So deluded is he—far more than his late wife—that he does not grasp his wretched status as a tattered remnant. The widower is a scrap of Hollywood notoriety as scorned and forgotten as the page of a 1980s newspaper blowing down an empty street.

For a few years after the wedding, Zsa Zsa and Frederic settled into a reasonable pattern. Sounding uncharacteristically sensible, he said, "This is a friendship marriage. We have much in common: animals, horseback riding, getting up early in the morning, working in the garden." They traveled extensively, Europe, Australia, South America, sometimes in the company of Eva and Merv Griffin. (Eva, having predicted a brief span for this marriage, finally accepted the status quo.) Both Zsa Zsa and Frederic achieved their goals, for she became a princess and he now had access to her Rolls-Royce, her bank account, and her famous friends, who nodded politely in his direction as though to a member of Zsa Zsa's household staff. Most important, he luxuriated in the afterglow of Zsa Zsa's celebrity, which, like a low-burning candle, seemed ready to flicker out.

Frederic's phrase, "a friendship marriage," perhaps carried more truth than he intended, or was generally capable of. Francesca—who always had Zsa Zsa's ear—claimed that the marriage was unconsummated. According to her, Zsa Zsa and the husband had an understanding. "I don't care what you do," she told him, "but don't bring it into my house." In spite of a few public kisses for the benefit of paparazzi, their body language suggested anything but passion. Convinced that her title conferred true royalty, Zsa Zsa reigned while Frederic followed a few steps behind. If she fancied herself on a par with Queen Elizabeth II, Frederic was not her Duke of Edinburgh but rather a groom from the imperial stables.

Zsa Zsa insisted on separate bedrooms, at home and when traveling. In New York for an appearance on *The Joan Rivers Show*, she demanded a two-bedroom suite at the Plaza. According to a hotel employee, she said, "Dahling, there is no way the prince can see me before I have my hair and makeup done."

And all the while, like Madame Defarge knitting as she awaits the French Revolution, Frederic waited for his day to come.

Chapter 34

He Who Gets Slapped

An astounding story, even by Gabor standards and those of Hollywood—magnificent, surreal, absurd, and bizarre, perhaps the greatest display of movie star courtroom drama since 1958 and Lana Turner's extreme emoting after her daughter, Cheryl Crane, stabbed to death Lana's gangster boyfriend.

On June 14, 1989, Zsa Zsa drove out of Bel Air in her white Rolls-Royce Corniche with no premonition that this warm day in late spring would be different from any other. The ensuing events, however, added so many layers of notoriety to the Gabor myth that when all else is forgotten, that day will live in tabloid infamy. Or will it be fondly remembered as the last great spectacle of post-studio Hollywood, a Gabor-tinged, eleventh-hour, pre-Internet cliffhanger when words such as "headlines" and "publicity avalanche" meant that the antics of a glamorous actress could upstage, in newspapers and magazines, on TV and radio, even the momentous collapse of the Iron Curtain, which was also taking place at the time?

The only undisputed fact is this: Zsa Zsa was driving on La Cienega Boulevard near West Olympic in Beverly Hills when a cop on a motorcycle pulled her over for an outdated registration sticker on her rear license plate. From that point on, the story becomes a shifting kaleidoscope of allegations, exculpatory denials, threats, contradictions, name calling, mud slinging, and great demented behavior. In the end, Zsa Zsa proved a point, if not exactly the point of her innocence: she showed the world her true calling, which was that of performance artist. This art she had so perfected by her seventh decade that she brought it off with the ease of a great ballerina or a high-wire acrobat.

Just as no one could upstage Anna Pavlova or the Flying Wallendas, no other actress could have slapped a cop and then parlayed it as CPR for a gasping career. Imagine Audrey Hepburn or Doris Day involved in such a thing! Even an outré former starlet like Mamie Van Doren would have lacked the nerve. Eva, known as "the nice Gabor," would have rolled down the window of her Rolls, smiled coquettishly, paid the fine, and said, "Dahling, thank you for spotting my, how do you say, *bottom tag*. My sister switched our license plates."

By the 1980s, the scandals of new Hollywood had become unimaginative and repetitive: drugs and sex, or both, and who really cared about the seedy private lives of a Tom Cruise or an Eddie Murphy? But a shameless old lady in a knock-down, drag-out fight with L.A. law enforcement—that was news plus old-school entertainment, and the story hung on for years to come. Some conspiracy theorists held the silly notion that Zsa Zsa engineered the cop slapping to get attention—which is like saying the *Titanic* was a publicity stunt. It's true that she reaped a windfall of media attention, though she declared, reasonably enough, "I don't need the publicity." One commentator gushed, "Zsa Zsa is again a household word!" But when wasn't she?

Looking back, we see that Zsa Zsa starred in a Fellini movie minus Fellini. Even so, her raucous trial is surely the only one in the annals of American jurisprudence that wanted a score by Nino Rota.

Zsa Zsa claimed to have mailed a check for one thousand dollars for a new registration sticker; either it didn't arrive, or her personal assistant forgot to attach it. She didn't notice the omission because she had been in Rome filming "a two-hour special for the Vatican in five languages." (I have found no record of this holy assignment, although Zsa Zsa wore a different bejeweled cross around her neck each day at her trial. "If one has a cross to bear," she sighed, "it might as well be diamonds.") Her driver's license also raised questions: it, too, had expired, and her date of birth was altered—most unconvincingly in ballpoint ink—to 1928. (The original date, 1923, was also erroneous.) Zsa Zsa explained this lapse by saying that Frederic usually drove them around town, and that "the studio sends for me a limousine," even though that perk had ended long ago.

The exchange between Zsa Zsa and the cop, even as he put in a call to the Beverly Hills police station to verify her license, remained in dispute. She claimed that, sitting in her car for the long while it took him to check her info, she became hot and uncomfortable. (She also needed access to a ladies' room.) Officer Paul Kramer, thirty-eight years old, six feet four inches tall, muscled, with a brush mustache and wearing dark glasses, could have doubled as a *Honcho* model. Although Zsa Zsa knew a hot number when she saw one, she did not flirt. He frightened her. (Seeing him on the witness stand when Zsa Zsa's case went to court later that year, one might share her disquiet, for he recalled the two malevolent birds in her past: the ill-omened one she buried in her back garden, and the "fuck you" bird from Neiman Marcus. That is to say, he had the sinister eyes of a velociraptor. Cross-examined by Zsa Zsa's attorney, Officer Kramer spoke in a baleful voice that somehow matched his twisted smirk.)

As the slow minutes dripped by on that hot midday in Beverly Hills, Zsa Zsa, impatient and growing angry, got out of her car and approached the officer to ask what was taking so long. "Why are you keeping me here? Am I free to go?" Perhaps more was said; did Zsa Zsa really call him an "asshole," as subsequently claimed?

Many times on television, Zsa Zsa quoted him as replying "fuck off" when she asked whether she could leave. (She demurely truncated his obscenity to "f. off" for talk-show consumption. On the witness stand, when her attorney said, "I apologize, Miss Gabor, but when you say 'f. off,' does that mean that Officer Kramer told you to 'fuck off'?" Zsa Zsa nodded shyly and cast her eyes to the floor, striking the pose of Caravaggio's *Penitent Magdalene*.) Having spoken English for sixty years, she nevertheless mistook the officer's meaning on that fateful day. She was certain it was cop lingo for "hit the road, sister." And so she touched the ignition and drove away.

Turning onto Olympic Boulevard, she heard the scream of sirens on La Cienega, saw flashing lights from the motorcycle. Zsa Zsa found herself in a chase as blood-curdling as Gene Hackman's in *The French Connection* or O.J. Simpson's in the white Bronco. She was soon caught and hauled out of her car. Furious and frightened, Zsa Zsa slapped the cop so hard that she knocked the dark glasses off his face. He handcuffed and arrested her, calling her names that she claimed singed her ears. A passing eyewitness, wondering whether he had happened on a drug bust, saw the cop sling the suspect to the rear of the Rolls. Her handbag went flying, her arms were pinned behind her back as the handcuffs went on. According to her subsequent court testimony, the tight handcuffs bruised her wrists, leaving them black and purple for weeks. He pushed her down onto the curb where she sat in the hot sun until the secondary police unit arrived, all the while making crude remarks to her and refusing to unloose the manacles for a moment so that she could adjust her skirt, which had lodged at mid-thigh in the hurly-burly. Zsa Zsa's high-pitched threat to have the officer fired, and to call her pals Ronald and Nancy Reagan, only fueled the combustion.

At the police station, she was charged with five offenses: battery upon an officer, disobeying an officer, driving without proper registration, driving without a license, and having an open container of alcohol, viz., a silver flask of vodka in the glove compartment. Zsa Zsa said it belonged to Frederic, who later explained that he sometimes added a drop to his Diet Pepsi.

The People vs. Zsa Zsa Gabor began in September 1989 and dragged on for weeks. The trial came to be known as such owing to a documentary video that was cobbled together and marketed, much to Zsa Zsa's displeasure. "When he was chasing me I thought of the Gestapo," Zsa Zsa testified through tears. "In Hungary we had the Nazis, we had the Russian tanks. But I was more scared on Olympic and La Cienega. I was screaming 'Help! Help!' I was afraid the police were going to shoot me."

Zsa Zsa, of course, left Hungary long before the arrival of the Gestapo or the Red Army. Apart from that exaggeration, however, it's hard to doubt the substance of her fear. Although the media mocked Zsa Zsa from every angle, a Los Angeles contributor to the *New York Times* placed the controversy in a more sober context. Writing on September 27, 1989, Anne Taylor Fleming first described the circus-like atmosphere of the trial, then followed with this caveat: "But for the locals, there is an angle beyond Miss Gabor's quips in an exaggerated Hungarian accent. That issue is the police and how they treat us: not just the celebrities, but any and all of us. Even as we giggle at Miss Gabor's predicament, we are also thinking about our own feelings and fears about the police and swapping stories about our encounters with them."

A retired police sergeant interviewed by Fleming told her, "You have to remember, cops hate losing face." In a sense, that was the fuse that Zsa Zsa lighted. Had she been less arrogant, less the grande dame, the result might have been different. Or maybe not: Officer Kramer had previously been accused of manhandling motorists.

Summing up, the *Times* journalist tipped the scale slightly in Zsa Zsa's favor: "So even though we have been having a good laugh over the whole thing, it is, for those of us who live here, much less of a farce than it might seem from a distance." Three decades later, in view of the daily atrocities committed by police across the United States, one wonders about Zsa Zsa's fate had she been a young male, or a person of color, a resident of Downey or East Los Angeles, and driving a nondescript vehicle. That trial might never have taken place— the officer's statement of self-defense for the killing would have ended the open-and-shut inquiry.

Fortunately for Zsa Zsa's career, the trial became not only a cause célèbre but her true Norma Desmond moment. And yes, DeMille might have filmed it had he been still alive, for it was the greatest Gabor show on earth. And the last one. It was Zsa Zsa's *Sunset Boulevard* played for laughs. Call it *La Cienega Boulevard*. Minus the anguish of a dead lover in the swimming pool, Zsa Zsa's version was still gothic and slightly ghoulish, for she seemed convinced that those cameras would never stop rolling. And she was almost right, for the moment she alighted from her car each morning at the courthouse the newsreel cameras made love to her image, reporters blocked her path, and she eagerly gave interviews on the sidewalk as though she were guest star on a plein-air talk show. Also like Norma Desmond, she had a German husband, for her entourage included Frederic, who stood by like a footman until called upon for confirmation; her attorney; her hairdresser; and various supporters and hangers-on.

Motley crowds greeted her outside the courthouse, some wearing "Free Zsa Zsa" T-shirts and hoisting placards with the same sentiment, and others with signs urging "Hang Zsa Zsa." An oddball woman hit Zsa Zsa up for money to pay her own legal bills; Zsa Zsa promised to help. A very convincing Eva Gabor imitator managed to seat herself in the courtroom beside Frederic until her fakery was discovered and a bailiff ushered her out. (The real Eva was mortified at these shenanigans. "It wouldn't have happened if you didn't talk so much," she scolded, much to Zsa Zsa's annoyance.)

Francesca, too, was in the crowd. She held up a wobbly hand-lettered "Free Zsa Zsa" sign that looked amazingly cheap for the daughter of a star. Watching all this on *The People vs. Zsa Zsa Gabor*, you see Zsa Zsa give Francesca an absentminded kiss; the scene is so weird you almost expect her to autograph Francesca's homemade sign, not quite realizing it belongs to her own daughter.

Zsa Zsa's arrest in 1989 rocketed her once more into the scandalsphere. The trial, which lasted for two weeks later that year, kept her in the headlines and newscasts well into the nineties. Arriving at court on the first day, Zsa Zsa wore a black Donna Karan dress with an enormous red silk corsage on her left shoulder. Next day, another DK original, this one a flashy leopard-spot design. Her daily fashion statements added to the *Day of the Locust* atmosphere, which spilled over into the courtroom.

During preliminary testimony, Zsa Zsa busied herself sketching witnesses, prosecutor, and Judge Charles Rubin. On the fourth day, she sketched Officer Kramer before she was called to reenact the incident. Cameras, never at rest, made the reenactment look like actors and director rehearsing a scene for a crime drama. At one point, however, Zsa

Zsa rushed out of court in tears but returned after a brief recess.

Zsa Zsa's testimony was not confined to the witness stand. Each day, upon arrival, she made snarky comments to the media about Officer Kramer, the judge, and others in her line of fire. As her comments became more inflammatory, the judge issued a gag order. Perhaps she didn't understand the term, for she continued her stream-of-consciousness narrative as before. The prosecution then called for a contempt citation. Judge Rubin instead gave Zsa Zsa what he called "my first and last warning. You are to say, 'No comment.'" The gag order included all members of the Beverly Hills Police Department. The prosecution, increasingly annoyed, raised the question of the defendant's mental competence. At that, Zsa Zsa grimaced and whispered in her attorney's ear.

When the trial finally ended, Judge Rubin sentenced Zsa Zsa to four days in jail, reduced to three owing to time served on the day of her arrest. He further imposed a two-year gag order and a fine of $12,937, along with 120 hours of community service and a psychiatric evaluation.

In July 1990, Zsa Zsa spent a weekend in the El Segundo City Jail. After her time behind bars, she was as visible on TV as a presidential candidate. To name only a few of the shows where she told her story, often changing details and even laughing at herself: *Good Morning America, A Current Affair, Entertainment Tonight, The Phil Donahue Show.*

The cop slapping followed her for the rest of her career. On an episode of *The Fresh Prince of Bel-Air* in 1991, she plays egotistical movie star Sonya Lamor, a neighbor of series regulars the Banks family. At a party, Vivian Banks says, "Miss Lamor, there's something I'm just dying to know—" To which Zsa Zsa replies, "Yes, I did it and he deserved to be slapped."

On an episode of *Empty Nest*, two of the female regulars—Carole and Laverne—end up in jail owing to a silly mix-up. In the adjoining cell is a woman with her head turned to the wall. "Why are you in jail?" Carole asks. The woman rolls over, and it's Zsa Zsa facing the camera. "Well, dahling, it all started when I was born. The doctor slapped me, and I slapped him back."

The notorious slap is her raison d'être in *The Beverly Hillbillies* (1993). The Clampetts end up behind bars, where they encounter none other than Zsa Zsa. In her final film, *A Very Brady Sequel*, Zsa Zsa threatens to slap a man who outbids her for an objet d'art at an auction.

The judge perhaps had a point when he ordered Zsa Zsa to undergo a psychiatric evaluation. Had her sanity really slipped, or was it that in her mind the year was always 1953? That question is valid because, when she tangled with the police back then, her studio squelched the story. George Sanders told it obliquely in his *Memoirs of a Professional Cad*: "Zsa Zsa succeeded in getting herself thrown out of jail, which takes a bit of doing. She was arrested for speeding in Santa Barbara and a rather poor view was taken of her truculent attitude by the arresting officer, who forthwith carted her off to the cooler where she put on a scene of such majestic proportions as quite pulverized the police force, who insisted that they were running a respectable jail. They threw her out with the greatest indignation."

Immediately after the trial, and before serving her sentence, Zsa Zsa appeared on *The Joan Rivers Show*.

Joan (mock serious): "When are you going to jail? That's what worries me."

Zsa Zsa: "Well, my lawyer found out last night—the judge

who of course never does his homework because he has makeup on and wants to look good on television—he said I have to make a psychiatric . . . I don't know how to say it in English, they have to check up if I'm normal or insane—"

Joan (a great guffaw): "You'll never go to jail! This is wonderful news for you!"

And Zsa Zsa joined the audience in a great cathartic belly laugh.

Chapter 35

Foul Deeds

Eva's death in 1995 removed the strongest barricade to Frederic's agenda, so that he now drew nearer to the throne. His advance brought control of the Gabor dynasty tantalizingly near, with its spectacular emoluments and bonuses. Zsa Zsa inherited millions from Eva's estate, which accrued to her own millions. Magda, in frail health, and Jolie, suffering from dementia and the ravages of extreme old age, both died in 1997. There now remained a single obstacle, and she a formidable one: Zsa Zsa's daughter. Frederic, like a spider inspecting a distracted moth, inventoried Francesca's vulnerabilities. And waited.

Those unfamiliar with the long tug-of-war between Frederic and Francesca might well inquire as to the provenance of this villainous stepfather, who eventually caught Zsa Zsa's daughter in his crosshairs. Hans Georg Robert Lichtenberg was born, according to some sources, on June 18, 1943, in Bad Kreuznach, Germany. Other sources suggest an earlier birthdate. His father was a policeman, his mother a housewife. In 1980, when Lichtenberg was thirty-six years old, he was adopted by Princess Marie-Auguste von Anhalt, who died three years later at the age of eighty-six. The adoption was a financial transaction, although whether Lichtenberg, financed by a wealthy patron, paid the old lady (according to some accounts, she was bankrupt) or whether she remunerated him to become her companion, remains unclear. Owing to countless fabrications on the part of shady characters in Germany and elsewhere, the story of Lichtenberg's metamorphosis became more tangled than any Gabor concoction, which is saying a lot. It is important to note, however, that in a republic such as Germany, holdover titles from long ago carry little weight except among the pretentious and the delusional.

Since I have no wish to quench von Anhalt's rabid thirst for publicity, I will abbreviate his unattractive biography except as necessary in relating Zsa Zsa's story and the sorrows visited on her daughter. Having met him on three occasions, I state my unequivocal dislike of the man, whom I found egomaniacal, coarse, and charmless.

Our first encounter was at lunch in August 2010, at the Caffé Roma in Beverly Hills, a meeting arranged by the late John Blanchette, who had been Zsa Zsa's publicist and who, after her incapacitation, ostensibly represented her while primarily publicizing Frederic. At the luncheon, we discussed my plans to write the Gabor biography. Frederic seemed to believe that the book would overwhelmingly feature him as source and subject. His references to Zsa Zsa that day were unflattering and suggested minimal affection for his wife. I was reminded of sour individuals encountered in low dives. Long before coffee was served, I realized his unreliablility as informant.

Our next meeting took place two years later, on August 19, 2012, in Zsa Zsa's house in Bel Air. The occasion, billed as a twenty-sixth anniversary celebration of their marriage, might more appropriately have been called O Come Let Us Adore

Frederic von Anhalt. Photographers, videographers, and TV journalists swarmed among the guests, with Frederic always on camera and repeating his tired yarns and opinions. Zsa Zsa, upstairs, in the throes of dementia and perhaps heavily sedated, seemed an afterthought to the merriment. Francesca, of course, was not invited.

My final encounter with Frederic was at Zsa Zsa's funeral. I will outline, in a later chapter, his nightmarish gaucherie on that occasion.

Francesca, an intelligent and perceptive woman, never took Frederic seriously, and never pretended to. Brutally frank at times, and despite the lessons in charm and demeanor taught her during her time in a Swiss school for young ladies, she refused to smile and say, "Oh, how interesting," when the response called for was, "Bullshit!" She laughed in his face when he brought out his medals and implied to hangers-on that he was heir to the Austro-Hungarian throne. This made him furious, of course, but he disciplined his fury as long as Zsa Zsa remained healthy and in control of her fortune.

In 2002, however, everything changed when Zsa Zsa was seriously injured in an automobile accident. During her hospital stay, open warfare broke out between Frederic and Francesca. The *New York Post* reported on November 30 that Francesca was "physically restrained from entering her mother's hospital room" by von Anhalt. She was able to visit only after hiring a lawyer who threatened legal action against Frederic and against Cedars-Sinai Medical Center in Los Angeles.

In a sense, Zsa Zsa never recovered from the car crash, neither physically, mentally, nor emotionally. She was not totally disabled, however, and so Francesca visited her and stayed in constant touch by phone. But the balance of power had shifted to Frederic. His legal rights as spouse exceeded Francesca's, for Zsa Zsa had designated him as power of attorney in the event of her inability to make decisions regarding health and finances. For several years he played public caregiver to Zsa Zsa, even though Francesca accused him of neglecting her mother.

Despite the hospital incident and other dustups, Francesca often visited Zsa Zsa at home, usually during Frederic's absence. On June 1, 2005, however, a lawsuit was filed in Zsa Zsa's name against Francesca. The plaintiff, of course, was in reality Frederic von Anhalt acting as his wife's representative. The suit claimed that Francesca had forged her mother's name and conspired with others to fraudently obtain a loan of $3.75 million on Zsa Zsa's house, and of subsequently purchasing a house for herself in the amount of two million dollars. It is implausible that Francesca, who was not shrewd in business matters, could have hoodwinked a financial institution for such an amount.

Francesca countersued, claiming that she suffered serious damages as a result of the false accusations. Given the state of Zsa Zsa's health at the time, it is unlikely that she herself initiated the legal action, or that she comprehended even the basics in the case. Two years later, a judge dismissed the Gabor-von Anhalt suit owing to Zsa Zsa's failure to appear in court and also to numerous misrepresentations. Francesca's attorney hinted at legal action against Zsa Zsa and Frederic for malicious prosecution if they attempted further litigation against his client. There the matter stood for several years.

In the meantime, Frederic pulled one bizarre publicity stunt after another in his overwrought quest for attention. He became the darling of TMZ and similar outlets for news of the celebrity grotesque. In 2007, with Anna Nicole Smith hardly cold in her grave—in fact, the day after her death—Frederic made the news with a proclamation that he "might be" the father of her five-month-old daughter. Claiming that he and Anna Nicole had made their rendezvous in hotels in New York, San Francisco, and Los Angeles, he inadvertently raised questions as to the quality of caregiving to his semi-invalid wife who was confined to a wheelchair. "You can have an affair in ten minutes," he said, then contradicted himself with the laughable statement, "I never talk about my private life. They will never know [about the Smith affair] because I don't talk." On the contrary, he rarely talked of anything but himself. Whether von Anhalt ever met Anna Nicole Smith remains in doubt.

Cindy Adams, a Gabor insider and longtime friend of the family, launched a scathing attack on Frederic in her *New York Post* column on February 13, 2007. After pointing out her credentials as Jolie's coauthor, as travel companion to Zsa Zsa in years past, and adding that she and her husband, Joey Adams, had worked with Zsa Zsa in nightclub acts, she unfurled a harrowing scenario. "Today Zsa Zsa exists as a prisoner in her Bel Air mansion. She can sit, she can stand, but she remains cloistered in her room. She sees no one. She watched the clownish performance of her husband of twenty years announce that he might have been on the conga line that could have fathered Anna Nicole's baby."

Adams stated that while Zsa Zsa's body was impaired, her mind was clear. She claimed firsthand knowledge of Zsa Zsa's distress over Frederic's outrageous claims to have fathered Anna Nicole Smith's baby. She also revealed that he had attempted to peddle an unflattering book on his years with Zsa Zsa. Before Zsa Zsa's incapacitation, Adams continued, when she gave an order Frederic jumped. "I was in that house when she told him, 'Go upstairs and put on your blue blazer and gray pants' and he obediently trotted upstairs and put on his blue blazer and gray pants. Now he's in charge."

According to Adams, Frederic padlocked the gates of Zsa Zsa's estate each time he left. Possessing the sole key to the grounds, he made sure his wife had no visitors in his absence. In addition, he disconnected the gate phone so that no one could enter when he was away. The columnist added further that he had fired Zsa Zsa's maid and that he monitored her phone calls as part of holding her virtual prisoner in her own home. Adams questioned, also, whether he had destroyed their prenuptial contract, which presumably would have granted various rights and responsibilities to Francesca.

In a bid for client sympathy, the publicist John Blanchette issued a press release stating that Frederic had collapsed from exhaustion owing to his continuous vigil at the bedside of his wife. Such devotion seemed inflated at best, given his regular visits to a gym, to restaurants, and to a particular Starbucks in West Hollywood. Zsa Zsa supposedly had round-the-clock nursing care, although Francesca doubted the accuracy of Frederic's claims in this regard. As for the Blanchette press release, it lacks the ring of truth. I liked John Blanchette, who was kind, well-mannered, and helpful. Still, his job, once Zsa Zsa had retreated to her bedroom, was to publicize Frederic in whatever unsavory project von Anhalt might dream up. Observing John and Frederic together on several occasions, it struck me that John felt embarrassed by his employer's crude behavior. It was equally clear that he dared not gainsay anything from Frederic's mouth.

Like the plot device of *Rashomon*—conradictory accounts of the same incident told from the point of view of several characters—the question of Frederic's devotion to Zsa Zsa during her long illness changes from one source to another. Francesca believed him negligent; John Blanchette offered the official version despite evidence that suggested otherwise. Betsy Jentz, who worked as Zsa Zsa's assistant from the 1970s until the early years of this century, had this to say: "There are many versions of Frederic, but his care of Zsa Zsa has the advantage over anything negative that one can say." She is convinced that he did everything necessary to make Zsa Zsa comfortable. His claims of Zsa Zsa's complicity in his stunts, however, leave Betsy skeptical. During our first interview, in April 2016, I asked, "Do you ever visit Zsa Zsa now?"

"Yes," she answered. "I was there for her birthday on February 6, when Frederic gave a party. He took me to her bedroom to say hello, but she didn't know who I was. Nor who anybody else was, in my opinion."

I followed with, "Does she recognize Frederic?"

"In my opinion, no. But he says yes."

"Does she speak to him at all?"

"I don't think she talks to anybody. I've only seen her twice in recent years, and to be perfectly honest I would have preferred not to see her this last time. I would rather remember her as the glamourous lady that she was, and the friend that she became when I worked for her."

If Frederic had not married Zsa Zsa and her wealth, he might have found employment as a headline writer for the supermarket tabloids. Even as his wife's condition deteriorated, his publicity schemes became increasingly perverse and distasteful. In 2011, CNN.com headlined ZSA ZSA GABOR TO BECOME NEW MOTHER AT 94, HUSBAND SAYS. According to Frederic, Zsa Zsa was to become a mother again using an egg donor, artificial insemination, and a surrogate mother. The exact biological avenues of such a conception were left untrodden. The CNN story added that von Anhalt was "working with Dr. Mark Surry of the Southern California Reproductive Center in Beverly Hills. CNN's calls to the center have not been returned." Technically, of course, one could claim to be "working with" a doctor based on a single phone call to his office, even if the call went unreturned.

Around the same time, he announced plans to run for governor of California. Even in the sideshow of American politics, this candidacy caused guffaws. Although a right-wing supporter of Reagan, Bush, and later of Trump, von Anhalt styled himself a "liberal independent." He withdrew his candidacy when he could milk no further coverage from it.

As Zsa Zsa's health declined, she suffered heart failure, a stroke, a heart attack, and amputation of her right leg. When death seemed imminent, Frederic made the ghoulish decision to preserve her body by plastination and put it on display— "so that her beauty will last forever," he said. Lured by his macabre carny show, the Golden Casket Company, a Connecticut firm, offered a solid gold coffin as a "pre-need gift" to Zsa Zsa. Pretending outrage, Frederic stated that he would accept the gift and have it melted into a ring. Reacting to Frederic's indignation, the company confirmed that John Blanchette had called to express interest on the part of his client, Frederic von Anhalt. "We have voicemail proof of this call," said Edward Balfour, head of sales at Golden Casket.

Along with his displays of hideous taste, Frederic ran a sideline of adopting adult males and turning them into "knights" and also the kind of princes that he himself was. For such entrée into the Teutonic nobility, they paid top dollar—though not top Deutsche Mark, such activity being illegal in the Federal Republic of Germany. Among the colorful names taken by Frederic's titular offspring are several Prince von Anhalts and a Prince Germany. At last report, Chancellor Angela Merkel did not feel threatened by a restored German throne operating out of California.

His next shenanigan reeks of amateur porn crossed with *The Dukes of Hazzard*. In this scenario, Prince von Charming stops his Rolls-Royce to help three damsels in distress. They are in a white Chrysler convertible with Florida license plates. As he drives by, the ladies recognize him as a stellar celebrity and flag him down. Is it for an autograph, he wonders, or to pose for selfies? Forgetting to ask, "Is that a gun in your purse?", he finds himself enmeshed in a robbery. They take his wallet, an expensive watch, $1,800 in cash, then they strip him naked and handcuff him to the steering wheel. Or so he said. A pathetic photo shows him bare-assed and bound, stretch marks shining, bent over the steering wheel though not handcuffed but tied with a white cloth. Like Clark Kent, however, he somehow managed, or so he said, to wiggle free and call police on a cell phone. Why he then retied himself to the steering wheel for a photo op was not explained, nor was the fact that the LAPD could find no handcuffs.

Worst scene of all, which ends this lamentable saga: On Zsa Zsa's ninety-fourth birthday, he brought photographers to the bedside where she lay, helpless and demented, and invited them to photograph her sans makeup, sans wig, sans beauty, sans everything. These pictures he sold to tabloids, who then flashed them around the world online. Francesca, horrified, said what anyone knows who knew Zsa Zsa at all: "She was never seen in public unless she looked like a movie star, and the last thing she wanted was to be old and helpless."

If there is karma in this world or the next, Zsa Zsa—along with Eva, Magda, Jolie, Vilmos, and Francesca—will see to it that Frederic's punishment, for this desecration of her image, goes on forever.

Chapter 36

Not Waving but Drowning

Among the bitter and baroque stories of Hollywood children, Francesca's eclipses most others. I can hardly write about her without a lump in the throat, for she was a dear friend. Thelma Ritter's reaction to Marilyn Monroe on the *All About Eve* set—"I adored that girl from the moment we met"—comes to mind when I recall my first encounter with Francesca. At sixtysomething, her life had been one rough patch after the next. Still, she was holding on, even though Frederic, in barring her from her mother's house, had made communication between her and Zsa Zsa virtually impossible. "My mother used to call me ten times a day," Francesca said during our initial conversation. "Then Frederic took away her phone."

Prior to that first meeting, I telephoned Francesca to seek her imprimatur for the book about her family. I said right off that without her approval I did not want to proceed, and she agreed to discuss the project. Arriving early at The Coffee Bean and Tea Leaf, 7915 Sunset Boulevard in Hollywood, I found the place crowded, the afternoon balmy, and so I took a table on the patio. Reading a newspaper, I was startled when she appeared behind me and said, "Sam?"

"How did you spot me?" I asked. A set-in-L.A. movie moment as a smile teased her lips: "I just knew." Francesca was not immediately recognizable as the scion of Hollywood glamour. She wore navy sweatpants and a bulky top, an outfit that partially disguised her weight. Light lipstick and blonde hair, slightly teased, recalled photos of an earlier, less bedeviled, Francesca Hilton. Although no surgeon's knife had come near her face, from certain angles the Gabor structure was detectable. She barely sipped her mineral water, so we talked. Or she talked, mostly about Frederic. I realize now that her obsession with him not only bankrupted her but also hastened her death on January 6, 2015. (She told me not long before she died that she had spent $400,000 in legal fees to obtain visiting rights with Zsa Zsa. Among Frederic's stated reasons for barring her: negativity.)

The deadly strife between Francesca and Frederic verged on Hollywood noir. Neither used a gun, although thoughts of murder surely darkened their dreams. As the afternoon wore on, a thunderstorm spread across Los Angeles. During one of Francesca's tirades, she mentioned the rumor that Frederic was in poor health. "Maybe he'll die!" she proclaimed. Just then there came a bulbous growl of thunder.

Any mention of "struck by lightning" would have been superfluous. We moved inside. There we remained for another hour, then she drove me in the rainstorm to my car several blocks away. Her dilapidated SUV, with a handicapped sign dangling from the rearview mirror, was piled high with papers, books, magazines, food scraps, electronic gadgets, paper bags with unknown content—in short, a foreshadowing of homelessness. She walked with some strain, although otherwise she didn't appear beset by ill health.

*   *   *

Disaster hit in the final months of 2014. I had not seen Francesca for several months, though we spoke often by phone. That fall, she told me that she had lost the lease on her rented house in Hollywood. She supplied only vague indications of her new address; mail went to a post office box. In late November I asked, as usual, about her cat. She replied in a voice of lead, "She died. It's okay, she was old." Knowing Francesca, I realized that she feared showing emotions that might elicit pity. I knew also that she, like all the Gabors, was a lover of animals and that the death of her cat would have brought staggering grief.

When I phoned her on Christmas Day 2014, she was napping so we chatted briefly. "I spent the day at a homeless shelter," she said. Unaware of her desperation—I later learned that she slept in her car during those final days—I took it to mean that she had volunteered to help serve Christmas dinner. This was a reasonable assumption, since her abrasive side was tempered by a compassionate heart. Such goodwill, however, she kept locked out of view. Twelve days later she died.

If I had been fully aware of her anguish, I would have sent her a plane ticket and insisted that she come to me for an indefinite stay.

Among Francesca's many burdens was the Gabor legend, which the Gabors expected her to assume as a natural legacy. She was groomed by masters. One of her childhood Christmas presents was a set of four dolls dressed and bewigged to resemble Jolie, Magda, Zsa Zsa, and Eva. These totems wore miniature copies of Dior gowns owned by the Gabors. Zsa Zsa claimed that she and Francesca's governess—as if inspired by the dark arts—had personally sewed the wardrobes for these miniature graven images. The cult-like objects, however, failed to cast a spell on the girl-child.

When Francesca rebelled, early on, against furs, jewels, flashy marriages and quick divorces, overstuffed headlines, haute couture, the Republican politics of her family, a slim waist and a camera-ready smile, Zsa Zsa was stunned. Their mother-daughter friction led to high-decibel fights that pealed across Bel Air; slammed doors and thrown objects; estrangements; and, in later years, lawsuits actual and threatened, followed by countersuits. But always, reconciliations.

Francesca's cousin put it this way: "She inherited all the liabilities and none of the benefits of the Gabor family." Jolie, who had micromanaged her daughters' lives from Budapest to New York to Hollywood, despaired of her insubordinate granddaughter. This grandmother, herself never a sylph, hounded Francesca to lose weight. When Francesca grew up, she avoided the nagging granny whenever possible. Despite the tensions, her tales of Grandmother Gabor's smash-bang driving could have furnished a skit for Carol Burnett and Vicki Lawrence. "She drove through a hurricane on Long Island with me in the car," Francesca recalled. "Even as a kid, I thought we were headed into the ocean." Her hair-raising account of Jolie's attempt to parallel park: "She banged the car in front, I screamed, then she slammed into the car behind." Francesca saw the absurd comedy in these stories. But when anger boiled over, Jolie became "that old cunt." (Eccentric driving ran in the family. Francesca swore that Zsa Zsa would turn her head to window-shop as she motored down Wilshire Boulevard.)

By the time of Eva's death, those wacky days were gone. Jolie and Magda died two years after Eva, leaving Francesca with a mere fragment of family. Only Zsa Zsa remained, and as usual she focused her attention on face, hair, glamourous outfits, gasp-worthy jewelry, her career or what was left of it, and Frederic.

*   *   *

For young Francesca, home life under Zsa Zsa seesawed from a child's wide-eyed fantasy to an opulent reign of terror. Life in a mansion, travel to storied cities with days of pleasure and hotel nights of great luxury, meals in high-gloss restaurants, doting nannies and schools to encourage every grace and enthusiasm. But also: shrill demands incomprehensible to a young girl; maternal fits of tears and screaming provoked by unknown cause; rigorous expectations laid out by movie star mother and aunt, and by the other aunt, Magda, who prefered poodles to children; unwelcome advice from a grandmother whose notions of child rearing stopped at the silver spoon. And what was this little girl to make of an elderly father who resembled her Hungarian grandfather, and who sent lavish presents but seldom permitted her to visit his home? What of the various "uncles" who made their entrances and exits and then were seen no more, gone before she could sort them out? Other children might wish for a pony (Francesca had one), but Francesca's mighty hope was for a daddy to counteract her mom. That intermittent mom, who kissed and embraced little Franci, then left for weeks and months to make pictures in far-off lands, returning for a day or a week before another TV show or another studio summoned her once more.

"I brought myself up," Francesca said in a tone that mixed bitterness and tough resignation. Her litany of sorrows began early and never found an end. "I couldn't bring home my friends," she said, "because my mother hit me every day. She also hit the help."

I hesitate to repeat this accusation, one reason being that corporal punishment—spankings and the like—was common during Francesca's childhood. Unless it took injurious forms, society looked upon it as a normal privilege of parenting, and it was also widespread in schools. A proverb oft repeated was "Spare the rod and spoil the child." For that reason, it seems unfair to condemn a parent of sixty or seventy years ago who could not have imagined that slapping a child's backside would someday be looked on as abuse. From Zsa Zsa's point of view, her daughter's cheekiness must be curbed.

As for hitting the help, Betsy Jentz, and also Nancy De-Jean, both employed by Zsa Zsa to assist in managing her big life, said nothing of the kind. Both women attended her funeral, and in a later conversation Nancy had this to say: "I want you to know she was a very generous lady. And loving, really kindhearted. There is no greater lady in my book than Zsa Zsa Gabor."

I asked how she came to work as Zsa Zsa's personal assistant. "I worked for an attorney who screamed a lot. Zsa Zsa happened to be one of his clients, and when she heard him yelling at me she said, 'Nancy, dahling, how can you let him speak to you this way? This is not healthy, this is no good. You should come to work for me.' A year or so later, she was in the office when it happened again. She said, 'Dahling, you're such a beautiful girl. You can have a job anywhere. Come with me. Leave this man.' You know what? I went to my computer, turned it off, grabbed my keys, left, and never went back."

Nancy was also fond of Francesca, whom she, like many family members and close friends, called Franci. "Our relationship was sisterly," she recalled. "Franci would call me to complain about her mom. When I scolded her for drinking too much, her response was, 'Oh shut up, you sound like her.'"

At some point Francesca, like Zsa Zsa, began to suffer the dizzying mood swings of bipolar disorder. Sometimes—perhaps when medicated—she was delightful, witty, the finest of friends. On other occasions, she would rant. Often on the telephone she raved for an hour, revisiting a lifetime of insults, injuries, and slights real or imagined. The immediate ones typically involved Frederic; others veered toward the

Gabors. Once she said, "I studied drama for years and Eva wouldn't give me a job on *Green Acres*." But Eva was not the show's producer. It's true that she could perhaps have influenced her bosses, but it's likely that Eva, always professionally correct, quailed at the thought of temperamental outbursts and the upsets that her niece might cause on the set and off.

Even in her bitterness, however, Francesca glowed with family pride. "My mother is Zsa Zsa Gabor," I heard her say more than once to an acquaintance who failed to recognize her right off. It seemed a pleasing fiction, if a brief one, to cast herself as the last of the glittering Gabors. Toward the end of her life, she added the fabled name to her own, so that her business card read "Constance Francesca Gabor Hilton."

"A lot of people ask what it's like growing up with Zsa Zsa Gabor as your mother," she told an interviewer in 1975. "Well, if you know nothing else, it's quite normal. My mother was very strict. I remember once being so embarrassed by my report card marks that I didn't want her to see it. The problem was, the parent had to sign the report card. So I took one of her 4-by-5 fan pictures that had been mass-copied with her autograph. I cut out the signature and taped it on. When I turned it in at boarding school, I said my mother had a broken arm."

Also during Francesca's teen years, Zsa Zsa, as if playing a helicopter mom on TV, would sometimes stand at the front door making small talk as Francesca tried to say good night to a date. Later on, Francesca found these intrusions funny, though at the time her resentment boiled over. The boys in question didn't come 'round again.

Zsa Zsa, of course, intended to be a doting mother. Her love for Francesca never wavered, and yet—with her model for motherhood as none other than Jolie, along with echoes of grandmother Franceska Tillemann, both of whom blended the talents of prison matron with mother love—what chance existed for this child of uncertain provenance? For not only was Conrad Hilton hesitant to claim her as his own. Rumors circulated in the Hilton family and beyond that her actual father was Nicky. Zsa Zsa herself claimed that she and her former stepson had a sexual relationship that began soon after her release from the sanitarium in 1945 and ended during his marriage to Elizabeth Taylor, a stretch of five years. Always maintaining that Conrad raped her during the final days of their marriage and was thus Francesca's father, Zsa Zsa unwittingly allowed, in her chronology, for the possibility that Nicky Hilton, not Conrad, fathered her child. He would thus have been Francesca's father and her half-brother.

Zsa Zsa's claim of an affair with Nicky Hilton might well have been planted and watered by Wendy Leigh, her notorious collaborator on *One Lifetime Is Not Enough*, that highly unreliable autobiography published in 1991. Earlier, when working with Gerold Frank in 1960 on *My Story*, Zsa Zsa's comment about her former stepson was this: "Any place he sees me he screams, 'Mother!' I think Nicky has a little hidden sort of crush on me." Frank omitted the statement from the published book, leaving it instead among the outtakes. Her "proof" of Nicky's crush meant little, however. Not only he, but Barron Hilton, as well, used the same sobriquet. During one of Zsa Zsa's Las Vegas shows, Barron said, "I'm going to catch Mother's act."

If Francesca had been Eva's daughter, the story would surely have ended differently. Early on, this aunt became Francesca's most steadying influence. Late in life, Eva said on television, "I wanted six children and couldn't have them. Believe me, I tried." (Her final marriage, to Frank Jameson, brought her stepchildren and stepgrandchildren who adored her, and she them. They, like Francesca, inherited money from Eva's estate.)

Interviewed while appearing in *Her Cardboard Lover* in 1951 at the Theatre by the Sea in Rhode Island, Eva sounded maternal.

"Let me tell you about my niece," she said. "She is such a little beauty. On the West Coast, we walked past a kiddie shop with toys and dolls in the window. 'Oh, Auntie Eva,' she said, 'aren't they beautiful?' When she and my sister visited New York last year, I took Francesca backstage at *The Happy Time*. There is a scene where Kurt Kasznar argues with another man in a very loud voice. When the play was over, my little niece walked right up to Kurt and said, 'I heard you. You were arguing and fighting with that man, and everybody could hear every word you said. If you act that way pretty soon people will not like you.'" Eva, laughing, added, "And then she shook her finger at him. She is such a darling child!"

Two years later, a photo in the *New York Daily News* showed Auntie Eva and six-year-old Francesca deplaning at LaGuardia. They had just flown in from Los Angeles, and Zsa Zsa had come to collect them.

Magda, although a more remote aunt than Eva, told a story about young Francesca that accords with Eva's account of their niece's sauciness. "One night at dinner with Zsa Zsa and George Sanders, when Francesca was three or four, my little niece headed off to bed. She said, 'Good night, Eva, good night, Magda, good night, Mommie, good night, Uncle George.' Then she walked to the door, turned around, and to George she said, 'You Russian!' And ran out of the room."

Magda thought it hilarious, but not George. "He couldn't even laugh at that," she said. By that time—around 1951— he was a changed man, according to Magda. "In earlier years," she added, "George was entirely different. He supported his family, who left Britain during the war. Not only his parents but also his sister, brother-in-law, and all their children. Nine or ten people in all." Magda hinted that marriage to Zsa Zsa, along with the pressures of a job he disliked—acting—brought on the change in his personality.

When Francesca grew up, Eva treated her as an adult, an equal. Zsa Zsa, on the other hand, fancied a thirty-year-old child kept in a doll's house, then a forty-year-old one, then fifty and beyond. Perhaps she dreamed of repairing earlier mistakes. Moreover, the younger the daughter in appearance and actions, the younger the mom. A demented extension of Zsa Zsa's rich fantasy life: John Blanchette told me that Zsa Zsa urged him to marry Francesca and produce a grandchild for her. Two obstacles obviated the match: he was gay and Francesca couldn't stand him.

Francesca's school years resemble a checkerboard—not one of orderly squares but rather a jigsaw of surreal triangles and trapezoids unnervingly juxtaposed. In other words, chaos. At various times she attended the Knox School on Long Island; the Château Montchoisi, a Swiss finishing school; Marymount, a Catholic girls' school in Los Angeles, from which she graduated in 1965. A person familiar with Francesca's time in Switzerland said, "That poor sweet girl— she had ball gowns but no underwear." A bit later, she made a brief stopover at UCLA.

In 1966, Leonard Lyons quoted Zsa Zsa in his syndicated column: "I am sending Francesca to another school—in Paris—to learn to be a woman of the world. In this school she will learn how to cook, paint, sew. The courses will include visits to Dior to learn haute couture, and to Van Cleef and Arpels. It is important for a woman to know about emeralds and rubies." Whether or not Francesca actually attended this Gaboresque institution remains unclear. It would surely have contradicted her interests.

In 1968, Zsa Zsa gave a farewell party for herself and Francesca. They were leaving for London, where Francesca had been admitted either to the Royal Academy of Dramatic Art or the Drama Centre acting school. Francesca herself claimed the latter, while newspapers reported the former. Admission to either suggests talent and promise in theatre and cinema. But like so many other intentions in Francesca's life, drama school didn't work out. One reason seems to have been drug use. She joked about marijuana: "While I was a student at the Knox School, I came back to L.A. with a marijuana seed that I planted in my mother's backyard in Bel Air. The gardener watered it and it grew. Then my mother had it pulled up!"

Unfortunately, she didn't limit herself to pot smoking. Swinging London in the late sixties, with hashhish, LSD, cocaine—it's easy to fill in the blanks. The story is all too common: the banal allure of drugs seducing unhappy people like Francesca, whose entire life hovered near a cliff. The miracle is that she didn't plunge off it until age sixty-seven. A person who knew Francesca for many years assured me that the house Zsa Zsa bought for her in Bel Air was lost "to drugs and a gigolo husband." Unlike Zsa Zsa and all the Gabors, she lacked a tough sense of money management. They worked hard; every penny must be accounted for. Francesca, by contrast, a child of plenty with time on her hands, failed to grasp the fragility of abundance. Before Frederic's arrival, Zsa Zsa might grouse but she would not let Francesca go wanting. Eva's legacy could have kept her niece in comfort for the rest of her life if only Francesca had learned how to invest, how to live within a budget.

Francesca's companion for several years in the early seventies was the actor and director Jack Starrett, who gave her a bit part in his 1973 film, *Cleopatra Jones*. She also worked as a production assistant on the picture. When they were no longer lovers, she recalled him with great fondness. "He's wonderful," she told an interviewer. "I still see him as a friend." In her proposal for the autobiography she never wrote, she called Starrett "one of the funniest men I ever met. He drank Jack Daniel's a lot and wore long wavy robes. Jack played the Gabby Hayes character in Mel Brooks's *Blazing Saddles*. Mel complained that Jack stole every scene he was in."

In that proposal, Francesca gave short shrift to her two marriages. "1988—I married Vincent Munden for six months. Got my first annulment." And, on the next line: "1993—Joe Piche, met him at a pool hall—Hollywood Athletic Club—married him a year and a half later." Her companion from 1997 until her death was Michael Nateece, whom she met in Las Vegas and who seems to have provided a stabilizing influence.

Her acting career went nowhere. After half a dozen bit parts from 1971 to 1999, including *Pterodactyl Woman from Beverly Hills*, Francesca wisely retreated from the cinematic side of show business. Later she tried stand-up comedy, with short-lived results. Her wittiest line onstage: "My mother and I get along great now that we're the same age." Zsa Zsa, in the audience, clapped hands and rolled with laughter.

Over the years, Francesca tried her hand at various jobs. She worked behind the counter in a Hollywood camera store. While in public relations, she managed Mickey Rooney Jr. for part of his brief film career. Her two main interests, however, were photography, which she began in childhood, and Hilton hotel management. The latter endeavor turned into a comic nightmare involving not only Barron Hilton, who ran the corporation after Conrad's death, but hotel employees in various cities. Like Zsa Zsa, Francesca seemed unable to occupy a hotel room without epic melodrama. Once in Madrid Zsa Zsa was pulled off a plane by Spanish police and charged with failure to pay her bill. Similar incidents took place elsewhere. Francesca, like her mother, felt entitled to royal treatment in any Hilton hotel, Zsa Zsa owing to marriage and Francesca to paternity.

At some point in the 1980s, after many a dead-end job, Francesca landed a minor position with the Hilton Hotel Corporation—in reality, a sinecure to pacify her as well as Zsa Zsa. For a time, Francesca received a free room in any Hilton hotel. That privilege ended when some in-room short-coming led to a fracas. She threatened to fire the manager, a call was made to corporate headquarters, and Miss Hilton no longer slept gratis under the family roof.

On another occasion, during a manic phase, she stripped naked at the pool of the Washington, D.C., Hilton, and was led away. Then, and on other occasions, her mania was further fueled by diet pills, which Francesca sometimes consumed in unhealthy doses. In 1987, Barron Hilton wrote to Francesca informing her that her monthly check from him would be reduced by half until the entire amount of $6,200, which he paid to the Las Vegas Hilton to cover bad checks she wrote, was reimbursed to him. The origin of this monthly stipend is unclear.

As a result of continuing clamor and disorder, she was eventually barred from all Hilton hotels, an interdict that left her undeterred. For years, and literally to her dying day, this was the saucy outgoing message on her phone: "This is Francesca Hilton of the Hilton Corporation. Please leave your name and number and a message and I will call you back. If you do not leave your name and a number I will not call you back."

Overmedication with appetite inhibitors led to a mephitic episode that caused a two-year rift between Francesca and Zsa Zsa during which they did not speak. In September 1984, the columnist Marilyn Beck reported that Francesca had entered Cedars-Sinai Medical Center in Los Angeles as a result of an overdose of diet pills. In a phone conversation with Zsa Zsa, Beck learned that Francesca had not slept in four weeks owing to the pills. "We had to get those uppers away from her," said Zsa Zsa. "She's doing fine in the hospital, finally getting some rest. I'm begging her to stay another week. I tell you, it's not easy being a mother today."

Two days later, Beck reported that "Constance Francesca Hilton phoned me to say that her stay at Cedars-Sinai is involuntary, that her mother had her committed to the psychiatric wing of the hospital against her will. She adds that she had not been taking diet pills, as Zsa Zsa claimed, and that she has informed her attorney that she wants to sue her mother for defamation of character."

Francesca referred to this horrific episode as her time in "the nut house," using the same terminology that her mother used to describe her own involuntary incarceration. In a late-night phone conversation a few years before her death, Francesca recalled being handcuffed in a police car after she had run amok in the streets of Bel Air.

After working on her autobiography for thirty years, with few pages written, she searched for a coauthor and was turned down by several prospects. Eventually she asked me to take on the assignment. "But Francesca," I said, "I can't spend months, maybe a year, in Los Angeles, and you won't come to me. So I have to say no, even though I would love to work with you." She then suggested Skype, and again I had to decline.

Her book's working title was *Hotels, Diamonds, and Me*. The six-page outline runs from birth to 2007, the year she put it aside. I suggested that, in view of her tribulations with the Hiltons and their hotels, she might have a bit of fun at Barron's expense. "Go back to your original title. Call it *Miss Hilton Prefers the Ritz*. Or," I added, "if not that, how about *Miss Hilton Regrets*?" I knew, however, that none of these would see print. In life, and on the page, just when success seemed at hand, she subverted it. In this respect, she copied her mother, who sacrificed her early career to hormones. But Zsa Zsa's implicit motto was "I won't be defeated," while Francesca's more poignant one might have been "Fate always intervened."

Was it fate, or Zsa Zsa, who stepped between Francesca and photojournalism? In the early 1970s, Francesca sold a few photographs to *People* magazine. In 1976 she traveled to the Middle East—Turkey, Iran, Syria, Lebanon—for her work. Arriving in Beirut during the Lebanese civil war, she landed just as Syrian troops invaded the country. Her photographs from this period are of museum quality. "I was in the middle of a war zone," she wrote in her book proposal, "and it was *not* a movie set. My mother called and pleaded with me to come home. I said, 'Hell no!' This is the real thing. Although I was terrified being there, it was fascinating to see it unravel before my eyes. I was the only photojournalist there and one of the photos I took ended up on the front page of the *New York Times*."

Two years later, Francesca and Zsa Zsa appeared together on Dinah Shore's syndicated talk show. Thirty-one at the time, Francesca conducted herself as a professional woman. Smartly attired in a black pantsuit, with light makeup and blonde hair stylishly done, she looked the antithesis of florid Gabor glamour. Nor did she resemble any of the Gabors, which surely pleased her. On this occasion, the only unsettling aspect was her leveled-out behavior: she seemed artificially calm, perhaps medicated, very different from the volatile woman of later years. The topic of that day's show was mothers and daughters. Dinah's other guests were Judy and Diana Canova, and Lee Grant with her daughter, Dinah Manoff. Of the three pairs, only Zsa Zsa and Francesca betrayed strains in their relationship.

Unlike Judy Canova and her daughter, or Lee Grant and hers, who seemed like chums, Francesca and Zsa Zsa bristled, though subtly enough to maintain the nonconfrontational style of Dinah Shore's show. When Zsa Zsa interrupted her daughter, Francesca snapped, "I understand the question!" For an instant, Zsa Zsa looked as if she had been bitten; next moment she was back to her shtick, fabulously giddy once more.

Then a cutaway to photos of each mother and daughter when the girls were very young. Zsa Zsa's commentary: "Franci was three or four, she was very good then, she didn't answer back, she was adorable. Now she has her own opinion about everything." This Zsa Zsa said with a laugh that betrayed low-level anger, as if to rebuke her daughter for daring to be an adult. Francesca replied sotto voce and Zsa Zsa muttered a retort. Their swashbuckling exchange was not picked up by microphones.

Another cutaway to Francesca's Middle East photographs. After half a dozen seen on camera, Dinah Shore and her guests applauded. Zsa Zsa did not, since Francesca's time in Lebanon had been a source of contention. On the show, Francesca said, "When I was in Lebanon, my mother demanded, 'Come home at once! You *will* come home, you *must* come home!' She was very upset. I didn't tell her I was there, she found out."

Zsa Zsa's anxiety, of course, was natural and certainly not blameworthy. Who wouldn't worry about a loved one in a war zone? Unfortunately, Zsa Zsa wanted total obedience. When she spoke ex cathedra as the mother, she expected compliance of the kind that she, Eva, and Magda gave to Jolie. But Francesca was not a Gabor sister, and so the lifelong conflicts grew and festered.

Whenever I traveled to Los Angeles, Francesca and I would often meet for breakfast in Hollywood at her favorite Starbucks. Her rhapsodic review of the lattes, the bagels with cream cheese, and all else on the predictable menu struck me as ironic, and a bit melancholy, in view of her lifelong experience with fine restaurants. On the last one of these occasions, I arrived early and took a seat outside to wait for her. Surrounded by millennials and others in thrall to every conceivable electronic device, I spotted Francesca on the sidewalk thirty or forty yards away. Just as I stood up to go and meet her, a cyclone of abuse erupted from her mouth that would startle a Billingsgate fishwife.

With gorgon furrows on her face, she slung her words at the man seated to my right, who raised a bewildered head from his laptop as if upbraided by a she-devil. "You fucking piece of shit!" she screamed. "Son of a bitch, you made up lies about me on TMZ, goddamn you, rotten sewer rat!"

Catching his breath, the middle-aged defendant yelled back something I didn't catch, although it sounded as accusatory as what Francesca charged him with. Dumbfounded though I was by such a scene—and before breakfast—I recall that no one seated at those tables outside Starbucks seemed surprised. Perhaps they imagined we were all extras in a movie.

I went over, greeted her, though she was too livid to do more than nod in my direction. The wildcat snarls back and forth grew louder even as I opened the door and guided her inside, making whatever anodyne small talk I could summon in the midst of such melodrama. "I'm hungry, aren't you?" I asked. Then, "How's your cat?" My relief was enormous when finally we found a table. Even so, Francesca's glare at her adversary threatened to melt the plate-glass window. Soon the man sidled away, perhaps to amplify whatever slander he had perpetrated on TMZ.

Francesca soon calmed down, and I noticed that the staff deferred to her as if she were the Grande Dame of Franklin Avenue. Were they intimidated, I wondered (as I was, a bit), or was it owing to her difficulty walking, that she received table service while the rest of us stood in line at the counter?

Looking back, I see this altercation as more than an embarrassing scene in public. In a sense, it was the Gabor *Götterdämmerung*, all other battles having been fought and many of them won. Now, however, Eva's ashes reposed in Westwood Village Memorial Park, Jolie's and Magda's farther away near Palm Springs, while Zsa Zsa, the last goddess of that fabled dynasty, lay slowly dying on a mountaintop in Bel Air, just a few miles from where Francesca battled demons—those invisible ones that plagued her body and mind, and the one of flesh and blood who had long since locked her out of paradise.

That day, that ordinary day in Hollywood, the great Gabor Valhalla began its final, fearsome fall.

Chapter 37

Could This Perhaps Be Death?

On June 2, 1995, Eva appeared on *Geraldo*, the syndicated talk show whose host was Geraldo Rivera. According to Wesley Hyatt, author of *The Encyclopedia of Daytime Television*, "Rivera was the first daytime talk-show host to emphasize sleazy subjects as his main selling point." By 1995, however, his lurid subject matter had become more pastel, his tawdry format having been co-opted by a swarm of vulgarians with even lower taste.

Appearing with Eva were three other women whose husbands had blatantly cheated on them: Ivana Trump, Melba Moore, and Beverly Sassoon. Despite their host, this segment remained above gutter level. Eva spoke of "her two big loves, Richard Brown and Frank Jameson." (She was married to Brown from 1959 to 1973, to Jameson from 1973 to 1983.)

Geraldo asked, "How did you find out Dick Brown was cheating on you?"

Eva answered, "I am so sensitive I *felt* it. I went to his secretary's house and there was Richard sitting. I slapped the poor girl. After the divorce, I had a collapse and a nervous breakdown. It took me a year to recuperate."

As to Frank Jameson: "We were in Paris. I got up in the night to have a glass of water, and I heard him talking on the phone: 'Darling, do you want to meet me in London or Washington? Mrs. Jameson has to go to Canada to work.' And Mrs. Jameson heard it! I was in a white satin nightgown—it was like a scene from a movie. I walked in and he had a brandy beside him. Even though I never drink, I tossed it down my throat and said, 'There is one thing I ask from you. Don't ever touch me again.'"

Frank Jameson, who predeceased Eva by two years, might have defended himself by repeating what he told an interviewer during the marriage. Eva's glamour became a burden not only to her but also to him. "We can't leave the house for a quick Chinese dinner or an ice cream cone," he said, "until my wife spends an hour or so on wardrobe and makeup." And so he searched elsewhere for streamlined companionship.

Seeing Eva on the *Geraldo* show, one might have guessed her age as forty, though she was in fact seventy-six. Only her eyes looked slightly tired. Close friends knew, however, that for some time she had been under emotional strain, owing mostly to her breakup with Merv Griffin. The word "breakup" in this case is purely platonic, for Griffin was gay and, after Frank Jameson, Eva pursued whatever romantic interests her busy life permitted.

On January 8, 1995, the *New York Post* ran an item about Princess Elizabeth of Yugoslavia, who had replaced Eva as Merv's "longtime escort on demand." Later that year another newspaper announced that Merv had "dumped Eva without any warning and that she was devastated." Perhaps they quarreled; if so, the reason remains unknown.

During the twelve years of their partnership, Eva appeared countless times on Griffin's talk show, occasionally filling in as host. On one of those occasions Zsa Zsa was a guest. Eva, trying to keep the show on track, found herself competing with Zsa Zsa's talk-show mode: cutting up, showing off, stealing every moment for herself. "You are very hard to take," said Eva.

"So are you!" Zsa Zsa shot back.

Eva accompanied Merv on business junkets and to openings of new hotels as he added them to his empire. Yet no one quite understood why Eva, who took her career so seriously, would lower herself to gimmicky appearances at Griffin's Atlantic City casino, where she performed such tasks as drawing raffle tickets from a fishbowl. Although well paid for her time in Griffin's entourage, Eva devolved to the status of a Hungarian Vanna White. Probably because she enjoyed his company, she continued the charade as Griffin's consort, even while earning her own millions as chairwoman of Eva Gabor International, the world's largest wigmaker, which she cofounded in 1972. Perhaps her own business, and Merv's, helped her survive the twilight of her career. Anyone so accustomed to public life as Eva would not be happy to stay home at night, even to see herself repeated on TV.

After *Green Acres*, Eva's career was a checkerboard of undistinguished television, occasional roles in regional theatre, personal appearances at convention centers and racetracks, and in department stores to sell more wigs. Regular disappointments rained down, e.g., *The Eva Gabor Show*, an unsuccessful 1977 pilot that no network would touch. In 1984, Merv Griffin signed both Eva and Zsa Zsa for a proposed comedy series, *Two Hungarian Maids*, which once again the networks orphaned. Sometimes, looking closely at Eva and other hard-to-employ entertainers in reruns of low-grade game shows (*Match Game*) or seeing her on the panel of *Hollywood Squares*, you glimpse an instant of profound sadness on her face. That look seems a lament that it's over as far as the dramatic roles she so craved but was never allowed to play. Through it all, however, she found time to raise money at charity events and to keep up her many friendships.

Eva's final strike-out came in 1990, when yet another pilot found no takers. This one, titled *Matchmaker* (aka *Close Encounters)* is notable mainly for Eva's consent to play the mother of a grown-up daughter who helps run Eva's matrimonial agency. Whether she agreed to this maternal role from desperation or mature judgment, it stands as unique on a Gabor résumé. Twenty years earlier, this volte-face might have resuscitated her career: picture Eva as one of Chekhov's aging actresses dealing with bothersome offspring; or as Regina Giddens in *The Little Foxes;* perhaps even a Tennessee Williams dragon lady like Violet Venable in *Suddenly, Last Summer*. (Could any Gabor outcamp Katharine Hepburn in the role?)

Eva's appearance on *Geraldo* in June 1995 was her last. One month later she was dead.

Emotionally depleted and physically exhausted, as well, Eva joined her stepdaughter, Mary Jameson, and other Jameson family members at their remote vacation property in Baja California during the second week of June. (She remained close to her stepdaughters and their children after her divorce from Frank Jameson.) There, in a ghastly repetition of Magda's accident three decades earlier, Eva fell down a staircase and broke a hip. Owing to the remote location, proper medical care was not immediately available. Soon after Eva entered a local hospital, the Jamesons realized that her condition was serious.

They arranged for an airlift to Los Angeles, where Eva entered Cedars-Sinai Medical Center on June 21. Her condition was listed somewhat ominously as "fair," although a hospital spokesman reported that "she is beginning to heal."

But her symptoms worsened. She developed pneumonia,

which failed to respond to antibiotics. Visitors to the hospital included Suzanne Pleshette and other close friends, and of course Zsa Zsa, Magda, and Francesca. Eva's fever spiked. Her breathing became labored, even with oxygen. When doctors ordered a respirator, they also broke the news to Zsa Zsa: the end was near, and it was Eva's stated wish not to stay alive by artificial means.

"Wait a few days," Zsa Zsa begged Ray Katz, Eva's manager for thirty-eight years who held Eva's medical power of attorney. She considered Katz "the brother I never had." Hoping for a miracle, Zsa Zsa despaired as Eva's condition grew more dangerous by the hour. Then Eva slipped into a coma.

Meanwhile Zsa Zsa, keeping vigil at Eva's bedside, complained of a pain in her arm. Then the arm went limp, causing her to fear a stroke. A doctor examined her and discovered that she herself required immediate medical care for a clogged carotid artery. As soon as possible after surgery, Zsa Zsa insisted on visiting Eva. A nurse rolled her to Eva's room in a wheelchair. There she found Francesca by the bedside, rubbing Eva's hands and feet. "You'll be all right, Auntie Eva," she intoned. At last Zsa Zsa said to Ray Katz, "Do what you must."

Eva Gabor died in the early morning hours of July 4, 1995.

She was cremated in full makeup, wig, and a gown that Suzanne Pleshette helped Zsa Zsa select. It was one that Eva loved. Owing to Zsa Zsa's own recent surgery and recovery period, Eva's memorial Mass was postponed until July 11. It took place on that date at the Church of the Good Shepherd in Beverly Hills, which Eva attended and where she often stopped in to pray.

(One could write a tract titled "How to Be a Gabor

Catholic." If such a denomination existed, it might be defined as the Hungarian version of Episcopalian. Whatever their religious beliefs, their credo seemed formulated as much by the Gabors themselves as by the Vatican. "I am very, very religious," Eva told an interviewer in 1978, "but I don't talk about it. Those kinds of things are private." On a table in Eva's bedroom was an icon of the Sacred Heart of Jesus. In front of it, a photograph of Jolie—ladies first, of course.)

Among the eulogists at Eva's service was Warren Cowan, the Hollywood publicist, who said, "Eva was a kind, big person. People felt better when they were around her." Eddie Albert, speaking from the pulpit, recounted stories about their years on *Green Acres*, some of which made the congregation rock with laughter. One day when she chose to wear a dress decorated with feathers, he chided her for it. "Ladies will see it on TV," he said, "and they'll want one. Thousands of birds will die."

Eva replied, "But Eddie, feathers don't come from birds."

"And where *do* they come from?"

"Dahling," said Eva—or was it Lisa Douglas speaking?— "feathers come from *pee-lowz*!"

She was joking, of course. As early as 1978, Eva expressed concern for the environment. "I particularly care about the ocean," she said, "so full of poisons that cause the fish and lovely animals to become—what is the word—extinct." The menagerie on her estate included dogs, cats, birds, and chickens.

Among other mourners at the memorial Mass were Johnny Mathis, Van Cliburn, Suzanne Pleshette, Merv Griffin, and Nancy Reagan. After the service, Magda, in a wheelchair, was lifted down the church steps by four men. Zsa Zsa, her face puffy from weeping, held Frederic's arm. Francesca followed behind.

Eva's remains were interred at Westwood Village Memorial Park. Her marker, with an incised cross on lower left and a rosebud on the right, reads:

OUR DARLING EVA
EVA GABOR
WE LOVE YOU
YOU ARE IN OUR HEARTS FOREVER
July 4, 1995

As Jolie passed a hundred, her mind dimmed. By degrees, she withdrew from the social life of Palm Springs that she had enlivened for many years. Eventually she required nursing care around the clock, although the family guarded this sad secret. After Eva's death, the Gabor family faced a dilemma: whether or not to tell Jolie.

Eventually Zsa Zsa said to Magda and Francesca, "The only way to keep Mother alive is to keep Eva alive. She must never know of Eva's death. We will leave it to Eva to break the news when they are reunited in heaven."

In moments of clarity during the twenty-one months remaining to Jolie, she would sometimes ask, "Where is Evika?" The answer varied somewhat: "She is making a picture in Europe. Soon she will return to us." Or, "Eva is visiting Budapest and sends her love. She will tell us about the many changes she found there."

Jolie Gabor died of pneumonia on April 1, 1997. She was buried in a pink and ivory casket on April 4. Mourners at the graveside service joined in singing Jolie's favorite song, one that she often sang at parties to her own piano accompaniment: "Never on Sunday." Her grave marker, at Desert Memorial Park in Cathedral City, bears the inscription:

OUR BELOVED MOTHER AND GRANDMOTHER
JOLIE GABOR DE SZIGETHY
WE LOVE YOU FOREVER
April 1, 1997

*   *   *

Just over two months later, Magda died of kidney failure. For the third time in two years, Zsa Zsa kept a bedside vigil. Realizing that her sister could not recover, Zsa Zsa tried to console her by recalling happy stories of their childhood. Although she could not ascertain Magda's level of awareness, she hoped that her words might bring comfort.

Zsa Zsa, as next of kin, made the decision to have life support withdrawn. When Magda died, Zsa Zsa wept as she had seldom done throughout her life, clutching Francesca as though unable to let go. "It was the hardest thing I ever did," she said again and again.

Magda Gabor's death came a few days before her eighty-second birthday. She was buried not far from Jolie, and her simple marker reads:

OUR BELOVED
MAGDA GABOR
JUNE 6, 1997

Chapter 38

They Are All Gone into the World of Light

Eva's death ended the Gabor show-business dynasty. Zsa Zsa's few remaining moments on camera were the dying wing beats of a rare bird no longer able to convince herself she was too young to be old. In 1996, Zsa Zsa did a cameo as herself in *A Very Brady Sequel*, her final role in a feature film. She made four television appearances in 1997, most memorably on *The Rosie O'Donnell Show*. At eighty, Zsa Zsa seemed strained from grief and weight loss. Around the eyes, a scooped-out, skeletal look suggested that tears had eroded the flesh.

Rosie mentioned Eva's death, adding, "Everyone loved her, no one more than you."

"I miss her so badly," Zsa Zsa said. "I can't tell you. We were very close. The press always said we fought and hated each other, but we didn't. We fought, but we always loved each other." Later that year, on *The Ruby Wax Show*, Zsa Zsa's decline was even more evident. Nevertheless, when Christie's held an auction of Eva's jewelry (other possessions not included), Zsa Zsa wrote a touching foreword for the beautifully illustrated catalogue.

In 1998, when she spoke about Eva on the *Lifetime* series *Intimate Portrait*, she had regained her looks, her poise, and her weight. Once again the phoenix, no more the go-away bird. In this episode devoted to Eva's life and career, Zsa Zsa recalled their happy times. At one point, however, she choked up and said, "I can't talk about it."

During the next eighteen years, Zsa Zsa was seen no more except in newsreel footage from earlier days. She had Frederic, whose comfort, such as it was, seemed better than none. He was rumored to spend long periods in Germany, during which Zsa Zsa and Francesca's rapprochement took place. Francesca urged her mother to ditch Frederic, but the thought of old age, followed by older age, terrified her. *How does one live alone?* she wondered, but found no reply.

She stopped going to parties, refused to make personal appearances, she no longer lunched with MGM girlfriends Kathryn Grayson, Ann Miller, Cyd Charisse, Esther Williams. "Why am I still here?" she wailed. She wept from grief and depression. More than ever, her dogs and cats brought comfort. ("I would sacrifice every diamond I own or ever have owned for the life of one of my animals," she said.) Francesca came to her almost daily, and drove her to doctors for treatment of the aches and pains of old age.

Like so many in Hollywood, Zsa Zsa liked to describe herself as a survivor. In her case, the claim was accurate. By the turn of the new century, she had resumed her travels with Frederic. She had begun once more to socialize, although with a smaller group of friends than before. These included Phyllis Diller, Quincy Jones, Larry King and his wife, Shawn King, Ruta Lee, and Alex Trebek. Having inherited many millions from Eva and Magda, she no longer felt compelled to work.

Then, on November 27, 2002, disaster struck. Zsa Zsa, a passenger in a Camaro driven by her hairdresser, was critically injured when the car swerved, jumped onto the curb, the driver lost control and crashed into a light pole on Sunset Boulevard. Although the driver received only minor injuries, Zsa Zsa was pinned in the car when the engine piled through the dashboard and crushed her legs. She suffered a broken arm and head injuries, as well.

For two months she remained hospitalized. Francesca feared that this was her mother's coup de grâce. But no. She pulled through, and after several weeks of recuperation at the Motion Picture and Television Country Home she returned to 1001 Bel Air Road. Photographed leaving the hospital, this Zsa Zsa looked strikingly different from the former one. The change no doubt startled even Zsa Zsa herself. Gone were the blonde bouffant wigs and much of the makeup. Departed, too, was the bold Gabor walk that had carried her across soundstages, TV studios, and nightclubs; into theatres, airplanes, palaces, mansions, and courtrooms. In its place, a wheelchair. Her face had narrowed, and her own long, white hair produced what would surely have been, had Zsa Zsa grasped the simile, an unwelcome resemblance to Jessica Tandy.

Zsa Zsa was unaware that Frederic had exploited her long hospitalization by inviting photographers from the *Globe*, the supermarket tabloid whose outrageousness matched his own, to photograph his wife as she lay in extremis. These pictures have a coffin-like ambiance: eyes closed, all color drained from her face, she shows no life at all. Frederic, predictably, hovers over the body, and the accompanying story—"Zsa Zsa's Brave Last Days"—quotes him at syrupy length: "I will be there for my wife; she is my world. With the prayers of every *Globe* reader she can and will get better."

In a later exclusive to that publication, Frederic revealed that in addition to Zsa Zsa's medications and physical therapy, he administered regular doses of the *Globe*. "I buy it every week and read it to her from cover to cover to exercise her mind," he said with no apparent irony.

*   *   *

A grievous side effect of the accident was Zsa Zsa's loss of her beloved dogs. At the insistence of her doctor she relinquished them to a dog breeder in Long Beach, the reason being the risk of tripping over one or the other while she still was able to walk. This suggests that the accident weakened Zsa Zsa's strong will as well as her body. Otherwise she never would have consented to give away an animal (except for the "fuck-you" bird).

I asked Betsy Jentz to recall Zsa Zsa's reaction to the doctor's orders. "She didn't like it," Betsy replied, "but she had a tendency always to believe the doctors." Zsa Zsa's enormous love of animals places her among other actresses known for animal rights activism, among them Doris Day, Tippi Hedren, Kim Novak, Brigitte Bardot, and Elizabeth Taylor. The media, however, seldom reported Zsa Zsa's efforts on behalf of animals, even though she was a Hollywood pioneer. In the early 1970s she and Francesca founded an animal shelter. She was a longtime member of Mercy Crusade, a Los Angeles organization that provides financial assistance for the neutering and spaying of cats and dogs, and of Love Unlimited, an animal welfare group. In 1972, she joined Doris Day and Richard Basehart in a campaign for the care of poorly treated domestic animals. Interviewed that year by a writer from *The Christian Science Monitor*, Zsa Zsa's compassion was perhaps more obvious than in any similar interview. (Although she often raised the issue of animals in TV appearances, interviewers invariably switched to the worn subject of men and matrimony.)

When she spoke about animals, Zsa Zsa left aside the usual Gabor shtick. In its place was a serious and deliberate message about their welfare. Herewith, a collage of her statements over the years. "Animals can't talk, but they are our best friends. That is proven to me since I'm born. I have always been saddened by the cruelty to animals that goes on in the world—since I was five I have been worried about it. When I raise the subject on television, it makes people say, 'Yes, but look what parents do to their own children.' True, but a little animal can't talk. A dog is born to love you, and he loves you better than he loves himself. A life without animals would be a life without beauty. If I wasn't an actress, I would have wanted to be a veterinarian. Anybody who has a heart loves animals."

When Zsa Zsa traveled, she called home every day to inquire about her pets and to speak to them. She would stop her car to pick up stray dogs, especially between Los Angeles and Palm Springs on visits to Jolie and Magda. And she loved horses as well as dogs and cats. In her later years, Zsa Zsa said, "I don't believe in wearing fur anymore."

One laments Eva's untimely death even more in light of how she might have prepared a better ending for Zsa Zsa. Had Eva been alive in 2002, she would have taken complete control of Zsa Zsa's care and comfort. In league with her powerful friends, she would have made Frederic an offer he couldn't refuse: a settlement in exchange for removing himself forever. Eva might well have taken Francesca in hand, despite the difficulty of that undertaking. But Eva was gone.

As the years flowed over Zsa Zsa, she spent her hours in bed dozing and watching television. She received the occasional visitor, spoke to Francesca by phone until Frederic ended the calls, and in 2007 suffered a stroke that debilitated her even further. Still she lived on, even as the larger public assumed she was dead. To the extent that her damaged consciousness took in Frederic's hijinks—his ludicrous claim to have fathered Anna Nicole Smith's baby, tabloid reports that he blacked out from exhaustion while caring for his bedridden wife, the arrival of fire trucks after he called in a questionable report of an eight-foot snake dangling from the front gate of their home, his declaration that Zsa Zsa lost millions to Bernie Madoff's fraud—the phantasmagoria must have compounded her confusion.

On several occasions an ambulance rushed Zsa Zsa to the hospital. Francesca believed some of these emergencies to be publicity stunts on Frederic's part to keep himself in the news.

On July 17, 2010, Zsa Zsa fell and broke a hip while attempting to sit down in a wheelchair that wasn't locked in place. She underwent hip replacement—a risky procedure for a ninety-three-year-old woman—and recovered sufficiently to return home on August 4. The following day she experienced chest pains. She was rushed back to the hospital, where doctors found and removed two blood clots, one of which was dangerously near the heart. By Saturday, August 7, she had improved and was able to speak. On Sunday morning her condition worsened, and she asked for a priest to administer the last rites of the Roman Catholic Church. (This sacrament, though popularly termed "the last rites," is more correctly designated as "extreme unction" or "the anointing of the sick." It is administered when death seems imminent.) After the rite, Zsa Zsa appeared to lapse into a coma.

A week later, she returned home once more, although her prognosis was unclear. She improved slightly, and began to eat small amounts of solid food. John Blanchette reported in a press release that she was "in and out of consciousness." On August 31, she was rushed once more to the hospital after Frederic found her "unresponsive and in distress." On September 2, she was released and returned home "in great pain," according to Blanchette. She had stopped eating and was receiving nutrition through a feeding tube.

On October 1, 2010, John Blanchette informed me by email that "Zsa Zsa's health is improving. The doctors removed the feeding tube today, she's eating a regular diet and getting stronger." Ten days later, in a phone call, he said that Frederic planned to take Zsa Zsa for a Sunday-afternoon drive to the ocean. Despite the unintentional Baby Jane Hudson echo, such news betokened prodigious improvement.

Meanwhile, the battle between Frederic and Francesca intensified. Between 2009 and 2012, Francesca paid several hundred thousand dollars to lawyers in attempts to gain some control over Zsa Zsa's care and finances, to prove that she and not Frederic was Zsa Zsa's designated legatee, and to secure the right to visit her mother's bedside after Frederic barred her from the house. In 2010, Francesca told me that she was allowed to go to the house and visit her mother only when Zsa Zsa's doctor was present. In 2012, Francesca filed a petition requesting that an independent conservatorship be established to monitor her mother's health and finances. A judge in Los Angeles granted the conservatorship, which pleased Francesca, but in a turnaround rebuff the judge made Frederic the temporary conservator of Zsa Zsa's finances, with the stipulation that such finances be used only for his wife's care. The judge also granted Francesca visiting rights every Tuesday, although each time I asked about the state of Zsa Zsa's health, she said, "My mother is always asleep when I go. I think it's because Frederic drugs her."

In January 2011, when it seemed that Zsa Zsa's perilous condition could decline no further, she developed a severe infection that did not respond to antibiotic treatment. She developed gangrene in the right leg, which was amputated as a life-saving measure. Not until two years later did she comprehend the loss, however dimly. Two months after the amputation, hearing on television of Elizabeth Taylor's death, Zsa Zsa suffered a panic attack that raised her blood pressure to a dangerous level. According to John Blanchette, Zsa Zsa feared that she would be the next star to die. (In long-held Hollywood superstition, star deaths occur in threes, and Jane Russell had died shortly before Elizabeth Taylor.) Once more an ambulance rushed Zsa Zsa to the hospital.

During 2012, Frederic permitted cast and crew of HBO's Liberace biopic *Behind the Candelabra* to shoot scenes in the house and to paint a swirling *L* on the bottom of the pool. On one of the Tuesdays of Francesca's scheduled visits, an altercation occurred with security guards. Without trying to find out who she was and why she was there, they attempted to oust her from her mother's home. She trembled with hurt and anger as she recounted this humiliating episode.

On August 19, 2012, Frederic hosted an elaborate party to celebrate the twenty-sixth anniversary of his marriage to Zsa Zsa. Several hundred people attended, including reporters from the U.S., Europe, and Australia. This, at last, was Frederic's own Norma Desmond moment—just him, the lights, and the cameras. After twenty-six years of waiting, he was overdue for his close-up.

According to John Blanchette's press release, the stars of *Behind the Candelabra*—Michael Douglas, Matt Damon, Debbie Reynolds—and director Steven Soderbergh had accepted invitations. If they turned up, I didn't see them, but the big arabesque *L* was still entwined across the bottom of the pool. Zsa Zsa, semiconscious in a faraway bedroom and attended by a nurse, knew nothing of the champagne celebration. Nor was Francesca ever on the guest list. Phyllis Diller, one of Zsa Zsa's few surviving friends, might have attended had her own health not been precarious. She was on hospice care and died on August 20, the day after the party.

In an earlier chapter I reported my final conversation with Francesca, which took place on Christmas Day 2014. Eleven days later, she died of an apparent stroke. Since her next of kin was Zsa Zsa, who lay near death herself, for days no one claimed the body, which remained in the Los Angeles County coroner's morgue. In a grotesque attempted beau geste, Frederic von Anhalt tried to claim Francesca's body and to make funeral and burial arrangements. The coroner denied the request. Eventually Stephen M. Hilton, one of Barron Hilton's sons and thus (depending on one's view of Conrad Hilton's paternity) Francesca's nephew, came forward to claim the body and arrange for burial.

Francesca's memorial Mass took place on January 21, 2015, at St. Ambrose Catholic Church in West Hollywood. The service was by invitation only, with this message printed on the card: "Per the family's wishes, this is a private service with no reception." Decoded, it meant that Frederic von Anhalt was denied entry. To make sure that he did not crash the service, two guards were stationed at the church entrance.

To no one's surprise, Frederic would not shut up. He opined to anyone who would listen that since the Hiltons claimed her body, "she should be buried next to her father in Texas and not here in Los Angeles. She always wanted to be with her father. That's what makes sense."

Francesca was cremated and her remains interred at Westwood Village Memorial Park, near Eva's. Perhaps the only decent thing to be said for Frederic von Anhalt is this: He made sure that Zsa Zsa never learned of Francesca's death.

By 2016, Zsa Zsa had lived so long, and been seen so often, that many considered her immortal. If Hollywood had a Mount Rushmore, her likeness would surely have been carved near the top. How apt was the title of her book, *One Lifetime Is Not Enough*, and how unfortunate that the book itself read like a dime novel.

On Sunday afternoon, December 18, 2016, the immortal Zsa Zsa Gabor finally died. Had she lived seven more weeks, she would have reached her desired goal of one hundred. Nor were her expectations misplaced. The Gabors were long-lived: Eva's death at seventy-six seemed premature, while Jolie passed a hundred by several years and Vilmos and Magda reached their eighties.

Zsa Zsa's death immediately became headline news around the world. A mere sampling:

**LEGENDARY SOCIALITE AND ACTRESS ZSA ZSA GABOR
DIES AT 99
MOULIN ROUGE ACTRESS ZSA ZSA GABOR DIES AGED 99
ZSA ZSA GABOR FALLECE A LOS 99 AÑOS
ZSA ZSA GABOR IST TOT
E MORTA ZSA ZSA GABOR, AVEVA 99 ANNI
ZSA ZSA GABOR N'EST PLUS
ELHUNYT GÁBOR ZSAZSA**

The *New York Times,* in a long obituary and a later appraisal, devoted more than a full page to Zsa Zsa. Among its reporting errors was the common one that she had been Miss Hungary in 1936. The appraisal, by staff writer Alessandra Stanley, led with the moldy cliché, "Long before the Kardashians, there were the Gabors." The writer's subsequent insights were equally lame.

As in life, so in death: controversy engulfed plans for the funeral and the disposition of Zsa Zsa's remains. The agent of dispute was of course the widower, whose grief did not obscure opportunites for the spotlight. A week before Zsa Zsa's funeral Mass, he released to the media a list of celebrities supposedly planning to attend. Among those named were Debbie Reynolds, Barbara Eden, Carol Channing, Larry King, Ruta Lee, and George Hamilton. The list, like so many of Frederic's inventions, bore no relation to reality. Those named on it, all of them friends of Zsa Zsa, wished to avoid the kind of sideshow that Frederic had become known for. Without him as ringmaster, they might all have attended the funeral.

Edward Lozzi, Zsa Zsa's longtime friend and former publicist and perhaps Francesca's closest friend—she was on the phone to him moments before her death—challenged Frederic's spurious announcement. From his PR firm, Lozzi sent a cease-and-desist letter to Frederic, as did Larry King. Lozzi's letter read in part, "A false media release is being sent to news agencies and celebrity publicists containing the names of stars who have no intention of attending." Lozzi said that his client Debbie Reynolds phoned him immediately to find out how to remove her name from the list. (In a development of staggering irony, Debbie herself died on December 28, two days before Zsa Zsa's funeral.) The others on Frederic's list also demanded removal of their names.

Countering what threatened to be an embarrassment to Zsa Zsa's memory, Lozzi announced plans for an alternative remembrance ceremony to be held at her gravesite. He, along with two dozen others of her friends, gathered at Westwood Village Memorial Park after the funeral. They expected her ashes to arrive there, since she owned a plot near Eva's and wished to be buried in it. Instead, Frederic took home the urn. According to Lozzi, he said, "These are my fucking ashes, and she was my fucking wife."

Edward Lozzi was always a fierce defender of Zsa Zsa and Francesca and of their respective legacies. It was he who sent me an invitation to Francesca's funeral (I was unable to attend), and his description of Frederic's intended "circus" left me in doubt whether or not to attend Zsa Zsa's funeral Mass. Knowing that I was at work on this book, he urged me to go. "You really can't afford not to," he said.

The service began at ten o'clock on the morning of December 30, 2016, at Church of the Good Shepherd in Beverly Hills. In front of the altar was a large portrait of Zsa Zsa from around 1994, and captioned "Farewell, My Love." For ten minutes before the service, Frederic received condolences while standing beside the portrait. His attire was bizarre; he wore a necktie but in place of a dark suit or a blazer and dark trousers, he chose a brown barn jacket. One might have mistaken him for a hay broker delivering straw for Zsa Zsa's horse.

Photographers swarmed over the sidewalk in front of the church. Cameras and audio equipment from networks and other media filled the choir loft, and in an example of postmodern bad taste, virtually every member of the congregation aimed smartphones to grab images for uploading to Facebook and YouTube. For Frederic, the crowning Norma Desmond moment had finally arrived. Unlike Norma, however, he *could* go on with the scene, and on and on beyond that. Whirring cameras elevated him to a higher plane of paradise than the one newly occupied by Zsa Zsa.

The opening hymn was "Amazing Grace," followed by the Roman Catholic liturgy comprising Bible readings, more music, and the Eucharist. Father Ed Benioff, who delivered the homily, spoke of Zsa Zsa's contributions to various charities and her great love of animals. "She supported those in distress and those less fortunate," he said, "and she gave much money to the Salvation Army. She had a big heart for the homeless. She helped their cause in many ways. And, as Jesus said, 'Do not let your left hand know what your right hand is doing,' Zsa Zsa did not talk about her good works."

The funeral Mass was properly dignified, comforting, and inclusive, perhaps a reflection of the leanings of the present pope. At the Eucharist, the priest invited everyone to gather at the altar, Catholics to receive Communion and others who wished a blessing to cross their arms over their chest.

In keeping with modern funeral tradition, near the end of the Mass came a time for Words of Remembrance. Typically, family members and close friends give a brief informal eulogy, often with anecdotes recalling happy times in the life of the departed. As if to subject poor Zsa Zsa to further crass narcissism, Frederic seized the opportunity to address his captive audience and the online millions in a rambling mono-

logue that resembled a medley of windbag speeches from
Oscar night.

Holding the urn with Zsa Zsa's ashes, he began his forty-
five-minute discourse by saying, "The church is not full because the timing is bad. But timing was always bad for my
wife. She could have died two weeks ago, or in January—
today, many are on vacation or out of town." (He omitted
the celebrity boycott.)

"I was famous in Germany," he continued, to the amaze-
ment of those familiar with his past, "then I came to Hollywood." At this point he held up a German magazine from
1983 with Zsa Zsa and him pictured on the cover. The speech
became more and more inappropriate for a church service, especially a Mass for the dead. Even so, his use of props took
on the lineaments of an infomercial. He held up the carrying
case that Zsa Zsa used for Macho Man, a shih tzu and one of
her favorite dogs, and pointed out a fancy yellow pillow
bought in Munich for the dog's comfort. Finally, he concluded—or so one thought with a sigh of relief—"Keep her
in your thoughts the way she was."

His tackiest moment, however, was yet to come. As the
clergy began their procession from the altar, Frederic interrupted—"Wait a minute"—to add a postscript about a horse
picture that Zsa Zsa painted, which he held up and proceeded to explicate like Kenneth Clark elucidating Giotto for
a PBS audience.

The priest, perhaps recalling martyrs of old, waited with
saintly patience for the art lecture to end, betraying no sign
of chagrin that a monster ego kept him standing for long
minutes with crucifix held aloft. Having upstaged Christ on
the Cross, Frederic then placed Zsa Zsa's ashes in Macho
Man's Louis Vuitton carrying case, proceeded down the aisle
and out of the church. The cantor began the recessional hymn,
"May Choirs of Angels," to the tune of "Londonderry Air."

Outside the church, as I spoke with Zsa Zsa's former assistants Betsy Jentz and Nancy DeJean, I overheard Frederic extolling the virtues of president-elect Donald Trump to any reporter left standing. And no wonder, for Frederic's own practices parallel those of fly-by-night Trump University, now defunct. For instance, Zsa Zsa's cousin József Gabor told an interviewer in Hungary that Frederic contacted him about the cost of a Hungarian funeral, with interrment of Zsa Zsa's ashes near the remains of her father in Budapest. József sent the estimated cost: two million forints, roughly seven thousand dollars. Frederic demurred, saying the grave of Vilmos was in bad condition. This József disputed. "After that, he disappeared," according to Zsa Zsa's cousin. As this book goes to press, Zsa Zsa's ashes remain in Frederic's custody.

It is doubtful that Zsa Zsa ever expressed the wish to die in Hungary, as Frederic claimed on TMZ, or that she would have wished her ashes to be sent there. Otherwise, why would she have purchased a plot at Westwood Village? Moreover, while she respected the Jewish faith of her ancestors and had many Jewish friends and one Jewish husband, she herself would not have desired a Jewish burial.

In this regard, as in so many others, Zsa Zsa often contradicted herself. Francesca would sometimes needle her: "We're Jewish, aren't we?" but Zsa Zsa was not amused. On the other hand, Betsy Jentz told this anecdote: "When I worked for Zsa Zsa, Frederic made a business deal that Zsa Zsa considered less than spectacular. She said to him, 'If you had one drop of Jewish blood in you, you would be able to deal with these people.'" And all of the Gabors worked on behalf of Jewish charities. Among Zsa Zsa's possessions sold at auction in 2018 was an award from the United Jewish Welfare Fund.

In 2017, *People* magazine revealed that according to probate court documents, Frederic was sole heir to Zsa Zsa's estate. Her will established a trust that consolidated all of her assets, with her husband as sole trustee. The trust stipulated that the amount of Zsa Zsa's estate not be disclosed. With exquisite irony, therefore, Zsa Zsa turned her final headline into an eclipse. One question hangs in the air, however: whether Zsa Zsa truly *willed* it this way. A previous document that went missing raised other possibilities, but of course anyone who might have challenged Zsa Zsa's last will and testament was forever silent.

In a sad coda to a lifetime collection, Zsa Zsa's possessions were sold at auction in April 2018. I decided not to catalogue the event and its contents in this book because Zsa Zsa's enormous absence cast a thick pall over the "going, going, gone." Her widower made roughly a million dollars from the sale. Those interested in the many items included in the auction may view them at the Heritage Auctions website, www.ha.com.

When a star extinguishes, what is left? According to romantic notions, traces of stardust drift from the sky. I prefer to think that the Gabor constellation shines unstoppably on, brightening an alternate universe—perhaps the same one that produced them and sent them to us in the first place.

A few years ago, a friend said to me, "Aren't you glad to have lived at a time when there were Gabors?"

This book is my answer.

Acknowledgments

How does anyone write a book without the generous assistance and goodwill of a company of friends, colleagues, acquaintances, and casual well-wishers? For me, it would be impossible. Minus that vast company, *Finding Zsa Zsa* would surely have been an incomplete biography.

My first stop on what became the Gabor superhighway was a telephone call in 2010 to Francesca Hilton, Zsa Zsa's daughter. Her cooperation and friendship convinced me to go forward with this lengthy and complex project. Francesca's death in 2015 was a terrible loss. Nevertheless, many of the details published here for the first time result from Francesca's confidence in me as a lifelong devotee of her family.

Also in 2010, I made the acquaintance of Tony Turtu, whose book *Gaborabilia* is unsurpassed. I devoured this museum of rarities—photographs, memorabilia, ephemera—in 2001, when the book was published. Then, at the outset of my own project, I wrote to him and he replied immediately. That was the beginning of a friendship without which my own book would surely have gone begging. *Finding Zsa Zsa* is dedicated to him and to the memory of Francesca.

Tony and two other authors, Ron Bowers and Richard Teleky, volunteered to read the chapters of *Finding Zsa Zsa* as I completed them. The sharp eyes and valuable suggestions of these three—friends, advisors, critics, comforters—contributed enormously to my final manuscript. Other friends also read sections along the way; they are Daniel Kusner, Glenn Russell, Leigh W. Rutledge, Robert Sanchez, and Ken Smith. I cite also film historian Foster Hirsch, a friend of long standing and a Gabor enthusiast whose insights and humor helped set the tone of this book. It was he who asked the haunting question that ends the final chapter: "Aren't you glad to have lived at a time when there were Gabors?"

I am grateful also to Mrs. Annette Lantos, Jolie Gabor's niece and thus first cousin to Zsa Zsa, Eva, and Magda, and to her daughter, Annette Tillemann-Dick, who welcomed me to their home and answered my many questions about the Gabors and other family members. Mrs. Lantos also supplied details of life in Budapest before and during the Holocaust.

Murat Belge, the son of Zsa Zsa's first husband, replied promptly to my many emails. His straightforward briefings helped to uncloud Zsa Zsa's fanciful narrative of her early years in Turkey.

Betsy Jentz and Nancy DeJean led me to an understanding of the private Zsa Zsa—the woman for whom they worked at various times as assistants and for whom they had the highest regard. Other friends of Zsa Zsa and Eva who shared memories are Juli Reding Hutner and Ruta Lee. Stephen Cox, who met Eva several times while writing *The Hooterville Handbook*, answered all questions about *Green Acres*. Kevin Sasaki, Eva's publicist, very kindly supplied details of his and Eva's trip to Budapest in the 1990s, her first visit to Hungary since her departure in 1939.

Research, in person and via email, took me to a number of libraries and archives whose staff members extended every courtesy. At New York Public Library, the Main Branch, I was indeed fortunate to receive the professional expertise of John Cordovez, Cara Dellatte, Tal Nadan, and Kyle Triplett.

At NYPL for the Performing Arts, at Lincoln Center, Sylvia Alicea, Jennifer Eberhardt, and Suzanne Lipkin were especially helpful. I am equally grateful to the following: Andrew Anderson, Dallas Public Library; Peter Balestrieri, Special Collections at the University of Iowa; Jane Klain and Patricia Lunde, at the Paley Center for Media in New York; Bob Tangney of the Seattle Public Library; Edith A. Sandler, Library of Congress; and Dr. Elizabeth B. White of the United States Holocaust Memorial Museum in Washington, D.C.

A special note of thanks to Amanda Smulowitz and Marisa Fine of Yad Vashem, the World Holocaust Remembrance Center in Jerusalem, for their efforts on my behalf in obtaining permission to quote a long passage from the Yad Vashem website.

A visit to Photofest in New York is always a happy experience. Howard Mandelbaum and Ron Mandelbaum seem to have memorized every photograph in their two-million-plus archive, and upon arrival I invariably found dozens of folders full of rarities unavailable elsewhere, some of which I have included in this book.

Several persons who spoke on condition of anonymity surely know the depth of my gratitude to them.

The following people and organizations contributed in myriad ways to what I hope is a three-dimensional portrait of the Gabors: Sara Abosch-Jacobson, the late Patrick Agan, Michael Ankerich, Barbara Bedevian, Jack Bedevian, Eva Beluska, the late John Blanchette, Tim Boss, Peter Carlson, Sarah Clothier, Ned Comstock, Judy Diamond, Joann Duff, Wendy W. Fairey, Roger Farabee, Bernard Fitzgerald, Heyd Fontenot, J.R. Giesen, Gene Gill, Michael Gilmore, Betty Abbot Griffin, Janet Groth, Mariel Hart, Ginger Haselden, Nicholas Haslam, Anastasia Hendrix, Robert Hickey, Patricia Hilton, Steven Hughes, Bobby Hyde, the late Vernon Jordan, the late Brian Kellow, Lana Kohler, Jokke Lagerspets, Steve Lambert, the late Robin Leach, Eszter Lesták, Shawn

Levy, the late Scott Lindsey, the late Al Lowman, Edward Lozzi, John Lukacs, Allison Littell McHose, Lucy Mallows, William J. Mann, Evan Matthews, Calvin Mingo, Linda Briscoe Myers, Dorie Nussbaum, Tom Nussbaum, Jerry Oppenheimer, James Robert Parish, Rubén Parra, Dennis Payne, Diane Pecknold, Jeffrey Prang, Glenn Russell, Tim Smith, Elke Sommer, Leonard Stanley, Kelli Strode, the late Ray Summer, Gabriela Tagliavini, Jim Tamulis, Gordon Taylor, Zenith Tillemann-Dick, Jason Tomes, Frederick Tucker, Robert Uher, Péter Váli, Hugo Vickers, Buddy Weiss, Susan Kohner Weitz, Robert T. Westbrook, and Wayne Wright.

Also, Eric Bradley, director of public relations, and Steve Lansdale, public relations specialist, at Heritage Auctions; and the Boris Karloff Information Centre.

I must emphasize that whatever strengths this book may have, they would be fewer without those named above. The flaws, however, are mine alone.

A disclosure, in the form of a nod to my late friend Pauline Kael: the phrase "refugee chic," in Chapter 13, is not original, though I wish it were. So perfectly does it describe Jolie Gabor at a particular moment that I borrowed it from Pauline's review, in *The New Yorker*, of the 1974 film *Les Violons du bal*.

Finally, at the end of this cavalcade, loud applause to my agent, Eric Myers of Myers Literary Management, whose enthusiasm and guidance lightened a difficult task. I also thank my editor, John Scognamiglio, for his generosity. And a deep bow to Carly Sommerstein, the ne plus ultra of copy editors.

Selected Bibliography

Aherne, Brian. *A Dreadful Man: The Story of Hollywood's Most Original Cad, George Sanders*. New York: Berkley Books, 1981 [orig. 1979].

Brady, Frank. *Citizen Welles: A Biography of Orson Welles*. New York: Scribner's, 1989.

Brown, Peter Harry. *Such Devoted Sisters: Those Fabulous Gabors*. New York: St. Martin's Press, 1985.

Caron, Leslie. *Thank Heaven: A Memoir*. New York: Viking, 2009.

Collins, Joan. *Past Imperfect*. New York: Simon & Schuster, 1984.

Cox, Stephen. *The Hooterville Handbook: A Viewer's Guide to Green Acres*. New York: St. Martin's Press, 1993.

Cronkite, Kathy. *On the Edge of the Spotlight: Celebrities' Children Speak Out About Their Lives*. New York: William Morrow, 1981.

Diderich, Bernard. *Trujillo: The Death of the Goat*. Boston: Little, Brown, 1978.

Eyman, Scott. *Ernst Lubitsch: Laughter in Paradise*. New York: Simon & Schuster, 1993.

Fenyo, Mario D. *Hitler, Horthy, and Hungary: German-Hungarian Relations, 1941–1944*. New Haven: Yale University Press, 1972.

Gabor, Eva. *Orchids and Salami*. Garden City, NY: Doubleday and Co., 1954.

Gabor, Jolie. *Jolie Gabor, as Told to Cindy Adams*. New York: Mason/Charter, 1975.

___. *Jolie Gabor's Family Cookbook*. (With Ted and Jean

Kaufman.) New York: Thomas Y. Crowell Company, 1962.

Gabor, Zsa Zsa. *How to Catch a Man, How to Keep a Man, How to Get Rid of a Man.* Garden City, NY: Doubleday, 1970.

___. *My Story: Written for Me by Gerold Frank.* Cleveland, OH: World Publishing Co., 1960.

___. *One Lifetime Is Not Enough.* New York: Delacorte, 1991.

Gazzara, Ben. *In the Moment: My Life as an Actor.* New York: Carroll and Graf, 2004.

Graham, Sheilah. *Hollywood Revisited: A Fiftieth Anniversary Celebration.* New York: St. Martin's Press, 1985.

___. *The Rest of the Story.* New York: Coward-McCann, 1964.

Griffin, Merv. *Merv: Making the Good Life Last.* New York: Simon & Schuster, 2003.

Grobel, Lawrence. *The Hustons: The Life and Times of a Hollywood Dynasty.* New York: Cooper Square Press, 2000 [orig. 1989].

Hammen, Scott. *John Huston.* Boston: Twayne Publishers, 1985.

Haslam, Nicholas. *Redeeming Features.* New York: Knopf, 2009.

Haycock, Dean A. *The Everything Health Guide to Adult Bipolar Disorder.* 3rd. ed. Avon, MA: Adams Media, 2014.

Heymann, C. David. *Poor Little Rich Girl: The Life and Legend of Barbara Hutton.* New York: Random House, 1983.

Hilton, Conrad. *Be My Guest.* New York: Fireside/Simon & Schuster, 1994 [orig. 1957].

Hope, Bob, and Bob Thomas. *The Road to Hollywood: My 40-Year Love Affair with the Movies.* Garden City, NY: Doubleday, 1977.

Horthy, Miklós. *Memoirs*. New York: R. Speller, 1957 [trans. of *Ein Leben für Ungarn*, 1953].

Hull, Cordell. *The Memoirs of Cordell Hull*. Vol. 2. New York: MacMillan, 1948.

Huston, John. *An Open Book*. New York: Knopf, 1980.

Ihrig, Stefan. *Atatürk in the Nazi Imagination*. Cambridge, MA: The Belknap Press of Harvard University Press, 2014.

Kaminsky, Stuart. *John Huston: Maker of Magic*. Boston: Houghton Mifflin, 1978.

Kennedy, Matthew. *Edmund Goulding's Dark Victory: Hollywood's Genius Bad Boy*. Madison, WI: University of Wisconsin Press, 2004.

Kertész, André. *Hungarian Memories*. Boston: Little, Brown, 1982.

La Mure, Pierre. *Moulin Rouge: A Novel Based on the Life of Henri de Toulouse-Lautrec*. New York: Random House, 1950.

LeRoy, Mervyn. *Take One*. New York: Hawthorn Books, 1974.

Levant, Oscar. *The Unimportance of Being Oscar*. New York: G.P. Putnam's Sons, 1968.

Levy, Emanuel. *Vincente Minnelli: Hollywood's Dark Dreamer*. New York: St. Martin's Press, 2009.

Levy, Shawn. *The Last Playboy: The High Life of Porfirio Rubirosa*. New York: HarperCollins, 2005.

Lewis, Norman. *The Changing Sky: Travels of a Novelist*. New York: Pantheon, 1959.

Long, Robert Emmet, ed. *John Huston: Interviews*. Jackson, MS: University Press of Mississippi, 2001.

Lord Kinross [John Patrick Douglas Balfour]. *Atatürk: A Biography of Mustafa Kemal, Father of Modern Turkey*. New York: William Morrow, 1965.

Lukacs, John. *Budapest 1900: A Historical Portrait of a City and Its Culture*. New York: Weidenfeld and Nicholson, 1988.

Mack, Gerstle. *Toulouse-Lautrec*. New York: Paragon House, 1989 [orig. 1938].

Marc, David. *Demographic Vistas: Television in American Culture*. Philadelphia: University of Pennsylvania Press, 1984.

Minnelli, Vincente, with Hector Arce. *I Remember It Well*. Garden City, NY: Doubleday, 1974.

Myers, Eric. *Uncle Mame: The Life of Patrick Dennis*. New York: St. Martin's Press, 2000.

Neagle, Anna. *Anna Neagle Says, "There's Always Tomorrow."* London: W.H. Allen, 1974.

Oppenheimer, Jerry. *House of Hilton: From Conrad to Paris: A Drama of Wealth, Power, and Privilege*. New York: Crown, 2006.

___. *Toy Monster: The Big, Bad World of Mattel*. New York: John Wiley & Sons, 2009.

Paar, Jack. *I Kid You Not*. Boston: Little, Brown, 1960.

Patai, Raphael. *The Jews of Hungary: History, Culture, Psychology*. Detroit: Wayne State University Press, 1996.

Pullen, Kirsten. *Like a Natural Woman: Spectacular Female Performance in Classical Hollywood*. New Brunswick, NJ: Rutgers University Press, 2014.

Reynolds, Debbie. *Make 'Em Laugh: Short-Term Memories of Longtime Friends*. New York: William Morrow/HarperCollins, 2015.

Sanders, George. *Memoirs of a Professional Cad*. New York: Putnam's, 1960.

Sebestyen, Victor. *Twelve Days: The Story of the 1956 Hungarian Revolution*. New York: Pantheon, 2006.

Slavitt, David R. *George Sanders, Zsa Zsa, and Me*. Evanston, IL: Northwestern University Press, 2009.

Staggs, Sam. *All About "All About Eve": The Complete Behind-the-Scenes Story of the Bitchiest Film Ever Made*.

New York: St. Martin's Press, 2000.

Stallings, Penny. *Forbidden Channels: The Truth They Hide from TV Guide*. New York: HarperCollins, 1991.

Taraborelli, J. Randy. *The Hiltons: The True Story of an American Dynasty*. New York: Grand Central Publishing, 2014.

Tauber, Diana Napier. *My Heart and I*. London: Evans Brothers Ltd., 1959.

Teleky, Richard. *Hungarian Rhapsodies: Essays on Ethnicity, Identity, and Culture*. Seattle: University of Washington Press, 1997.

Tucker-Jones, Anthony. *The Battle for Budapest 1944–1945*. South Yorkshire, UK: Pen and Sword Books, 2016.

Turtu, Anthony, and Donald F. Reuter. *Gaborabilia*. New York: Three Rivers Press, 2001.

VanDerBeets, Richard. *George Sanders: An Exhausted Life*. Lanham, MD: Madison Books, 1990.

Vickers, Hugo. *Cecil Beaton: A Biography*. Boston: Little, Brown, 1985.

Weaver, Tom. *Interviews with B Science Fiction and Horror Movie Makers: Writers, Producers, Directors, Actors, Moguls, and Makeup*. Jefferson, NC: McFarland, 1988.

Williams, John. *Chasing Pig's Ears: Memoirs of a Hollywood Plastic Surgeon*. Victoria, BC, Canada: Trafford Publishing, 2007.

Wilson, Earl. *Show Business Laid Bare*. New York: Putnam's, 1974.

A Note on Sources

In view of the millions of words about the Gabors printed in dozens of languages, it is unfortunate that so much of it is repetitive and of little value. The Gabors themselves were responsible for many of the clichés, for they stuck to the press-release versions of their lives. No studio publicist was more imaginative than they.

I was fortunate indeed to have Francesca Hilton's testimony as a counternarrative to the autobiographies of Zsa Zsa, Eva, and Jolie. Ironically, however, those very autobiographies served by necessity as primary *print* resources for this book. (The oral accounts other than Francesca's are listed in my acknowledgments.) In using those questionable resources, however, I kept in mind Mark Twain's sly evaluation of an autobiography. In a letter to William Dean Howells, he called it "the truest of all books; for though it eventually consists mainly of extinctions of the truth, shirkings of the truth, partial revealments of the truth, with hardly an instance of plain straight truth, the remorseless truth is there, between the lines, where the author-cat is raking dust upon it, which hides from the disinterested spectator neither it nor its smell . . . the result being that the reader knows the author in spite of his wily diligences."

My eyes often ached from squinting between the lines until Tony Turtu, author of *Gaborabilia*, came to my rescue with bio/career chronologies of Zsa Zsa (219 pages), Eva (192), Jolie and Magda combined (55). These annotated documents are unique because they include virtually every appearance onscreen, onstage, and in person of these four unstoppable women.

The first attempt at a book-length biography of the Gabors was Peter Harry Brown's *Such Devoted Sisters: Those Fabulous Gabors*, published in 1985. He told their story more or less accurately in the broad strokes, in spite of an enormous handicap: the Gabors, and their lawyers, were ready to pounce if he revealed one syllable too much. Although he acknowledged Zsa Zsa's "cooperation and candor," they were minimal owing to her impending ninth marriage and a hectic career kept afloat through sheer willpower. The book is not well written; it sinks under a cargo of perfumed prose.

I have praised Tony Turtu's *Gaborabilia* elsewhere as a "museum of rarities," the world's premier assemblage of everything Gabor. His book, of course, does not purport to be a full biography except as a photographic chronicle beginning in the 1920s, when the Gabor sisters were approaching adolescence.

David Slavitt's *George Sanders, Zsa Zsa, and Me* relies mostly on a rehash of Sanders's own book and of Zsa Zsa's two autobiographies. Slavitt muddles various facts, and the "Me" overshadows both George and Zsa Zsa.

Eva Gabor an Amazing Woman: Unscrupulous is the peculiar title of an even more peculiar book by Camyl Sosa Belanger, who was employed by Eva for several years. I quote from two reviews on amazon.com of this self-published muddle: "Quite possibly the worst book ever written"; "*Unscrupulous* is unreadable." Enough said, except to add "incoherent."

Is it possible to outdo the Gabors in the matter of unreliable narration? Indeed it is, as proven by *Those Glamorous Gabors: Bombshells from Budapest*, an obese, self-published tome by Darwin Porter. Lacking bibliography, notes, acknowledgments except of the most spurious kind, and style, Porter's book is the biographical equivalent of mad cow disease. Much of it is sheer fiction. One of his most shocking inventions is the claim that during the Nazi invasion of Hungary in 1944, Adolf Eichmann raped Magda Gabor, then slapped her face and called her a "Jew bitch." Totally unsubstantiated, Porter's pathetic attempt at Nazi porn insults those who actually suffered such war crimes.

As for those non-Gabors who played significant roles in the lives of Zsa Zsa, Eva, Magda, and Jolie—e.g., George Sanders, Porfirio Rubirosa, Merv Griffin, Ernst Lubitsch —I have referred in the text to the sources that I found most useful.

My own lifelong scrutiny of every Gabor, from birth to death, has given me a keen instinct for fact vs. myth. Although *Finding Zsa Zsa* relies largely on the reports of those closely connected to the Gabors, my own research includes sources in Hungarian, a language I studied long before I imagined its usefulness vis-à-vis those over-the-top Hungarians who charmed my childhood and eventually became, from a distance, mine for life.

Index